"Nothing shapes how we interpret and apply the Bible as much [as our] understanding of *covenant*. Richar[d Barcellos grounds his] biblical exegesis and theological ref[lection in a covenant] theology for God's relationship wit[h His people. Although] this book's discussion is framed by c[ertain debates, the is-]sues are of great consequence to all  [Christians of sin-]cerity. It serves as an effective antidote to New Covenant Theology, which, though saying many good things, can still do considerable damage to the church with regard to living out the Christian life practically and experientially. This is a welcome book written in an irenic spirit, and I pray that it will do much good in our day of great need to remain faithful to the biblically and carefully constructed covenant theology of our Puritan forebears. I am grateful that Dr. Barcellos underscores with clarity the vital importance of getting right the scriptural teaching on the covenant of works and on the Lord's Day."

> **Dr. Joel R. Beeke**
> President and Professor of Systematic Theology and Homiletics
> Puritan Reformed Theology Seminary
> and a pastor of the Heritage Reformed Congregation
> Grand Rapids, Michigan

"Richard Barcellos presents a compelling critique of New Covenant Theology. His work integrates biblical, historical, and systematic theology. His arguments are irenic but nevertheless potent as he demonstrates the important links between the covenant of works, the Sabbath, and eschatology. His research is deep, his exegetical spadework is thorough, and his arguments cogent. Anyone interested in uncovering the deficiencies in New Covenant Theology should definitely read this book."

> **J. V. Fesko**
> Academic Dean
> Professor of Systematic and Historical Theology
> Westminster Seminary California

"If exegesis is the queen of our biblically-birthed theology and practice, then biblically-formed hermeneutics is the king. There is a crisis in biblical hermeneutics today, both of ignorance and consistent application, which hinders agreement and unity among all evangelicals, but especially among reforming Baptists. What is needed is a clear voice to explain sound hermeneutics and irenically to examine the hermeneutical errors of New Covenant Theology, which hinders the full reformation of grace-based Baptist churches. I find a loss of words to advocate the importance of Dr. Barcellos' work, *Getting the Garden Right*, concerning the present status of biblical and historical reformation today among reforming Baptist students, pastors, and churches. It should be required reading in every Baptist seminary. The 'Doctrines of Grace' doth not a full reformation make. The rise of New Covenant Theology from the 1970s to the present day has challenged the biblical and confessional tenets of the Reformed faith, both for credobaptists and paedobaptists (e.g., covenant theology, the law and the gospel, the Sabbath, sanctification, etc.). Having dealt with the spreading teachings of New Covenant Theology since the late 1970s to the present day, I believe that its faulty hermeneutic has truncated the full Baptist reformation of a return to the more biblical faith and practice of our forefathers which so many of us had hoped for in the 70s. Dr. Barcellos has given us an irenic and thorough examination of New Covenant Theology's hermeneutical errors, clear exegetical answers to most of its errors, and a robust defense of our historical Baptist faith. Therefore, first, I commend Dr. Barcellos himself for the highest level of Reformed hermeneutics, accurate biblical exegesis of texts involved, and an irenic theological correction to New Covenant Theology and some of its leaders. Second, I recommend Dr. Barcellos' work with the highest commendation I can give: (1) I wish that I possessed the gifts and energy to have written it; (2) I believe every Baptist student and pastor should read it in light of today's theological differences and confusion; and (3) I believe that it brings glory to our triune God for the cause of His revealed Truth. Dr. Barcellos' thorough research and composition has given Reformed Baptists (and all evangelicals) a convincing apologetic for the faith of our Reformed Baptist forefathers which would advance a robust unity and reformation in our Baptist churches today. We have needed this work for a long time."

    Fred A. Malone, Ph. D.
    Pastor of First Baptist Church, Clinton, Louisiana
    Author of *The Baptism of Disciples Alone*

"Pastors and theologians have been called 'God's water treatment specialists,' protecting the churches from bad water and subsequent bad health. In the history of Christianity, faithful pastors and theologians who have engaged and critiqued bad theology were doing 'polemical theology.' All pastors and theologians are called to serve the churches in this way and protect them from both bad doctrine and wrong teachers. Sadly, in our postmodern culture, few pastor-theologians engage in polemics and even fewer still do it well. Dr. Richard Barcellos is a welcome exception. He puts the churches in his debt in this *tour de force* examination of how God's revelation in the garden of Eden plays itself out through the rest of the Bible. Irenically, and yet firmly, the author examines New Covenant Theology and finds it wanting in regards to the biblical revelation and the history of Reformed theology. I find this a great example of Christian scholarship in service to the churches. It is methodologically sound, respectful to those with whom it disagrees, and clearly written. The chapter on hermeneutics alone is worth the price of the book. I highly commend this book to all Reformed pastors and theologians, especially Baptist and 'New Covenant' pastors and theologians. I pastored for over 30 years in Reformed churches and this book would have helped the people of my church wanting to know why we were different from the church down the road and it would have been great to give to my New Covenant brethren with whom I dialogued for over 25 years. If all works of polemics were done like this, there would be more light on problematic doctrinal issues and greater unity and joy in the churches."

Steve Martin
Coordinator of the Association of Reformed Baptist Churches of America (ARBCA)

"*Getting the Garden Right* is no garden-variety theology book. More fruitful than fault-finding, it produces the biblical testimony lushly, apprehended best in the tradition of Reformed orthodoxy, that God is blessing His creation toward a redemptive end which is indeed better than the beginning. The seeds of His purpose were all sown in Eden. The light of all Scripture helps us see them now. They bud, flourish, and flower in the Promised Seed, even our Lord Jesus Christ, who is the abundant fruition of God's righteousness, gracious presence, and Sabbath rest. Even without a special interest in New Covenant Theology, reverent readers will appreciate this meditation on the paradise God has prepared for those who love Him. Were more dialogue about doctrinal differences conducted this way, more light would illumine our hearts, the breaches among brothers would decrease, and God would be more glorified. I would especially urge pastors to plow through these verdant fields of theological insight and to reap a harvest of enrichment for their own ministries of the Word."

D. Scott Meadows
Pastor of Calvary Baptist Church (Reformed)
Exeter, New Hampshire

"This book will serve the reader well from several vantage points. It provides a clean window into present discussion concerning New Covenant Theology and Covenant Theology. This issue has deeply important implications for understanding aspects of coherence, continuity, and discontinuity over the whole biblical corpus. Barcellos speaks to friends, not to enemies, and makes a transparently honest attempt to present the New Covenant view according to its own best arguments. He then seeks to focus the discussion around places where he discerns missteps or inconsistencies in interpretation or theological development. Although there is agreement on a multitude of doctrines—very important Reformation doctrines—among the adherents of both parties in the discussion, Barcellos isolates the issues of the covenant in the garden of Eden and the theme of Sabbath rest, Christologically perceived, as keys to sorting out differences, with the hope that greater agreement can be attained. Barcellos provides a model of how to integrate tight contextual issues, broadly conceived hermeneutics, biblical theology, and systematic theology into a covenantal framework, an important issue for both groups participating in this discussion. I believe this is a great step forward in defining Covenant Theology *vis a vis* New Covenant Theology and will help establish a foundation for more focused and edifying interaction."

>   Tom Nettles
>   Retired Professor of Historical Theology
>   The Southern Baptist Theological Seminary
>   Louisville, Kentucky

"Polemical writings frequently are like well-honed blades. An author enters the fray with his sword honed to a fine sharp edge and wields it seeking to destroy his opponent. But occasionally, one finds a writer who seeks to win his battle with kind and gracious words. In this polemical work, Dr. Richard Barcellos does just this. Examining some of the key tenets of a recently proposed system called 'New Covenant Theology,' he presents a well-considered, carefully constructed, and thoughtful engagement with several of the proponents of that system. Barcellos carefully exegetes Scripture in conversation with the past and present, presenting an evaluation and refutation, along with an exhortation to its adherents, of several central ideas of New Covenant Theology. Both friend and foe will profit from this book."

>   James M. Renihan, Ph.D.
>   Dean and Professor of Historical Theology
>   Institute of Reformed Baptist Studies
>   Westminster Seminary California
>   Escondido, California

"In *Getting the Garden Right*, Richard Barcellos not only draws a clear line of hermeneutical differences between New Covenant Theology and Covenant Theology, but so thoroughly dismantles the former while defining and defending the latter that the reader is left with one direction in which to move—toward a more biblical understanding of the garden of Eden, and therefore of the Christian faith. Careful exegesis, precise theology, and a kind spirit make this book a challenging and joyful read."

>**Joe Thorn**
>Lead Pastor of Redeemer Fellowship
>St. Charles, Illinois

"Richard Barcellos has given us a real gem in his *Getting the Garden Right*. I know of no contemporary book like it. It is worth its weight in gold. Barcellos defends the confessional understanding of the covenant of works and the Sabbath rest through hermeneutics, exegesis, biblical theology, historical theology, and systematics. While the context for the book is discussion of these central doctrines with theologians within the New Covenant Theology movement, the book should be of interest to the wider Reformed community beyond Baptist circles. Barcellos has written theology as it ought to be written. *Getting the Garden Right* is polemical theology at its gentle best. I heartily recommend this volume for its depth of theological argumentation seasoned with grace, for its delineation and vindication of the doctrine of the covenant of works and the continuing validity of a Sabbath rest in this age, and for its clear example of theological method. You must not only read the cover of this book. Get the book, consume it, digest it, and then return to it annually and as often as you need."

>**Rev. Jeffrey C. Waddington, Ph.D.**
>Stated Clerk & Archivist—Presbytery of Philadelphia
>The Orthodox Presbyterian Church
>Stated Supply & Ministerial Adviser—Knox OPC
>Lansdowne, Pennsylvania

"Contentions about issues like covenant theology and the first day of the week, the Lord's Day, are too often bitter and negative, not to mention complex and confusing. Rich Barcellos' newest offering on these topics is careful without being pedantic, thorough without being exhausting, thoughtful without being speculative, academic without being abstruse, fair without being soft, and pointed without being nasty. Rich builds gradual momentum through his book, digging ever deeper through the various strata of biblical, historical, and systematic theology to develop his case. Those who more or less agree with him will find this a helpful confirmation and a useful prompt to further careful study. Those who more or less disagree will find that this is no casual contribution, but a significant effort and a serious challenge to any who overlook, neglect or even carelessly dismiss the patterns, purposes, and privileges of the Lord's Day as it is understood in the context of creation, fall, redemption, and coming glory."

Jeremy Walker
Pastor of Maidenbower Baptist Church
Crawley, England

Getting the Garden Right

Adam's Work and God's Rest In Light of Christ

By
Richard C. Barcellos

 Founders Press

Cape Coral, Florida

Published by
Founders Press

P.O. Box 150931 • Cape Coral, FL 33915
Phone (239) 772-1400 • Fax: (239) 772-1140
Electronic Mail: founders@founders.org
Website: http://www.founders.org

©2017 Founders Press

Printed in the United States of America

13 ISBN: 978-1-943539-08-6

All rights reserved. No part of this publication may be reproduced, stored in a retrieval system or transmitted in any form by any means, electronic, mechanical, photocopy, recording or otherwise, without prior permission of the publisher, except as provided by USA copyright law.

Scripture quotations taken from the NEW AMERICAN STANDARD BIBLE®, Copyright® 1960, 1962, 1963, 1968, 1971, 1972, 1973, 1975, 1977, 1995 by The Lockman Foundation. Used by permission.

Contents

    Foreword 3

    Preface 5

    Introduction 9

1. What Is New Covenant Theology 13
2. The Importance of Hermeneutics in Theological
   Formulation 19

Part I: Adam's Work in Light of Christ

3. A Covenant of Works in the Garden:
   The New Covenant Theology Perspective 31
4. A Covenant of Works in the Garden:
   The Confessional Formulation 38
5. A Covenant of Works in the Garden:
   The Scriptural Arguments 53

Part II: God's Rest in Light of Christ

6. The Doctrine of the Christian Sabbath:
   The New Covenant Theology Perspective 81
7. The Doctrine of the Christian Sabbath:
   The Confessional Formulation 99
8. The Doctrine of the Christian Sabbath:
   Adam's Identity and Vocation 110
9. The Doctrine of the Christian Sabbath:
   The Beginning and the End 145
10. The Doctrine of the Christian Sabbath:
    Genesis 2:1–3 156
11. The Doctrine of the Christian Sabbath:
    Exodus and the Prophets 181

12.	The Doctrine of the Christian Sabbath: New Testament Fulfillment 198
13.	The Doctrine of the Christian Sabbath: Hebrews 4:9–10 231
14.	The Doctrine of the Christian Sabbath: Revelation 1:10 260

Conclusion 270

Appendix 273
A review of *New Covenant Theology: Description, Definition. Defense* by Tom Wells and Fred Zaspel

Index of Scripture References 283

Index of Names and Subjects 295

Bibliography 301

Foreword

Dr. Thomas K. Ascol

This is an important book. Dr. Barcellos tackles a subject that is crucial for a right understanding of the Bible and he does so in a very careful way. Both the conclusions that he advocates and the methods by which he reaches them are instructive. The Bible tells the story of God's salvation of sinners in Christ. But that story does not begin in Bethlehem. It begins, well, at the beginning. At creation. Misunderstand God's work at the beginning and you will not fully appreciate what He has done since.

Barcellos recognizes this and so takes a careful look at the garden of Eden. God's work in that place sets the stage for His work for the rest of history. With a scholar's eye and a pastor's heart, Barcellos carefully examines the relationship that God established with Adam in the garden with its stated stipulations and threat as well as its implied promise. The purpose of that covenantal arrangement, and Adam's failure to maintain it, establishes the trajectory for all subsequent revelation and the promise of eternity.

Barcellos writes as a Reformed Baptist who is convinced of the covenantal structure of biblical revelation. To get at key issues involved in this study, he interacts with other Calvinistic Baptists who do not share that conviction. Most of the proponents of this so-called "New Covenant Theology" (NCT), have, until recently, been hesitant to acknowledge that God established a covenant with Adam at the beginning. Barcellos gives their arguments a gracious hearing while exposing their weaknesses and failures to understand biblical and historical texts. One of the key points of disagreement between NCT and covenant theology (including the Reformed Baptist version) is the perpetuity of the weekly Sabbath. In acknowledgment of this, and because it is a crucial part of the order that God established at creation, Barcellos devotes the second half of the book to that question. His arguments for an abiding Sabbath principle in the Christian Lord's Day are exegetically sound, theologically robust and pastorally wise.

In a day when the idea that God calls us to set aside one day in seven as a Sabbath rest sounds archaic to the large majority of evangelical Christians, the case presented here needs to gain a wide hearing.

In this book Dr. Barcellos has given us a wonderful example of exegetical, historical, systematic, polemical and pastoral theology. He has served the church well by calling attention to an essential ingredient for reading the Bible rightly and by doing so with humility, rigor and grace. I hope that it will gain a wide reading not only by those who already hold his conclusions, but especially by those who, though they do not, nevertheless share his love for God's Word. May this book bring glory to the One who succeeded where Adam failed and whose life, death and resurrection guarantee that everything that was originally promised in the beginning will infallibly come to pass.

Thomas Ascol
Cape Coral, Florida
August 2017

Preface

In 2001, my *In Defense of the Decalogue: A Critique of New Covenant Theology (IDOTD)* was published by Founders Press. In 2002, my friends Tom Wells and Fred Zaspel published *New Covenant Theology: Description, Definition, Defense*. Fred sent me a copy and signed it with these words:

Richard,

To the guy who made us go to all this work! Trust you will enjoy and learn!

Fred

I was very thankful for the book and for its attempt to set the record straight about what New Covenant Theology (NCT) asserts. A review of the Wells/Zaspel book has been included as an appendix to this book. The review was first published in the *Reformed Baptist Theological Review (RBTR)* in 2004. Since much has transpired since *IDOTD*, the Wells/Zaspel book, and my review, it was determined that a new book was needed.

The idea for a new book, a second and expanded edition of *IDOTD*, was presented to me several years ago. I had been content to let the first edition stand on its own (even with the faults I admit in the review of the Wells/Zaspel book), though realizing it was outdated at points. Since *IDOTD* is out of print, and since my own thinking and that of NCT has developed and matured, I thought it best to work on a second edition. As the work began, I came to the conclusion that what was needed was not a second edition, but rather a book that interacts with NCT on some foundational issues on a deeper level than that offered by *IDOTD*. This book is offered as an attempt to reflect upon some of the discussions that have taken place since *IDOTD* was published, focusing on three issues—hermeneutics, the covenant of works, and the Sabbath. The arguments used by NCT adherents, particularly against the doctrines of the covenant of works and of the Sabbath, are held by many in our day, and thus are worthy of interaction.

The analysis of NCT contained herein in no way pretends to be exhaustive. It reflects my own limited understanding of NCT. As I stated in 2001, it is still somewhat difficult to critique NCT because it is not a monolithic movement. There is also no agreed-upon NCT confession of faith. New Covenant theologians differ on some of the finer nuances involved with their system, as will become obvious in later discussions. These facts serve to alert the reader that NCT is a movement still in progress, which I think is a good thing.

As will become evident, the book utilizes hermeneutical principles contained in the Second London Confession of Faith of 1677/89 (2LCF) and seeks to defend two doctrinal formulations of that confessional document. Both the hermeneutical principles and the two doctrinal formulations are also found in the Westminster Confession of Faith (WCF) and the Savoy Declaration (SD). The justification for utilizing the 2LCF will be given in Chapter 2.

This book has been written primarily for pastors and theological students, though it is hoped that any studious Christian will profit from its contents. Those not interested in technical, secondary points may skip the footnotes (something I never do). The reader should know, however, that the footnotes also contain crucial justification for arguments made in the main text, as well as further interaction with those arguments.

I want to thank various pre-publication readers who offered helpful comments and push-back. The Lord knows who you are. Christ Reformed Baptist Church, Vista, California, sent students from the Institute of Reformed Baptist Studies to fill my pulpit for a whole month in 2016, and I thank them for doing so.

Special thanks to my long-time friend Pastor James P. Butler of Free Grace Baptist Church, Chilliwack, British Columbia. Jim read each chapter of the book in a timely fashion and offered many suggestions that ended up in the book. I hope he does not accuse me of plagiarism.

Thanks also to my own church, Grace Reformed Baptist Church, Palmdale, California. Though we are not many nor mighty, we are Christ's and he cares for us faithfully.

My wife, Nan, is to be thanked for understanding that writing books means late nights and early mornings.

I want to express my deep appreciation to Founders Press for expressing interest in this book. Special thanks go to Dr. Thomas K. Ascol.

May the Lord continue to bless the labors of Founders Press and bring about a theological and practical reformation not only in the Southern Baptist Convention, but throughout the world and in all of Christ's true churches.

Soli Deo gloria!

Richard C. Barcellos
Grace Reformed Baptist Church
Palmdale, California
September 2016

Introduction

This book, in one sense, concentrates on hermeneutics and theological method. I contend that NCT gets the covenant of works and the Sabbath wrong because it gets the garden of Eden wrong, and it gets the garden of Eden wrong because it gets crucial aspects of hermeneutics wrong. The garden of Eden (and its surrounding context in the Genesis narrative) contains "the principal themes of biblical theology displayed in epigrammatic brevity" and "these simple but far-reaching affirmations…become the presuppositions of the rest of the sacred story."[1] Eden sets the stage for the drama of redemption revealed to us in subsequent Holy Scripture. Though Eden was glorious, Adam failed his task as the representative of man and fell short of the glory of God. He fell short of something he did not possess via creation.

The redemptive stream of Holy Scripture takes creation to its intended end, the eternal state of glory. The agent appointed by God to do this is our Lord Jesus Christ. The last Adam, our Lord, takes His seed where the first Adam failed to take his. Adam had a goal to obtain, a goal he failed to achieve. Adam fell from the righteous state in which he was created and did not enter glory due to his sin. Though the potential for attaining glory was endowed upon him by his Creator, he never reached it. This means that eschatological potential existed from the beginning. Eden, though a glorious place, was not the end, but the beginning to an end. It had within it the seeds of a better world; a better world where sin could not enter and which could never lapse into a cursed condition. In the words of William J. Dumbrell, "Eden is the representation of what the world is to become…"[2]

---

[1] Gordon J. Wenham, *Genesis 1-15*, Word Biblical Commentary (Waco, TX: Word, 1987), 39.
[2] William J. Dumbrell, "Genesis 2:1-17: A Foreshadowing of the New Creation," in *Biblical Theology: Retrospect & Prospect*, ed. Scott J. Hafemann (Downers Grove, IL: InterVarsity Press, 2002), 61.

What the world is to become is what we call the eternal state of glory, the new heavens and the new earth. This being the case, a proper understanding of the garden is crucial for understanding many scriptural doctrines, such as God as both Creator and divine exemplar, man's identity and vocation, the law of nature, the covenant of works, the Sabbath, and even Christology and eschatology. Those who get the garden wrong end up robbing themselves of the foundational doctrines necessary to make proper sense of redemptive history. In order to properly understand the promise of Genesis 3:15, the unfolding and function of the biblical covenants, the function of old covenant Israel, and the new covenant inaugurated by our Lord, one must understand creation and its various doctrinal and ethical entailments. Indeed, as Dumbrell asserts, "the foundational factor in biblical theology is a creation theology."[3] The redemptive story line of the Bible assumes and develops from the original revelation of the state of Adam and Eve before the fall. Going astray at the level of the foundation creates problems when trying to assemble the structure of the Bible's teaching on many crucial subjects.

Why the Covenant of Works and the Sabbath?

I chose to interact with NCT on the covenant of works and the Sabbath because, as will be argued, both of these doctrines are revealed to us in the beginning of the Bible and both are denied or modified by NCT advocates. In addition, the formulation of these doctrines demands the application of hermeneutical principles with which most NCT adherents agree, though, as will also be argued, they apply them inconsistently. The ongoing nature of the Sabbath under the inaugurated new covenant, in many respects, is the most obvious doctrine wherein NCT and Covenant Theology disagree. The covenant of works is probably second to the Sabbath in this regard. The formulation of these doctrines will serve as test cases to illustrate the differences in hermeneutics utilized by NCT and Covenant Theology.

The Structure of the Book

The first two chapters deal with defining NCT (Chapter 1), the importance of hermeneutics in theological formulation, and charting a course of study for the main sections of the book (Chapter 2). Part I is entitled "Adam's Work in Light of Christ." This section discusses NCT's view of

---

[3] Dumbrell, "Genesis 2:1-17: A Foreshadowing of the New Creation," 65.

God, Adam, and covenant (Chapter 3), the confessional formulation of the doctrine of the covenant of works (Chapter 4), and the scriptural arguments in favor of the doctrine (Chapter 5). Part II, "God's Rest in Light of Christ," is more involved. After a chapter discussing NCT's position on the Sabbath (Chapter 6), and a chapter on the confessional formulation of the doctrine (Chapter 7), seven chapters are devoted to the scriptural arguments for a Christian Sabbath (Chapters 8–14). The reason so much attention is given to the issue of the Sabbath is due to its foundational place at creation and its subsequent function in both the Old and New Testaments. The biblical doctrine of the Sabbath begins at creation and follows the story line of the Bible to the consummation. Understanding it properly requires the examination of many biblical texts. Because of this book's particular focus on the problems within NCT, the present writer has attempted to provide significant interaction with those who agree and disagree with the confessional position advocated herein.

Why Read this Book?

The book contains exegesis, biblical theology, systematic theology, and historical theology. It is crucial that the subject matter of this book be addressed through these methodological disciplines. This book will deal with texts, seek to help the reader understand those texts in their immediate contexts and the wider context of the entire Bible, and interact with systematic and historical theological concerns along the way. Interacting with voices from the past keeps the discussion within the bounds of Christian orthodoxy, where the Spirit of Christ has been helping the people of Christ understand the Word of Christ for thousands of years.

Some of the chapters are long and contain sustained arguments that must be followed carefully. Each chapter assumes and builds upon previous discussion. Readers are encouraged to read carefully and recall previous discussion often.

Though NCT is primarily a Calvinistic Baptist phenomenon, some of its tenets are held by others who do not identify with that theological tradition. There are Presbyterians who deny (or modify) the covenant of works and the Sabbath, though these doctrines are contained in the Westminster Standards. There is also a school of thought known as Progressive Covenantalism which denies (or modifies) these same doctrines. Progressive Covenantalism is relatively new. Books advocating its distinctives are just coming off the press. More time is needed for them to articulate their views and for others to listen carefully to them before interacting on a substantive level, though some interaction with it will be provided here. These things being the case, this book is not aimed at Baptists alone. My hope is that it will benefit any inquiring mind on the issues discussed. If you are interested in hermeneutics, theological method, biblical theology, creation and its ethical entailments, man in the image of God, the covenant of works, the Sabbath, the old and new creations, and the relationship between protology, eschatology, redemptive history, and Christology, you are invited to read carefully and prayerfully the pages before you.

1

What Is New Covenant Theology?

In order to conduct the following study properly, it is only fair to define NCT. I attempt to do that in this chapter, allowing its own writers to speak for themselves. Since I will argue that hermeneutics is of great importance concerning the issues to be discussed, in the next chapter I will introduce readers to some of the principles of interpretation utilized in this book and chart our course of study, indicating what will be discussed and why.

What is New Covenant Theology?

In *IDOTD*, the following was asserted:

> The critique in no way pretends to be exhaustive. It reflects my own limited, and certainly fallible, understanding of New Covenant Theology. Frankly, it is somewhat difficult to critique New Covenant Theology for at least three reasons. *First*, New Covenant Theology is not a monolithic movement. New Covenant theologians differ on some of the nuances involved with defining New Covenant Theology. *Second*, New Covenant Theology is a relatively new school of thought. Though there is much in print on New Covenant Theology, there is no definitive work, as of yet.... Because of these things, a critique can become quickly outdated.[1]

---

[1] Richard C. Barcellos, *In Defense of the Decalogue: A Critique of New Covenant Theology* (Enumclaw, WA: WinePress Publishing, 2001), 7.

The Preface to *New Covenant Theology* by Tom Wells and Fred Zaspel, published in 2002, agrees with this assessment. After quoting my words above, the authors say:

> This analysis is right on target. It is too soon to know how these difficulties will be reconciled, but if NCT proves to be a viable understanding of the Scriptures, the work could well extend into the period beyond our lifetimes.[2]

Recently, NCT advocate Gary D. Long says of NCT:

> [NCT] as a theological system in America…is a recent development[3] having different explanations, especially due to diverse—sometimes, sad to say, even heterodox—writings on the Internet which lack the discipline of biblical hermeneutics. The time has come for those who hold to the need for NCT to unify, explain and demonstrate what it is as a developing theological system exegetically based on sound principles of biblical interpretation.[4]

I appreciate Long's assessment. NCT is a recent, developing system.[5] Neither is it a monolithic movement. Because there is no agreed-upon creedal document subscribed by NCT advocates, it is hard for outsiders to offer critique. John Reisinger has even gone so far as to say, "Currently, New Covenant Theology has no clearly defined hermeneutic."[6] Elsewhere, he says, "I have yet to discover what a 'true new covenant theologian' is."[7] Though there is probably some rhetorical overkill in Reisinger's statements, his words reveal that even NCT advocates realize their formulations are somewhat recent and developing.[8] This makes what I asserted in 2001, and what the Wells/Zaspel book affirmed in 2002, still applicable.

---

[2] Tom Wells and Fred Zaspel, *New Covenant Theology: Description, Definition, Defense* (Frederick, MD: New Covenant Media, 2002), 4.

[3] Kirk M. Wellum agrees with Long at this point. In A. Blake White, *What is New Covenant Theology? An Introduction* (Frederick, MD: New Covenant Media, 2012), endorsement page iii, Wellum identifies NCT as a "relatively new theological formulation…"

[4] Gary D. Long, *NCT: Time for a More Accurate Way* (n. p., 2013), 1. The book is available at Amazon.com and CreateSpace.com.

[5] A. Blake White says, "New Covenant Theology is a developing system of theology.…" See White, *What is New Covenant Theology?*, 1.

[6] John G. Reisinger, *New Covenant Theology and Prophecy* (Frederick, MD: New Covenant Media, 2012), 7.

[7] John G. Reisinger, "Foreword," in A. Blake White, *The Law of Christ: A Theological Proposal* (Frederick, MD: New Covenant Media, 2010), 3, n. 1.

[8] I don't think developing one's system is necessarily a bad thing. In *IDOTD*,

The safest way to define NCT is to allow their writers to speak for themselves. However, since it is still developing, what one writer sees as a crucial element of the system, another might not. For example, in *IDOTD*, I asserted that "One key text for New Covenant Theology is found in Matthew 5:17–20."[9] John Reisinger takes issue with my claim:

> While NCT does believe in a redemptive-historical shift in law, we do not present this text as a key text to support the idea. We usually only refer to this text in relation to that shift when someone else raises it as an objection. To present it as one of our key texts is akin to saying, "One of the key texts for those who believe in free will is Romans 9," and then proceeding to show how Romans 9 teaches sovereignty and refutes free will. Arminians do not use Romans 9 as a key text. Barcellos' point is similar to stating that 1 John 2:2 is a key text for those who believe in limited atonement, and then demanding an explanation from them of the phrase *the whole world*. It would seem that Barcellos has chosen texts that he himself wants to discuss, and then has stated that he is using those particular texts because they are important texts to NCT. While it is legitimate for him to feel that a given text is important in this discussion, it is not fair to put words in our mouth and then refute them. If the phrase "One key text for New Covenant Theology" means "this is a key text that NCT must explain," then Barcellos has made a fair request. If he means that the text he identifies is one that New Covenant theologians use as a key text, then he has misrepresented NCT.
>
> Matthew 5:17–20 is important to this discussion because Covenant theologians make it a key text in their refutation of NCT. Again, I acknowledge that NCT must explain that text, as well as any other salient text, but that does not mean that we make it a foundational text for our view.[10]

This was published in 2008. The Wells/Zaspel book was published in 2002. Its full title is *New Covenant Theology: Description, Definition, Defense*. Four of its fifteen chapters, written by Fred Zaspel, treat Matthew 5:17–20 (the discussion is more extensive than those verses alone). *IDOTD* is not referenced in those chapters. Zaspel himself says of Matthew 5:17–

---

for example, I purposefully stayed clear of various doctrinal formulations found in my confession of faith (2LCF) that I was still "developing" in my own thinking. Where I have landed on those issues is not relatively new ground, however. Also, to be fair, some of the tenets of NCT predate its designation.

[9] Barcellos, *IDOTD*, 12.

[10] John G. Reisinger, *In Defense of Jesus, the New Lawgiver* (Frederick, MD: New Covenant Media, 2008), 59-60.

20, "Indeed, the whole NT theology of law grows out of this pivotal statement of Jesus."[11] In the Foreword to that book, Douglas J. Moo says, "… Zaspel concentrates on a careful exegesis of key New Testament texts — especially the pivotal Matthew 5:17–20."[12] Most of what Zaspel wrote on Matthew 5 was written prior to *IDOTD*.[13] Since that is the case, he was not responding to my book simply because I brought up that text. This would mean that what I said about this passage in *IDOTD* was accurate, at least as Zaspel sees NCT. Interestingly, Gary Long's list of "NCT Characteristics" published in 2013, what he identifies as "some of the major NCT characteristics,"[14] includes the following: "The Law of God is both absolute and covenantal (Matt. 5:17–20)"[15] and "The law of Christ is not to be equated with the Decalogue."[16] He then cites Matthew 5 three times in support. It is clear that Long sees Matthew 5 as important for NCT. In addition, John Reisinger wrote a whole book on the Sermon on the Mount, first published in 1989.[17] Maybe I assumed more than I ought to have in light of that book by Reisinger, but it seems clear to me that the Wells/Zaspel book and Long's book both view Matthew 5 as important to the system of thought advocated by NCT.

This brief caveat was included to highlight that defining NCT is not easy, especially for an outsider. Indeed, as Gary Long asserts, NCT "is a recent development having different explanations."[18] Though I will attempt to state a working definition of NCT, I fully realize some might take issue with aspects of it.

If I understand NCT correctly, the chapter titles of A. Blake White's *What is New Covenant Theology?* may go some way toward a working definition. NCT is a developing system of doctrine which advocates the following:

Chapter 1: One Plan of God Centered in Jesus Christ

Chapter 2: The Old Testament Should Be Interpreted in Light of the New Testament

---

[11] Wells and Zaspel, *NCT*, 78.

[12] Ibid., xiii.

[13] This has been confirmed to me through personal correspondence with Fred Zaspel.

[14] Long, *NCT*, 4.

[15] Ibid., 5.

[16] Ibid., 7.

[17] John G. Reisinger, *But I Say Unto You* (Southbridge, MA: Crown Publications, Inc., 1989).

[18] Long, *NCT*, 1.

What Is New Covenant Theology?

Chapter 3: The Old Covenant Was Temporary by Divine Design

Chapter 4: The Law is a Unit

Chapter 5: Christians are not Under the Law of Moses, but the 'Law' of Christ

Chapter 6: All Members of the New Covenant Community are Fully Forgiven and Have the Holy Spirit

Chapter 7: The Church is the Eschatological Israel.[19]

As stated and without explicit elucidation, I agree with all seven points. But, as will be demonstrated below, some of the nuances articulated by NCT adherents in the way these statements are explained is where I will take issue. For example, though I agree that the Old Testament should be understood in light of the New Testament, I maintain that the Old Testament ought to be understood in light of itself as well. Though my hunch is that NCT adherents will agree with me at this point, I have not seen this worked out on a consistent basis in the various books I have read by them.

Gary Long offers the following brief definition of NCT: *"God's eternal purpose progressively revealed in the commandments and promises of the biblical covenants of the OT and fulfilled in the New Covenant of Jesus Christ."*[20] He then offers what he calls its "major themes…summarily described" as follows:

- *God's eternal purpose of redemption:* covenantally revealed and administered through biblical covenants beginning with a pre-fall covenant of obedience with Adam (Rom. 5:12–19; Eph. 2:12)[21] and a post–fall covenant of promise (Gen. 3:15);

- *Hermeneutics:* consistent interpretation of the OT in light of the NT (Luke 24:27; II Cor. 1:20);

---

[19] White, *What is New Covenant Theology?*, Table of Contents.

[20] Long, *NCT*, 2; emphasis original.

[21] This is an interesting place to reference Ephesians 2:12. If intentional by Long, it makes that text to include what he calls "a pre-fall covenant of obedience with Adam," which would make that covenant one of the covenants of promise mentioned by Paul. Ephesians 2:12 speaks of "the covenants of promise." Paul says that Gentiles "were at that time [i.e., when they were not Christians] separate from Christ, excluded from the commonwealth of Israel, and strangers to the covenants of promise, having no hope and without God in the world." Long includes the "pre-fall covenant of obedience with Adam" among "the covenants of promise." This seems unwarranted from the Ephesians text and broader considerations. It could be that the reference to Ephesians 2:12 belongs with Long's words "and a post-fall covenant of promise (Genesis 3:15)."

- *The people of God:* all the elect of God throughout time first constituted as the church at Pentecost (Acts 1:4–5), but not before (John 7:39; 17:21–22; Col. 1:26–27; Heb. 11:39–40), as one corporate spiritual body in union with Christ (I Cor. 12:13; Eph. 2:19–21; Col. 1:18, 24); and

- *The law of God:* the two great commandments of God—love of God and neighbor (Matt. 22:36–40)—are innate law known instinctively by man (Rom. 2:14–15) created in God's image (Gen. 1:27). Upon these two great commandments all of God's covenantally written laws depend as administered under biblical covenants, which culminate in the New Covenant (NC) law of Christ (I Cor. 9:20–21; Romans 13:8–10; Galatians 6:2; Heb. 8:6; James 2:8; I John 5:3). Innate law is righteous and unchanging. Covenantal law is written, righteous and changeable (Heb. 7:12) worked out in history in accordance with God's eternal purpose (Eph. 1:11; 3:11; II Tim. 1:9).[22]

Some of these major themes of NCT as offered by Long are not agreed upon by other NCT advocates, as will be shown below. What is of interest at this point in our discussion is his suggestion that there are two covenants revealed in the early chapters of Genesis: a pre-fall covenant of obedience with Adam and a post-fall covenant of promise announced in the curse upon the serpent (Genesis 3:15). It is also of interest to note that this is not typical of many NCT writers. Finally, notice Long's distinction between innate law and covenantal law, which will be discussed below.

These two samples of what constitutes the major tenets of NCT from two of its writers illustrate what some of its advocates admit: NCT is a developing system. One of my intents in this book is to nudge NCT adherents in this admitted development.

---

[22] Long, *NCT*, 2–3.

2

The Importance of Hermeneutics In Theological Formulation

Having mentioned a hermeneutical issue in the previous chapter (i.e., the OT use of the OT), it is important to lay my hermeneutical cards on the table. We will consider the importance of hermeneutics in theological formulation and then look at the road ahead for our study.

Hermeneutics and Theological Formulation

In the 1980s, one of my seminary professors said something like this: "The differences between covenant theology and Dispensationalism are, at bottom, hermeneutical differences." I think he was right. I also think that the differences between much of what NCT advocates and a covenantal Baptist (i.e., Second London Confession of Faith) perspective are, at bottom, hermeneutical ones. We read the same texts through different interpretive lenses. Several years ago, I asked Dr. Vern Poythress, "Dr. Poythress, is it true that if you get the garden wrong, you get eschatology wrong?" He responded, "If you get the garden wrong, you will get everything wrong." Though there is probably hyperbole in Dr. Poythress' answer, he is essentially correct.

I will argue below that NCT gets major aspects of the Bible's teaching on various issues wrong because it gets the garden wrong, and it gets the garden wrong because it gets crucial aspects of hermeneutics wrong. This ends up affecting their system adversely (though there is movement in a better direction by some NCT writers). I will argue, among other things, that a proper hermeneutic leads to affirming the following: 1) the covenant of works in the garden of Eden and 2) the perpetuity of a Sabbath day to be kept under the inaugurated new covenant due to the function of the Creator's rest first revealed to us in Genesis 2. It will be shown that NCT denies or distorts these crucial doctrines due to a faulty hermeneutic.

This book is an attempt to present a better way to understand much of the covenantal theology of the Bible than what NCT offers. Understanding the Bible's teaching on covenants is crucial. In agreement with this sentiment, C. H. Spurgeon said:

> The doctrine of the covenant lies at the root of all true theology. It has been said that he who well understands the distinction between the covenant of works and the covenant of grace, is a master of divinity. I am persuaded that most of the mistakes which men make concerning the doctrines of Scripture are based upon fundamental errors with regard to the covenants of law and grace.[1]

The seventeenth-century Particular Baptist Nehemiah Coxe, while discussing God's transactions with Adam, said, "If a man misses the right account of this, he is certainly bewildered in all further searching for that truth which most concerns him to know."[2] I agree with these men about the importance of getting the covenant theology of the Bible right.

It will be helpful to remind ourselves of some hermeneutical principles utilized by those who formulated the 2LCF, the Westminster Standards (its Confession [WCF] and Catechisms), and the Savoy Declaration (SD). NCT writers often disagree with doctrinal formulations contained in these documents, especially where they assert the covenants of works and grace and issues related to the law of God. As will be explained below, on the issues of the covenant of works and the Sabbath, I think these old documents got it right (though the 2LCF differs with the WCF and SD at points which will be discussed below). The hermeneutical principles utilized by the men who wrote those creedal documents pre-date the Westminster Assembly, going all the way back to the canonical writers of the Hebrew Scriptures, though space does not permit me to prove such. In the history of Christian thought, these principles are what we might label

---

[1] This comes from C. H. Spurgeon, "Sermon XL, the Covenant," *The Sermons of Rev. C. H. Spurgeon of London*, 9th Series (New York: Robert Cater & Brothers, 1883), 172, as quoted in Pascal Denault, *The Distinctiveness of Baptist Covenant Theology: A Comparison Between Seventeenth-Century Particular Baptist and Paedobaptist Federalism* (Birmingham, AL: Solid Ground Christian Books, 2013), 6, n. 4.

[2] Nehemiah Coxe and John Owen, *Covenant Theology From Adam to Christ*, ed. Ronald D. Miller, James M. Renihan, and Francisco Orozco (Palmdale, CA: Reformed Baptist Academic Press, 2005), 42.

The Importance of Hermeneutics in Theological Formulation 21

as pre-critical or pre-Enlightenment.³ They were utilized by the catholic theological tradition from the early centuries of Christian reflection upon Scripture through the post-Reformation era. In that sense, they are not exclusively Reformed or Protestant. It is of interest to note that these pre-critical hermeneutical principles were the interpretive foundations from which the great creeds, confessions, and catechisms of the church were formed. Four principles are worthy of noting at this time. Space will not allow me to illustrate all of these from the Scriptures in the brief discussion below, though they (and others) will be illustrated throughout the book where I seek to give scriptural explication of various doctrinal formulations found in the 2LCF.

*The Holy Spirit is the Only Infallible Interpreter of Holy Scripture.*⁴

As an example of this principle, John Owen says, "The only unique, public, authentic, and infallible interpreter of Scripture is none other than the Author of Scripture Himself…that is, God the Holy Spirit."⁵ Nehemiah Coxe says, "…the best interpreter of the Old Testament is the Holy Spirit speaking to us in the new."⁶ This meant that they saw the Bible's interpretation and use of itself as infallible and with interpretive principles embedded in it. When the Bible comments upon, or utilizes itself in any fashion (e.g., direct quotation, allusion, echo, or fulfillment in the OT or NT), it is God's interpretation and, therefore, the divine understanding of how texts should be understood by men. This often means that later texts shed interpretive light on earlier texts. This occurs not only when the New Testament uses the Old Testament, but it occurs in the Old Testament

---

³ See David C. Steinmetz, "The Superiority of Pre-Critical Exegesis," *Theology Today* (April 1980): 27–38, for an introduction to pre-critical hermeneutics. See also Moisés Silva, "Has the Church Misread the Bible?," in *Foundations of Contemporary Interpretation*, gen. ed. Moisés Silva (Grand Rapids: Zondervan Publishing House, 1996).

⁴ The material under the next four sub-headings is taken (with permission and slight modification) from Richard C. Barcellos, "Getting the Garden Right: From Hermeneutics to the Covenant of Works," in *By Common Confession: Essays in Honor of James M. Renihan*, ed. Ronald S. Baines, Richard C. Barcellos, and James P. Butler (Palmdale, CA: RBAP, 2015), 201–05. I think most NCT adherents will agree with much of what is discussed here.

⁵ John Owen, *Biblical Theology or The Nature, Origin, Development, and Study of Theological Truth in Six Books* (Pittsburgh, PA: Soli Deo Gloria Publications, 1994), 797.

⁶ Coxe and Owen, *Covenant Theology*, 36.

itself, which will be illustrated in our discussion below. Alternatively, we could put it this way: subsequent revelation often makes explicit what is implicit in antecedent revelation.[7] This principle led the older theologians to three more related concepts.

The Analogy of Scripture (Analogia Scripturae)

Here is Richard A. Muller's definition of *analogia Scripturae*: "the interpretation of unclear, difficult, or ambiguous passages of Scripture by comparison with clear and unambiguous passages *that refer to the same teaching or event*."[8] An example of this would be utilizing a passage in Matthew to help understand a passage dealing with the same subject in Mark. This principle, as with the first one, obviously presupposes the divine inspiration of Scripture. The principle of *analogia Scripturae* gained confessional status as follows: "The infallible rule of interpretation of Scripture is the Scripture itself…" (2LCF 1.9).

The Analogy of Faith (Analogia Fidei)

Muller defines *analogia fidei* as follows:

> The use of a general sense of the meaning of Scripture, constructed from the clear or unambiguous *loci* [i.e., places]…, as the basis for interpreting unclear or ambiguous texts. As distinct from the more basic *analogia Scripturae*…, the *analogia fidei* presupposes a sense of the theological meaning of Scripture.[9]

This principle has not always been understood properly. For example, Walter C. Kaiser Jr. fails to distinguish properly between *analogia Scripturae* and *analogia fidei* and advocates what he calls "The Analogy of (Antecedent) Scripture."[10] While analyzing the principle of the analogy of faith,

---

[7] See Vern S. Poythress, "Biblical Hermeneutics," in *Seeing Christ in all of Scripture: Hermeneutics at Westminster Theological Seminary*, ed. Peter A. Lillback (Philadelphia: Westminster Seminary Press, 2016), 14, where he says: "The later communications build on the earlier. What is implicit in the earlier often becomes explicit in the later."

[8] Richard A. Muller, *Dictionary of Latin and Greek Theological Terms* (Grand Rapids: Baker Book House, 1985, Second printing, September 1986), 33; emphasis added.

[9] Ibid., 33.

[10] Walter C. Kaiser, Jr., *Toward An Exegetical Theology* (1981; reprint, Grand Rapids: Baker Book House, Sixth printing, January 1987), 134ff.

he says, "Our problem here is whether the analogy of faith is a hermeneutical tool that is 'open [theological] sesame' for every passage of Scripture."[11] While discussing his proposal for "The Analogy of (Antecedent) Scripture," Kaiser confidently asserts:

> Surely most interpreters will see the wisdom and good sense in limiting our theological observations to conclusions drawn from the text being exegeted and from texts which preceded it in time.[12]

In the conclusion to his discussion, he says:

> However, in no case must that *later* teaching be used exegetically (or in any other way) to unpack the meaning or to enhance the usability of the individual text which is the object of our study.[13]

This is, at worst, a denial of the historic understanding of *analogia fidei* and, at best, a very unhelpful and dangerous modification of the principle. This would mean, for example, that we cannot utilize anything in the Bible outside of Genesis 1–3 to help us interpret it. Since there is nothing in the Bible antecedent to Genesis 1–3, interpreters are left with no subsequent divine use, no subsequent divine explanation of how to understand those chapters. This method ends up defeating itself when we consider that Genesis (like all other books of the Bible) was never intended to stand on its own.[14] As well, the Bible itself (OT and NT) comments on antecedent

---

[11] Kaiser, *Toward An Exegetical Theology*, 135; bracketed word original.

[12] Ibid., 137.

[13] Ibid., 140; emphasis original.

[14] The OT is not an end itself; it is heading somewhere and demands answers to various issues left unfulfilled. It sets the stage for God's future acts of redemption and assumes that God will follow his redemptive acts with corresponding redemptive-revelational words. The OT cannot stand on its own; it is an open-ended book and must be interpreted as such. The NT provides the rest of the story. See Dennis E. Johnson, *Him We Proclaim: Preaching Christ from All the Scriptures* (Phillipsburg, NJ: P&R Publishing, 2007), 160, n. 51, where he takes Kaiser to task for claiming that the OT can stand on its own. In Walter C. Kaiser, Jr., *Preaching and Teaching from the Old Testament: A Guide for the Church* (Grand Rapids: Baker, 2003), 27, he claims: "The Old Testament can stand on its own, for it has done so both in the pre-Christian and the early Christian centuries." Johnson replies: "As will be argued in Chapter 6, the preacher to the Hebrews saw in the Old Testament Scriptures themselves various indications that the Old Testament and its institutions could not 'stand on their own[']' but testified to a better, more 'perfect' order to come." Johnson's book is highly recommended. Reading and interpreting the OT on its own is like reading the Gospels without

texts, helping its readers understand the divine intention of those texts. Kaiser's method seems to imply that the exegesis of a given biblical text is to be conducted as if no subsequent biblical texts exist. We must realize that, in one sense, we have an advantage that the biblical writers did not have—we have a completed canon. But we must also realize that the Bible's use of itself (whenever and however this occurs) is infallible. If this is so, then the exegete, using tools outside of the biblical text under consideration, ought to consult *all* possible useful tools, which includes how the Bible comments upon itself no matter where or how it does so. If the Holy Spirit is the only infallible interpreter of Holy Scripture, then certainly exegetes ought to utilize biblical texts outside of Genesis to aid in the understanding of it. It seems to me that Kaiser's proposal would give warrant for exegetes to consult fallible commentaries on Genesis to aid in its interpretation, but deny the use of the Bible itself (which contains inspired and infallible commentary) to that same end.

An example of the proper understanding and use of the analogy of faith would be identifying the serpent of Genesis 3. We can say with utter certainty that the serpent is the devil and Satan. We know this because God tells us via subsequent Scripture in Revelation 12:9, "And the great dragon was thrown down, the serpent of old who is called the devil and Satan" and 20:2, "And he laid hold of the dragon, the serpent of old, who is the devil and Satan." So, according to the analogy of faith, we can affirm that the serpent of Genesis 3 is the devil and Satan.

The inspired and infallible rule of faith is the whole of Scripture, whose textual parts must be understood in light of its textual-theological whole. This insures that the theological forest is not lost for the individual textual trees. It should keep us from doing theology concordance-style, doing word-studies as an end-all to interpretation, and counting texts that use the same words and drawing theological conclusions from it. These methods often do not consider the meaning of the text (or word) under

---

the Epistles, the Epistles without the Gospels, the Prophets without the Pentateuch, the Pentateuch without the Prophets, and the NT without the OT. Kaiser's position seems to entail reading and interpreting the OT without the New. If this is the case, it would give the appearance of over-emphasizing the human authorial element of Holy Scripture. The apostle Peter informs us, concerning the writing prophets of the OT: "It was revealed to them that they were not serving themselves, but you, in these things which now have been announced to you through those who preached the gospel to you by the Holy Spirit sent from heaven—things into which angels long to look" (1 Peter 1:12). The prophets wrote with a future-oriented messianic consciousness. What they predicted happened when our Lord came and the NT interprets our Lord in light of the OT.

investigation in light of the various levels of context (i.e., phrase, clause, sentence, pericope, book, author, testament, canon) in which it occurs. The principle of the analogy of faith also warrants that, when we are seeking to understand any text of Scripture (e.g., Genesis 1–3), all texts of Scripture are fair game in the interpretive process. It could also be stated this way: the context of every biblical text is all biblical texts.

The principle of *analogia fidei* gained confessional status as follows:

> The infallible rule of interpretation of Scripture is the Scripture itself; and therefore, when there is a question about the true and full sense of any Scripture (which is not manifold, but one), it must be searched by other places that speak more clearly. (2LCF 1.9)

The Scope of Scripture (Scopus Scripturae)

Terms such as *Christ-centered* and *Christocentric* are used often in our day. But what do they mean? The older way of naming the concept these terms point to, the target or end to which the entirety of the Bible tends, is encapsulated by the Latin phrase, *scopus Scripturae* (the scope of the Scriptures). This concept gained confessional status in the WCF, the SD, and the 2LCF in 1.5, which, speaking of Holy Scripture, say, "…the scope of the whole (which is to give all glory to God)…"

Reformation and post-Reformation Reformed theologians understood *scope* in two senses. It had a narrow sense—i.e., the scope of a given text or passage, its basic thrust—but it also had a wider sense—i.e., the target or bull's-eye to which all of Scripture tends.[15] It is to this second sense that we will give our attention.

Scope, in the sense intended here, refers to the center or target of the entire canonical revelation; it is that to which the entire Bible points. Whatever that is, it must condition our interpretation of any and every part of Scripture. For the federal or covenant theologians of the seventeenth cen-

---

[15] See the discussion in Richard A. Muller, *Post-Reformation Reformed Dogmatics: The Rise and Development of Reformed Orthodoxy, ca. 1520 to ca. 1725, Volume Two – Holy Scripture* (Grand Rapids: Baker Academic, 2003 [Second Edition]), 206–23, where he discusses these distinctions. See also James M. Renihan, "Theology on Target: The Scope of the Whole (which is to give all glory to God)," *RBTR* II:2 (July 2005): 36–52; Richard C. Barcellos, "*Scopus Scripturae*: John Owen, Nehemiah Coxe, our Lord Jesus Christ, and a Few Early Disciples on Christ as the Scope of Scripture," *Journal of the Institute of Reformed Baptist Studies* [*JIRBS*] (2015): 5–24; and Stephen J. Casselli, *Divine Rule Maintained: Anthony Burgess, Covenant Theology, and the Place of the Law in Reformed Scholasticism* (Grand Rapids: Reformation Heritage Books, 2016), 102–07.

tury, the scope of Scripture was the glory of God in the redemptive work of the incarnate Son of God.[16] Their view of the scope of Scripture was itself a conclusion from Scripture, not a presupposition brought to it, and it conditioned all subsequent interpretation.[17]

William Ames, for example, said, "The Old and New Testaments are reducible to these two primary heads. The Old promises Christ to come and the New testifies that he has come."[18] Likewise, John Owen said, "Christ is…the principal end of the whole of Scripture…"[19] He continues elsewhere:

> This principle is always to be retained in our minds in reading of the Scripture,—namely, that the revelation and doctrine of the person of Christ and his office, is the foundation whereon all other instructions of the prophets and apostles for the edification of the church are built, and whereunto they are resolved… So our Lord Jesus Christ himself at large makes it manifest, Luke xxiv. 26, 27, 45, 46. Lay aside the consideration hereof, and the Scriptures are no such thing as they pretend unto,—namely, a revelation of the glory of God in the salvation of the church…[20]

Coxe said, "…in all our search after the mind of God in the Holy Scriptures we are to manage our inquiries with reference to Christ."[21]

Their Christocentric interpretation of the Bible was a principle derived from the Bible itself, and an application of *sola Scriptura* to the issue of hermeneutics. In other words, they viewed the Bible's authority as extending to how we interpret the Bible. It could also be stated this way: they saw the authority of Scripture extending to the interpretation of Scripture.[22]

These hermeneutical principles (and others) will be utilized throughout this book. I hope to show that some of NCT's theological formula-

---

[16] See my forthcoming *The Doxological Trajectory of Scripture: God Getting Glory for Himself through what He does in His Son — An Exegetical and Theological Case Study*, Chapter 5, "Christ as Scopus Scripturae — John Owen and Nehemiah Coxe on Christ as the Scope of Scripture for the Glory of God."

[17] I am sure many, if not most or all, NCT adherents would agree with this point.

[18] William Ames, *The Marrow of Theology* (Durham, NC: The Labyrinth Press, 1983), 1.38.5 (202).

[19] John Owen, *The Works of John Owen*, 23 vols., ed. William H. Goold (Edinburgh: The Banner of Truth Trust, 1987 edition), 1:74.

[20] Owen, *Works*, 1:314–15.

[21] Coxe and Owen, *Covenant Theology*, 33.

[22] See Poythress, "Biblical Hermeneutics," 11, where he says: "We use the Bible to derive hermeneutical principles. Then we use hermeneutics to interpret the Bible."

The Importance of Hermeneutics in Theological Formulation

tions do not follow these time-tested and biblically-grounded principles consistently. I believe their faulty doctrinal conclusions stem from a faulty hermeneutic, or at best an inconsistent one.

The Road Ahead for our Study

Since I am a confessional Reformed Baptist subscribing the 2LCF, it will serve as my working theologically-formulated basis to which I will compare some of NCT's doctrinal assertions, whether affirmations or denials. Though some might scoff at such a method, it may help to know that what I subscribe, I do so believing it is the teaching of the Bible. It also means that what I believe the Bible teaches on the subjects discussed is not my personal opinion or an opinion with little (or only recent) historical and ecclesiastical support. My views are neither novel nor private. At each doctrinal place with which NCT is compared, however, I will give attention to prove its scriptural basis. I do this not only to confirm that what the Confession asserts is biblical, but also to challenge those who deny the confessional affirmations addressed.

This study is not an exhaustive critique of NCT. It is purposefully selective. At this point, it is important to say without qualification that those NCT adherents mentioned in this book also affirm very orthodox and agreed-upon doctrines on many fronts. This book addresses some tenets of NCT upon which I think its adherents need to do more thinking. As will become apparent and as stated above, I chose to interact with NCT on the following doctrinal fronts: 1) the covenant of works in the garden of Eden and 2) the perpetuity of a Sabbath day to be kept under the inaugurated new covenant due to the function of the Creator's rest first revealed to us in Genesis 2. Some subjects I chose not to treat in this book were covered in *IDOTD*; others will have to wait for future discussions.

Not only do I not treat every area in which I disagree with NCT, I do not interact with all the literature on the subject by its proponents. I chose to interact with those authors who seem to me to be the major spokesmen for NCT in the United States and who apply the denominator "NCT" to themselves. The book also interacts with others who may not use this denominator, simply to show that what NCT teaches on various issues is also adhered to by others in our day. This fact has given NCT some traction in the last 15 years that it did not have before. The topics to be discussed were chosen due to my belief that NCT gets the beginning (i.e., the garden) wrong. The book ends with a conclusion seeking to briefly recapitulate some of what has been discussed and to tie up any loose ends.

The reader will notice that much of the discussion in the book deals with confessional doctrines denied (or distorted) by NCT. It is only fair to remind ourselves that NCT adherents do not subscribe the 2LCF, but it is also fair to note that much of their polemical writing interacts with doctrines affirmed by the 2LCF and other public confessions of faith and catechisms (especially the Westminster Standards). Along with their denials come affirmations, and I will attempt to be fair in identifying and stating those.

This is a polemical book, which means it will interact with views that I think are wrong. When I state opposition to certain NCT views, however, I will provide arguments in place of those views. In light of the polemical flavor of the book, it may be good to remind ourselves that views are ideas held by persons. One can disagree with another's views without attacking the person. This is what I hope to do. May the Lord help me to this end. I have no itch to attack my brothers (or sisters) and make them look silly or impugn them with less than desirable motives. I believe the NCT adherents with whom I interact in this book are well-meaning believers in Christ. Though I believe they are wrong on various issues (and they believe the same about me), this does not mean I think they are damnable heretics, nor does it mean I ought to treat them with anything less than respect and fairness, accurately reflecting their views. I trust my desires are evident in what follows.

Part One

Adam's Work
In Light of Christ

3

A Covenant of Works in the Garden

THE NEW COVENANT THEOLOGY PERSPECTIVE

Before discussing NCT and the garden of Eden, let me inform readers of my method of approach in the ensuing chapters. The sections where NCT's views are offered are comprised largely of quotations from its adherents and a few from others who hold the same view though do not use the denominator NCT for self-identification. I will attempt to refrain from providing too much comment until the chapters, or sections of chapters, where I offer alternative views from NCT. When reading the words of NCT proponents, it is interesting to notice, not only what they assert (by way of either affirmation or denial), but also the rhetorical power with which they advocate their views.

New Covenant Theology on the Garden of Eden: In Covenant and not in Covenant

It is no secret that NCT denies the 2LCF's formulation of the covenant of works. As will be illustrated below, however, some NCT advocates are proposing an Edenic covenant of (or with) creation, including Adam. This, I believe, is a move in the right direction, since, as Gary D. Long asserts, "God's covenants with man reveal how He governs creation and man in history."[1]

---

[1] Long, *NCT*, 14.

A. Blake White, though denying the covenant of works as understood by confessional Reformed theology, concedes "the viability of a covenant with creation." He says,

> While "covenant" does not occur in the opening chapters of Genesis, many have seen an implicit covenant in the chapters, though the matter is much debated. While not affirming the Reformed notion of a covenant of works or grace in Genesis 1–3, the evidence does demonstrate the viability of a covenant with creation in these chapters.[2]

Long, similar to White, though filling in the details a bit more, says,

> *NCT agrees with CT that there was both a pre-fall covenant and post-fall covenant with Adam, but NCT rejects the traditional covenant of works explanation of CT as taught by the majority of Reformed theologians…*[3]

Long prefers calling this covenant "a pre-fall covenant or creation covenant."[4] Elsewhere, he labels it "a pre-fall covenant of obedience with Adam."[5] He even cites Hosea 6:7 as proof for a pre-fall covenant with Adam.[6] In a footnote in his discussion, Long concedes that some NCT adherents deny any pre-fall covenant with Adam, but then he follows with a very important and perceptive caveat:

> Some who genuinely claim to teach NCT do not hold to a pre-fall covenant with Adam because the word for covenant does not occur until Genesis 6:18. But doctrinally, the denial of a pre-fall covenant will, *if consistently* carried out, eventually undermine—as history has demonstrated, e.g., in New England Theology (1750–1900)—the whole doctrine of imputation of Adam's original sin and Christ's righteousness, indeed of substitutionary atonement. God forbid![7]

Both White and Long affirm some sort of covenant in the garden or at creation while also denying the traditional Reformed understanding of a covenant of works. Long seems to base this covenant on Romans 5:12–19,

---

[2] A. Blake White, *The Newness of the New Covenant* (Frederick, MD: New Covenant Media, 2008), 7.

[3] Long, *NCT*, 11; emphasis original.

[4] Ibid., 12.

[5] Ibid., 2 and 92. On page 92, he says, "I prefer using the generic term *"pre-fall"* covenant of obedience"; emphasis original.

[6] Ibid., 12–13. We will discuss Hosea 6:7 in Chapter 6.

[7] Ibid., 11, n. 6; emphasis original.

The New Covenant Theology Perspective 33

Hosea 6:7, and other considerations,[8] while White opts for basing it upon Genesis 6:18a (along with Hosea 6:7 and other considerations).[9]

Other NCT writers clearly deny a covenant of works. Notice the rhetorical power of some of these statements. For example, John Reisinger says:

> [Covenant Theology] assumed that covenants were the key to understanding Scripture, and then discovered two covenants in Genesis: a Covenant of Works with Adam before he fell, and a Covenant of Grace with Adam after he fell. Neither of these covenants is found in Genesis (or anywhere else in Scripture); neither is based on clear textual evidence.[10]

Reisinger denies a covenant in the garden altogether.

In a paper which is dated 2004, answering the question, "A Covenant of Works?" Reisinger says:

> I view the situation in the Garden of Eden as follows: Suppose I put you on a large farm and tell you that everything on it was for your personal use and enjoyment. I promise to pay all of the bills for everything, the fertilizer, the animal's feed, the electric bill, etc. You need only work the farm and you may sell or use all the produce, animals, etc. for yourself. There is only one condition. There is a small building out back of the barn that belongs to me and you may not go into it. The day you go in that building, you are going to be thrown off the farm. That is exactly like the arrangement that God made with Adam. Those are the same promises, conditions and terms laid on Adam in Eden. Everything in the Garden was Adam's to do with as he chose. The only restriction was to not eat of one tree.[11]

Later in the same piece he says, "I always thought Eden was a pretty good deal that did not need any improvements. I think Adam had everything any heart could desire."[12] This comes while denying the traditional Reformed understanding that the covenant of works proffered life

---

[8] Long, *NCT*, 11–14 and 105–107.
[9] White, *Newness*, 7–11. White views the Noahic covenant as a sort of recapitulation of the creation covenant (11–12).
[10] Reisinger, *In Defense of Jesus*, 39.
[11] John G. Reisinger, "A Covenant of Works?" http://resources.grantedministries.org/article/covenant_of_works_j_r.pdf. Accessed 31 March 2016.
[12] Reisinger, "A Covenant of Works?"

to Adam as a reward for his obedience. He counters this with these words: "But He [*sic*] already had life!"[13]

In his book, *New Covenant Theology: questions answered*, Steve Lehrer says:

> NCT does not believe that it is wise to refer to God's relationship with Adam as a "covenant." NCT holds that God gave Adam a command with a promise of punishment if broken. And because this situation is not called a covenant by the authors of Scripture, we must think twice about describing it by that name ourselves.
>
> Let's consider that most important and foundational question "Is it biblical?" Even if the relationship between God and Adam in the Garden is technically a covenant, God places no importance on that fact. If Scripture does not use the term "covenant" when referring to God's relationship to Adam but uses it of other pivotal events, perhaps we should reserve the term for those events God calls covenants.[14]

Notice Lehrer's words, "Even if the relationship between God and Adam in the Garden is technically a covenant, God places no importance on that fact." If the relationship is "technically a covenant" (and I believe it is), the only way we could know this is due to divine revelation. And if it is divinely revealed, it is very important. Lehrer's statement obviously contradicts Long and White, who believe subsequent revelation demands we call Adam's relationship to God a covenantal one. Both Lehrer and Reisinger seem to deny not only a covenant in the garden but also any offered reward for obedience as well. Long also denies that the covenant with Adam proffered a type of life he did not have via the creative act of God. Instead, he says, "…if [Adam] continued obedient, he would continue in his [then] present state of *earthly* bliss."[15] I am of the opinion that NCT advocates need to think more on this important issue.

Though there is rethinking and reformulating going on with some NCT advocates on this issue, the traditional Reformed formulation of the covenant of works is still clearly denied.

---

[13] Reisinger, "A Covenant of Works?" See Chapters 5 and 6 for a discussion of the covenant of works and the promise of life as a reward.

[14] Steve Lehrer, *New Covenant Theology: questions answered* (n. p., 2006), 41.

[15] Long, *NCT*, 88; emphasis original.

Denying the Covenant of Works: An Illustration of "Biblicism"?

From the quotations above, it is obvious that NCT categorically denies the doctrine of the covenant of works in the garden as formulated in the 2LCF (Chapters 4 and 5 of this book investigate the covenant of works in the 2LCF and the Bible.). This type of denial from NCT reflects a tendency toward a "biblicist" mentality which demands that a doctrine must be spelled out explicitly in the text of Scripture. However, as I hope to show below, there are many times when a scriptural doctrine or concept may be observed without the specific wording required by biblicists.[16] One example of a biblicist mentality by a NCT author can be found in these words by A. Blake White: "NCT strives to limit itself to using the language of the Bible."[17] In the endorsement section of White's book, Jim Elliff says, "What attracts me to this way of seeing Scripture is its determination to use Bible words for Bible concepts…"[18] John G. Reisinger informs us, "The Ten Commandments are never once called the moral law by any writer of Scripture…."[19] Similarly, Gary D. Long says, "It should be noted that the word '*moral*' does not occur in the original languages of the Bible. Therefore, it is better not to refer to God's law as 'the *moral* law of God'…"[20] Long rejects the term moral because it is not in the Bible, yet he asserts elsewhere that "Biblical law may be rightly explained under two distinctive categories: the *absolute law of God and the covenantal law of God*…."[21] Neither of these phrases occur in the original languages of the Bible, however. Elsewhere, Long asserts the following about some NCT advocates:

---

[16] For informed discussions on biblicism see James M. Renihan, "Person and Place: Two Problems with Biblicism," in *Southern California Reformed Baptist Pastors' Conference Papers*, Volume I (2012), ed. Richard C. Barcellos (Palmdale, CA: RBAP, 2012), 111–27 and Michael Allen and Scott R. Swain, *Reformed Catholicity: The Promise of Retrieval for Theology and Biblical Interpretation* (Grand Rapids: Baker Academic, 2015), 84ff. and 117–41.

[17] White, *What is New Covenant Theology?*, 6. White's book, ironically, contains many words not used in the Bible to explain the Bible.

[18] Ibid., iii.

[19] Reisinger, *In Defense of Jesus*, 330. See John G. Reisinger, *Abraham's Four Seeds: A Biblical Examination of the Presuppositions of Covenant Theology and Dispensationalism* (Frederick, MD: New Covenant Media, 1998), ii, 20, 38–39, 45, 46.

[20] Long, *NCT*, 171.

[21] Ibid., 131; emphasis original.

> ...some within NCT deny that a covenant existed between God and Adam because the word *covenant* does not occur until Genesis 6:18. However, this is too simplistic for such a position does not take into account the characteristics of a divine covenant present in the original creation and more fully revealed and explicitly taught in the movement, the organic nature, of redemptive history.[22]

Consistent biblicism (which NCT is not) rejects doctrinal formulations which use words not used *explicitly* by the Bible. If one uses words not utilized by the Bible in the formulation of a given doctrine (e.g., "covenant of works"), the consistent biblicist rejects that doctrine because it does not use Bible words. This is a classic example of the word-concept fallacy, which asserts that if a word is not present, then the concept it embodies is not present. As we will see below, the writers of Scripture did not fall prey to this fallacy and, in fact, sometimes referred to concepts in earlier texts using words not found in the earlier passage. For example, in Acts 2:31, Peter says David "...looked ahead and spoke of the resurrection of the Christ..." in Psalm 16. The psalm, however, has neither the word *resurrection* nor the word *Christ* in it. Peter is describing *concepts* from Psalm 16 in *words* not used by Psalm 16. Later texts can, and do, describe earlier *concepts* with different *words*.

Some of the statements above would force (at least some) NCT advocates to argue against the covenant of works in the garden on various fronts. First, neither the word "covenant" nor the word "works" occurs in the narrative of Genesis 1–2, which, though not a deal-breaker for all NCT advocates on this account alone, causes serious doubt in some that a covenant was imposed upon Adam in the garden.[23] Second, though some are advocating a "covenant of creation" or "covenant of obedience," they deny the works aspect of the traditional Reformed doctrine of the covenant of works, especially the promise of life conditioned upon obedience.[24] How should we respond to this?

In Chapter 5 I want to illustrate the proper hermeneutical principles discussed above and how these have led and continue to lead to the doctrine of the covenant of works. Not all of the arguments in favor of a covenant of works will be offered, however. I also want to suggest a better way ahead for NCT. Prior to looking at the Bible, it may help to examine the 2LCF and its doctrinal formulation of the covenant of works. This will

---

[22] Long, *NCT*, 85. Long does not provide any names of NCT advocates who argue this way.

[23] See above.

[24] See Long, *NCT*, 88ff. and Lehrer, *New Covenant Theology*, 41.

provide us with what NCT denies and what I hope to show (in Chapter 5) is grounded in the text of Scripture itself.

4

A Covenant of Works in the Garden
THE CONFESSIONAL FORMULATION

In order to understand what NCT denies about the covenant of works as formulated in the 2LCF and to understand what must be proven from Scripture to affirm such a doctrine, this chapter focuses on the Confession. A working definition of the covenant of works is necessary in order to begin. The covenant of works is that divinely sanctioned commitment or relationship God imposed upon Adam in the garden of Eden. Adam was a sinless representative of mankind (i.e., a public person), and an image-bearing son of God. The covenant God made with him was for the bettering of man's state, conditioned upon Adam's obedience, with a penalty for disobedience. Here we have: 1) sovereign, divine imposition; 2) representation by Adam (i.e., federal headship), a sinless image-bearing son of God; 3) a conditional element (i.e., obedience); 4) a penalty for disobedience (i.e., death); and 5) a promise of reward (i.e., eschatological potential). It is important to keep this definition in mind as we work our way through this chapter and the next.

How the Confessional Doctrine of the Covenant of Works was Formulated[1]

Before tracing the confessional formulation of the covenant of works, let's consider how it was *not* formulated.

---

[1] The material under this heading is taken (with permission and modification)

How the Doctrine of the Covenant of Works was Not Formulated

The doctrine of the covenant of works was not formulated by the Westminster divines inventing a theory and then trying to find it in the Bible, forcing biblical texts into a pre-conceived theological system. The same is true for the Savoy and Particular Baptist divines. This is contrary to what I was taught during my seminary days in the late 1980s, which was that the theology of the seventeenth-century divines stood over the Bible as its interpretive lord.

Some think that a theology of the garden including the covenant of works was only constructed in the minds of men, and then a hermeneutic was invented to justify it. In other words, an extra-biblical theology led to an extra-biblical hermeneutic, which led to an extra-biblical confessional formulation.[2] Again, in this view, their theology and hermeneutical principles stood over the Bible as interpretive lord.

It is certainly true, however, that the hermeneutics (interpretive principles) used by covenant theologians did indeed lead to their covenant theology (what they said the Bible teaches). However, their theology and their hermeneutical principles, though in part distinguishable, were not separate, unrelated categories, one derived from special revelation (i.e., Scripture) and the other (i.e., hermeneutics) exclusively from general revelation. Rather, part of their theology was hermeneutics.

In other words, *their interpretive principles came, in part, from what they believed the Bible said about itself and how it interpreted itself.* They saw texts (that is, the authors of texts and/or those speaking in the texts) interacting with texts (authored by others) and further explaining them, sometimes using new words to describe the concepts contained in the text being referenced (Cf. Acts 2:31 and Psalm 16, as noted above). In our day, we would say they saw inner-biblical exegesis occurring in the Bible; that is, they saw later texts interpreting and applying earlier texts, and they accounted

from Barcellos, "Getting the Garden Right: From Hermeneutics to the Covenant of Works," 198–201.

[2] Having studied the theological method of seventeenth-century Reformed orthodoxy (especially as it relates to covenant theology and the interpretation of redemptive history), I am convinced from the primary sources that anyone who makes this claim has either not read the proper sources or does not understand what they read. This claim gives the appearance of being nothing less than a dismissal tactic. It might carry rhetorical weight with uninformed readers, but it has no basis in the facts of history. See Richard C. Barcellos, *The Family Tree of Reformed Biblical Theology: Geerhardus Vos and John Owen — Their Methods of and Contributions to the Articulation of Redemptive History* (Owensboro, KY: RBAP, 2010), 53–107.

for it in the way they understood other texts. In other words, they did not impose a wholesale extra-biblical theory of hermeneutics upon the Bible, thus producing their covenant theology. Their approach to hermeneutics instead sought to reflect what they saw transpiring in the Bible, and in this sense came from Scripture itself, not some extra-biblical source.

How the Doctrine of the Covenant of Works Was Formulated

How did the older covenant theologians go from the garden to the covenant of works? The answer is that they utilized long-acknowledged hermeneutical principles somewhat typical of the entire Christian theological tradition from the early centuries to the post-Reformation era.[3] In other words, as noted in Chapter 2, they utilized a pre-critical or pre-Enlightenment method of interpreting Scripture. They believed that the Bible was not to be interpreted like any other book. They believed the Bible was the written Word of God and that it was its only infallible interpreter. They not only believed the writers of Scripture to be God's penmen, but they also saw them to be infallible theologians as they wrote, due to the doctrine of the divine inspiration of Holy Scripture. They believed that the Bible often interpreted itself and that later texts often used earlier texts in a way that gave the divine, and therefore infallible, interpretation of those earlier texts.

The Doctrine of the Covenant of Works in the Confession of Faith

There was a time when I thought the 2LCF was substantially different from the WCF and SD on the doctrine of the covenant of works. The reasoning was simple. The 2LCF does not say what the other confessions say about the covenant of works in Chapter 7. Both the WCF and the SD assert in 7.2: "The first covenant made with man was a covenant of works, wherein life was promised to Adam; and in him to his posterity, upon condition of perfect and personal obedience." The 2LCF does not contain this paragraph (see the text of the 2LCF 7.1–2 below). The conclusion was that the Particular Baptists must have held to a different view of Adam in the garden. I now believe I was wrong. Others hold this view or something similar to it: since 7.2 of the WCF and SD was deleted by the Baptists, their theology of the garden was different. Such a view is incorrect for several reasons which will be discussed below.

---

[3] A good case can be made that the principles they used predate post-apostolic reflection and are imbedded in the text of Scripture (OT and NT) itself. Proving this, however, is beyond the scope of this book.

The Confessional Formulation

At this point, six observations will be offered upon the 2LCF 7.1–2 to aid in understanding what it asserts concerning the covenant of works. These paragraphs were chosen for three reasons: first, the title of Chapter 7 is "Of God's Covenant"; second, the language of the 2LCF 7.2 is not the same as the WCF and SD, which has caused some to conclude that the doctrine of the covenant of works is absent or considerably altered; and third, although the phrase "covenant of works" is absent, the concept is present. We will then move to broader considerations of the 2LCF which will be offered to prove that its formulation, though differing in form (i.e., the way it is stated), is materially (i.e., the substance that is stated) the same as the WCF and SD.

Six Observations Upon the 2LCF 7.1–2

Here are the paragraphs which will be examined below followed by six observations:

> The distance between God and the creature is so great, that although reasonable creatures do owe obedience to him as their creator, yet they could never have attained the reward of life but by some voluntary condescension on God's part, which he hath been pleased to express by way of covenant. (2LCF 7.1)

> Moreover, man having brought himself under the curse of the law by his fall, it pleased the Lord to make a covenant of grace, wherein he freely offereth unto sinners life and salvation by Jesus Christ, requiring of them faith in him, that they may be saved; and promising to give unto all those that are ordained unto eternal life, his Holy Spirit, to make them willing and able to believe. (2LCF 7.2)

1. It is important to realize the confessional context of this chapter. Chapter 7, "Of God's Covenant," comes after the chapter on creation, Chapter 4, "Of Creation," and after the chapter on sin, Chapter 6, "Of the Fall of Man, of Sin, and of the Punishment Thereof." Chapter 7 comes before Chapter 8, "Of Christ the Mediator."[4] The order is creation, fall, covenant, and then the Mediator of salvation.[5]

---

[4] See the helpful outline of the 2LCF in James M. Renihan, "Covenant Theology in the First and Second London Confessions of Faith," *Recovering a Covenantal Heritage: Essays in Baptist Covenant Theology*, ed. Richard C. Barcellos (Palmdale, CA: RBAP, 2014), 61–62.

[5] I noted the order to show the progressive development of doctrinal formulation in the Confession. The later chapters assume the former and the former

2. It is important to understand the flow of thought in 7.1–2. Here is my attempt at an outline of part of 7.1–2.

A. The Absolute Necessity of God's Covenant (2LCF 7.1)

   1. Because of the Creator/creature distinction (2LCF 7.1a); *The distance between God and the creature is so great, that although reasonable creatures do owe obedience to him as their creator*

   2. Because the reward of life could never be attained apart from the condescension of God (2LCF 7.1b); *yet they could never have attained the reward of life but by some voluntary condescension on God's part, which he hath been pleased to express by way of covenant*

B. The Essential Characteristics of God's Covenant (2LCF 7.2)

   1. Its Subsequent Necessity (2LCF 7.2a); *Moreover, man having brought himself under the curse of the law by his fall*

   2. Its Divine Basis (2LCF 7.2b); *it pleased the Lord*

   3. Its Gracious Nature (2LCF 7.2c); *to make a covenant of grace*

   4. Its Specific Elements (2LCF 7.2d, e); *wherein…*

Notice that the necessity of God's covenant with man is grounded in two realities. The first is the Creator/creature distinction ("The distance between God and the creature is so great, that although reasonable creatures do owe obedience to him as their creator"). The second is the necessity of condescension on God's part for the attaining of "the reward of life" ("yet they could never have attained the reward of life but by some voluntary condescension on God's part, which he hath been pleased to express by way of covenant"). Reasonable creatures owe God obedience (2LCF 4.2–3), but the reward of life is added or promised "by some voluntary condescension on God's part." This "voluntary condescension" God "hath been pleased to express by way of covenant."

3. It is important to understand how 7.2 relates to 7.1. Notice the word "Moreover" in paragraph 2. This means something like in addition to what

prepare for the later. This means that Chapter 7 assumes the chapters prior to it and the doctrinal assertions therein. As will be argued below, the 2LCF 7.1–2 does not use the phrase "covenant of works" for at least two reasons: first, it is assumed from 2LCF 4 and 6 and second, 2LCF 7 concentrates primarily upon the covenant of grace, especially paragraphs 2 and 3.

has been said, further, or besides. It is an expansion on what has been said in light of Adam's fall into sin (2LCF 6.1). The implication is that God voluntarily condescended "by way of covenant" for the attaining of "the reward of life" (see 2LCF 7.1 and 6.1, "…gave him a righteous law, which had been unto life had he kept it…"), but man fell in Adam and was brought "under the curse of the law by his fall," thus necessitating "a covenant of grace." The "curse of the law" in 7.2 refers to the threatened death of Genesis 2:16–17.

4. Notice to what the following words refer: "The distance between God and the creature is so great, that although reasonable creatures [see 2LCF 4.2] *do owe obedience to him as their creator" (2LCF 7.1a).* These words refer to what man as creature owes to God as Creator.[6] Here the Creator/creature distinction is expressed. Reasonable creatures owe obedience to God because He is their Creator, specifically due to the constitution of man as made in the image of God, which will be noted below.

5. Notice the words, "yet they could never have attained the reward of life but by some voluntary condescension on God's part" (2LCF 7.1b). The clause means that "the reward of life" is not based exclusively on the Creator/creature relationship stated in 7.1a. This becomes clear by the next observation and explanation.

6. Notice that the words, "which he hath been pleased to express by way of covenant," tell us what God's "voluntary condescension" is. The clause "which he hath been pleased to express by way of covenant" tells us to what God's "voluntary condescension" refers, which in turn contains the promise of "the reward of life." This principle of "the reward of life" being related to "some voluntary condescension on God's part" implies a covenantal revelation beyond and subsequent to Adam's created status.[7] This is what has been termed "the covenant of works."

Though man as a reasonable or rational creature owes God obedience because he is created,[8] "the reward of life" for obedience is a covenantal stipulation, not a strictly or absolutely creational one. In other words, there were two pre-fall states in which Adam existed—as a reasonable creature

---

[6] See the discussions by Robert Shaw, *An Exposition of the Westminster Confession of Faith* (Fearn Ross-shire, Scotland: Christian Focus Publications, 1998), 123, and A. A. Hodge, *The Confession of Faith* (1869; reprint, Edinburgh; Carlisle, PA: The Banner of Truth Trust, 1983), 120–21.

[7] This will be discussed below.

[8] The 2LCF 7.1 cites Luke 17:10, which says, "So you too, when you do all the things which are commanded you, say, 'We are unworthy slaves; we have done *only* that which we ought to have done.'" Man owes God obedience because he is a reasonable or rational creature of God.

of God, owing obedience to his Creator, and as a reasonable creature of God in covenant with Him, owing obedience to his covenantal Lord.[9] A. A. Hodge, commenting on WCF 7.1 says, "The very act of creation brings the creature under obligation to the Creator, but it cannot bring the Creator into obligation to the creature."[10] Robert Shaw, commenting on the same text, says, "God entered into a covenant with Adam in his state of innocence."[11] This seems to imply that Adam existed in a state of innocence and, while existing in that state, God entered into a covenant with him. Is this what is intended by the WCF, SD, and 2LCF?

Where did God enter into a covenant with Adam?[12] Consider the fact that man was made before the garden into which he was placed. Genesis 2:7–8 says,

> Then the LORD God formed man of dust from the ground, and breathed into his nostrils the breath of life; and man became a living being. The LORD God planted a garden toward the east, in Eden; and there He placed the man whom He had formed.

Genesis 2:15 says, "Then the LORD God took the man and put him into the garden of Eden to cultivate it and keep it." Man was created, then placed in the garden. Man's Edenic vocation was not absolutely coeval with his creation. This distinction between man as creature of God and man in covenant with God in the garden seems to be what the WCF, SD, and 2LCF teach. The Westminster Larger Catechism (WLC), Q. 20 says:

> Q. 20. *What was the providence of God toward man in the estate in which he was created?*
> A. The providence of God toward man in the estate in which he was created, was *the placing him in paradise*, appointing him to dress it, giving him liberty to eat of the fruit of earth; putting the creatures under his dominion, and ordaining marriage for his help; affording him communion with himself; instituting the Sabbath; *entering into a covenant of life with him*, upon condition of personal, perfect, and perpetual obedience, of which the tree of life was a pledge; and forbidding to eat of the tree

---

[9] See the discussions in Rowland S. Ward, *God & Adam: Reformed Theology and the Creation Covenant* (Wantirna, Australia: New Melbourne Press, 2003), 59–66 and 99–103. Ward uses the language "two pre-fall states" on p. 61 (see also 99ff.). Casselli, *Divine Rule Maintained*, 69ff. points out the careful distinctions made by the seventeenth-century Reformed theologians on this issue.

[10] Hodge, *Confession of Faith*, 121.

[11] Shaw, *Exposition*, 124.

[12] This question obviously assumes that God entered into covenant with Adam for the sake of the discussion about the Confession.

of the knowledge of good and evil, upon the pain of death. (emphasis added)

Notice that the WLC discusses the covenant of works under the doctrine of divine providence, which begins at Q. 18. ("What are God's works of providence?") and comes after the questions dealing with creation (i.e., questions 15–17). The Westminster Shorter Catechism (WSC) and the Baptist Catechism (BC) do the same thing. In the estate in which man was created, God revealed to him what is termed "a covenant of life," which is a synonym for the covenant of works, after "placing him in paradise." The covenant of works, then, is not absolutely coeval with the act of man's creation.[13] Man was created *for* covenant, but strictly speaking not *in* the covenant of works.[14] The creation of man and man in the covenant of works with God can be distinguished but they should not be separated.[15] The *matter* of the covenant of works, the law written on Adam's heart due to man being created in the image of God, is present at his creation, however, the *form* of the covenant of works was revealed to him by God as found in (at least) Genesis 2:16–17.[16] Though beyond the scope of this chapter's discussion, it is important to realize that the Confession asserts that man, male and female, was "made after the image of God, in knowledge, righteousness, and true holiness [citing Ecclesiastes 7:29 and Genesis 1:26];

---

[13] See Barcellos, *The Family Tree*, 164–66, under the heading "EXCURSUS: The Temporal Revelation of the Covenant of Works in Owen — Absolutely or Relatively Coeval with Creation?" and Ward, *God & Adam*, Chapter 4, entitled "Emergence of a post-creation, pre-fall covenant," 59–66 and Chapter 11 entitled "Law and covenant: the two states of the pre-fall Adam," 99–103.

[14] Thanks to Samuel Renihan for first mentioning this formulation to me. See Joel R. Beeke & Mark Jones, *A Puritan Theology: Doctrine for Life* (Grand Rapids: Reformation Heritage Books, 2012), 223–24, under the heading, "Made *In* or *For* a Covenant?" The 2LCF hints at this distinction in these words: "After God had made all other creatures, he created man, male and female, with reasonable and immortal souls, rendering them fit *unto* [emphasis added] that life to God *for which* [emphasis added] they were created…" (2LCF 4.2a). Man was created "fit unto that life for which they were created…" This seems to imply the distinction for which I am arguing. Whether that is the case or not, in the next chapter it will become clear that many seventeenth-century (and subsequent) Reformed theologians viewed the covenant of works as offering a quality of life not endowed upon man at his creation.

[15] Ward, *God & Adam*, 99.

[16] According to Ward, this is the view found in Edward Fisher's *The Marrow of Modern Divinity*. See Ward, *God & Adam*, 102. Thanks to Dabney Olguin for stimulating discussions on this issue.

having the law of God written in their hearts [citing Romans 2:14–15]…" (2LCF 4.2). Adam's responsibility to obey God is based on creation; once put in the garden, however, a positive[17] aspect of his obedience is added by the words of Genesis 2:16–17. This is reflected in 2LCF 6.1 and 19.1.

> Although God created man upright and perfect, and gave him a righteous law, which had been unto life had he kept it, and threatened death upon the breach thereof [citing Genesis 2:16–17], yet he did not long abide in this honour; Satan using the subtlety of the serpent to subdue Eve, then by her seducing Adam, who, without any compulsion, did willfully transgress the law of their creation, and the command given unto them, in eating the forbidden fruit, which God was pleased, according to his wise and holy counsel to permit, having purposed to order it to his own glory. (2LCF 6.1)

> God gave to Adam a law of universal obedience written in his heart [echoing 2LCF 4.2, quoted above], and a particular precept of not eating the fruit of the tree of knowledge of good and evil [echoing 2LCF 6.1]; by which he bound him and all his posterity to personal, entire, exact, and perpetual obedience; promised life upon the fulfilling, and threatened death upon the breach of it, and endued him with power and ability to keep it. (2LCF 19.1)

As stated above, Adam's created state and covenantal state unto life may be distinguished but ought not to be separated. This distinction is reflected in the WCF, SD, 2LCF, WLC, WSC, BC, and in many writers of that era.[18]

---

[17] "Positive" refers to that which is in addition to nature or creation. The law written on the heart of man at creation and the obedience owed the Creator is natural; the positive law, being in addition to nature, brings man formally into covenant with his Creator.

[18] Another way the distinction was maintained has to do with the concept of man's restipulation. For example, Coxe says: "…a covenant relationship to God and interest in him does not immediately result from the proposal of a covenant and terms of a covenant relationship to man. But it is by restipulation that man actually enters into covenant with God and becomes an interested party in the covenant. It is a mutual consent of the parties in covenant that states [To instate or establish in covenant.] and completes a covenant relationship." See Coxe and Owen, *Covenant Theology*, 35. The bracketed words are an editorial footnote in the Coxe and Owen book. The concept of restipulation, according to some, does not apply universally or to all biblical covenants. For example, the Noahic covenant is a covenant of unconditional promise. No one had to do any work of the law or believe in the gospel for the promise of that covenant to be fulfilled. The concept

The Confessional Formulation

Man's obedience is naturally necessary due to his being created by God and in His image. Anything above this, such as "the reward of life," comes from God's "voluntary condescension…, which he hath been pleased to express by way of covenant" (2LCF 7.1). Casselli, commenting on the view of Westminster Assembly member Anthony Burgess, says, "Adam by virtue of creation owes perfect obedience to God, which obedience strictly merits nothing from God, but which God graciously chooses to reward on the basis of the covenant established by Him."[19] Coxe says that God added to the law written on Adam's heart a positive law in the garden of Eden. Recall that man was placed in the garden after he was created. Here are Coxe's own words:

> It pleased the Sovereign Majesty of Heaven to add to this eternal law [i.e., the internal law written on man's heart via the creative act of God] a positive precept in which he charged man not to eat of the fruit of one tree in the midst of the garden of Eden.[20]

Coxe also says,

> In this lies the mystery of the first transaction of God with man and of his relationship to God founded on it. *This did not result immediately from the law of his creation but from the disposition of a covenant according to the free, sovereign, and wise counsel of God's will.* Therefore, although the law of creation is easily understood by men (and there is little controversy about it among those that are not degenerate from all principles of reason and humanity), yet the covenant of creation, the interest of Adam's posterity with him in it, and the guilt of original sin returning on them by it, are not owned by the majority of mankind. Nor can they be understood except by the light of divine revelation.[21]

> *It is not from any necessity of nature that God enters into covenant with men* but of his own good pleasure. Such a privilege and nearness to God as is included in covenant interest *cannot immediately result from the relationship which they have to God as reasonable creatures*, though upright and in a perfect state.[22]

---

of restipulation is also termed dipleuric. For discussion on the terms monopleuric and dipleuric in the context of covenantal revelations of God to man see Barcellos, *The Family Tree*, 91, 97, 98, 101, 163, 164, 165, 187, and 204, and the sources cited there. For definitions of these terms see Muller, *Dictionary*, 120 and 122.

[19] Casselli, *Divine Rule Maintained*, 72.
[20] Coxe and Owen, *Covenant Theology*, 43.
[21] Ibid., 49; emphasis added.
[22] Ibid., 36; emphasis added.

The "voluntary condescension" of God was an act of His kind providence, not formally included in the initial act of man's creation. The promise of "the reward of life" is in addition to man's created status. The type of life to be rewarded was not what Adam possessed via creation, but what he failed to attain via covenant or, as the WCF says, the "fruition of [God] as their blessedness and reward" (WCF 7.1). It is this quality of life that our Lord Jesus merited by His covenantal obedience as the last Adam, and which He brings to and confers upon all gospel-believing sinners (see Chapter 5). This is termed the *covenant of grace*, and is the focus of Chapter 7 of the 2LCF.

Though Chapter 7 of the 2LCF does not use the phrase "covenant of works," the doctrinal concept of it is clearly implied in all three paragraphs (see below for brief discussion of the 2LCF 7.3). It is also implied in 4.3, 6.1, Chapter 8, and 19.1 as well. The phrase is used explicitly in 19.6 (twice) and 20.1.

The 2LCF Contains the Same Doctrine of the Covenant of Works as the WCF and SD

Taking a wider look at the 2LCF in order to see the doctrinal assertions, the assumptions of earlier formulations within the document, and the explicit terminology used at various places will bring with it the conclusion that its basic doctrine of the covenant of works comports with the WCF and SD. Six reasons for this claim are offered below.

1. Because the explicit language "covenant of works" occurs in the Confession (19.6 [twice] and 20.1).

> Although true believers be not under the law as a *covenant of works*, to be thereby justified or condemned, yet it is of great use to them as well as to others, in that as a rule of life, informing them of the will of God and their duty, it directs and binds them to walk accordingly; discovering also the sinful pollutions of their natures, hearts, and lives, so as examining themselves thereby, they may come to further conviction of, humiliation for, and hatred against, sin; together with a clearer sight of the need they have of Christ and the perfection of his obedience; it is likewise of use to the regenerate to restrain their corruptions, in that it forbids sin; and the threatenings of it serve to shew what even their sins deserve, and what afflictions in this life they may expect for them, although freed from the curse and unallayed rigour thereof. The promises of it likewise shew them God's approbation of obedience, and what blessings they may expect upon the performance thereof, though not as due to them by the law as a *covenant of works*; so as man's doing good and refraining from evil, because the law encourageth to the one and deterreth from the other,

is no evidence of his being under the law and not under grace. (2LCF 19.6; emphasis added)

The *covenant of works* being broken by sin, and made unprofitable unto life, God was pleased to give forth the promise of Christ, the seed of the woman, as the means of calling the elect, and begetting in them faith and repentance; in this promise the gospel, as to the substance of it, was revealed, and [is] therein effectual for the conversion and salvation of sinners. (2LCF 20.1; emphasis added)

There is no reason from the Confession or the writings of Nehemiah Coxe, a likely co-editor (possibly even senior editor) of the Confession, or any other Particular Baptist connected to the Confession (as far as I am aware) to think they meant anything different from what their Presbyterian and Congregational brothers meant by the phrase "covenant of works." Pascal Denault, supporting this claim, says, "The writings of the [seventeenth-century Particular] Baptists show that they shared this same conception of the Covenant of Works as their paedobaptist contemporaries."[23] Also, in the Preface to the Confession, entitled, "*To the Judicious and Impartial Reader*," we are assured that the editors used

the very same words with them both [i.e., Presbyterians and Congregationalists] in these articles (which are many) wherein our faith and doctrine are the same with theirs; and this we did the more abundantly to manifest our consent with both in all the fundamental articles of the Christian religion… And also to convince all that we have no itch to clog religion with new words… (xiii)

It is likely this applies to, among other things, the phrase and doctrine of the covenant of works. There is no evidence in the primary document or any secondary documents that I am aware of that they meant anything different from what others in their day meant by the phrase.

2. *Because the doctrine of the covenant of works is contained or implied without the phrase "covenant of works" in at least five places in the Confession.* First, 2LCF 6.1 says:

Although God created man upright and perfect, and gave him a righteous law, which had been unto life had he kept it, and threatened death upon the breach thereof, yet he did not long abide in this honour; Satan

---

[23] Denault, *The Distinctiveness of Baptist Covenant Theology*, 29. See Renihan, "Covenant Theology in the First and Second London Confessions of Faith," 45–70.

using the subtlety of the serpent to subdue Eve, then by her seducing Adam, who, without any compulsion, did willfully transgress the law of their creation, and the command given unto them, in eating the forbidden fruit, which God was pleased, according to his wise and holy counsel to permit, having purposed to order it to his own glory.

This is the doctrine of the covenant of works without the phrase. Notice the context in which it occurs—the fall into sin. If we lived in the seventeenth century, we would immediately think "covenant of works" while reading 6.1.

Second, 2LCF 7.1 says:

The distance between God and the creature is so great, that although reasonable creatures do owe obedience to him as their creator, yet they could never have attained the reward of life but by some voluntary condescension on God's part, which he hath been pleased to express by way of covenant.

This implies "the reward of life" (not a gift at Adam's creation, but a quality of life to be attained via covenant) spoken of in 2LCF 6.1 came by God's "voluntary condescension…by way of covenant."

Third, 2LCF 7.2a says, "Moreover, man having brought himself under the curse of the law by his fall." As noted above, "Moreover" should be taken to mean something like in addition to what has been said, further, or besides. It is an expansion on what has already been said in light of Adam's fall into sin. What had already been said? Both 2LCF 7.1 and 2LCF 6.1. The implication is that God voluntarily condescended by way of covenant for the attaining of the reward of life but man fell in Adam and was brought under the curse of the law.

Fourth, 2LCF 7.3b says, "man being now utterly incapable of acceptance with God upon those terms on which Adam stood in his state of innocency." The necessity of the covenant of grace is predicated upon the fact that man is incapable of acceptance with God upon the terms Adam stood upon in his state of innocency (see 2LCF 6.1), and according to 2LCF 7.1, those terms included God's "voluntary condescension…by way of covenant."

Fifth, 2LCF 19.1 says:

God gave to Adam a law of universal obedience written in his heart, and a particular precept of not eating the fruit of the tree of knowledge of good and evil; by which he bound him and all his posterity to personal, entire, exact, and perpetual obedience; promised life upon the fulfilling, and threatened death upon the breach of it, and endued him with power and ability to keep it.

This is the doctrine of the covenant of works without the phrase.

3. Because of the title and emphasis of Chapter 7.[24] Notice the slightly shortened form of this title as compared with the WCF and SD, which read, "Of God's Covenant with Man." The Baptist title is "Of God's Covenant," which gives the appearance of concentrating on one covenant, which is exactly what happens in 2LCF 7. It concentrates on the covenant of grace and either assumes or implies the covenant of works, making its explicit mention superfluous.

4. Because of the order of the chapters and the shift that takes place at Chapter 7. Chapter 6 is about the fall into sin and its consequences. Chapter 7 introduces us to the covenantal framework of salvation—the covenant of grace. Chapter 8 introduces us to the covenant servant of salvation. Chapters 9–20 cover both the accomplishment (via the covenant of redemption, 2LCF 8.1) and application of redemption. The point is that Chapter 7 is foundational and forward-looking.[25] It assumes the broken covenant of works and introduces us to God's remedy—"a covenant of grace," wherein all its benefits are procured or earned by the incarnate Son of God and conferred upon believing sinners apart from their own works.

5. Because Nehemiah Coxe clearly taught the doctrine of the covenant of works in his "A Discourse of the Covenants that God made with men before the law"... Coxe utilized the same terms, phrases, concepts and sources as his paedobaptist brothers. His treatise is "structured after the federal model, utilizes Reformed orthodox theological nomenclature, concepts, and sources, and is semantically Reformed orthodox..."[26] Like others in his day, he called it the covenant of creation,[27] covenant of works,[28] covenant of friendship,[29] and a covenant of rich bounty and goodness.[30]

---

[24] Dr. James M. Renihan is to be credited with reasons 3 and 4 (and much more).

[25] See Renihan, "Covenant Theology in the First and Second London Confessions of Faith," 66, where he says of 2LCF 7, "Its paragraph 3 is a wonderful redemptive-historical overview of the covenantal purpose of God in the gospel." He goes on to discuss "the emphasis on the forward movement of redemptive history..." reflected in 7.3. He also discusses the forward-looking motif of the covenant theology of the 2LCF in his conclusion (69).

[26] Barcellos, *The Family Tree*, 94. See Coxe and Owen, *Covenant Theology*, 71–140.

[27] Coxe and Owen, *Covenant Theology*, 39, 46, 49, 53, 58.

[28] Ibid., 45, 49, 53.

[29] Ibid., 49, 51. This seems to be dependent upon Cocceius.

[30] Ibid., 49.

6. Because (as far as I am aware) no seventeenth-century Particular Baptist connected to the Confession denied the covenant of works or thought it needed recasting. The extant evidence, in fact, is clearly to the contrary. If there is no evidence from the literature of the Particular Baptists of that day that they thought differently about the covenant of works, and there is evidence that they agreed with the basic tenets of the doctrine, saying they denied it or thought it needed recasting contradicts what they said. Not only that, it displays a poor method of interpreting documents of antiquity, imposing one's scruples upon an old document and interpreting it in light of those scruples. This is anachronistic, and a very poor method of historical interpretation.

Conclusion

Though it could be argued that the changes in the 2LCF were both intentional and theologically strategic, this does not necessarily imply these changes were an attempt to alter the doctrine of the covenant of works, or to distance the Particular Baptists from the theology of the covenant of works as found in either the WCF or SD, nor was it to satisfy the scruples of fellow Particular Baptists. There were no such scruples concerning the doctrine of the covenant of works to satisfy.

Now that we have examined the 2LCF on the covenant of works, the next chapter will attempt to show that Holy Scripture teaches a covenant made by God with Adam in the garden of Eden.

5

A Covenant of Works in the Garden
THE SCRIPTURAL ARGUMENTS

Before offering some scriptural arguments in favor of the covenant of works, it may help to interact with a typical objection to this doctrine as well as offer a working definition along with some brief discussion.

A Typical Objection to the Covenant of Works[1]

Perhaps the most obvious, and common objection, to the covenant of works is that the word *covenant* does not appear in the first two chapters of Genesis. In fact, the Hebrew word for covenant, *berith*, is not found in the book of Genesis until Chapter 6. These observations lead to the conclusion, so goes the objection, that there is no covenant in the Bible until Genesis 6. A covenant of works in the garden, then, lacks biblical evidence and is, in fact, unbiblical.[2] It is an extra-biblical, human construct imposed on the Bible to justify one's theological system, which obviously needs recasting. The covenant of works has human origins, not divine origins, so it is claimed. It is man's theology, not God's. Put in the form of a question, this objection can be stated as follows: How can there be a covenant in

---

[1] Some of the material in this chapter is taken (with permission and expanded) from Barcellos, "Getting the Garden Right: From Hermeneutics to the Covenant of Works."

[2] See Richard L. Mayhue, "New Covenant Theology and Futuristic Premillennialism," *The Master's Seminary Journal*, 18.2 (Fall 2007): 221 and 225 for this kind of argumentation.

Genesis 2 if Moses does not say so? My short answer to this legitimate question would be because God says so. But to be fair to any objectors, this question will be answered under three points of consideration.

The Objection Answered

First, this objection assumes that if a word is not in a text, its concept cannot be there either. This is the word-concept fallacy. The Bible itself sees concepts in texts and then uses words that do not occur in the text being referenced to describe those concepts, as we have seen. Consider Acts 2 again, where Peter references Psalm 16:8–11. Acts 2:22–31 says:

> "Men of Israel, listen to these words: Jesus the Nazarene, a man attested to you by God with miracles and wonders and signs which God performed through Him in your midst, just as you yourselves know—this *Man*, delivered over by the predetermined plan and foreknowledge of God, you nailed to a cross by the hands of godless men and put *Him* to death. "But God raised Him up again, putting an end to the agony of death, since it was impossible for Him to be held in its power. "For David says of Him, 'I SAW THE LORD ALWAYS IN MY PRESENCE; FOR HE IS AT MY RIGHT HAND, SO THAT I WILL NOT BE SHAKEN. 'THEREFORE MY HEART WAS GLAD AND MY TONGUE EXULTED; MOREOVER MY FLESH ALSO WILL LIVE IN HOPE; BECAUSE YOU WILL NOT ABANDON MY SOUL TO HADES, NOR ALLOW YOUR HOLY ONE TO UNDERGO DECAY. 'YOU HAVE MADE KNOWN TO ME THE WAYS OF LIFE; YOU WILL MAKE ME FULL OF GLADNESS WITH YOUR PRESENCE.' "Brethren, I may confidently say to you regarding the patriarch David that he both died and was buried, and his tomb is with us to this day. "And so, because he was a prophet and knew that GOD HAD SWORN TO HIM WITH AN OATH TO SEAT one OF HIS DESCENDANTS ON HIS THRONE, he looked ahead and spoke of the resurrection of the Christ, that HE WAS NEITHER ABANDONED TO HADES, NOR DID His flesh SUFFER DECAY.

Notice particularly what he does in 2:31. Peter uses words that are not in the Psalm to describe *concepts* from the Psalm. He says that David "looked ahead and spoke of the resurrection of the Christ." The words *resurrection* and *Christ* do not occur in the Psalm. Peter uses these words to describe concepts implicit in the Psalm though the terms themselves are not used explicitly by the psalmist. The point is that concepts can be present in texts without the words we normally use to describe them. If I said, "Base hit, home run, strike three, and walk-off single," you would, most likely, reduce those phrases and the concepts indicated by them to a single word—*baseball*—yet I did not use the word *baseball*.

Second, there are words used outside of the garden narrative to describe Adam and his Edenic vocation which are not contained in it. For example, in Luke 3:38, Adam is called "the son of God." However, Moses does not call Adam the son of God in Genesis and, in fact, the word *son* first occurs in Genesis 4:17 with reference to Enoch's son. If God tells us Adam was a son of God, it does not matter where He tells us. The case is settled, even if He tells us in Luke 3. Also, Adam did not first become a son of God when Luke penned his Gospel. He was constituted as such long before. The concept of Adam as a son of God, therefore, is implicit in the Genesis narrative, even though the word *son* is not found there. How do we know this? God tells us in subsequent written revelation, the only infallible interpretation of Holy Scripture we possess.

In Romans 5:14, Adam is called "a type of Him who was to come." However, Moses does not call Adam a type of Christ in Genesis and, in fact, the word *type* first occurs in the Bible in Romans 5:14. If God tells us Adam was a type of Christ, it does not matter where He tells us. The case is settled, even if He tells us in Romans 5. Also, Adam did not first become a type of Christ when Paul penned Romans. The concept of Adam as a type of Christ, therefore, is implicit in the Genesis narrative, even though the word *type* is not found there. How do we know this? God tells us in subsequent written revelation, the only infallible interpretation of Holy Scripture we possess.

In 1 Corinthians 15:22, Paul says, "For as in Adam all die…" However, Moses does not tell us that Adam was the representative of men in the Genesis narrative. The phrase "in Adam" is not in the book of Genesis or anywhere else in the Old Testament. As a matter of fact, the phrase "in Adam" occurs only in 1 Corinthians 15:22. If God tells us "in Adam all die," it does not matter where He tells us. The case is settled, even if He tells us in 1 Corinthians 15. Also, all did not die in Adam when Paul penned 1 Corinthians 15. The concept of Adam as the representative man in the garden, therefore, is implicit in the Genesis narrative, even though the phrase "in Adam" is not found there. How do we know this? God tells us in subsequent written revelation, the only infallible interpretation of Holy Scripture we possess.

Third, the Bible itself, looking back upon Adam in the garden, uses the explicit language of covenant. Since this is an important link in the argument for the scriptural doctrine of the covenant of works, we will explore this in the next major heading in some detail. For now, let me draw a conclusion to this typical objection.

I think the objection is cleared, though more counter-arguments could be offered. The account of Genesis 1–3 contains more than meets the eye. It is a narrative, not an exhaustive theological essay drawing out all the implications embedded or assumed in its terms. It is one of those texts that ends up being referenced many times in subsequent written revelation. Other texts assume it and draw out of it what is implied in it. What is implicit in it becomes explicit by the subsequent written Word of God. The biblical writers were theologians after all. They not only quoted (and alluded to) biblical texts, they often articulated the meaning of ancient texts in their own words. As stated above, subsequent revelation often makes explicit what is implicit in antecedent revelation. In other words, the Bible often comments upon and explains itself, and in the case of Adam in the garden, this is exactly what happens in both the Old and New Testaments.

A Working Definition of the Covenant of Works

Prior to offering scriptural arguments in favor of the doctrine of the covenant of works, a working definition will be offered in order to establish what must be proved. Consideration will be given to defining divine covenants with men and then a proposed definition of the covenant of works will follow.

A Brief Definition of Covenant When It Relates to God and Man

A divine covenant with man is a divinely-sanctioned commitment or relationship. In this sense, covenants come from God to man. They are not contracts between equal business partners. They are not up for negotiation. They are imposed by God upon man and are, as Coxe says, "[for] the advancing and bettering of his state.[3]" The divine covenants are not intended to merely sustain man in the condition he was in prior to those covenants being revealed to him.

Think of the Noahic covenant. Prior to its revelation as found in Genesis 6–9, the earth was potentially subject to a universal flood due to the justice of God being executed on the earth against the wickedness of man. We know this for certain because that is exactly what happened. The Noahic covenant, which includes man (Noah and his descendants), also involves every living creature (Genesis 9:9–10, 15, 16). It embraces and benefits the earth as well (Genesis 8:22 says, "While the earth remains, seedtime and harvest, and cold and heat, and summer and winter, and day and night shall not cease"; see also Genesis 9:13, "I set My bow in the cloud, and it shall be for a sign of a covenant between Me *and the earth*" [emphasis added], as well as Jeremiah 33:20, 25, which alludes to

---

[3] Coxe and Owen, *Covenant Theology*, 36.

the Noahic covenant: "My covenant for the day and My covenant for the night"[4]). That divine covenants are revealed to man for "the advancing and bettering of his state" can also be said of all other divine covenants with man throughout the Bible. Abraham (along with his carnal and spiritual seed) was better off for the covenant revealed to him. The Israelites were better off for the covenant revealed to them. It promised them blessings from God that were not promised to them prior to its promulgation. David and the Israelites were better off for the covenant revealed to them, and believers of all ages are much better off for the revelation of the new covenant in its promissory form in the Old Testament and in its concluded, or historically ratified, form in the New Testament. Coxe also says this while defining covenants between God and man:

> [They involve a] declaration of his sovereign pleasure concerning *the benefits he will bestow on them*, the communion they will have with him, and the way and means by which this will be enjoyed by them.[5]

Note that Coxe says covenants are imposed on man by God "[for] the advancing and bettering of his state" and that they concern "the benefits he will bestow on them." Improvement and betterment, in some sense, are built into all covenants that God makes with man, and the covenant of works is no exception.[6] As we will see below, the improvement that the covenant of works proffered was eschatological in nature, something which Adam failed to attain but that which Christ, the last Adam, attained.

The Definition of the Phrase "Covenant of Works"

Our working definition of the covenant of works is as follows: that divinely sanctioned commitment or relationship God imposed upon Adam, who was a sinless representative of mankind (or a public person), an image-bearing son of God, conditioned upon his obedience, with a penalty for disobedience, all for the bettering of man's state. Here we have the following: 1) sovereign, divine imposition; 2) representation by Adam (i.e., federal or covenantal headship), a sinless image-bearing son of God; 3) a conditional element (i.e., obedience); 4) a penalty for disobedience (i.e., death); and 5) a promise of reward (i.e., eschatological potential or "bet-

---

[4] See Michael G. Brown and Zach Keele, *Sacred Bond: Covenant Theology Explored* (Grandville, MI: Reformed Fellowship, Inc., 2012), 78–79 for this interpretation of Jeremiah 33.

[5] Coxe and Owen, *Covenant Theology*, 36; emphasis added.

[6] I am indebted to Samuel Renihan for helping me state my thoughts more clearly on this issue.

terment"). It is important to keep this definition in mind as we work our way through the discussion below. It is also important to recognize that the covenant of works was made with a representative, sinless image-bearing son of God. It could only be fulfilled by a representative, sinless, image-bearing son of God, since disobedience violates its terms, which happened with Adam and all those he represented. Its curse affects Adam and his progeny, but its promised reward is impossible to attain since man is now in a fallen, sinful condition. In order to fulfill its condition and receive its promised reward, another like Adam is necessary.

Scriptural Arguments for the Covenant of Works

The scriptural arguments in favor of a covenant of works in the garden offered below are not exhaustive. In large part, the arguments are framed to help illustrate the hermeneutical issues mentioned above. It was stated in previous discussion that NCT gets the garden wrong because it gets hermeneutics wrong. The arguments below are attempts to offer a better way of interpreting the garden. The seven arguments, stated as considerations, are as follows:

- Consider Moses' subsequent and inspired, and therefore infallible, reflection upon the acts of God at creation as recorded for us in Genesis 2:4ff.

- Consider the words of the prophet Isaiah.

- Consider the words of the prophet Hosea.

- Consider why it is denominated the "covenant of works."

- Consider the fact that Adam was "a type of Him who was to come."

- Consider the fact that Adam sinned and fell short of something he did not possess via creation.

- Consider the fact that Christ, upon his resurrection, entered into glory.

These considerations reflect a redemptive-historical method, on the main, which seeks to interpret the events in the garden via subsequent divine comment in the Bible on those very events. As will become evident, the considerations quickly become Christological. The reason for this will become obvious as one reads through the discussion.

The Scriptural Arguments

What J. V. Fesko asserts about his book, *Last Things First: Unlocking Genesis 1—3 with the Christ of Eschatology*, applies to the discussion below, and to most of the discussion in the rest of this book. Fesko says,

> Many come to the chapters [i.e., Gen. 1–3] thinking they know what occurs therein — creation, man, fall — and they then move along never realizing that they have entered the shadowlands, the land of the types of Christ and his work. This book represents my efforts to explain Genesis 1—3 in the light of Christ and eschatology.[7]

The considerations below are an attempt to do what Fesko did, with the rest of this chapter concentrating on the covenant of works. Subsequent chapters will discuss the function of the Creator's rest using the same method. The arguments below are cumulative. Each consideration is to be taken on its own, then in concert with the others.

The Words of Moses in Genesis 2:4ff.

It is important to understand the relationship between God's acts and the Holy Scripture. In large part, Holy Scripture is the recording, interpretation, and application of God's previous acts. In other words, the Scripture writers don't simply record God's acts; they interpret them and apply them in their own words—i.e., they do theology. For example, our Lord Jesus Christ lived and died before the final divine interpretation of His sufferings and glory were given to us in the form and unique words of the New Testament. Likewise, the creating act of God occurred prior to Moses' writing about it (as did all the events subsequent to creation recorded in the Pentateuch).

In Genesis 2:4, Moses goes from the term *Elohim* for God to the phrase *Yahweh Elohim*, Yahweh being the covenantal name of God (cp. Genesis 1:1, 2, 3, 4, 5, 6, 7, 8, 9, 10, 11, 12, 14, 16, 17, 18, 20, 21, 22, 24, 25, 26, 27, 28, 29, 31; 2:2, 3 with Genesis 2:4, 5, 7, 8, 9, 15, 16, 18, 19, 21, 22). Many believe that at 2:4, Moses goes from creation in general to the apex of the terrestrial creation, man in God's image, and his covenantal responsibility to God. In other words, Moses goes from the creation of man, male and female, to the Edenic vocation of Adam. The use of *Yahweh* here could indicate a covenantal act of God toward Adam. This suggests that covenant and Adam's Edenic vocation or calling go together. Moses, reflecting upon God's act of creation and its immediate aftermath, uses the

---

[7] J. V. Fesko, *Last Things First: Unlocking Genesis 1–3 with the Christ of Eschatology* (Fearn, Ross-shire, Scotland: Mentor Imprint by Christian Focus Publications, 2007), 9.

covenantal name of God in the context of discussing Adam and his Edenic vocation.[8] To modern readers, this might not seem to be an issue worth noting. However, for ancient readers/hearers of this passage, they would most likely have noticed the shift in language, a shift with theological and covenantal implications, whether they recognized it or not.[9]

Before moving to the next consideration, it will help to remember what was discussed briefly in Chapter 4. There I pointed out that the WCF, SD, 2LCF, and the WLC, WSC, and BC view the covenant of works as formally revealed in the garden. A distinction between man's created state and man in covenant with God was observed to be the teaching of the Confessions and Catechisms. Man was made, and then the garden was made into which man was placed (Genesis 2:7–8, 15). In Genesis 1:27, Moses informs us that "God [*Elohim*] created man in His own image, in the image of God He created him; male and female He created them." At Genesis 2:4, Moses begins using the compound phrase, *Yahweh Elohim*. It is the compound divine name that is used when describing the making of man in Genesis 2:7, the making or planting of the garden in 2:8, and the placing of man into it in 2:15. Reminding ourselves that Moses wrote Genesis as a sort of preface to the books of Exodus through Deuteronomy, using this compound name gives the appearance of an intentional shift to identify the Creator as the covenant Lord of Israel. The shift from creation at large, to the creation of man, and then to man's Edenic vocation seems to instill what follows with covenantal implications. If the covenant of works was revealed formally through the positive law of Genesis 2:16–17 and if the place of this revelation to Adam was the garden, then obviously *Yahweh Elohim* formally entered into covenant with Adam at that time and in that place. The explicit identification of the Creator as *Yahweh Elohim* does not communicate to Adam his vocation. Moses was not writing for Adam. Adam's vocation was revealed to him long before Moses wrote the book of Genesis.[10]

---

[8] See the discussion on Moses' use of the covenantal name of God in Brown and Keele, *Sacred Bond*, 47–48 and the brief discussion on "the compounding of the two divine names" in John D. Currid, *A Study Commentary on Genesis*, Volume 1: *Genesis 1:1–25:18* (Darlington, UK: Evangelical Press, 2003), 96–97.

[9] I say "whether they recognized it or not" because the text meant and means what it does irrespective of the understanding of its original recipients. Meaning is not in the eye of the beholder.

[10] Because Moses' treatment is sparse in terms of what Adam knew about his identity (image bearer) and vocation (the covenant of works), it could be argued that I am reading too much into the account. Let me address this briefly. First, my method of interpretation seeks to draw out of Moses' narrative what subsequent written revelation does. I am not imposing my thoughts on the narrative. I am imposing God's thoughts as recorded for us by the inspired words of Scripture writ-

The Words of the Prophet Isaiah

> The earth is also polluted by its inhabitants, for they transgressed laws, violated statutes, broke the everlasting covenant. Therefore, a curse devours the earth, and those who live in it are held guilty. Therefore, the inhabitants of the earth are burned, and few men are left. (Isaiah 24:5–6)

The curse, which extends to the entire earth, came about due to "transgressed laws, violated statutes," and a broken covenant. Since the earth was cursed due to Adam's sin as our representative, Adam broke covenant with God in the garden of Eden and the effects of his covenant-breaking affects "those who live on the earth," that is, everyone. E. J. Young's comments support this interpretation:

> It must be noticed, however, that those who have frustrated the eternal covenant are not merely the Jews but the world generally. The frustrating of the covenant is something universal. For this reason we may adopt the position that the eternal covenant here spoken of designates the fact that God has given His Law and ordinances to Adam, and in Adam to all mankind.[11]

Echoing Young's words, "in Adam to all mankind," Michael Brown and Zack Keele say:

> For all mankind to be under such a covenant, it must be the same covenant God made with Adam as the father of all humanity. Isaiah, then, assumes the covenant of works in order to apply it to all fallen humanity.[12]

---

ers. Second, it appears that Adam fell into sin relatively soon after being placed in the garden, certainly before Eve bore a child as far as we can know (see Genesis 4:1). It could be that Yahweh revealed more to Adam than Moses informs us (or even knew about). Cain and Abel brought offerings to the LORD, but Moses does not tell us how they knew to do this (Genesis 4:3–5). Something similar happens with Noah (Genesis 8:20). The best way to account for this is that the LORD must have revealed more to those in the early history of man than Moses records for us.

[11] Edward J. Young, *The Book of Isaiah, Chapters 19–39*, vol. 2 (Grand Rapids: Wm. B. Eerdmans Publishing Co., 1969), 155–60. See also John N. Oswalt, *The Book of Isaiah: Chapters 1–39*, NICOT, ed. Robert L. Hubbard Jr. (Grand Rapids: Wm. B. Eerdmans, 1986), 446, where he says: "While the eternal covenant may have specific reference to the Noahic covenant in Gen. 9:1–17 with its prohibition of bloodshed, its broader reference is to the implicit covenant between Creator and creature, in which the Creator promises life in return for the creature's living according to the norms laid down at Creation."

[12] Brown and Keele, *Sacred Bond*, 53.

Here is a prophet, writing long after Adam was created and long after Moses wrote, utilizing principles that first started with Adam to explain the universal guilt of man. In this sense, Isaiah is very Pauline; or better yet, Paul is very Isaianic. This later text makes explicit what is implicit in an earlier text. This passage will be discussed under the next consideration as well.

The Words of the Prophet Hosea

> But like Adam they have transgressed the covenant; There they have dealt treacherously against Me. (Hosea 6:7)

The translation of this text is disputed. The NASB's is to be preferred, in my opinion. The translation "like Adam" has a long pedigree, going back, at least, to Jerome. B. B. Warfield states that due to Jerome's translation, "to the Christians of the West it [Hosea 6:7] spoke of a covenant of God with Adam."[13] This is most likely why Muller asserts, "The text indicated, as virtually all of the patristic and medieval commentators concluded, a prelapsarian covenant made by God with Adam and broken in the fall."[14] This proves that the seventeenth-century covenant theologians did not invent the concept of a covenant with Adam, nor was it novel to use Hosea 6:7 as biblical support for such a concept. They stood on the shoulders of others who predated them. Warfield notes that the fifteenth-century Portuguese Jewish Bible commentator Isaac Abarbanel held this view, quoting him as follows: "The meaning is that they have acted like Adam, or the first man, whom I put in the Garden of Eden and he transgressed my covenant."[15] In the seventeenth century, Herman Witsius cited this text in

---

[13] Benjamin B. Warfield, "Hosea VI.7: Adam or Man," in *Selected Shorter Writings: Benjamin B. Warfield*, I, ed. John E. Meeter (Phillipsburg, NJ: P&R Publishing, Fourth Printing, January 2001), 117. Warfield's discussion is highly recommended for those interested in the history of the interpretation of Hos. 6:7. See also Bryon G. Curtis, "Hosea 6:7 and Covenant-Breaking like/at Adam," in *The Law is not of Faith: Essays in Works and Grace in the Mosaic Covenant*, ed. Bryan D. Estelle, J. V. Fesko, and David VanDrunen (Phillipsburg, NJ: P&R Publishing, 2009), 170–209; and Fesko, *Last Things First*, 88–91. Fesko agrees with Warfield that "like Adam" is preferred over "like men" or "at Adam."

[14] Muller, *PRRD*, 2:437.

[15] Warfield, "Hosea VI.7: Adam or Man," 117–18. The quote comes from Husen's annotations on Abarbanel, cited as "Ed. Husen (Leiden, 1686), p. 270. Husen's annotations may be found on p. 282." Warfield adds, "The great name of Rashi may be quoted for the same view" (118). Rashi was an eleventh-century French rabbi who wrote commentaries on the Jewish *Tanakh*, what we call the OT.

The Scriptural Arguments 63

support of the covenant of works, as did Wilhelmus a' Brakel and others.[16]

In Hosea 6:7, Israel is likened unto Adam. "But like Adam they have transgressed the covenant..." (Hosea 6:7). Fesko says, "The most natural reading of the verse is a comparison between Adam, God's son (Luke 3:38), and Israel who is also God's son (Exodus 4:22–23)." Warfield comments,

> No such exegetical objections [previously discussed by Warfield] lie against the rendering, 'Like Adam.' Any difficulties that may be brought against it, indeed, are imported from without the clause itself. In itself the rendering is wholly natural. Nor is it without commendations of force. The transgressing of Adam, as the great normative act of covenant-breaking, offered itself naturally as the fit standard over against which the heinousness of the covenant-breaking of Israel could be thrown out. And Hosea, who particularly loves allusions to the earlier history of Israel (cf. ii. 3, ix. 10, xi. 8, xii. 4), was the very prophet to think here of the sin of our first father.[18]

Warfield then cites Franz Delitzsch's comments on Job 31:33, where he cites Hosea 6:7.

> 'They have ['like Adam'] transgressed the covenant,' consists in this 'that Israel is accused of a transgression which is only to be compared to that of the first man created; here as there, a like transgression of the expressed will of God' (as also according to Rom. v. 14 Israel's transgression is that fact in the historical development of redemption which stands by the side of Adam's transgression).[19] And the mention of Adam in Hosea cannot surprise one, since he also shows himself in other respects to be familiar with the contents of Genesis and to refer back to it.[20]

---

[16] See Herman Witsius, *The Economy of the Covenants Between God and Man: Comprehending A Complete Body of Divinity*, 2 vols. (Escondido, CA: The den Dulk Christian Foundation, re. 1990), 1:135; Wilhelmus a' Brakel, *The Christian's Reasonable Service*, 4 vols. (Grand Rapids: Reformation Heritage Books, 1992, Third printing 1999), 1:365–67; Francis Turretin, *Institutes of Elenctic Theology*, 3 vols., ed. James T. Dennison, Jr., trans. George Musgrave Giger (Phillipsburg, NJ: P&R Publishing, 1992–97), 1.3.8 (1:576); and Ward, *God & Adam*. Ward's book is highly recommended.

[17] Fesko, *Last Things First*, 90.

[18] Warfield, "Hosea VI.7: Adam or Man," 128.

[19] Warfield has a footnote at this point which reads: "Hofmann, *Schriftbeweis*, I. p. 412." It looks like this comes from Delitzsch quoting Hofmann.

[20] Warfield, "Hosea VI.7: Adam or Man," 128.

Then Warfield cites Given from *The Pulpit Commentary*:

> *They like Adam have transgressed the covenant*: this rendering, supported by the Vulgate, Cyril, Luther, Rosenmüller and Wünsche, is decidedly preferable and yields a suitable sense. God in his great goodness had planted Adam in Paradise, but Adam violated the commandment which prohibited his eating of the tree of knowledge, and thereby transgressed the covenant of his God. Loss of fellowship with God and expulsion from Eden were the penal consequences that immediately followed. Israel like Adam had been settled by God in Palestine, the glory of all lands; but ungrateful for God's great bounty and gracious gift, they broke the covenant of their God, the condition of which, as in the case of the Adamic covenant, was obedience. Thus the comparison projects the shadow of a coming event, when Israel would leave the land of promise.[21]

Both Adam and Israel broke a covenant imposed upon them by God. They both disobeyed. They sinned, violating the covenants they were under. Both covenants were conditional, requiring the obedience of those in the covenant to enjoy the benefits of the covenant. As Moses says, "…in the day that you eat from it you will surely die" (Genesis 2:17; see Exodus 19:5–6 for the conditional nature of the Mosaic covenant). There are other parallels between Adam and Israel which will be developed in later discussion.

Here is another prophet, looking back at previous written revelation, making explicit what was implicit in it. Remember, subsequent revelation often makes explicit what was implicit in antecedent revelation. The inspired words of the prophet give us God's infallible knowledge of similarities between ancient Israel and Adam. Both had a covenant imposed on them by God and both transgressed their covenants. Also, as with Isaiah above, the prophet's inspired words (e.g., in the case of Hosea, "transgressed" and "covenant") describe concepts first revealed by Moses, though in different words from Moses. As Brown and Keele say, "Once more, the prophet's interpretation of Genesis 2–3 peeks through his prophecy, and it reveals that Adam was in covenant with God."[22]

If the interpretations of the Isaiah and Hosea texts are correct, either one or both of them, we have an example of the revelation of a covenant with Adam without the term being used to describe it in the Genesis account. The covenant with Adam is first revealed, though without the term *covenant* being used to describe it, then it is explicitly identified as such

---

[21] Warfield, "Hosea VI.7: Adam or Man," 128–29. The Given quote is cited as "*The Pulpit Commentary*, on Hos. vi. 7 (p. 169)."

[22] Brown and Keele, *Sacred Bond*, 54.

The Scriptural Arguments

by subsequent written revelation. This same phenomenon occurs with the revelation of the Davidic covenant. It is first revealed without the word *covenant* being used, then explicitly identified as a covenant by subsequent revelation. Let's compare 2 Samuel 7 with 2 Samuel 23 and Psalm 89:

> "Now therefore, thus you shall say to My servant David, 'Thus says the LORD of hosts, "I took you from the pasture, from following the sheep, to be ruler over My people Israel. I have been with you wherever you have gone and have cut off all your enemies from before you; and I will make you a great name, like the names of the great men who are on the earth. I will also appoint a place for My people Israel and will plant them, that they may live in their own place and not be disturbed again, nor will the wicked afflict them any more as formerly, even from the day that I commanded judges to be over My people Israel; and I will give you rest from all your enemies. The LORD also declares to you that the LORD will make a house for you. When your days are complete and you lie down with your fathers, I will raise up your descendant after you, who will come forth from you, and I will establish his kingdom. He shall build a house for My name, and I will establish the throne of his kingdom forever. I will be a father to him and he will be a son to Me; when he commits iniquity, I will correct him with the rod of men and the strokes of the sons of men, but My lovingkindness shall not depart from him, as I took *it* away from Saul, whom I removed from before you. Your house and your kingdom shall endure before Me forever; your throne shall be established forever."'" In accordance with all these words and all this vision, so Nathan spoke to David. (2 Samuel 7:8–17)

The "last words of David" (2 Samuel 23:1) are recorded for us in 2 Samuel 23:1–7. There David reflects on the account given to us in 2 Samuel 7. Notice what happens in verse 5 of 2 Samuel 23:

> Truly is not my house so with God? For He has made an everlasting covenant with me, ordered in all things, and secured; For all my salvation and all *my* desire, will He not indeed make *it* grow? (2 Samuel 23:5)

David identifies what transpired as recorded in 2 Samuel 7 as the revelation of a covenant. The same thing occurs in Psalm 89:

> "I have made a covenant with My chosen; I have sworn to David My servant, I will establish your seed forever and build up your throne to all generations." Selah. (Psalm 89:3–4)

The psalmist evokes 2 Samuel 7, identifying a divine revelation of a covenant to David, though the first recording of that transaction is not identified explicitly as such. Meredith G. Kline notes this phenomenon while referencing Isaiah 24:5 and Hosea 6:7.

> Actually, it is possible that the Bible itself, in later references back to Genesis 1–3, applies the term *berith* [i.e., covenant] to the situation there, just as 2 Samuel 23:5 and Psalm 89:3 refer to God's covenantal revelation to David as a *berith*, though the term is not employed in the account of it in 2 Samuel 7. Isaiah 24:5 and Hosea 6:7 have been suggested as instances of this. Although the meaning of both passages is disputed, the everlasting covenant of Isaiah 24:5 definitely appears to refer to the creational arrangements and Hosea 6:7 probably refers to Adam as the breaker of a covenant.[23]

Could it be that what occurs in 2 Samuel 23:5 and Psalm 89:3 also occurs in Isaiah 24:5 and Hosea 6:7? I think this is exactly what is happening. Narrative accounts of earlier written revelation are evoked by subsequent authors of Scripture, identifying in explicit words the concepts implicit in those accounts. The case presented above illustrates a pattern of inner-biblical interpretation. We saw this happening with Moses in Genesis 2:4ff. In fact, this phenomenon occurs throughout the Old Testament. Earlier recorded revelatory acts of God are explained by later writers in words not used by the authors of the earlier recorded revelatory acts. Since the writings of the later authors are inspired, as are the former, what we have is the divine explanation of the previous revelatory acts of God. And since we have a divine explanation, we also have an infallible interpretation.

It is Denominated the "Covenant of Works"

It is called the "covenant of works" due to the fact that it was conditioned on Adam's obedience, or his works. The term *works* in the phrase "covenant of works" is a synonym for obedience. It is a term that communicates biblical, and therefore infallible, reflection upon Adam's Edenic vocation (see Romans 5:12–21). Romans 5:19 justifies this term when it says, "For as through the one man's *disobedience* the many were made sinners, even so through the *obedience* of the One the many will be made righteous" (emphasis added). The opposite of "disobedience" is "obedience." A legitimate synonym for *obedience* is *works*.

The term *works* is also a good word choice because it contrasts with *grace* and *gift* in Romans 5:17. Paul says there,

---

[23] Meredith G. Kline, *Kingdom Prologue: Genesis Foundations for a Covenantal Worldview* (Overland Park, KS: Two Age Press, 2000), 14.

> For if by the transgression of the one, death reigned through the one, much more those who receive the abundance of *grace* and of the *gift* of righteousness will reign in life through the One, Jesus Christ. (Romans 5:17; emphasis added)

Adam's disobedience brought death. Christ's obedience brings life, a quality of life Adam did not have, i.e., eternal life (John 17:3; Romans 5:21).

Prior to leaving this brief discussion on why the denominator "covenant of works" is appropriate, note that, in this consideration and in the three following, there is a heavy dependence upon the words of the apostle Paul. The reason for this is that Paul often offers theological commentary on Adam's vocation, his disobedience, and the effects of his disobedience upon mankind. Commenting on Westminster divine Anthony Burgess' method of understanding Genesis, Casselli says, "Burgess explained plainly that Genesis is only properly read through Paul…"[24] The apostle Paul takes center-stage in the writings of the New Testament as the one providing the most mature theological reflection upon Adam's vocation and the implications of it for mankind, Christ, and believers in Christ.

Adam, "a Type of Him Who Was to Come"

> Nevertheless death reigned from Adam until Moses, even over those who had not sinned in the likeness of the offense of Adam, who is a type of Him who was to come. (Romans 5:14)

Let me first present some very brief comments on typology. First, a type is an historical person, place, institution, or event designed by God to point to a future historical person, place, institution, or event. An example of this would be the sacrificial system revealed to us in the Old Testament. That institution was designed by God to point to Christ's once-for-all sacrifice. Second, the object to which a type points is always greater than the type itself. For example, "the blood of bulls and goats" could point to Christ but could not and did not do what Christ's sacrifice did—take away sins (Hebrews 10:4, 11–14). Third, types are both like and unlike their antitypes. The blood of animals was shed; the blood of Christ was shed. The blood of animals did not take away sins; the blood of Christ takes away sins. Fourth, antitypes tell us more about how their typical antecedents

---

[24] Casselli, *Divine Rule Maintained*, 71, n. 140. We could extend this further by saying that Genesis is only properly read through the lens of the entire Bible.

function as types. The blood of Christ takes away sins; the blood of animals pointed to that.[25]

It is important to note some specific considerations in light of Adam as a type of Christ. I agree with Herman Bavinck when he says, "Adam, the son of God [see Luke 3:38], was a type of Christ."[26] He was a type of Christ in his prelapsarian state (Romans 5:14). Adam was a type of Christ as a public person (1 Corinthians 15:22, i.e., federal or covenantal representation). Adam's failure is seen in the fact that he disobeyed or he failed to obey (Romans 5:12ff.). He did not obey, and thus did not attain to the better state of existence to which the covenant of works pointed (more on this below). But what if he had obeyed? Would he have remained in the state in which he was created—able to sin and able not to sin? I don't think so and, I think, for good reason. Let me add that this is not an impractical, speculative, or abstract question, the answer to which cannot be known. It is a question related to the fact that Adam was a type of Christ. Let's explore this in more detail.

In Romans 5:21, God says, "even so grace would reign through righteousness to eternal life through Jesus Christ." The righteousness that is "to eternal life" comes as a gift to sinners and is based on Christ's obedience. The life-unto-death obedience of Christ constitutes a righteousness "to eternal life." In other words, according to His sinless human nature as the antitype of Adam, Christ, our Mediator, earned eternal life for us.

---

[25] For helpful discussions on typology see G. K. Beale, *Handbook on the New Testament Use of the Old Testament: Exegesis and Interpretation* (Grand Rapids: Baker Academic, 2012), 13–25; G. P. Hugenberger, "Introductory Notes on Typology" and Francis Foulkes, "The Acts of God: A Study of the Basis of Typology in the Old Testament," in *The Right Doctrine from the Wrong Texts? Essays on the Use of the Old Testament in the New*, ed. G. K. Beale (Grand Rapids: Baker Books, 1994), 331–71 (The essay by Foulkes is exceptionally helpful.); James, M. Hamilton, Jr., *What is Biblical Theology? A Guide to the Bible's Story, Symbolism, and Patterns* (Wheaton, IL: Crossway, 2014); Paul M. Hoskins, *Jesus as the Fulfillment of the Temple in the Gospel of John* (Eugene, OR: Wipf and Stock Publishers, 2006), 18–36; Silva, "Has the Church Misread the Bible?," 57–61; Daniel J. Trier, "Typology," in *Dictionary for Theological Interpretation of the Bible*, gen. ed. Kevin J. Vanhoozer (Grand Rapids: Baker Academic, 2005), 823–27; Richard M. Davidson, *Typology In Scripture: A study of study of hermeneutical τύπος structures* (Berrien Springs, MI: Andrews University Press, 1981); and Leonhard Goppelt, *TYPOS: The Typological Interpretation of the Old Testament in the New* (1939; reprint, Grand Rapids: William B. Eerdmans Publishing Company, 1982).

[26] Herman Bavinck, *Reformed Dogmatics*, gen. ed. John Bolt, trans. John Vriend (Grand Rapids: Baker Academic, 2004, Third printing, July 2008), 2:562.

His righteousness was "*to* eternal life" (emphasis added). Guy Waters comments:

> The fact that Christ purchased eternal "life" for his own, and that he did so for those who were eternally "dead" in Adam means that Christ's work was intended to remedy what Adam had wrought (death), and to accomplish what Adam had failed to do (life). Paul emphasizes disparity in his argument precisely in order to underscore the breathtaking achievement of what Christ has accomplished in relation to what Adam has wrought. This means that if Adam by his disobedience brought eternal death, then his obedience would have brought eternal life. In other words, Christ's "obedience" and its consequence ("eternal life") parallel what Adam ought to have done but did not do. The life that Adam ought to have attained would have been consequent upon Adam's continuing, during the period of his testing, in obedience to all the commands set before him, whether moral or positive. This life, it stands to reason, could be aptly described "eternal."[27]

Eternal life was earned by Christ, the antitype of Adam, for us and given by Christ to us. The quality of life Christ attains for us and gives to us is not what Adam had and lost, but what Adam failed to attain. Adam did not possess "eternal life" via creation. Robert Shaw, commenting on the covenant of works, says:

> There is a *condition* expressly stated, in the positive precept respecting the tree of knowledge of good and evil, which God was pleased to make the test of man's obedience. There was a *penalty* subjoined: 'In the day thou eatest thereof, thou shalt surely die.' There is also a *promise*, not distinctly expressed, but implied in the threatening; for if death was to be the consequence of disobedience, it clearly follows that life was to be the reward of obedience. That a promise of life was annexed to man's obedience, may also be inferred from…our Lord's answer to the young man who inquired what he should do to inherit eternal life: 'If thou wilt enter into life, keep the commandments' (Matthew 19:17); and from the declaration of the apostle, that 'the commandment was ordained to life' (Romans 7:10).[28]

Just as Adam's disobedience brought upon him a status not his by virtue of creation (cp. Genesis 2:17 with Genesis 3:8ff.; Romans 5:12ff.; and 1 Corinthians 15:22), so his obedience would have brought upon him

---

[27] Guy P. Waters, "Romans 10:5 and the Covenant of Works," in *The Law is not of Faith*, 230.

[28] Shaw, *Exposition*, 124–25.

a status not his by virtue of creation. Christ, as antitypical Adam, the last Adam, takes His seed where Adam failed to take his. As will be argued below, Christ takes His seed to glory (Hebrews 2:10), something to which Adam fell short.

Adam Fell Short of the Glory of God, Something He Did Not Possess Via Creation

> for all have sinned and fall short of the glory of God (Romans 3:23)

In Paul's writings, it is clear that Adam was the first man who sinned. The first man sinned and fell "short of the glory of God" (Romans 3:23), something which he did not possess or experience via his created status. As John Murray notes:

> [to fall short of the glory of God]...refers to a condition, not to an action, though, of course, the condition may arise from the absence of action which would have remedied or prevented the condition.[29]

Adam was not created in a condition or state that could be called "glory" and he fell short of it by sinning. He failed to attain that state because he sinned. In other words, Adam was created in a state that could have been improved, with God being the ultimate cause and Adam's obedience the instrumental cause of the improvement. He was created in a mutable state, a changeable condition (2LCF 4.2). He was righteous, but he could sin. His obedience would have brought him to a higher state, an immutable state, conferred upon him by God out of his voluntary, condescending kindness expressed in the covenant of works (2LCF 7.1). Adam was not created with eternal life. Adam's obedience could have attained something with which he was not created, "the reward of life" in the words of the Confession (2LCF 7.1). In other words, Adam had an eschatology before the need of soteriology. The soteriological strand of revelation comes because the eschatology of the garden was never attained by Adam. Or, in the words of Geerhardus Vos, "The eschatological is an older strand in revelation than the soteric."[30] The soteriological (i.e., redemptive) strand of Scripture takes us to the eschatological (i.e., the goal) that was imbedded in the protological (i.e., the beginning).

---

[29] John Murray, *Epistle to the Romans* (1959, 1965; reprint, Grand Rapids: Wm. B. Eerdmans Publishing Co., one-volume edition, 1984), 112.

[30] Geerhardus Vos, *Biblical Theology: Old and New Testaments* (1948; reprint, Grand Rapids: Wm. B. Eerdmans Publishing Company, 1988), 140.

The Scriptural Arguments

Because the subject of Edenic eschatology might be new to some readers, and is a debated issue in Reformed thought, let me take a brief excursus to show you that what is being asserted is not new in the history of Reformed theology.[31] Take, for example, Nehemiah Coxe. According to Coxe, Adam had "the promise of an eternal reward on condition of his perfect obedience to these laws."[32] The tree of life functioned sacramentally as "a sign and pledge of that eternal life which Adam would have obtained by his own personal and perfect obedience to the law of God if he had continued in it."[33] As noted above, God sovereignly proposes covenants with men in order to bring them to an advanced or better state than they are in when the covenant is revealed to them, and ultimately "to bring them into a blessed state in the eternal enjoyment of himself."[34] Adam, Coxe says, "was capable of and made for a greater degree of happiness than he immediately enjoyed [which] was set before him as the reward of his obedience by that covenant in which he was to walk with God."[35]

According to Witsius, the covenant of works (or of nature, or of the law), as it functioned in the garden, "…promised eternal life and happiness if [Adam] yielded obedience."[36] Witsius sees Adam in a probationary state

---

[31] For further discussion on the eschatological motif in the garden narrative in seventeenth-century Reformed theologians, see my *The Family Tree*, 90–106. In later chapters of that book, I show the same motif in Geerhardus Vos and John Owen.

[32] Coxe and Owen, *Covenant Theology*, 44–45. Coxe gives three proofs with discussion for the promise of a reward on pages 45–46. Later in his discussion, he says, "He [fallen Adam] could no longer claim a right in, or hope for, that reward which was promised on condition of his perfect obedience to the law of that covenant which God had made with him" (51).

[33] Ibid., 45. Coxe justifies this function of the tree of life as follows: "The allusion that Christ makes to it in the New Testament (Revelation 2:7).… The method of God's dealing with Adam in reference to this tree after he had sinned against him and the reason assigned for it by God himself [i.e., Genesis 3:22ff.].… This also must not be forgotten: that as Moses' law in some way included the covenant of creation and served for a memorial of it (on which account all mankind was involved in its curse), it had not only the sanction of a curse awfully denounced against the disobedient, but also a promise of the reward of life to the obedient." Here Coxe is articulating Owen's (and others') view of the relation of the covenant of works to the Mosaic covenant. Notice that Coxe utilizes subsequent revelation to aid in the interpretation of antecedent revelation.

[34] Ibid., 36.

[35] Ibid., 47.

[36] Witsius, *Economy of the Covenants*, 1:150. The covenant of works has been termed the covenant of creation, nature, and the law by various older authors. They all refer to the same doctrinal formulation.

and capable of arriving at a higher, more blessed state of existence. He says:

> That man was not yet arrived at the utmost pitch of happiness, but [was] to expect a still greater good, after his course of obedience was over. This was hinted by the prohibition of the most delightful tree, whose fruit was, of any other, greatly to be desired; and this argued some degree of imperfection in that state, in which man was forbid the enjoyment of some good.[37]

The more blessed state of existence was "eternal life, that is the most perfect fruition of himself [i.e., God; this echoes the WCF 7.1], and that forever, after finishing his course of obedience..."[38] This promise of life flowed out of God's goodness and bounty, not out of any strict necessity.[39] God voluntarily condescended in the revelation of the covenant of works, offering a reward to Adam for his obedience. The garden of Eden, according to Witsius, was a pledge, a type, and a symbol, both temporary and anticipatory of a better state yet to be enjoyed.[40] In other words, protology is eschatological, or the eschatological is embedded in the protological. Adam had an eschatology that he failed to attain.

Let's get back to Romans 3:23. Notice that John Owen references this verse in this quotation:

> Man, especially, was utterly lost, and came short of the glory of God, *for which he was created*, Rom. iii. 23. Here, now, doth the depth of the riches of the wisdom and knowledge of God open itself. A design in Christ shines out from his bosom, that was lodged there from eternity, to recover things to such an estate as shall be exceedingly to the advantage of his glory, infinitely above what at first appeared, and for the putting of sinners into inconceivably *a better condition than they were in before the entrance of sin.*[41]

For Owen, "the glory of God" here does not refer exclusively to what God possesses, but to what God *confers*.[42] The eschatological state, glory, is that

---

[37] Witsius, *Economy of the Covenants*, 1:69; see also 1:123–24.
[38] Ibid., 1:73.
[39] Ibid., 1:76ff.
[40] Ibid., 1:106ff., esp. 1:109.
[41] Owen, *Works*, 2:89; emphasis added.
[42] Murray mentions this view as one of four options. He describes this view in the following words: "to fail of the consummated glory that will be dispensed to the people of God at the coming of Christ." He cites 2 Thessalonians 2:14 and Hebrews 2:10, among other texts. These texts will be mentioned in our discus-

The Scriptural Arguments

"for which…[man] was created." The state of existence to which Christ takes elect sinners is "inconceivably *a better condition than they were in before the entrance of sin.*" Christ takes elect sinners to a state of existence that is better than the beginning.[43]

Now listen to Paul in Romans 5:1–2, "Therefore, having been justified by faith, we have peace with God…and we exult *in hope of the glory of God*" (emphasis added). Charles Hodge says:

> It is a[n]…exultation, in view of the exaltation and blessedness which Christ has *secured for us*.… The glory of God may mean that glory which God gives, or that which he possesses. In either case, it refers to the exaltation and blessedness *secured to the believer*, who is to share the glory of his divine Redeemer.[44]

Likewise, John Gill comments:

> by the glory of God, is not meant the essential glory of God; not that which we ought to seek in all that we are concerned, and which we are to ascribe unto him on the account of his perfections and works; but that everlasting glory and happiness which he has prepared for his people, has promised to them, and has called them to by Christ, and will bestow upon them…[45]

---

sion below. Murray opts for a different view, however. See Murray, *Romans*, 113. Charles Hodge mentions the view advocated above, though he opts for a different one. He says, "Others again say that the glory of God here means that glory which God promises to the righteous, as in v. 2." See Charles Hodge, *The Epistle to the Romans* (1835; reprint, Edinburgh; Carlisle, PA: The Banner of Truth Trust, Reprinted 1983), 90. We will note Hodge's comments on Romans 5:2 below. Sanday and Hedlam recognize the view advocated here in William Sanday and Arthur C. Headlam, *A Critical and Exegetical Commentary on the Epistle to the Romans*, The International Critical Commentary, eds. S. R. Driver, A. Plummer, and C. A. Briggs (1895; reprint, Edinburgh: T & T Clark, Fifth Edition, 1971), 84–85. They cite Romans 5:2; 8:18 and 30; and 2 Timothy 2:10. John Gill seems to hint at the view above in John Gill, *Exposition of the Old and New Testaments*, 9 vols. (1809; reprint, Paris, AR: The Baptist Standard Bearer, Inc., 1989), 8:438.

[43] See Richard C. Barcellos, *Better than the Beginning: Creation in Biblical Perspective* (Palmdale, CA: RBAP, 2013), where I argue this at length.

[44] Hodge, *Romans*, 133, emphases added. See Murray, *Romans*, 161–62, where Murray hints at the view I am advocating. Sanday and Hedlam, in *Romans*, 121, acknowledge a future transformation of "man's whole being" from the text of Romans 5:2.

[45] Gill, *Exposition*, 8:449. See Douglas J. Moo, *The Epistle to the Romans*, The New International Commentary on the New Testament (Grand Rapids: William B. Eerdmans Publishing Company, 1996), 301–02.

We get glory, a state of existence, because it is conferred upon us, having been secured for us by Christ. This is why we can "exult in hope of the glory of God." Since we have been justified, glory awaits. This "glory" is that to which Adam fell short.

Christ, Upon His Resurrection, Entered Into Glory

The Old Testament speaks about the Messiah who would come, suffer (due to Adam's sin and ours in him), and enter into glory. Consider these inspired and infallible theological reflections on the Old Testament:

> Was it not necessary for the Christ to suffer these things and to enter into His glory? (Luke 24:26)

> and He said to them, "Thus it is written, that the Christ would suffer and rise again from the dead the third day" (Luke 24:46)

> "So, King Agrippa, I did not prove disobedient to the heavenly vision, but *kept* declaring both to those of Damascus first, and *also* at Jerusalem and *then* throughout all the region of Judea, and *even* to the Gentiles, that they should repent and turn to God, performing deeds appropriate to repentance. "For this reason *some* Jews seized me in the temple and tried to put me to death. "So, having obtained help from God, I stand to this day testifying both to small and great, stating nothing but what the Prophets and Moses said was going to take place; that the Christ was to suffer, *and* that by reason of *His* resurrection from the dead He would be the first to proclaim light both to the *Jewish* people and to the Gentiles." (Acts 26:19-23)

> As to this salvation, the prophets who prophesied of the grace that *would come* to you made careful searches and inquiries, seeking to know what person or time the Spirit of Christ within them was indicating as He predicted the sufferings of Christ and the glories to follow. It was revealed to them that they were not serving themselves, but you, in these things which now have been announced to you through those who preached the gospel to you by the Holy Spirit sent from heaven—things into which angels long to look. (1 Peter 1:10–12)

The Son of God incarnate, according to His human nature, both suffered and entered into glory (i.e., a glorified state) via His resurrection and as a reward for His righteousness, which, according to Paul, was "to eternal life." In other words, Christ, according to His human nature, became what He was not at the resurrection (the beginning of His exaltation).

The Scriptural Arguments

Suffering and glory is another way of saying humiliation and exaltation. Paul speaks of the Son's humiliation and exaltation in Romans 1:1–4 and Philippians 2:6–9.

> Paul, a bond-servant of Christ Jesus, called *as* an apostle, set apart for the gospel of God, which He promised beforehand through His prophets in the holy Scriptures, concerning His Son, who was born of a descendant of David according to the flesh, who was declared the Son of God with power by the resurrection from the dead, according to the Spirit of holiness, Jesus Christ our Lord (Romans 1:1–4)

> who, although He existed in the form of God, did not regard equality with God a thing to be grasped, but emptied Himself, taking the form of a bond-servant, *and* being made in the likeness of men. Being found in appearance as a man, He humbled Himself by becoming obedient to the point of death, even death on a cross. For this reason also, God highly exalted Him, and bestowed on Him the name which is above every name (Philippians 2:6–9)

The resurrection of our Lord marks a new phase of messianic lordship (see Acts 2:36). Commenting on Romans 1:4 ("who was declared the Son of God with power by the resurrection from the dead, according to the Spirit of holiness"), Murray says:

> The apostle is dealing with some particular event in the history of the Son of God incarnate by which he was instated in a position of sovereignty and invested with power, an event which in respect of investiture with power surpassed everything that could previously be ascribed to him in his incarnate state.[46]

> Just as "according to the flesh" in verse 3 defines the phase which came to be through being born of the seed of David, so "according to the Spirit of holiness" characterizes the phase which came to be through the resurrection. And when we ask what that new phase was upon which the Son of God entered by his resurrection, there is copious New Testament allusion and elucidation (*cf.* Acts 2:36; Eph. 1:20–23; Phil. 2:9–11; I Pet. 3:21, 22). By his resurrection and ascension the Son of God incarnate entered upon a new phase of sovereignty and was endowed with new power correspondent with and unto the exercise of the mediatorial lordship which he executes as head over all things to his body, the church. It is in this same resurrection context and with allusion to Christ's resurrection endowment that the apostle says, "The last Adam was made a

---

[46] Murray, *Romans*, 10. See Moo, *Romans*, 47–51 for a very similar view to Murray's.

life-giving Spirit" (I Cor. 15:45).... Christ is now by reason of the resurrection so endowed with and in control of the Holy Spirit that, without any confusion of the distinct persons, Christ is identified with the Spirit and is called "the Lord of the Spirit" (II Cor. 3:18). Thus, when we come back to the expression "according to the Spirit of holiness," our inference is that it refers to that stage of pneumatic endowment upon which Jesus entered through his resurrection. The text, furthermore, expressly relates "Son of God with power according to the Spirit of holiness" with "the resurrection from the dead" and the appointment can be none other than that which came to be by the resurrection.... What is contrasted is not a phase in which Jesus is not the Son of God and another in which he is. He is the incarnate Son of God in both states, humiliation and exaltation, and to regard him as the Son of God in both states belongs to the essence of Paul's gospel as the gospel of God. But the pre-resurrection and post-resurrection states are compared and contrasted, and the contrast hinges on the investiture with power by which the latter is characterized.[47]

Christ's representation in the state of humiliation started at His conception and ended at His death and burial. Upon His death/burial, because of His obedience to the point of death, God "highly exalted Him…" (Philippians 2:9). The incarnate Son of God, according to His human nature, obeyed and suffered due to our sin, and then entered into glory as a result of or reward for His obedience. He did both as the sinless last Adam, representing those given to Him by the Father before the world began (Ephesians 1:4). All believers in Christ will be transformed and conformed to that state of existence. Paul says our Lord "will transform the body of our humble state into conformity with the body of His glory, by the exertion of the power that He has even to subject all things to Himself" (Philippians 3:21).

Adam failed to comply with the conditions of the covenant God imposed upon him and brought with that the ruin of the human race. He fell short of the glory of God, a permanent state of existence in God's special presence, which he did not possess via creation. But here is the good news—another came: the last Adam, our Lord Jesus Christ, who suffered, then entered into glory at His resurrection, and who is the agent through whom many sons will be brought to glory (Hebrews 2:10), who will also "gain the glory of our Lord Jesus Christ" (2 Thessalonians 2:14). Owen says, on 2 Thessalonians 2:14, "'The glory of our Lord Jesus Christ,' or the obtaining a portion in that glory which Christ *purchased* and *procured* for them…"[48] Christ *purchased* glory for all He came to save. He did so as the

---

[47] Murray, *Romans*, 11–12.
[48] Owen, *Works*, 11:203; emphasis added.

last Adam. He suffered to satisfy the justice of God, and His obedience unto death resulted in His exaltation, an entrance into glory, and all those who are His will enter into that same glory as well. The last Adam takes His seed where the first Adam failed to take his. Adam sinned, violating the covenant of works, and thus fell short of the glory of God. Christ did not sin; He perfectly upheld the stipulations of the covenant of works imposed upon Him (precepts and penalties) and entered into glory as our forerunner. Our Lord not only lived and died for us, but His resurrection was for us as well.

This is the doctrine of the covenant of works, and I think the 2LCF is correct to include it. It is a doctrinal formulation with ample scriptural and historical support.

Conclusion

Moses, writing after the divine acts of creation, utilizes the covenantal name of God, *Yahweh*, while discussing Adam's Edenic vocation (Genesis 2:4ff.). Isaiah utilizes concepts that started with Adam to explain the universal guilt of man, while using the word "covenant" (Isaiah 24:5–6). Hosea, looking back upon previous written revelation, makes explicit what was implicit in it. The prophet's inspired words give us God's infallible knowledge of one of the similarities between ancient Israel and Adam: both had a covenant imposed on them by God and both transgressed their covenants (Hosea 6:7). Paul, while reflecting on Adam's Edenic vocation, contrasts the disobedience of Adam and its results with the obedience of Christ and its results (Romans 5:19). The term *works* in the phrase "covenant of works" contrasts with "grace" and "gift" in Romans 5:17. Paul asserts that Adam was a type of Christ (Romans 5:14). Adam sinned and fell short of the glory of God (Romans 3:23). Christ did not sin (Hebrews 4:15), and, upon His resurrection, entered into glory (Luke 24:46; Acts 26:19–23; 1 Peter 1:10–12), a quality of life conferred upon Him due to His obedience (Romans 5:21). This is the life He confers upon all believers.

These scriptural realities, understood by the utilization of the hermeneutical principles of the Holy Spirit as the only infallible interpreter of Holy Scripture, the *analogia Scripturae*, the *analogia fidei*, and the *scopus Scripturae*, led to the confessional formulation of the doctrine of the covenant of works.

NCT denies this doctrine as formulated above and in the 2LCF. Chapter 3 made that clear in the words of some of its own writers. It is hoped that NCT adherents (and others) will consider not only the progressive proposals of Gary Long and Blake White, but also the arguments above, and continue to develop and refine, as they admit they are doing.

I applaud those NCT writers (and others) who now affirm a covenant with Adam, and I trust this discussion will help nudge some toward a more carefully defined, robust doctrinal formulation of this crucial issue. With that in mind, if there was a covenant imposed upon Adam in the garden, are we to insist that it was designed to keep him (and his progeny) in the state in which he was created? If so, this would seem to imply that divine covenants (at least this one) are designed to maintain man in the condition in which they come to him. Is this, in fact, the way the biblical covenants function? I think not. It seems clear that biblical covenants are imposed on men to bring them to a better state of existence. If there was a covenant imposed upon Adam in the garden, then it was so for his good, unto a better state of existence for himself and for all those he represented. Adam was created morally upright, yet mutable. He was not created in a state that could be called "glory," as indicated above.

Another important aspect of the creation account and Adam's vocation involves God's rest recorded for us in Genesis 2:1–3. The next nine chapters will discuss this vital subject.

Part Two

God's Rest
In Light of Christ

6

The Doctrine of the Christian Sabbath

THE NEW COVENANT THEOLOGY PERSPECTIVE

NCT's view of the Sabbath is well-attested in its literature, which will become clear to readers in this chapter. The subject normally comes up in their discussions concerning what they do not believe about it.

NCT believes the Sabbath was a sign of the Mosaic covenant. It came with ancient Israel's covenant and left with it. It had a covenantal beginning and ending with that covenant. When the Mosaic covenant came, the Sabbath came; and when it went, the Sabbath went with it because it was fulfilled by Christ. It had a temporary function from Sinai to the cross as the sign of the Mosaic covenant, but it also pointed to the rest brought in by our Lord. Though it had an eschatological function, the Sabbath command no longer functions as a requirement for the new covenant church in terms of keeping one day in seven holy to the Lord. The Sabbath, according to NCT, did not begin at creation, is not relevant to all men, does not have anything to do with Christian ethics, and is not to be commended for others to keep. The Lord's Day is not the Christian Sabbath. The Lord's Day might be the day of Christ's resurrection, the first day of the week, but Christians are free to gather on any day for public worship.[1] Though the first day may be preferred, it is not required. These things will become evident as we examine NCT's view on the Sabbath.

---

[1] I am not sure this is the view of all NCT writers. See Lehrer, *NCT*, 190.

NCT on the Sabbath

It is not hard to understand the NCT view on the Sabbath. They write quite clearly on the subject, as the following quotations will demonstrate. After considering these statements, I will interact with a book written by Tom Wells devoted to the issue of the Sabbath, and then examine the view of New Testament scholar Thomas Schreiner. Though Schreiner, as far as I can tell, does not self-identify as a NCT proponent, his arguments are very similar to NCT, thus serving as an example of a contemporary scholar who advocates the same basic view.

Various NCT Authors on the Sabbath

NCT author A. Blake White says,

> ...the New Testament clearly teaches that we are no longer bound to the Sabbath Commandment, which is the fourth of the Ten Commandments. If Paul thought that new covenant Christians were still bound to obey the Sabbath, do you think he would have ever said: "One person esteems one day as better than another, while another esteems all days alike. Each one should be fully convinced in his own mind" (Rom 14:5). Paul is a Sabbath relativist! He says to make up your own mind regarding the matter. This is a far cry from "Remember the Sabbath Day to keep it holy" (Exod 20:8). Do you remember the man who was stoned for gathering wood on the Sabbath? Clearly times have changed in the new covenant.[2]

White later references Colossians 2:16–17 and Galatians 4:8–11 (in that order) in support of his view. These passages, along with Romans 14:5, are often cited in support of NCT's views on the Sabbath.

> Therefore no one is to act as your judge in regard to food or drink or in respect to a festival or a new moon or a Sabbath day—things which are a mere shadow of what is to come; but the substance belongs to Christ. (Colossians 2:16–17)

> However at that time, when you did not know God, you were slaves to those which by nature are no gods. But now that you have come to know God, or rather to be known by God, how is it that you turn back again to the weak and worthless elemental things, to which you desire to be enslaved all over again? You observe days and months and seasons and years. I fear for you, that perhaps I have labored over you in vain. (Galatians 4:8–11)

---

[2] White, *What is New Covenant Theology?*, 29.

After citing the Colossians text, White says, "Christ has come! The reality is here. We are no longer slaves to the elemental spirits of the world—which includes observing the Sabbath (Gal 4:8–11)."[3] The cited texts are assumed to teach exactly what White asserts, but without much exegesis of the texts themselves in their contexts and in light of antecedent or subsequent written revelation.[4] Notice that White says "the New Testament clearly teaches that we are *no longer* bound to the Sabbath Commandment, which is the fourth of the Ten Commandments. If Paul thought that new covenant Christians were still bound to obey the Sabbath…" and "We are *no longer* slaves to the elemental spirits of the world—which includes observing the Sabbath…" (emphasis added). He says similar things in his *The Law of Christ*. For example:

> Finally, (as with circumcision) the Sabbath command is abrogated in the New Testament. This command creates problems for those who believe that the Ten Commandments are directly binding on believers. The New Testament is clear that we are *no longer* bound to obey the Sabbath command. The Sabbath was the sign of the old covenant, which has passed away with the death and resurrection of Christ. So just as believers are *no longer* bound to the old covenant, neither are they bound to the sign of that covenant….
>
> As we saw above, the book of Hebrews views the Sabbath as a type of the eschatological rest brought about by Jesus (Heb 3:7–4:11). For new covenant believers, the command to obey the Sabbath is a command to believe the gospel.[5]

If Christians are "no longer bound" to keep the Sabbath, this appears to assume that they once were.[6] This poses a difficulty for NCT, since the Sabbath, in their thinking, was given as a sign of the Mosaic covenant which was delivered by God through Moses to Israel, and not to first century Gentiles. We will discuss this more below.

---

[3] White, *What is New Covenant Theology?*, 30.

[4] In A. Blake White, *Theological Foundations for New Covenant Ethics* (Frederick, MD: New Covenant Media, 2013), 37–38, he mentions Romans 14, Galatians 4, and Colossians 2. In each case, the verses mentioned are assumed to prove his assertion, but with very little interaction with the texts and no interaction with literature from those who take a differing view. See also p. 98 for the same (i.e., assertions without proof). At the end of his brief discussion on the Sabbath on pp. 37–38, he says, "Again, exegesis must inform our theology" (38). Exegesis and citing texts, however, are not one and the same.

[5] White, *The Law of Christ*, 138–39; emphasis added.

[6] It is most likely that White is referring to believing Jews in the first century, though he does not make himself clear on this point.

Notice also that White says the Sabbath was "a type of the eschatological rest brought about by Jesus." But "the eschatological rest brought about by Jesus," as will be argued in subsequent chapters of this book, is only fully enjoyed by the resurrected Mediator until the second coming. The Sabbath did not typify the interadvental period on the earth exclusively. It pointed to and, as will be argued, points to the eternal state, the age of consummation, when all the elect will enjoy the fullness of the Creator's rest, along with the One (i.e., our Lord) who is the agent through whom they are brought to glory (Hebrews 2:10). The type does not give way to its antitype until its antitype comes in fullness and completeness. Until the eternal state, there is a type pointing to it in the Sabbath institution. Believers this side of the cross and resurrection of our Lord live in the already/not-yet tension of the interadventual age, not in the eternal state.

Finally, notice that White says, "For new covenant believers, the command to obey the Sabbath is a command to believe the gospel." This has a certain ring to it, but I am not sure what it means. The Sabbath is law; the gospel is not. I suppose the intent is that Jesus is the Sabbath, or something similar to that. The Sabbath, as will be shown in later discussion, is not a person but ultimately points to a condition of existence for man, the eternal state. Our Lord takes us to that condition, that state of existence, but is Himself not that state of existence, though He has entered it via His resurrection.[7]

Gary Long says, "The Fourth Commandment, the Sabbath commandment, being the sign of the Mosaic Covenant (Exod. 31:15–17), is not a creation ordinance as taught by CT [Covenant Theology]."[8] Later in the same book, he says:

> Under the New Covenant, the law of Christ also incorporates nine of the Ten Commandments including fulfillment of the fourth commandment, the Sabbath commandment, resulting in "Sabbath rest" for the people of God (Heb. 4:9).[9]

Long denies the Sabbath as a creational ordinance and advocates a fulfillment motif that does away with the fourth commandment under the inaugurated new covenant as prescribing a day of sacred rest for Christians.

---

[7] Just as the sacrificial system points, not absolutely to a person, but inclusively to the work of that person and the benefits that come to believing sinners in light of that person's work, so the Sabbath points to the work and benefits of the same.

[8] Long, *NCT*, 6. We will discuss the Sabbath as a creational ordinance in Chapter 10.

[9] Ibid., 170.

Fred Zaspel asserts similar things as above. Under the heading, "The Sabbath in the New Covenant," he says:

> ...the New Testament writers consistently treat the Sabbath as having served an anticipatory function, a purpose and usefulness exhausted in the person and work of Christ. Under the new covenant all of life has been made holy, and as a result there are no special holy days (Rom. 14; Gal. 4:9–11; Col. 2:16–17). In particular, the Sabbath day pictured a rest now realized in Christ (Matt. 11:28–30; Col. 2:16–17; Heb. 4), and according to Galatians 4:9–11 a return to Sabbath-keeping is wholly inconsistent with the Christian profession....
>
> ... Nor should we expect the sign of the old covenant, which in its first instance was the function of the Sabbath (Exod. 31), to be carried over into the new. Reading our Bibles as we do we are not surprised to find that the Sabbath is no longer a day to be observed but a rest enjoyed every day (Rom. 14:5) in Christ. The Sabbath is not thereby destroyed; it is fulfilled (Matt. 5:17).
>
> ... So in this new covenant age we "keep the Sabbath" not in the observance of a day of the week as holy but in our faith-rest in Christ. This is the shape of Sabbath-keeping in the new covenant. And thus, we observe the Sabbath today in the way we observe all the old covenant law—in light of Christ, its fulfillment.[10]

Zaspel cites the same texts as others in defense of his position. He advocates an anticipatory function of the Sabbath, which has been "exhausted in the person and work of Christ." The Sabbath is now "a rest enjoyed every day (Romans 14:5) in Christ." With the arrival of Christ, to whom the Sabbath pointed, fulfillment came as well, and thus the Sabbath must be understood in light of that fulfillment. It seems to me that this is an over-realized eschatology of the interadvental period. As we have seen and will see below, the rest that Christ takes believers of all ages to is not the interadvental period, but the eternal state. The rest enjoyed now is a taste of that which is to come, a rest our Lord has entered into already via His resurrection. We will come back to this issue in subsequent chapters.

John G. Reisinger says many of the same things other NCT authors say on this issue. He correctly points out that the Sabbath "functioned as the sign of the [Mosaic] covenant (Ex. 31:12–18)."[11] He then adds:

---

[10] Fred G. Zaspel, *The New Covenant and New Covenant Theology* (Frederick, MD: New Covenant Media, 2011), 38–39.

[11] John G. Reisinger, *Continuity and Discontinuity* (Frederick, MD: New Covenant Media, 2011), 71.

> When the New Covenant fulfilled and replaced the Old Covenant, of which the Sabbath was the ceremonial sign, the entire Ten Commandments ceased to be covenant terms, and thus lost their major relevance. The Sabbath, as one of the ten, was fulfilled and done away with—it lost all of its significance as a holy day.[12]

At the beginning of his discussion, he says, "…God did not reveal the concept of a Sabbath until Sinai (recorded in Ex. 16)."[13] Technically speaking, however, the account of Exodus 16 records events in "the wilderness of Sin, which is between Elim and Sinai…" (Exodus 16:1; we will consider this text in Chapter 11). The concept of a Sabbath was revealed to Israel prior to Mount Sinai. Reisinger's point seems to be that the Sabbath was for ancient Israel under the Mosaic covenant and for Israel alone. Elsewhere he says, "I believe that God gave the Sabbath only to Israel."[14] He argues the same thing in his *Tablets of Stone & the History of Redemption*.[15]

Finally, Steve Lehrer discusses the Sabbath in his book, *New Covenant Theology*. He begins his chapter dealing with this issue as follows:

> There are three major points by which the NCT position on the Sabbath can be summarized:
>
> 1. The Old Covenant has passed away and none of the commands of the Mosaic Law are binding on believers today, including the command to keep the Sabbath holy.
>
> 2. There is not a "1 in 7 pattern" of rest and work that believers in the New Covenant era are obligated to follow because there is no such command in Scripture.
>
> 3. Although the early church may have regularly met on Sundays (the first day of the week) as a way of commemorating the resurrection, there is no command to meet on that day. In addition, early church patterns are not binding on believers. Therefore God's people are free to gather any day or days of the week that they so choose to gather.[16]

---

[12] Reisinger, *Continuity and Discontinuity*, 71.
[13] Ibid.
[14] Reisinger, *In Defense of Jesus*, 252.
[15] John G. Reisinger, *Tablets of Stone & the History of Redemption* (Frederick, MD: New Covenant Media, 2004), 69–71. To his credit, Reisinger not only cites Colossians 2:16 in his discussion, but he also offers two pages of interaction with the text in its context. Because this text will be discussed in more detail in subsequent chapters, I will not interact with Reisinger at this point.
[16] Lehrer, *NCT*, 181.

Lehrer adds:

> As I explained above, the entire Mosaic Law, including the Ten Commandments, are no longer binding on believers because the Old Covenant in its entirety is null and void and has been replaced by the New Covenant. This commandment in the Decalogue [i.e., the fourth] is as applicable to us today as the commandment, "Do not mate different kinds of animals" (Leviticus 19:19), which is also part of the Mosaic Law.[17]

Commenting on the fact that some "believe that the Sabbath was a command given at creation" (see Genesis 2:2–3, where Moses tells us that God "rested on the seventh day" and "blessed the seventh day and sanctified it"), he says:

> It is clear that God rested on the seventh day and because that was the day that He finished His work, He blessed that day and made it holy. But these verses don't tell us to do anything in particular with the seventh day. What does it mean in this passage for the seventh day to be "holy"? Does it necessarily entail some sort of Sabbath for mankind? It seems to me that the text is silent on the issue. Therefore, we are not able to say this is a command.[18]

Concerning Genesis 2:2–3, it must be admitted that no explicit command for man is given in that text. Lehrer asks an important question about the seventh day being made holy or sanctified by God. He asks, "Does it necessarily entail some sort of Sabbath for mankind?" As was pointed out in previous discussion, and will be illustrated below, to understand the primal history of man in the early chapters of Genesis properly, we must allow subsequent Scripture to have a place at the table of interpretation in determining its meaning, assuming it comments upon those chapters. This is exactly what happens. As with the covenant of works, so with the Creator's rest: subsequent revelation makes explicit what is implicit in antecedent revelation. This will be discussed in more detail in subsequent chapters, especially Chapter 10.

Tom Wells' Book, *The Christian and the Sabbath*

Tom Wells wrote a book on this issue entitled, *The Christian and the Sabbath*.[19] Many of the points made above by others are made and ampli-

---

[17] Lehrer, *NCT*, 186.
[18] Ibid., 185.
[19] Tom Wells, *The Christian and the Sabbath* (Frederick, MD: New Cove-

fied by Wells. After the Foreword and establishing the basis for the book in its first chapter, Wells discusses the Old Testament on the Sabbath. He addresses what he calls the argument from creation based on Genesis 2:1–3 or what many call creation ordinances. He says:

> Perhaps you have heard someone say that the Sabbath is a creation ordinance. What did they mean by that? Those who use the phrase appear to mean that at creation God gave commands to be carried out by all men and women throughout history. Often three are cited: marriage, labor and Sabbath. But if creation ordinance implies that all men and women must do these things, even if we suppose that Jesus needed to be an obvious exception, Paul shows us that it is not necessary that all normal people get married. In fact, he expressed a preference for singleness like his (1 Cor 7:7–8). So also the Sabbath could be an exception.[20]

I am not sure if any who advocate creation ordinances claim that marriage as first instituted is a mandate for all men and women, *no matter what circumstances might come onto the world-scene subsequently*. If that were the case, then Jesus and Paul sinned. This would be similar to arguing that the only legitimate vocation is that of Edenic garden-tending. I think the point of those who advocate creation ordinances is simply that if and when men and women unite in marriage, they are to do so monogamously. Also, though creation-based ethics (i.e., creation ordinances) are age-long ethics, the fall into sin does complicate matters. For instance, in Matthew 19, Jesus argues from the creation account to lifelong monogamous marriage. However, he also acknowledges that sin has complicated matters and thus there is a modified application of the creation ordinance of marriage in a fallen world. In fact, due to the fall into sin and the curse, the creation ordinance of labor looks different in its postlapsarian application (Genesis 3:17–19). Could it be the same for the Sabbath? Could it be that the Sabbath takes on various temporary nuances due to the presence of sin and God's purposes in the unfolding drama of redemption? Obviously, I think this is the case and will attempt to prove this below. Due to God's purposes in creation and redemption (i.e., new creation), the Sabbath takes on redemptive-historical nuances as it is incorporated into and applied in

---

nant Media, 2010). Interested readers may want to see Richard C. Barcellos, "*The Christian and the Sabbath*, Tom Wells: A Review Article (Part I)," *RBTR* VII:1 (Spring 2010): 81–93 and Richard C. Barcellos, "*The Christian and the Sabbath*, Tom Wells: A Review Article (Part II)," *RBTR* VII:2 (Fall 2010): 131–49. Some of the material in this section of the book comes from those articles and is used with permission.

[20] Wells, *The Christian and the Sabbath*, 26.

The New Covenant Theology Perspective

differing eras of redemptive history. Though sin may complicate or change the application of creation ordinances, it does not negate them.

While discussing Genesis 2:1–3, Wells says:

> To begin we see that there is nothing in Genesis 2:1–3 that commands a Sabbath for anyone. I have already said that the verses would fit in nicely with such a command. Does this prove that there was no such command? Of course not. Still there is no such command in the passage. People may imagine they hear one, but even a casual look shows that it is not there.
>
> If we ask why people find a command here, they may tell us these verses do not stand alone but are joined with other verses in the Mosaic writings. When we look in those we find that each speaks only of what Israelites and people living in her land must do. Moses is silent on others.[21]

First, concerning the argument that since there is no command, there is no command, it does have a *prima facie* appeal to it. There is no command, therefore there is no command! Case closed, end of debate, right? I don't think so. There are many things not commanded in the creation narrative that most (all?) Christians believe were nonetheless commands (call them moral requirements, ordinances, or whatever) for Adam and Eve *and* for all subsequent men and women. For instance, would Wells want to argue that since there is no command in the creation narrative concerning truth-telling, truth-telling was not commanded or required of Adam and Eve and all subsequent men and women? There is nothing in the creation narrative that explicitly commands truth-telling. It would fit in quite well, but there is none. People may imagine they hear one, but even a casual look shows that it is not there. The same goes for monotheism, idolatry, honoring God-ordained human authorities, murder, coveting, etc. Here's the point: Wells' argument is a *non sequitur*—it does not follow—and it actually proves too much. Wells is asking too much of a narrative. The Genesis creation account tells the story of creation; it is not an explicit, detailed ethical code. As a matter of fact, the creation narrative is scant when it comes to ethical injunctions compared to many other portions of Scripture. Also, even though it is not an explicit ethical code, that does not mean it does not *imply* ethics. For instance, we know that being an image-bearer of God has ethical implications. This is hinted at in the creation narrative (Genesis 1:26ff.) and teased-out for us elsewhere in subsequent revelation (see Romans 1–2; Ephesians 4:24; Colossians 3:10; James 3:9).

In other words, creational revelation is implicitly imperatival, at least some of it. The act of creation warrants, even demands, man's proper re-

---

[21] Wells, *The Christian and the Sabbath*, 26.

sponse. "Let all the inhabitants of the world stand in awe of Him," says Psalm 33:8. But why? Verse 9 says, "For He spoke, and it was done; He commanded, and it stood fast." To what does "it" refer? "By the word of the LORD the heavens were made..." (Psalm 33:6a). In other words, the fact and act of creation is implicitly imperatival. This also shows us, once again, that subsequent revelation often makes explicit what is implicit in antecedent revelation. The Bible often expounds upon and applies itself, drawing out of previous revelation implications for the present that were always there. Sometimes, the implications the Bible draws out are highly conditioned upon the era of redemptive history in which one lives (e.g., Exodus 20:8ff.; Mark 2:28; 1 Timothy 2:11ff.; Revelation 1:10). Wells seems to forget about general revelation and the ethical implications of creation *imago Dei*, which will be discussed in Chapter 8 of this book.

Second, Wells says, "these verses [Genesis 2:1–3]…do not stand alone but are joined with other verses in the Mosaic writings" and "[w]hen we look at those we find that each speaks only of what Israelites and people living in her land must do."[22] What are we to make of this? First of all, Genesis 2:1–3 is not only "joined with other verses in the Mosaic writings," it is connected to and further explained by other portions of Holy Scripture outside of the Pentateuch.[23] There are at least allusions to Genesis 2:1–3 outside of the Mosaic writings and these must be taken into account when seeking to understand it (see Mark 2:27 and Hebrews 4:4, 9). Interestingly, Wells says elsewhere, "What could I tell others about the meaning of my keeping a Sabbath if all I had was Genesis 2:1–3?"[24] This, too, is a *non sequitur*—it does not follow that since you can't say much, therefore you can't say anything. But more importantly, we have much more revelation than simply Genesis 2:1–3, and limiting ourselves to that

---

[22] Wells, *The Christian and the Sabbath*, 26.

[23] This phenomenon is called intertextuality. It is defined in Arthur G. Patzia & Anthony J. Petrotta, *Pocket Dictionary of Biblical Studies* (Downers Grove, IL: InterVarsity Press, 2002), 63, as follows: "The phenomenon that all texts are involved in an interplay with other texts, which results in the interpretive principle that no text can be viewed as isolated and independent. This interplay is particularly true of biblical literature, since each document, or text, is self-consciously part of a stream of tradition. The study of intertextuality pays attention to the fragments, or 'echoes,' of earlier texts that appear in later texts, examining texts that share words and themes." The basic thought here is that all biblical texts are, at some level, involved with all other biblical texts in revealing a cohesive story. This is illustrated, for instance, in the sharing of words, phrases, concepts, and/or themes from antecedent revelation by subsequent revelation. With reference to the Bible, intertextuality is assured by the fact of divine inspiration.

[24] Wells, *The Christian and the Sabbath*, 26.

passage alone is simply dangerously myopic and a really poor hermeneutical move. The only infallible interpreter of the Holy Scripture is the Holy Spirit in the Holy Scripture. We must allow the Bible to speak concerning the canonical meaning of Genesis 2:1–3 lest we impose our own conjectures or arguments from silence upon it.

Wells' book discusses many other issues, some of which I interacted with in the *RBTR* articles noted above. Since many of the issues Wells brings up will be discussed in later chapters of this book, I will refrain from further interaction with his arguments for now. One issue I did not interact with in the *RBTR* articles that I think needs mention at this point concerns John Owen on the Sabbath. In subsequent discussion, Owen will be consulted on this issue. Since Owen is recognized as possibly the greatest English theologian ever, it is appropriate for us to study his views carefully.[25] Wells discusses Owen in one of the later chapters of his book. Attempting to prove that there is controversy on the issue of the Sabbath in the churches due to leaning too heavily on creeds, Wells says of Owen:

> I fear that John Owen himself illustrates this. I mentioned that I estimate Owen's defense of the Sabbath runs to as much as 90,000 words…. Surely in doing this Owen discussed the relevant biblical material very thoroughly indeed!
>
> But sadly the evidence shows otherwise. And the evidence is not debatable….
>
> What does Owen say on Galatians 4:10–11? Nothing. According to the index to the seven volumes of the commentary on Hebrews which includes the essay on the Sabbath, Owen makes no significant reference to this major Sabbath passage whatever, in the commentary proper or in the essay.
>
> What does Owen say about Romans 14:5–6, the passage in which Paul shows his conviction that days are a matter of indifference? Surely one cannot offer a New Covenant Sabbath day without referring to each of these two passages—but Owen does it.
>
> And what of Colossians 2:16? Here Owen is not completely silent. In his essay on the Sabbath he cites this verse in passing at least twice.[26]

---

[25] See my *The Family Tree*, 51–52, "The Legacy of John Owen."

[26] Wells cites Owen's Hebrews commentary at this point as follows: "Owen, 2:281, 363." The version of Owen on Hebrews Wells cites from is entered in the bibliography of his book as "Owen, John, *An Exposition of Hebrews*, Evansville, IN: Sovereign Grace Publishers, 7 vols (bound in four), repr. 1980. [Footnote references are to the 7 volumes.]" (136). Thanks to Pastor Donald R. Lindblad for helping me confirm that the version of Owen that Wells used, Sovereign Grace Publishers, and the version I used, Banner of Truth, corresponded in pagination and indices.

In addition he has a fuller discussion worthy of study and comment.[27]

At this point, Wells interacts with Owen on Colossians 2:16, then draws this conclusion.

> We do not know Owen's motives, but I think he felt how little this explained Colossians 2:16. He writes, "This place must be afterwards considered…"[28] He never made good on that promise—not in the Commentary (with its essay), the Works or the Biblical Theology. (In each case I had to judge this, of course, from the indexes.)[29]

These are startling claims. As will become obvious in subsequent discussion in this book, I think Owen got the Sabbath right. But what can be said about Wells' assertions? First of all, I agree with Wells that Owen did not "afterwards" consider the Colossians text in his *Biblical Theology* as promised in his essay on the Sabbath. The reason why is because Owen's *Biblical Theology* was published in 1661 and the first volume of the Hebrews commentary was published in 1668.[30] I read Owen on the Sabbath in 1993 and again in 2016. In 1993, I was especially interested in how he dealt with Romans 14, Galatians 4, and Colossians 2. I wrote in the margins each time these texts were discussed. So when I read Wells in 2010, his claims piqued my interest. My hunch at that time has been confirmed by a second read of Owen's essay and the use of the indices for the Hebrews commentary. Wells makes unsubstantiated assertions about Owen and does so with a rhetorical style in an attempt, seemingly, to discredit him.

Taking the Pauline texts cited in the order Wells dealt with them above, what do we learn? Wells claims that Owen says nothing about the Galatians 4 passage. He says, "According to the index to the seven volumes of the commentary on Hebrews which includes the essay on the Sabbath, Owen makes no significant reference to this major Sabbath passage whatever, in the commentary proper or in the essay." He then adds, "What does Owen say about Romans 14:5–6, the passage in which Paul shows his conviction that days are a matter of indifference? Surely one cannot offer a New Covenant Sabbath day without referring to each of these two passages [i.e., Galatians 4 and Romans 14]—but Owen does it." However,

---

[27] Wells, *The Christian and the Sabbath*, 110. Wells cites Owen's Hebrews commentary at this point as follows: "Owen, 2:381–385."

[28] Wells cites Owen's Hebrews commentary at this point as follows: "Owen, 2:382."

[29] Wells, *The Christian and the Sabbath*, 111.

[30] See the discussion in Barcellos, *The Family Tree*, 50.

The New Covenant Theology Perspective

Owen does discuss both Galatians 4:10 and Romans 14:5 in the essay on the Sabbath, although those texts do not occur as entries in the index.[31] One wonders if Wells read the essay or merely based his assertion on the index.

What about Colossians 2:16? I am not sure why Wells limited himself to verse 16. Owen deals with Colossians 2:16 in the two places cited by Wells, as well as on pages 398–99, a reference Wells missed, which once again is not in the index. Wells claims this of Owen: "We do not know Owen's motives, but I think he felt how little this explained Colossians 2:16. He writes, 'This place must be afterwards considered…' He never made good on that promise—not in the Commentary (with its essay), the Works or the Biblical Theology. (In each case I had to judge this, of course, from the indexes.)" Wells cites Owen's essay at page 382, where Owen says, "This place must be afterwards considered."[32] To what does "this place" refer? Turning back to the previous page in Owen, we find Colossians 2:16–17 cited, and on the very page Wells referenced. My hunch when first reading this in Owen led me to the conclusion that he would deal with either Colossians 2:16 or 17 or both in the commentary. Reading Owen's comments carefully, he makes the referent to "this place" clear. He is referring back to Colossians 2:17, specifically to those who take it to mean

> that there is nothing moral in the observation of the Sabbath, seeing it was a mere type and shadow, as were other Mosaical institutions, as also that it was absolutely abolished and taken away in Christ.[33]

So it is clear that "this place" refers to Colossians 2:17, most likely to be further discussed in the commentary.

Wells claims that Owen "never made good on that promise—not in the Commentary (with its essay), the Works or the Biblical Theology." Is this, in fact, the case? In this case the index shows "iv. 257" and "vi. 421" entered under Colossians 2:17. Remember Wells said, "In each case I had to judge this, of course, from the indexes." He obviously overlooked these two entries. The first entry comes in Owen's commentary on Hebrews 4:3, while discussing the typology of Canaan. Here's what he says there:

> But both the land and all the institutions to be observed in it were types of Christ, with the rest and worship of believers in and by him. They were "shadows of things to come, the body whereof was Christ," Col. ii. 17.[34]

---

[31] See Owen, *Works*, 18:425–26.
[32] Ibid., 18:382.
[33] Ibid.
[34] Ibid., 20:257.

The second entry comes in Owen's commentary on Hebrews 10:1. He argues that Colossians 2:17, "a *mere* shadow of what is to come," is the same as Hebrews 10:1, "the Law, since it has *only* a shadow of the good things to come." He says,

> "They are a shadow of things to come," is the same with this, "The law hath a shadow of good things to come;" for it is the law with its ordinances and institutions of worship concerning which the apostle there discourseth, as he [Owen believed Paul wrote Hebrews] doth in this place.[35]

Owen then discusses the function of such shadows.

Why should we take the time to deal with this issue of historical theology? The reason is at least two-fold. First, I think Wells' treatment of Owen illustrates something I said above about some NCT writers. They often write in such a way that gives the appearance of bolstering their assertions. In other words, they sometimes make their assertions with powerful rhetorical flair. Wells does this above. Second, NCT writers sometimes display a faulty view of historical theology and thereby reveal that they do not always understand their debate partners.[36] This is illustrated

---

[35] Owen, *Works*, 22:421.

[36] The issue of the Sabbath in Owen is not the first time Wells misrepresented him in print. See my "John Owen and New Covenant Theology: Owen on the Old and New Covenants and the Functions of the Decalogue in Redemptive History in Historical and Contemporary Perspective," in Coxe and Owen, *Covenant Theology*, 317–54. I argued that Wells misunderstood Owen on issues related to the old and new covenants. In the conclusion to that piece (p. 354), I said,

> We have examined Owen in light of Owen, his historical and theological context, and Tom Wells' claims that align him with John G. Reisinger and NCT. In light of the discussion above, it is safe to say that Owen cannot be claimed by NCT on the grounds Wells claims him. He held views with which NCT is sympathetic. But his views did not change, at least as far as the perpetuity of the Decalogue under the New Covenant goes, nor were they contradictory or novel. The novelty in all of this appears to be NCT's method of abrogating the Decalogue from the New Covenant. It does this upon the grounds of it being a unit of law applicable to Old Covenant Israel as a body politic and applicable to them alone. This leads NCT to view the Old Covenant as a covenant of works in itself and unrelated to the Edenic covenant of works. Radical antinomians eliminate the Decalogue because it is law. Doctrinal antinomians eliminate it because it is Moses' Law and not Christ's. This has detrimental implications for the identity of the Natural Law, the basis of the covenant of works, the perpetuity of the Moral Law, the Sabbath, the active obedience of Christ, and

above, not only in Wells, but in how the covenant of works was formulated, and will become evident in our discussion of the Sabbath in the 2LCF and, especially in the Bible. I do not want to be too critical of Wells, but he did make some serious claims that are simply not true.[37]

John Reisinger is another example of a NCT author who has either displayed ignorance of the position of those he is critiquing, or who has put words and meanings into their minds and mouths. For example, while discussing the question of the existence of a moral law of God and the language used by the WCF, he says:

> Every time someone uses the term *the moral law*, I am tempted to reply, "I assume by *the moral law* that you mean the opposite of *the immoral law*." ... Theologians have created a new and unique use of the word *moral* in order to justify a preconceived theological position. They have made the opposite of *moral* to *be ceremonial and civil*.... They insist that the law of Moses can be divided into three distinct lists: the *moral* list; the *ceremonial* list; and the *civil* list.[38]

Reisinger goes on, attempting to prove his case by citing a 2002 edition of *Webster's Dictionary* on the word *moral*. After listing six explanations of its adjective form, three of its noun form, and a list of synonyms, he concludes as follows: "As you can see, there is no hint that the word *moral*

> the imputation of righteousness—indeed, the gospel itself. The issues are far-reaching and have very practical relevance.
>   In closing, it is important to remember what was said at the outset. Owen can be easily misunderstood if not followed very carefully and if his statements are not examined in light of his systematic thought and the historical and theological context in which he wrote. It appears that both John G. Reisinger and Tom Wells did just that. May we all learn from this to be careful when making claims about another's position, especially someone who carries as much theological weight as John Owen. In making such claims, we may be making sweeping generalizations unawares and leading others to believe that which is simply not true.

[37] I have done the same, unfortunately. In my review of the Wells/Zaspel book, published in *RBTR* I:1 (January 2004): 163–69, I admitted the following on p. 164: "… I learned that I misrepresented Fred Zaspel in my book *In Defense of the Decalogue* (*NCT*, 188, n. 263). I stand corrected and regret this careless, though not intentional misrepresentation." The review is also contained in Samuel E. Waldron with Richard C. Barcellos, *A Reformed Baptist Manifesto: The New Covenant Constitution of the Church* (Palmdale, CA: Reformed Baptist Academic Press, 2004), 93–102.

[38] Reisinger, *In Defense of Jesus*, 325.

ever means the opposite of or different from ceremonial or civil."[39] This is anachronistic. If one wants to consult a dictionary to help define theological terms from the sixteenth and seventeenth centuries, he should either consult the *Oxford English Dictionary* or Muller's *Dictionary* (cited above). Muller's book seeks to define terms and phrases as they were utilized in the literature of the day. In order to understand the concepts embodied by the terms *moral, ceremonial,* and *civil* and the threefold division of the law as utilized by Reformed theologians of the past, *Webster's Dictionary* is not sufficient. We must remind ourselves that common words can be and are often used by Christians and infused with technical theological meaning. In fact, most words which are contained in the Bible predate its writing. The same goes for technical terms used in the history of Christian thought. The word *Trinity* has had a technical theological meaning for many centuries, but the word and its cognates predate its technical theological sense. The same applies to the phrase "New Covenant Theology." The three words utilized in that phrase all predate its technical meaning, which now describes a theological movement in the late twentieth and early twenty-first centuries. Reisinger commits an anachronistic fallacy, attributing meaning to historically conditioned terms and phrases based on a modern dictionary definition.[40] Sadly, I could multiply examples.

Thomas R. Schreiner on the Sabbath and Christians

Thomas R. Schreiner is a well-known and respected New Testament scholar. I have profited from many of his writings. His book, *The Law and Its Fulfillment: A Pauline Theology of Law,* has many excellent observations and displays careful scholarship, though I disagree with some aspects.[41] In 2010, his *40 Questions about Christians and the Law* was published.[42] He devotes a chapter to this question: "Is the Sabbath Still Required for Christians?" In Schreiner's summary on the chapter dealing with the Sabbath in his 2010 book, we read the following:

---

[39] Ibid., 328. A definition and discussion of the phrase "moral law" will be included in Chapter 7.

[40] A very helpful book dealing with the interpretation of history and the fallacies often made while doing so is Carl R. Trueman, *Histories and Fallacies: Problems Faced in the Writing of History* (Wheaton, IL: Crossway, 2010).

[41] Thomas R. Schreiner, *The Law and Its Fulfillment: A Pauline Theology of Law* (Grand Rapids: Baker Books, 1993).

[42] Thomas R. Schreiner, *40 Questions about Christians and the Law* (Grand Rapids: Kregel Publications, 2010).

> Believers are not obligated to observe the Sabbath. The Sabbath was the sign of the Mosaic covenant. The Mosaic covenant and the Sabbath as the covenant sign are no longer applicable now that the new covenant of Jesus Christ has come. Believers are called upon to honor and respect those who think the Sabbath is still mandatory for believers. But if one argues that the Sabbath is required for salvation, such a teaching is contrary to the gospel and should be resisted forcefully. In any case, Paul makes it clear in both Romans 14:5 and Colossians 2:16–17 that the Sabbath has passed away now that Christ has come. It is wise naturally for believers to rest, and hence one principle that could be derived from the Sabbath is that believers should regularly rest. But the New Testament does not specify when that rest should take place, nor does it set forth a period of time when that rest should occur. We must remember that the early Christians were required to work on Sundays. They worshiped the Lord on the Lord's Day, the day of Jesus' resurrection, but the early Christians did not believe the Lord's Day fulfilled or replaced the Sabbath. The Sabbath pointed toward eschatological rest in Christ, which believers enjoy in part now and will enjoy fully on the Last Day.[43]

Schreiner's arguments are very similar to those of the NCT writers we have discussed. Because the "Sabbath was the sign of the Mosaic covenant" and because the "Mosaic covenant..." is "no longer applicable now that the new covenant of Jesus Christ has come," the Sabbath is "no longer applicable." By "no longer applicable," it appears Schreiner means that the believing Jews who were members of the old covenant at the time of Christ's coming, death, and resurrection, were no longer under the Sabbath command once the new covenant was formally inaugurated. Romans 14:5 and Colossians 2:16–17, in Schreiner's thought, are clear Pauline witnesses against a new covenant Sabbath. A principle of rest may be derived from the Sabbath, but the New Testament does not direct us as to what day or how long this rest should be. Though early Christians worshiped on the Lord's Day, they did not view it as a fulfillment of or replacement for the seventh day Sabbath of the Mosaic covenant. "The Sabbath pointed toward eschatological rest in Christ, which believers enjoy in part now and will enjoy fully on the Last Day." Schreiner and NCT are one on this issue. Further interaction with a more recent publication by him will be included in a subsequent chapter of this book.

---

[43] Schreiner, *40 Questions*, 216–17.

Conclusion

The NCT position on the Sabbath has been made clear. As with the covenant of works, so with the Sabbath; NCT does not appear to allow the Bible its proper place in helping us understand man's creation and vocation, God's rest, and what those meant for Adam and what they mean for Christ and His people. As will be argued below, man was created in the image of God, which has ethical implications from his creation onwards. Also, as it will be argued, the garden of Eden was the first temple on the earth and Adam was the earth's first prophet, priest, and king. The garden was the first earthly expression of the kingdom of God and Adam was the earth's first created ruler of the earth. Both Adam's identity as image-bearer of God and his vocation as priest relate him to God, the divine exemplar. As exemplar, God worked, then rested. He created a temple, then sat enthroned over that temple, and He called Adam to do the same on a creaturely level. Adam was to work, then enter God's rest, but he failed to do so. We will discuss these issues later in this book.

This brief discussion illustrates two more areas in which I think NCT needs to keep developing. First, what does it mean for Adam, for us, and for Christ that Adam was a sinless image-bearer of God who represented others and failed his calling? Second, does God's act of creation in six days, followed by resting, have anything to do with Adam, the rest of mankind, and our Lord and His people? As will be seen in the next chapter, the 2LCF grounds the Sabbath at creation, when God rested. Thus, in subsequent chapters, I will attempt to connect the Sabbath with God's example at creation, Adam as the image of God, and Adam's vocation as the covenantal head of the human race. Finally, I will attempt to show, once again, that what Adam failed to do, our Lord did. It will be argued that to the degree we understand Adam's identity and vocation, we may better understand the incarnation, sufferings, and glory of our Lord. Also, to the degree we understand what the Creator's rest meant for God and what it means for man, we may better understand the incarnation, sufferings, and glory of our Lord.

7

The Doctrine of the Christian Sabbath
THE CONFESSIONAL FORMULATION

In order to understand what NCT denies about the Christian Sabbath as formulated in the 2LCF and to understand what must be proven from Scripture to affirm such a doctrine, this chapter focuses on the Confession itself. The next seven chapters are devoted to the scriptural argument for a Christian Sabbath.

The Doctrine of the Christian Sabbath in the Confession of Faith

The 2LCF's explicit formulation of the doctrine of the Christian Sabbath is found in Chapter 22, paragraphs 7–8. For our purposes, the discussion will concentrate on 22.7, because that paragraph seeks to establish the doctrine and 22.8 discusses its practice. I will offer an outline of 22.7–8a, discuss the doctrinal assumptions and technical terms of paragraph 7, then briefly discuss the assertions made in that paragraph. The paragraph reads as follows:

> As it is the law of nature, that in general a proportion of time, by God's appointment, be set apart for the worship of God, so by his Word, in a positive-moral, and perpetual commandment, binding all men, in all ages, he hath particularly appointed one day in seven for a sabbath to be kept holy unto him, which from the beginning of the world to the resurrection of Christ was the last day of the week, and from the resurrection of Christ was changed into the first day of the week, which is called the Lord's day: and is to be continued to the end of the world as the Chris-

tian Sabbath, the observation of the last day of the week being abolished. (Exodus 20:8; 1 Corinthians 16:1, 2; Acts 20:7; Revelation 1:10)

The Outline of 2LCF 22.7–8a

A. The Foundation of the Sabbath Day (2LCF 22.7)
   1. The Law of Nature requires a Sabbath Day (2LCF 22.7a); *As it is the law of nature*
      a. Its essence: *that in general a proportion of time*
      b. Its author: *by God's appointment*
      c. Its goal: *be set apart for the worship of God*
   2. The Word of God commands a Sabbath Day (2LCF 22.7b)
      a. Its revelation: *so by his Word*
         1) A positive commandment: *in a positive… commandment*
         2) A moral commandment: *in a…moral…commandment*
         3) A perpetual commandment: *in a…perpetual commandment*
      b. Its scope
         1) As to persons: *binding all men*
         2) As to times: *in all ages*
      c. Its essence
         1) Concerning its time: *he hath particularly appointed one day in seven*
         2) Concerning its sanctity: *to be kept holy*
         3) Concerning its object: *unto Him*
      d. Its identity
         1) From creation to Christ's resurrection: *which from the beginning of the world to the resurrection of Christ was the last day of the week*
         2) From Christ's resurrection to the consummation: *and from the resurrection of Christ was changed into the first day of the week*
      e. Its present implications
         1) The Lord's Day is the first day of the week: *which is called the Lord's day*

2) The Lord's Day is to be continued to the end of the world: *and is to be continued to the end of the world*

3) The Lord's Day is the Christian Sabbath: *as the Christian Sabbath*

4) The seventh-day Sabbath has been abolished: *the observation of the last day of the week being abolished*

B. The Sanctification of the Sabbath day (2LCF 22.8)

One can easily see the progression of thought in the outline above. The Sabbath is based on the law of nature and the Word of God. It applies to all men of all ages. It requires one day in seven to be kept holy to the Lord. Its beginning goes all the way back to the creation of the world. Its perpetuity extends to the end of the world. The particular day to be kept holy to the Lord was the last day of the week from creation to the resurrection of our Lord, and is the first day of the week from the resurrection of Christ to the end of the world. The Sabbath day since the resurrection of Christ is called the Lord's Day. The last day of the week as a Sabbath to the Lord has been abolished.

The Doctrinal Assumptions and Technical Terms of 2LCF 22.7

Entering Chapter 22 of the Confession, we do not start over theologically. This chapter, as with others, assumes or utilizes many assertions made prior to it and cannot be understood properly without identifying and understanding those assumptions or assertions and the terms associated with them. As will be noted, it assumes Chapter 19, "Of the Law of God" and Chapter 4, "Of Creation" especially. This ties the theology of the Christian Sabbath in the Confession to the law of God and creation. The Christian Sabbath is part and parcel with the system of doctrine contained in the Confession. To understand the confessional formulation properly at this point, we must understand the creation and constitution of man and the law of God in its various functions. To take exception to the Confession's doctrine of the Christian Sabbath is no minor thing. Denying the formulation of 22.7 necessarily affects other doctrinal formulations within the Confession. Philip S. Ross, while discussing taking exception to the Sabbath by adherents to the WCF, comments,

> …let me say that biblical law, with its Sabbath, is no easily dispensable part of the Reformed doctrinal infrastructure…. Attempts at performing a precision strike on the Sabbath produce an embarrassing amount

of unintended damage. Strike out the Sabbath and you also shatter the entire category of moral law and all that depends on it.[1]

Ross likens the Confession to a garment in the following words:

> Were the Westminster Confession a garment, you would not want to pull this 'minor' thread, unless you wanted to be altogether defrocked.
> ...Unbuckle the Sabbath, and you are well on your way to mastering theological escapology.[2]

These are strong words. Ross' point is that the Confession contains a system of doctrine. Pull one string out of it and you tamper with other aspects of the garment. Understanding the assumptions and technical terms and phrases in 22.7 makes this clear.

The first clause of 22.7 illustrates the fact that technical terms are used which possess technical meaning and evoke previous confessional assertions. The first clause is as follows: "As it is the law of nature." The "law of nature" is synonymous with "natural law" and had technical theological meaning when the Confession was written. To what does it refer? Here is Richard Muller's entry for natural law:

> **lex naturalis**: *natural law*; also **lex naturae**; *law of nature*; the universal moral law either impressed by God upon the mind of all people or immediately discerned by the reason in its encounter with the order of nature. The natural law was therefore available even to those pagans who did not have the advantage of the Sinaitic revelation and the *lex Mosaica* [i.e., Mosaic law, which includes the natural law, though in a different form] with the result that they were left without excuse in their sins... The scholastics argue the identity of the *lex naturalis* with the *lex Mosaica*...according to substance, and distinguish them...according to form. The *lex naturalis* is inward, written on the heart and therefore obscure [due to sin], whereas the *lex Mosaica* is revealed externally and written on tablets and thus of greater clarity.[3]

The natural law is universal because God is the Creator of all men. Natural law is "founded on the natural right of God...(being founded on the very holiness and wisdom of God)."[4] These laws are "just and good anteced-

---

[1] Philip S. Ross, *From the Finger of God: The Biblical and Theological Basis for the Threefold Division of the Law* (Fern, Ross-shire, Scotland: Christian Focus Publications Ltd., Mentor Imprint, 2010), 5–6.

[2] Ibid., 5. Ross is interacting with a statement made by Tim Keller.

[3] Muller, *Dictionary*, 174–75.

[4] Turretin, *Elenctic Theology*, 2.11.1 (2:2).

ently to the command of God…"⁵ They are commanded because they are just and good in light of who God the Creator is and what man is as His image-bearing creature. Natural law is "the practical rule of moral duties to which men are bound by nature."⁶ Due to man's created constitution, this law is written on his heart (2LCF 4.2–3), though now obscured by sin (2LCF 6). Natural law is not acquired by tradition or formal instruction. This law was, however, promulgated (i.e., formally published) on Sinai, which differs from the natural law in form, though it is identical to it in substance. Protestant Orthodoxy taught that the Decalogue summarily contains the moral law and is the inscripturated form of the natural law, as to its substance.

A distinction was made between *substance* and *form*. *Substance* is one; *form* (and function) may vary. For example, when the WLC Q. 98. says, "The moral law is summarily comprehended in the ten commandments," it refers to the fact that the *substance* (i.e., the underlying matter) of the moral law is assumed in the propositions of the Decalogue as contained in Exodus 20 and Deuteronomy 5. The *form* (and function) fits the redemptive-historical circumstances in which it was given. The *substance*, or underlying principles, are always relevant and applicable to man because he is created in the image of God. The application may shift based on redemptive-historical changes, such as the inauguration of the new covenant, but the *substance* and utility never changes. For example, the application of the second commandment under the inaugurated new covenant is different from its application under the Mosaic covenant, but its substance is the same. We must worship God as God has revealed, and since the fall into sin, through a Mediator and in accord with His revealed will.

The first clause of 22.7 evokes 2LCF 4.2–3, where we read:

> After God had made all other creatures, he created man, male and female, with reasonable and immortal souls, rendering them fit unto that life to God for which they were created; being made after the image of God, in knowledge, righteousness, and true holiness; having the law of God written in their hearts, and power to fulfil it, and yet under a possibility of transgressing, being left to the liberty of their own will, which was subject to change. (Genesis 1:27; Genesis 2:7; Ecclesiastes 7:29; Genesis 1:26; Romans 2:14, 15; Genesis 3:6)
>
> Besides the law written in their hearts, they received a command not to eat of the tree of knowledge of good and evil, which whilst they kept,

---

⁵ Turretin, *Elenctic Theology*, 2.11.1 (2:2).
⁶ Ibid.

they were happy in their communion with God, and had dominion over the creatures. (Genesis 2:17; Genesis 1:26, 28)

According to the Confession, the law of nature or natural law refers us back to the creation of man, made in God's image, male and female, "having the law of God written in their hearts" (2LCF 4.2). In 4.3, we read, "Besides the law written in their hearts." So, 2LCF 22.7 assumes 4.2–3, which identifies the "law of nature" as that which was written in Adam and Eve's hearts. Chapter 19, "Of the Law of God," opens with these words: "God gave to Adam a law of universal obedience written in his heart." Then, paragraph 2 mentions "The same law that was first written in the heart of man." Taking these things into consideration, this would mean that "in general a proportion of time, by God's appointment, [ought to] be set apart for the worship of God" is something man knows intuitively or innately by virtue of and in light of his creation by God, though since the fall into sin, he has suppressed that law unrighteously (Romans 1:18).

When 2LCF 22.7 uses the words *positive* and *moral*, it is evoking previous discussions (see also 2LCF 28.1 for the use of the technical term *positive* in the context of baptism and the Lord's Supper). When 2LCF 19.1 says, "God gave to Adam a law of universal obedience written in his heart, and a particular precept of not eating the fruit of the tree…," the second clause is referring to the concept of positive law. The 2LCF 6.1 also refers to the concept of positive law in these words: "Although God created man upright and perfect, and gave him a righteous law." The second clause refers to a positive law revealed to Adam recorded in Genesis 2:16–17. And finally, 2LCF 4.3 refers to the concept of positive law, stating, "Besides the law written in their [i.e., Adam and Eve's] hearts, they received a command not to eat of the tree of knowledge of good and evil" (Genesis 2:17). Once again, the second clause refers to the concept of positive law. To what does the phrase "positive law" refer? Positive laws are those laws added to the natural or moral law (to be defined below). They are dependent upon the will of God. These laws are "good because God commands them." They become just, because they are commanded by God. The first revelation of positive law was delivered to Adam in the garden (Genesis 1:28; 2:17; see 2LCF 4.3; 6.1; 7.1–3; 19.1). Subsequent positive laws are spread throughout the Old and New Testaments. Positive laws can be abrogated for various reasons. They are not necessarily universal or perpetual. Some obvious examples of positive law in the Old Testament are circumcision and the laws of sacrifice. Two New Testament illustrations are baptism and the

---

[7] Turretin, *Elenctic Theology*, 2.11.1 (2:2).

Lord's Supper (2LCF 28.1, "Baptism and the Lord's supper are ordinances of positive and sovereign institution…"). Neither circumcision, sacrifices, baptism, nor the Lord's Supper are universal or perpetual. The ceremonial laws of the Old Testament, as well as the judicial law of old covenant Israel, are also examples of positive law. Ceremonial law is not based on creation, but is conditioned upon God's purpose to remedy the plight of man due to sin. It is positive law, law added to the natural or moral law and, in this case, for the purposes of redemption. The judicial law (also positive law) refers to the civil laws revealed through Moses for ancient Israel as God's nation in the land of promise. Though the underlying principles of these laws (i.e., their general equity) are still of moral use (2LCF 19.4), the laws as universal, positive laws for God's covenant people have expired along with the theocracy.

The last clause of 2LCF 22.7, "the observation of the last day of the week being abolished," also evokes previous confessional assertions. In 2LCF 19.3–4, we read:

> Besides this law, commonly called moral, God was pleased to give to the people of Israel ceremonial laws, containing several typical ordinances, partly of worship, prefiguring Christ, his graces, actions, sufferings, and benefits; and partly holding forth divers instructions of moral duties, all which ceremonial laws being appointed only to the time of reformation, are, by Jesus Christ the true Messiah and only law-giver, who was furnished with power from the Father for that end abrogated and taken away. (Hebrews 10:1; Colossians 2:17; 1 Corinthians 5:7; Colossians 2:14, 16, 17; Ephesians 2:14, 16)
>
> To them also he gave sundry judicial laws, which expired together with the state of that people, not obliging any now by virtue of that institution; their general equity only being of moral use. (1 Corinthians 9:8–10)

The words "Besides this law, commonly called moral" take us back to 2LCF 19.2. There the Confession asserts:

> The same law that was first written in the heart of man continued to be a perfect rule of righteousness after the fall, and was delivered by God upon Mount Sinai, in ten commandments, and written in two tables, the four first containing our duty towards God, and the other six, our duty to man. (2LCF 19.2)

The "law, commonly called moral" (2LCF 19.3) refers to the formal publication (i.e., promulgation) of the natural law "delivered by God upon

Mount Sinai in ten commandments" (2LCF 19.2). Muller defines moral law in Protestant Orthodox thought as follows:

> [S]pecifically and predominantly, the *Decalogus*, or Ten Commandments; also called the *lex Mosaica*..., as distinct from the *lex ceremonialis*...and the *lex civilis*, or civil law. The *lex moralis*, which is primarily intended to regulate morals, is known to the *synderesis* [i.e., the innate habit of understanding basic principles of moral law] and is the basis of the acts of *conscientia* [i.e., conscience—the application of the innate habit above]. In substance, the *lex moralis* is identical with the *lex naturalis*...but, unlike the natural law, it is given by revelation in a form which is clearer and fuller than that otherwise known to the reason.[8]

As noted above, the moral law is summarily comprehended in the Decalogue, not exhausted by it. Though the formal promulgation of the moral law had a unique redemptive-historical context and function, it is nothing other than the natural law incorporated into the Mosaic covenant in a new form.[9] This Mosaic covenantal function is one of its uses in the Bible, though it does not exhaust its uses (cf. Jeremiah 31:33).[10]

The Confession further asserts:

> Besides this law...God was pleased to give to the people of Israel ceremonial laws: all which...laws being appointed only to the time of reformation, are, by Jesus Christ the true Messiah and only law-giver... abrogated and taken away. (2LCF 19.3)

The moral law, because it is grounded in creation, is not abrogated when the new covenant is formally inaugurated. The ceremonial laws are "abrogated and taken away." The inaugurated new covenant changes the positive laws for God's people while assuming the perpetuity of moral law.

Finally, at the end of 2LCF 22.7, we read, "...the observation of the last day of the week being abolished." The coming of Christ and, specifically, His resurrection, changes the Sabbath day from the last day of the week to the first day of the week. The resurrection of Christ is assumed to be an epoch-changing event. As we will note below, it is the inauguration of the new creation, the entering into rest by the Mediator on behalf and for the benefit of believers.

---

[8] Muller, *Dictionary*, 173–74.

[9] The positive aspect of the Decalogue in its unique context and function, its Mosaic covenant form and function, is abrogated.

[10] See Barcellos, "John Owen and New Covenant Theology."

The Assertions Contained in 2LCF 22.7

Several of the main statements of 2LCF 22.7 are worth noting. These are the assertions with which NCT disagrees and the same ones that must be shown to find their origin in the Bible, or else the confessional formulation must be denied or changed. I will state the assertions in my own words.

- The law of nature, written on man's heart from creation, indicates that time must be taken from normal labor and devoted to the worship of God. This is not only so because of the constitution of man, but also because of the acts of God at creation and how man was to relate to them.

- God appointed the seventh day of the week as the Sabbath day for man early on in man's history, recorded for us in Genesis 2:2–3.[11]

- The resurrection of Christ is the redemptive-historical basis upon which the Sabbath day is changed from the last day of the week to the first day of the week.

- The first day of the week is called the Lord's Day in the New Testament and is the Christian Sabbath.

Conclusion

The confessional formulation of the Christian Sabbath has been claimed by some to be an invention of English Puritanism.[12] Jon English Lee, however, shows that "the English Puritans were not original in their understanding of the Lord's Day as the 'Christian Sabbath.'"[13] Lee demonstrates that the English Puritan Sabbath doctrine has immediate precedent in earlier Reformed writers, even Continental authors. This should not surprise us. The English Puritans were working conscientiously within a stream of theological discussion that predates them. Their creedal formulation of the Christian Sabbath was not an invention, but a codification reflecting discussions that had been taking place for a long, long time.

---

[11] Though the 2LCF does not cite Genesis 2:2–3, it is cited by the WCF 21.7 and it is discussed in the literature of the day. This will be illustrated in Chapter 10.

[12] See the discussion in Jon English Lee, "An Examination of the Origins of English Puritan Sabbatarianism," *Puritan Reformed Journal* 7, 1 (2015): 103–19. Lee's article is highly recommended.

[13] Ibid., 103.

NCT disagrees with the confessional formulation on various fronts. It denies that the Sabbath was made for man at the time of his creation. It denies that it was ordained by God as the seventh day of the week prior to ancient Israel. It denies that it applies to all men in all ages. Though it does affirm that the seventh-day Sabbath was abrogated by the coming and kingdom of Christ, it denies that the Lord's Day, the first day of the week, has any connection to the fourth commandment in terms of a command to keep a day holy under the inaugurated new covenant and affirms that it is not to be called the Christian Sabbath in any sense.

The confessional formulation of the Sabbath assumes a distinct doctrine of man, both his identity or constitution and his vocation or calling. It assumes a doctrine of the law of God that affirms its beginning with the creation of man, its being added to at various times in the history recorded for us in the Old Testament, and its very different appearance (in terms of positive laws) under the inaugurated new covenant. The confessional formulation of the Sabbath also assumes something about God as the divine exemplar for man, both in terms of the six days of divine labor and the one day of divine rest. Though the Confession does not tease out much on this issue, it does assume it. Both the issue of man's identity and vocation and the issue of God as exemplar for man must be discussed in the following chapters in order to get the bigger picture behind the confessional formulation. In the last several decades, there has been much work on these very issues, as will become obvious in the next few chapters. In all discussions of confessional formulation, it should be noted that the proof texts cited by the Confession were not included in it to be an end-all in the discussion of the doctrine. They were included as windows into the exegetical bases for the doctrinal formulations, which were to be found in the commentaries and theological treatises of that day and prior to that day.[14] Since the writing of the Confession, however, there has been much exegetical

---

[14] For a discussion on the function of the proof texts in the Westminster Standards, see Richard A. Muller and Rowland S. Ward, *Scripture and Worship: Biblical Interpretation & The Directory for Worship* (Phillipsburg, NJ: P&R Publishing, 2007), 81–82. Muller says: "…the confession and the catechisms cite texts by way of referencing an exegetical tradition reaching back, in many cases, to the fathers of the church in the first five centuries of Christianity and, quite consistently, reflecting the path of biblical interpretation belonging to the Reformed tradition as it developed in the sixteenth century and in the beginning of the seventeenth" (81). The Westminster Standards do not contain doctrinal formulations thought up on the spur of the moment, and neither does the 2LCF. As we saw with the doctrine of the covenant of works, Hosea 6:7 had a long interpretive history indicating a covenant between God and Adam. Muller discusses why Hosea 6:7 did not make it into the Standards as a proof for the covenant of works on pp. 73–74.

and biblical-theological work done on the pertinent issues related to the doctrine of the Christian Sabbath. In the next several chapters, that will become evident.

8

The Doctrine of the Christian Sabbath
ADAM'S IDENTITY AND VOCATION

The issue of the Sabbath is huge and multi-faceted. Many who approach the doctrine of the Christian Sabbath to argue against it are quick to run to Romans 14, Galatians 4, or Colossians 2, as though these texts are trump cards that overrule every other argument in favor of the doctrine. This approach, however, does not take proper account of the flow and progress of redemptive history concerning the Sabbath and the phenomenon of inner-biblical interpretation. It typically asserts, then assumes, that the Sabbath has only two functions in redemptive history—as a sign between God and old covenant Israel, and as a shadow of Christ to come. Once the Mosaic covenant goes when Christ comes to inaugurate the new covenant, the Sabbath as a day to be kept goes. This is an insufficient and myopic approach to a more complex issue with far-reaching implications for God's people. Owen points out the insufficiency of this approach.

> Slight and perfunctory disquisitions will be of little use in this matter; nor are men to think that their opinions are firm and established when they have obtained a seeming countenance unto them from two or three doubtful texts of Scripture. The principles and foundations of truth in this matter lie deep, and require a diligent investigation.[1]

This issue demands thorough investigation and sustained thought. As will become clear, I will assert that the Bible teaches that the Sabbath points

---

[1] Owen, *Works*, 18:273.

to our hope of glory—a condition, or state of existence, proffered from the beginning, and symbolized in and typified by a weekly day from creation to consummation. The case for this understanding takes time to build. Some of the foundations for it were laid in previous chapters. As with many other biblical discussions, a few proof texts either for or against the Christian Sabbath will not do.

My aim is to examine the Old Testament's teaching on the Sabbath, and then consider the New Testament, though I will not be exhaustive.[2] I will approach the study utilizing a biblical-theological or redemptive-historical method, which seeks to examine a subject in the historical (and usually canonical) order in which it is presented in Scripture. I will also be applying the hermeneutical principles discussed in Chapter 2 and applied in Chapter 5 to the doctrine of the covenant of works. This will demonstrate the doctrine's inception, the various stages of its application and modification (i.e., how the Scripture writers interpreted it in their given contexts), and how aspects connected to it under the Mosaic covenant are abrogated by fulfillment due to the coming, sufferings, and glory of our Lord. This method helps us to see the doctrine's basis, to identify its unique redemptive-historical applications in redemptive history, to address the question of continuity and discontinuity in the biblical materials, and to see the doctrine as it relates to our Lord Jesus and his people under the inaugurated new covenant. It gives us a panoramic view of the doctrine's development within the Bible itself. It identifies how the Creator's rest relates to God and man, Adam, Israel, Christ, and the people of God living under the inaugurated new covenant.

When the doctrine of the Sabbath is approached in this manner (as we approached the doctrine of the covenant of works), the case for a present Christian Sabbath, a day to keep holy, becomes not only clear, but also, in

---

[2] For a recent book which treats all the relevant passages on the Sabbath in both the Old and New Testaments, see Robert Paul Martin, *The Christian Sabbath: Its Redemptive-Historical Foundation, Present Obligation, and Practical Observance* (Montville, NJ: Trinity Pulpit Press, 2015). Of the many fine qualities of Dr. Martin's (who is now absent from us but present with our Lord) book, four stand out. First, he treats all the relevant texts of Scripture, showing ample ability in both Hebrew and Greek. Second, he shows acute awareness of the history of interpretation concerning the texts he addresses. Third, he shows very discerning, careful scholarship while interpreting the patristics on this issue. Fourth, he presents critical discussions in the body of the work, and especially in the footnotes, of the book edited by D. A. Carson, *From Sabbath to Lord's Day: A Biblical, Historical, and Theological Investigation* (reprint ed., Eugene, OR: Wipf and Stock Publishers, 1999). Martin's interaction with the work edited by Carson is worth the price of the book.

my opinion and the opinion of many others, compelling. As noted above, the Sabbath is not a person; ultimately, it is a state of existence, one which was proffered to Adam but never attained by him. This state of existence is that which our Lord earns for and confers upon His people. The Sabbath rest of the Creator, as will be argued, is an invitation for Adam to be like his Maker, working as a temple-builder and then, upon final completion of the task assigned to him, entering the rest of God. It is a symbol of a state of creaturely existence to be entered into after the creature's faithful work. Adam's Edenic vocation, which assumes his created identity, was the beginning point, a beginning that had an end or goal, the consummative rest of God. As G. K. Beale says, "…the ultimate goal of humanity was to enter into the kind of consummative rest into which God himself had entered (Gen. 2:2)."[3] If Beale is right, then the covenant of works and the Sabbath are related and both entail an eschatological motif from the beginning. We will see these connections made by John Owen and others below. This would also mean that the Sabbath, though a this-world ordinance, functions as a that-world symbol and type. A hymn written by John Newton reflects this view.

> Safely through another week God has brought us on our way;
> Let us now a blessing seek, Waiting in his courts today;
> Day of all the week the best, Emblem of eternal rest:
> Day of all the week the best, Emblem of eternal rest.[4]

Not wanting to get too far ahead of myself, I will leave it at that and return to these issues in later chapters. Before doing so, the words of Geerhardus Vos may help prepare our way. Vos argues that the Sabbath principle symbolizes and typifies "the eschatological structure of history" and "was true before, and apart from, redemption."[5] Then comes one of the most important and far-reaching statements made by Vos in all of his writings (quoted in Chapter 5 above): "[t]he eschatological is an older strand in revelation than the soteric."[6] He goes on to say "[t]hat the…'Covenant

---

[3] G. K. Beale, *A New Testament Biblical Theology: The Unfolding of the Old Testament in the New* (Grand Rapids: Baker Academic, 2011), 780.

[4] John Newton, "Safely through another week," in *Trinity Hymnal—Baptist Edition* (Suwanee, GA: Great Commission Publications, Inc., 1995), #320.

[5] Vos, *Biblical Theology*, 140. See Barcellos, *The Family Tree*, 158–59, from which this is taken, and 205–07 for further discussion on Vos on the fourth commandment.

[6] Ibid. It is of interest to note that this statement comes in the context of Vos discussing the Sabbath.

Adam's Identity and Vocation

of Works' was nothing but an embodiment of the Sabbatical principle."[7] If the probation of the covenant of works had "been successful, then the sacramental Sabbath would have passed over into the reality it typified…"[8] In other words, protology is eschatological and eschatology precedes soteriology. The priority of eschatology over soteriology is something found in many post-Reformation Reformed writers through the doctrine of the covenant of works as illustrated in Chapter 5. Viewing the end as better than the beginning (which contained the seeds of eschatology) is a concept that predates Vos and the post-Reformation writers, going all the way back (at least) to the early Christian writers. For example, in the seventh century, Anastasius of Sinai said, "Indeed, God in his wisdom prepared all things (cf. Psalm 103 [104]:24) in the heavens and on earth as a type and sketch of the new existence."[9] I mention this to show that what Vos stated was not an invention of something new, but a reflection of thought that predated him, a discovery made by many others before him.

Prior to addressing the issue of the Sabbath directly, I will discuss Adam's identity and vocation, assuming the doctrine of the covenant of works presented in Chapter 5. In previous discussion I said, "to the degree we understand Adam's identity and vocation, we may better understand the incarnation, sufferings, and glory of our Lord. Also, to the degree we understand what the Creator's rest meant for God and what it means for man, we may better understand the incarnation, sufferings, and glory of our Lord." I will attempt to make the basis for these claims clear to readers in the discussion which follows.

As with the preceding discussion concerning the covenant of works, the Bible will be given due place in seeking to explicate Adam's identity and vocation, as well as what the Creator's rest meant for God and what it means for man. As mentioned previously, Adam had an eschatology before he fell into sin. This will become clearer as we consider his identity and vocation and what God's rest means for man. One way to express what I am trying to prove in the next several chapters is this: *The redemp-*

---

[7] Vos, *Biblical Theology*, 140.

[8] Ibid.

[9] The statement by Anastasius is quoted in Paul M. Blowers, *Drama of the Divine Economy: Creator and Creation in Early Christian Theology and Piety* (Oxford: Oxford University Press, 2012), 132. This gives us a glimpse into the thought-world of the early church. It also confirms that viewing protology as imbedded with eschatological potential has a long and rich history. Though the *way* the early church theologians argued for this will not always be convincing to others, the *fact* that they did is important to acknowledge. As will become clear, this world, at its creation, had a that-world potential in its womb.

tive motif of Scripture tends toward the eschatological, which was imbedded in the protological. In other words, that state to which Christ takes his people via redemption was proffered to Adam (and us in him) at the beginning. It could also be stated this way: *The end is the beginning glorified, an end to which the beginning pointed.*

Considering Adam's identity and vocation, I will present exegetical and theological considerations indicating that 1) man is the apex of the terrestrial creation, focusing on what it means that he was created in the image of God, 2) draw some implications from this, 3) make some further observations upon Adam's identity and calling, and then 4) briefly consider God's remedy for Adam's sin. Reminding ourselves of the remedy, the last Adam, will shed further light on the identity and vocation of the first Adam, since antitypes tell us more about how their antecedents function as types. Prior to the conclusion to this chapter, an important question will be asked and answered: *Does creation in the image of God warrant following the divine exemplar without explicit commands recorded for us in Scripture?*

Man is the Apex of the Terrestrial Creation

Man is the apex of the terrestrial creation (i.e., the creatures whose natural habitation is earthly) and has a unique calling as such.[10] What does it mean for man, male and female, to be created in the image of God? The first time we read of man's creation in the image of God is in Genesis 1:26. "Then God said, 'Let Us make man in Our image, according to Our likeness…'" (Genesis 1:26a). We are told *that* man was made in the image of God, but we are not told *what* it means. In order to flesh out a definition of being made in the image of God, we need more information. Also, more information is needed in order to determine if being made in the image of God has ethical implications for man. The Bible provides such information. It shows the various implications for man's identity and calling which flow from being created in the image of God.

High-Level Contextual Considerations Concerning the Importance of Man

Before looking at Genesis 1:26–27, some high-level contextual considerations which indicate the importance of man from the early chapters of Genesis will be considered. In Genesis 1:1, we are told that "God cre-

---

[10] Some of the material is taken and adapted from my *Better than the Beginning* and is used with permission.

ated the heavens and the earth." The subsequent narrative shows escalation from the more basic to the more complex, from creation *ex nihilo* to the forming of things from things. There were created things, then things created (or formed) from the things already created. An example of this is man's body: "Then the LORD God formed man of dust from the ground…" (Genesis 2:7). This type of creation is called *mediate* creation by some theologians.[11] By "mediate," Turretin, for example, means that "which is made indeed from some matter."[12] Immediate creation is *ex nihilo simpliciter* (i.e., simply, directly, in and by itself [e.g., Genesis 1:1]). The material being of man comes from the product of creation *ex nihilo*, but not immediately or directly by the *ex nihilo* act of divine power. In other words, the material aspect of man predates the form of man.

William Ames traces the progress of the creation narrative from simple to complex, terminating upon the creation of man, creation's apex.

> 27. The creation of the world is divided according to the parts of the world. Although the world is one in numerical unity and in unity of order and end, yet it has parts distinguishable by position and by essence and existence.
>
> 28. The creation of these parts of the world did not occur at one and the same moment, but was accomplished part by part in the space of six days.[13]
>
> 46. The rude and incomplete existence was in that mass which in the beginning was created without form, void, and wrapped in darkness, which is called the earth, the waters, the deep.[14]
>
> 51. The order of creation was this: In the first day after the constituting of the highest heavens, the angels, and the unformed mass, the most delicate part of that mass was called upward and became light, i.e., a shining fire.
>
> 52. On the second day, air was made out of that very delicate part nearest to the light.
>
> 53. On the third day the thicker parts of the mass were divided so that the sea stood forth by itself as the greatest part of the waters gathered in hollows. And the earth appeared adorned with herbs and trees.
>
> 54. On the fourth day were made the luminaries of heaven to give light to the earth.

---

[11] E.g., Turretin, *Elenctic Theology*, 5.1.6 (1:432). Ames distinguishes between active and passive creation in Ames, *The Marrow of Theology*, 1.8.3–4 (100).

[12] Turretin, *Elenctic Theology*, 5.1.6 (1:432).

[13] Ames, *The Marrow of Theology*, 1.8.27–28 (102).

[14] Ibid., 1.8.46 (103).

55. On the fifth day fishes and birds, living in the water and the air, were brought forth.

56. On the sixth day all terrestrial living creatures were brought forth, first the unreasoning animals and then man....[15]

62. He [man] was the last of the creatures contingently perfect and was thus of them and above them, in the intention of God.

63. Therefore man is said to be created in a different manner from other creatures; they were brought forth by a word only, *Let there be light, Let there be a firmament*, but man was brought forth, as it were, with greater counsel and deliberation, *Let us make man*, Gen. 1:26.[16]

That the narrative reflects purposed divine actions toward a goal is echoed by Douglas F. Kelly.

> The work of these days then indicates strong purposive movement in the divine activity: God is preparing the stage with the intended purpose of making a home for His image bearers: Adam and Eve and their descendants.[17]

The divine activity at creation was directed toward the well-being of man on the newly created earth.

In Genesis 1:3, 6, 9, 11, 14, 20, and 24, the words "Then God said" occur. In each instance, they are followed by the words "Let there be," or something similar. However, in Genesis 1:26, after the words "Then God said," these words occur: "Let Us make." Something is unique about man. From Genesis 2:4 onward, though aspects of the initial creation are repeated, the focus is on man (2:7, 8, 15–25). In Genesis 5, where we have a genealogy that ends with Noah, the beginning of it reminds us of the creation of man (Genesis 5:1–2). In Genesis 9, in the covenant with Noah, God reminds him of man's creation (Genesis 9:6). Again, something is unique about man.

The most striking and mysterious teaching of the Bible about the uniqueness of man, however, is found in the New Testament:

> And the Word became flesh, and dwelt among us, and we saw His glory, glory as of the only begotten from the Father, full of grace and truth. (John 1:14)

---

[15] Ames, *The Marrow of Theology*, 1.8.51–56 (104).

[16] Ibid., 1.8.62–63 (105).

[17] Douglas F. Kelly, *Creation and Change: Genesis 1:1–2:4 in the Light of Changing Scientific Paradigms* (1997; reprint, Fearn, Ross-shire, Scotland: Christian Focus Publications, Mentor Imprint, 2010), 184.

Adam's Identity and Vocation

But when the fullness of the time came, God sent forth His Son, born of a woman, born under the Law. (Galatians 4:4)

Have this attitude in yourselves which was also in Christ Jesus, who, although He existed in the form of God, did not regard equality with God a thing to be grasped, but emptied Himself, taking the form of a bond-servant, *and* being made in the likeness of men. Being found in appearance as a man, He humbled Himself by becoming obedient to the point of death, even death on a cross. (Philippians 2:5–8)

Therefore, since the children share in flesh and blood, He Himself likewise also partook of the same, that through death He might render powerless him who had the power of death, that is, the devil, and might free those who through fear of death were subject to slavery all their lives. For assuredly He does not give help to angels, but He gives help to the descendant of Abraham. Therefore, He had to be made like His brethren in all things, so that He might become a merciful and faithful high priest in things pertaining to God, to make propitiation for the sins of the people. For since He Himself was tempted in that which He has suffered, He is able to come to the aid of those who are tempted. (Hebrews 2:14–18)

Therefore, when He comes into the world, He says, "SACRIFICE AND OFFERING YOU HAVE NOT DESIRED, BUT A BODY YOU HAVE PREPARED FOR ME; IN WHOLE BURNT OFFERINGS AND *sacrifices* FOR SIN YOU HAVE TAKEN NO PLEASURE. THEN I SAID, 'BEHOLD, I HAVE COME (IN THE SCROLL OF THE BOOK IT IS WRITTEN OF ME) TO DO YOUR WILL, O GOD.'" After saying above, "SACRIFICES AND OFFERINGS AND WHOLE BURNT OFFERINGS AND *sacrifices* FOR SIN YOU HAVE NOT DESIRED, NOR HAVE YOU TAKEN PLEASURE *in them*" (which are offered according to the Law), then He said, "BEHOLD, I HAVE COME TO DO YOUR WILL." He takes away the first in order to establish the second. By this will we have been sanctified through the offering of the body of Jesus Christ once for all. (Hebrews 10:5–10)

By common confession, great is the mystery of godliness: He who was revealed in the flesh, was vindicated in the Spirit, seen by angels, proclaimed among the nations, believed on in the world, taken up in glory. (1 Timothy 3:16)

For God so loved the world, that He gave His only begotten Son, that whoever believes in Him shall not perish, but have eternal life. (John 3:16)

Why did God send His Son to become man? Why such condescension? Why become one of us? What is man, to be given such love, such mercy, such grace? What a strange design. "He does not give help to [fallen] angels," but He does to man. There must be something about man in which God is vitally interested, but what is it? It is the fact that man was created in the image of God and is, therefore, the apex or jewel of God's creative work. It must be that God loves His image such that He became one of us to repair it and bring it to glory. Hear John Owen.

> …what heart can conceive, what tongue can express, the glory of that condescension in the Son of God, whereby he took our nature upon him, took it to be his own, in order unto a discharge of the office of mediation on our behalf?[18]

Surely man is important, being God's image.

A Closer Look at Genesis 1:26–27

> Then God said, "Let Us make man in Our image, according to Our likeness; and let them rule over the fish of the sea and over the birds of the sky and over the cattle and over all the earth, and over every creeping thing that creeps on the earth." God created man in His own image, in the image of God He created him; male and female He created them. (Genesis 1:26–27)

Notice first, *the divine announcement of man's creation*: "Let Us…" There are at least three views explaining the plural "Us."[19] Some see "Us" as referring to a heavenly court, inclusive of the angels. However, angels did not create; God did. Also, "Our image" and "Our likeness" is further described for us in the next verse as "God created man in His own image." If that's not clear enough, Moses adds, "in the image of God He created him; male and female He created them." God is clearly the exclusive creator, not a heavenly court inclusive of angels, "as if God had a sanhedrim in heaven…"[20]

Others see "Us" as a plural of majesty, noting that in the ancient world kings used to speak of themselves in the plural, seeking to engender respect from their subjects. However, it has been shown by scholars that the plural of majesty was introduced by the Persians long after Moses wrote Genesis.[21]

---

[18] Owen, *Works*, 1:325.
[19] See Fesko, *Last Things First*, 40–45.
[20] Owen, *Works*, 17:222. The spelling of *sanhedrim* is original in Owen.
[21] See Fesko, *Last Things First*, 44.

The third view understands this verse as a rudimentary, or not fully-developed, reference to the Trinity—the three distinct Persons of the Godhead all sharing the one essence of divinity or deity. The Bible is clear—the Father, the Son of God, and the Spirit of God all executed divine power in the act of creation (Hebrews 1:1–2 [Father and Son]; John 1:3 and Colossians 1:16 [Son]; and Genesis 1:2 and Job 33:4 [Spirit]). Genesis 1:2 says, "…and the Spirit of God was moving over the surface of the waters." This is the function of the Spirit of God in creation.[22] Some shy away from this view claiming that the original readers would not have known that. However, we are not interested in speculating about how the original readers understood this.[23] Psalm 33:6 seems to reflect a Trinitarian activity at creation: "By the word [i.e., Son] of the LORD [i.e., Father] the heavens were made, and by the breath [i.e., Spirit] of His mouth all their host." The Scripture, which is our only infallible guide, is clear that each Person of the Godhead executed divine power in the creation of all things. I think this view of Genesis 1:26 is correct, and it is the more commonly held view over the centuries. What we have here is an intra-Trinitarian, executive divine counsel.[24] Here is a vague hint at something the rest of the Bible unfolds and the church recognized over time: "there is a richness of interpersonal life within the Godhead, which Christians came to call 'the Trinity.'"[25]

Second, notice *the superlative action in man's creation*. Three times in Genesis 1:27, Moses uses the verb "created" and each time, God is the subject, the Creator, and man is the object, that which was created. "God created man in His own image, in the image of God He created him; male and female He created them" (Genesis 1:27). Why is this threefold use of the word only used in the creation of man? Fesko suggests, "The repetition most likely indicates the superlative, namely, that man is the apex of God's creation."[26] Moses could have said it once, but he repeats himself. The repetition highlights the uniqueness of man. It points to the fact that though God made the heavens and the earth, the sea, the land, the stars, the sun, the moon, plants, animals, and angels, man is unique. Man is special, something different from the rest of God's creation.

---

[22] In Blowers, *Drama of the Divine Economy*, 114, he lists Tertullian, Origen, Basil, Athanasius, and many others as forming "an emerging consensus" of early theologians who held this view.
[23] See Fesko, *Last Things First*, 45.
[24] See Kelly, *Creation and Change*, 193.
[25] Ibid., 193.
[26] Fesko, *Last Things First*, 51.

Third, notice *the exclusive terminology of man's creation*. Moses writes, "Our image…Our likeness…His own image…the image of God." No other aspect of creation is so designated. Whatever this means, we know this much; man is the apex of God's terrestrial creation. God takes special counsel in man's creation and He makes man in His own image, to reflect Him on the earth, to be like Him (according to his creaturely capacities) in ways no other creature of God is able or for which they are responsible.

What constitutes man as unique, so privileged, and so different from all other created entities is the fact that he alone is created in God's image. Though everything that is, outside of God, was created by God, man is the apex, the pinnacle, the Mount Everest of what He has made. This is so due to man's creation—male and female—in the image of God. But what does this mean?

Notice the terminology of man created in God's image. Moses says, "Then God said, 'Let Us make man in Our image, according to Our likeness…'" (Genesis 1:26a). In the next verse, he says, "God created man in His own image, in the image of God He created him; male and female He created them" (Genesis 1:27). Notice that in verse 27, the word *likeness* is not used. Verse 26 says, "…Our image,…Our likeness…" In Genesis 5:1–2, Moses refers back to man's creation.

> This is the book of the generations of Adam. In the day when God created man, He made him in the likeness of God. He created them male and female, and He blessed them and named them Man in the day when they were created. (Genesis 5:1–2)

Moses does not use the word *image* here. In Genesis 9:6, he uses *image* and not *likeness*: "Whoever sheds man's blood, by man his blood shall be shed, for in the image of God He made man." Paul uses the term *image* to refer to creation in 1 Corinthians 11:7a: "For a man ought not to have his head covered, since he is the image and glory of God…" In this text, whatever "image of God" means, it is what man *is*, not what man *possesses*. Also notice that Paul does not use the term *likeness*. James 3:9 says, "With it [i.e., our tongue] we bless *our* Lord and Father, and with it we curse men, who have been made in the likeness of God." Notice that James says "likeness" and does not use the word *image*. Also, this text indicates that man, even after the fall into sin, is still the "likeness" of God. This interchange of the terms *image* and *likeness* indicates that they are basically synonymous.[27] Whatever it means to be the image of God, being the likeness of God means the same thing.

---

[27] John Trapp, Matthew Poole, Herman Bavinck, Louis Berkhof, Douglas F. Kelly, and J. V. Fesko take this view.

Fourth, what is *the meaning of man's creation in the image of God?* The fact of man's creation in the image of God argues for man as the apex of creation. But what does it mean to be created in God's image? There are at least three ways one could seek to define creation in God's image. The first is to go to Genesis 1:26–27, identify the terms which describe man as created, then consult a Hebrew lexicon or English dictionary to determine the meaning of those words. Once the lexical or dictionary definition is found, it would be applied to the text. But both words in this case (i.e., *image* and *likeness*) mean basically the same thing. Man is like God, in some sense, due to how he has been made. A second way would be to go to other texts that use the same words. However, we would find the same thing—both words mean basically the same thing. A third way would be to go to texts that explain what these terms mean or what they imply. This third way is the best method because it allows God to tell us what these terms mean. This method of investigation will now be applied in order to determine the meaning of these terms. We will look at several texts that end up giving us the Bible's explanation of what it means to be created in God's image. This is an example of inner-biblical exegesis.

Our first text is Ecclesiastes 7:29, which says, "Behold, I have found only this, that God made men upright, but they have sought out many devices." This could mean that God made man physically "upright." Man at creation took his first breath standing. This would mean, however, that seeking "out many devices" would refer to the many ways since man's creation that he seeks not to be physically upright. The author is contrasting being made upright (evoking the creation of man) with seeking out many devices (evoking the fall of man). Though it is true that since man's creation he has sought out many ways of not being physically upright, there is not anything inherently wrong with that. The author of these words is not talking about physical uprightness, since there is nothing wrong with crawling or lying down, for instance. It is best to understand this as referring to man's original moral uprightness.[28] Man was originally holy. He had integrity of soul. He was righteous. The devices we all seek are sinful devices, sinful ways. This seeking "out many devices" is wrong. It is not in accord with man's original state of integrity. Man was made morally upright, but something happened. Creation *imago Dei* included moral integrity.

Colossians 3:10 is another text that sheds light on being created *imago Dei*. That text reads, "and have put on the new self who is being renewed to a true knowledge according to the image of the One who created him." It

---

[28] Interestingly, the 2LCF cites Ecclesiastes 7:9 at 4.2 while discussing the creation and constitution of man. This suggests that utilizing this text to help flesh-out what it means to be created in the image of God has a long history.

is important to note that Paul is talking about what happened to believers in Christ in this passage. Specifically, he is talking about the work of the renovation of man by God or, as the older writers put it, the work of the reparation of human nature. "Being renewed" may be translated "being renovated" or "repaired." This work of renovation involves "being renewed to a true knowledge." Something is wrong with our minds. They have been stained or deprived by sin. They need renovation by the Spirit of God to a true knowledge of God. Notice that this work of renovation, or reparation, is "according to the image of the One who created him." It is a renovation in which believers are made to be like God, according to His image, with reference to their minds, and in accordance with how God made man in the beginning. So Adam and Eve were given the true knowledge of God at their creation and believers in Christ have that true knowledge restored, "according to the image of the One who created him" (see 2 Peter 1:3). Sin deprives man of true knowledge; the grace of Christ restores it. Grace repairs, and actually elevates, nature.

Ephesians 4:24 is a similar text. It says, "and put on the new self, which *in the likeness of* God has been created in righteousness and holiness of the truth." As in Colossians, Paul is talking about what happened to believers in Christ. He is talking about the work of the renovation of man. This work of renovation, or reparation, is "*in the likeness of* God" or literally "according to God."[29] It is a renovation in which believers are made to be like God in a way they were not prior to being renovated. This implies that unbelievers are not like God in this sense. This work of renovation involves a creation: "…has been created…" I do not think this refers to the initial creation. Paul is dealing with what he calls "a new creation" in 2 Corinthians 5:17: "Therefore if anyone is in Christ, *he is* a new creature ["creation" in many versions]; the old things passed away; behold, new things have come." Being a part of this new creation has to do with one's relationship to Christ. This work of renovation involves being "created in righteousness and holiness of the truth." To be righteous means to be rightly related to God due to being rightly related to God's law. To be holy means to be pure of mind, heart, and will. Man was made righteous and holy. He was morally pure.

For Adam, then, being the image of God meant his mind was stocked with and able to process true knowledge of God. His heart was morally pure; he was made upright. His will acted in accordance with the law of God. Romans 2:14–15 teaches us that all men have the law of God written on their hearts due to having been created. This was certainly true of the first man, Adam. This is why the 2LCF 4.2 says, "…being made after the

---

[29] The Greek text reads: τὸν κατὰ θεὸν κτισθέντα (*ton kata theon ktisthenta*). This could be rendered literally, "the according to God having been created."

image of God, in knowledge, righteousness, and true holiness; having the law of God written on their hearts." This confessional formulation evokes Colossians 3, Ephesians 4, and Romans 2.[30] In fact, these texts are commonly discussed in Reformed discussions on the doctrine of man's creation and the relation of the law of God to man as created.[31]

Some Implications of Man Created in the Image of God

First, though man is not God, man is God's creation, in His image, which means God has claims upon man. Body and soul, we belong to God, the Creator. These things are gifts of which we are stewards, not the basis for doing as we please with them. The universe exists because God called it into being for His glory (Romans 11:36). He does not give us the right to act as if He does not exist. There is a law of God which comes with our being (Romans 2:14ff.). It comes with the territory of who we are. It is according to this law that we are accountable to God as creatures. Understanding what it means to be created in the image of God makes this clear. Being His image means that we are accountable to Him.

Second, being created in the image of God, Adam and Eve had true knowledge of God, were morally upright, and loved His law. This is clear from the discussion above. But what happened? Is it the case that all men and women today have true knowledge of God, are morally upright and pure of heart, and love His law? Obviously not. In fact, the Bible asserts in many places that our minds are futile, our hearts are polluted, that we do not and cannot subject ourselves to the law of God, that there is none righteous, and that our wills are bound to sin (John 6:44; Romans 1:18–32; 3:9–12; 8:7; Ephesians 2:1–3; 4:17–19). When Adam and Eve sinned, human nature was scarred, marred, shattered, twisted, distorted, mangled, and made unfit to be and do what it was made to be and do.

---

[30] For my most recent treatment of Romans 2:14–15, see Richard C. Barcellos, "The Ten Commandments and the Christian," in *Going Beyond the Five Points: Pursuing a more Comprehensive Reformation*, gen. ed. Rob Ventura (n.p., 2015), 41–46. The conclusion I came to in that discussion is as follows: "A careful exegesis of Romans 2:14–15 demonstrates that the moral law is summarily contained in the whole Decalogue and is at the same time common to all men through general revelation" (46). This view has a long history.

[31] For example, see William Perkins, *A Golden Chain, or The Description of Theology* (1597; reprint, n.p., Puritan Reprints, 2010), 17; Ames, *The Marrow of Theology*, 1.8.73 (106); Thomas Watson, *A Body of Divinity: Contained in Sermons upon the Westminster Assembly's Catechism* (Edinburgh: The Banner of Truth Trust, Reprinted 1986), 119; Turretin, *Elenctic Theology*, 5.9–10.5 (1:462–70) and 11.1.12 (2:4); and Bavinck, *Reformed Dogmatics*, 2:531–32.

Third, this understanding of the image of God and man's fall into sin explains all the sorrow and pain experienced all over the world every day. It explains all the heartaches, all the troubles, all the wars, all the violence, all the lying, cheating, stealing, adultery, fornication of various sorts, hatred, and idolatry throughout man's history. We are not in the same condition in which we were made, "for all have sinned and fall short of the glory of God" (Romans 3:23). We have all sought out many devices (Ecclesiastes 7:29). We need help and we are unable to provide it for ourselves. We need to be repaired. We need renovation. We need a permanent fix to our perpetual plight. Though man had a good start, things have changed drastically since then. Adam sinned and his sin affected everyone (Romans 5:12–21). The entire human race was plunged into an unnatural, deformed state of existence. Death came as a result of sin. Curse came as a result of sin. Distortion and discordance came as a result of sin. The image-bearing apex of creation brought catastrophic change into the arena of the world due to sin. And what did God do? He pronounced judgment upon them and the serpent (Genesis 3:13–19). He banished Adam and Eve from the garden (Genesis 3:23); He exiled them. Adam and Eve were kicked out of God's Edenic house. A dramatic event occurred early in man's history that has infected and affected all.

Fourth, this understanding of the image of God sheds light on the glorious news of the gospel. The drama does not stop with exile from God's favorable presence. The chilling account of man's banishment from the special presence and favor of God in the garden of Eden, man's loss of communion with God and his loss of righteousness, is not the end of the story. In the midst of this dark scene of God's curse, a ray of hope and promise emerges in a most peculiar manner. God says this to the serpent, "And I will put enmity between you and the woman, and between your seed and her seed; He shall bruise you on the head, and you shall bruise him on the heel" (Genesis 3:15).[32] In this judgment upon the Serpent there lies a promise, a glimmer of hope for the future of man. One born of a

---

[32] For a Messianic interpretation of Genesis 3:15 by a contemporary author, see Michael Rydelnik, *The Messianic Hope: Is the Hebrew Bible Really Messianic?*, NAC Studies in Bible & Theology, vol. 9 (Nashville: B&H Publishing Group, 2010), 129–45. Rydelnik's book is highly recommended, if for nothing else than his interpretive method utilized throughout the book. Concerning the antiquity of this view, Rydelnik says: "A messianic interpretation was offered by the LXX, ancient Jewish Targumim (*Pseudo-Jonathan, Neofiti, Onqelos*) and the church fathers Justin and Irenaeus" (134–35). This is the understanding of Genesis 3:15 contained in the 2LCF 7.3 and 20.1. For proof that many in the post-Reformation era held this view, see Barcellos, *The Family Tree*, 90 (Cocceius), 93–106 (Coxe, Witsius, and Edwards), and 172–74 (Owen).

woman will come and destroy the works of the devil. He will rescue the image of God which was shattered, marred, and scarred by the fall into sin. Paul says, "Now the promises were spoken to Abraham and to his seed. He does not say, 'And to seeds,' as referring to many, but rather to one, 'And to your seed,' that is, Christ" (Galatians 3:16) and "But when the fullness of the time came, God sent forth His Son, born of a woman, born under the Law, so that He might redeem those who were under the Law, that we might receive the adoption as sons..." (Galatians 4:4–5). John says, "The Son of God appeared for this purpose, to destroy the works of the devil" (1 John 3:8b). And then there is Hebrews 2:10–18, which says:

> For it was fitting for Him, for whom are all things, and through whom are all things, in bringing many sons to glory, to perfect the author of their salvation through sufferings. For both He who sanctifies and those who are sanctified are all from one *Father*; for which reason He is not ashamed to call them brethren, saying, "I WILL PROCLAIM YOUR NAME TO MY BRETHREN, IN THE MIDST OF THE CONGREGATION I WILL SING YOUR PRAISE." And again, "I WILL PUT MY TRUST IN HIM." And again, "BEHOLD, I AND THE CHILDREN WHOM GOD HAS GIVEN ME." Therefore, since the children share in flesh and blood, He Himself likewise also partook of the same, that through death He might render powerless him who had the power of death, that is, the devil, and might free those who through fear of death were subject to slavery all their lives. For assuredly He does not give help to angels, but He gives help to the descendant of Abraham. Therefore, He had to be made like His brethren in all things, so that He might become a merciful and faithful high priest in things pertaining to God, to make propitiation for the sins of the people. For since He Himself was tempted in that which He has suffered, He is able to come to the aid of those who are tempted.

The Son of God became man that He might suffer for us and be the agent through whom many sons are brought to glory. He assumed our nature, duties, and liabilities. God loved His image so much that the Son of God was sent to assume human nature in order to repair and perfect us. This is, indeed, good news.

Observations Upon Adam's Identity and Calling

In light of Adam's identity as image-bearer of God, what did God give him (and Eve) to do? Man's calling was the highest calling of all of God's earthly creatures, being created in the image of God. But just what was Adam to do as God's image?

We will approach this question by making observations about both Adam's identity and calling, then looking briefly at God's remedy for his failure. Looking at the remedy sheds light on the problem. We will focus primarily on Adam due to Paul's words in Romans 5:12–19.

> Therefore, just as through one man sin entered into the world, and death through sin, and so death spread to all men, because all sinned— for until the Law sin was in the world, but sin is not imputed when there is no law. Nevertheless death reigned from Adam until Moses, even over those who had not sinned in the likeness of the offense of Adam, who is a type of Him who was to come. But the free gift is not like the transgression. For if by the transgression of the one the many died, much more did the grace of God and the gift by the grace of the one Man, Jesus Christ, abound to the many. The gift is not like *that which came* through the one who sinned; for on the one hand the judgment *arose* from one *transgression* resulting in condemnation, but on the other hand the free gift *arose* from many transgressions resulting in justification. For if by the transgression of the one, death reigned through the one, much more those who receive the abundance of grace and of the gift of righteousness will reign in life through the One, Jesus Christ. So then as through one transgression there resulted condemnation to all men, even so through one act of righteousness there resulted justification of life to all men. For as through the one man's disobedience the many were made sinners, even so through the obedience of the One the many will be made righteous.

This is an important passage. It helps us understand Adam's vocation. It is divine commentary on such. Paul is making theological statements based on his reflection on Adam's Edenic vocation. Adam was a public person. He stood as a representative of others. As he went, so went the rest of us. This is important to understand in order to understand Adam's vocation. It is also crucial to understand the vocation of our Lord Jesus Christ, the last Adam.

First, *Adam was an image-bearer, which placed ethical demands upon him.* As stated above, being created in the image of God has ethical implications for man's conduct. Adam was to be like God according to the abilities with which he was endowed at his creation (i.e., his creaturely capacities). As Kline says:

> Man's likeness to God is a demand to be like God; the indicative here has the force of an imperative. Formed in the image of God, man is informed by a sense of deity by which he knows what God is like, not merely that God is (Rom 1:19ff.).[33]

---

[33] Kline, *Kingdom Prologue*, 62.

Adam's Identity and Vocation

Even man's sense of the divine has ethical implications before and after the fall.

Second, *Adam was sinless*. Adam possessed moral integrity as a direct result of creation. The retributive justice of God had no claims on him, because he was without sin.

Third, *Adam was told to be fruitful and multiply, and fill the earth, and subdue it*. "God blessed them; and God said to them, 'Be fruitful and multiply, and fill the earth'" (Genesis 1:28). There are three things worth noting at this point. First, Adam and Eve were to produce children. Second, they were to fill the earth, and the implication is that they would have passed this commission on to their children. In this sense, Adam was the first spokesman for God on the earth, the first prophet, the first human to speak to man on behalf of God.[34] Third, Adam was told to subdue the earth. Genesis 1:28 says, "God blessed them; and God said to them, 'Be fruitful and multiply, and fill the earth, and subdue it...'" Adam's calling was not limited to the garden of Eden. He was to subdue the earth and fill it with others like him—image-bearers who were sinless and who would be fruitful and multiply and fill the earth. Recall Isaiah 45:18, which says:

> For thus says the LORD, who created the heavens (He is the God who formed the earth and made it, He established it *and* did not create it a waste place, *but* formed it to be inhabited), "I am the LORD, and there is none else." (Isaiah 45:18)

The earth was created to be inhabited by man.

Fourth, *Adam was told to rule over other creatures*. Genesis 1:28 continues, "...rule over the fish of the sea and over the birds of the sky and over every living thing that moves on the earth." Adam was appointed king of creation, God's created viceroy.

Fifth, *Adam was formed of dust with the breath of life breathed into him*. "Then the LORD God formed man of dust from the ground, and breathed into his nostrils the breath of life; and man became a living being" (Genesis 2:7). Adam was comprised of body and soul. As a sinless image-bearer, comprised of body and soul, who was both a spokesman for God (i.e., prophet) and a ruler (i.e., king), Adam was told to fill the earth with others like him.

---

[34] For a fruitful discussion arguing that Adam passed this commission on to others, see Beale, *A New Testament Biblical Theology*, 29–87. Beale distinguishes carefully between the commission in its pre-fall and post-fall state. See also G. K. Beale, *The Temple and the Church's Mission: A biblical theology of the dwelling place of God* (Downers Grove, IL: InterVarsity Press, 2004), 93–121.

Sixth, *Adam was the first created son of God*. Luke 3:38 says, "…the son of Enosh, the son of Seth, the son of Adam, the son of God." Adam was God's sinless son, an image-bearer of God, called to be fruitful and multiply, fill the earth, and subdue it—starting in the garden of Eden.

Seventh, *Adam was made outside the garden, which was the earth's first temple, then put in it*. "The LORD God planted a garden toward the east, in Eden; and there He placed the man whom He had formed" (Genesis 2:8). Genesis 2:15 says, "Then the LORD God took the man and put him into the garden of Eden to cultivate it and keep it." The garden was the place of God's special dwelling on the earth with man. It was in the garden that Adam and Eve "heard the sound of the LORD God walking…" (Genesis 3:8). G. K. Beale comments:

> The same Hebrew verbal form (stem) *mithallek*…used for God's 'walking back and forth' in the Garden (Gen. 3:8), also describes God's presence in the tabernacle (Lev. 26:12; Deut. 23:14[15]; 2 Sam. 7:6–7).[35]

God's walking in the garden indicates His special presence among men. In this sense, the garden of Eden was a temple, a special dwelling place of God on earth among men. The garden of Eden was the earth's first sanctuary.

Since this may be a new concept for some Christians, it is important to consider this a bit further. Was the garden the earth's first temple? Was the garden a special dwelling place of God among men on the earth? The text of Genesis 2 and 3 does not use those words to describe the garden of Eden, but as we have already seen, it does utilize language used elsewhere in Scripture that describes God's presence in Israel's tabernacle. Does the Bible look back upon the garden of Eden and indicate that it was, in fact, a temple, a sanctuary, the first special dwelling place of God on earth among men? I think it does, as do many others.

Consider Ezekiel 28:11–19, especially verses 13–14, 16, and 18:

> Again the word of the LORD came to me saying, "Son of man, take up a lamentation over the king of Tyre and say to him, 'Thus says the Lord GOD, "You had the seal of perfection, full of wisdom and perfect in beauty. You were in Eden, the garden of God; Every precious stone was your covering: the ruby, the topaz and the diamond; the beryl, the onyx and the jasper; the lapis lazuli, the turquoise and the emerald; and the gold, the workmanship of your settings and sockets, was in you. On the day that you were created they were prepared. You were the anointed cherub who covers, and I placed you *there*. You were on the holy mountain of God; You walked in the midst of the stones of fire. You were blameless

---

[35] Beale, *The Temple and the Church's Mission*, 66.

in your ways from the day you were created until unrighteousness was found in you. By the abundance of your trade you were internally filled with violence, and you sinned; Therefore I have cast you as profane from the mountain of God. And I have destroyed you, O covering cherub, from the midst of the stones of fire. Your heart was lifted up because of your beauty; You corrupted your wisdom by reason of your splendor. I cast you to the ground; I put you before kings, that they may see you. By the multitude of your iniquities, in the unrighteousness of your trade You profaned your sanctuaries. Therefore I have brought fire from the midst of you; It has consumed you, and I have turned you to ashes on the earth in the eyes of all who see you. All who know you among the peoples are appalled at you; You have become terrified and you will cease to be forever.""

Notice that verse 13 is speaking explicitly of Eden: "You were in Eden, the garden of God." Verses 14 and 16 call Eden "the holy mountain of God." We will note later that "...from the beginning of the Bible, mountains are sites of transcendent spiritual experiences, encounters with God or appearances by God."[36] Beale says of mountains:

> The prophet Ezekiel portrays Eden on a mountain (Ezek. 28:14, 16). Israel's temple was on Mount Zion (e.g., Exod. 15:17), and the end-time temple was to be located on a mountain (Ezek. 40:2; 43:12; Rev. 21:10).[37]

Identifying Eden as "the holy mountain of God" indicates God's special presence among men on the earth. In verse 18, the prophet Ezekiel says, "You profaned your sanctuaries." Beale comments upon this passage as follows:

> ...it should not be unexpected to find that Ezekiel 28:13–14, 16, 18 refer to 'Eden, the garden of God...the holy mountain of God', and also alludes to it as containing 'sanctuaries', which elsewhere is a plural way of referring to Israel's tabernacle (Lev. 21:23) and temple (Ezek. 7:24; so also Jer. 51:51). The plural reference to the one temple probably arose because of the multiple sacred spaces or 'sanctuaries' within the temple complex (e.g., courtyard, holy place, holy of holies)...Ezekiel 28 is probably, therefore, the most explicit place anywhere in canonical literature where the Garden of Eden is called a temple.[38]

---

[36] "Mountain," in *Dictionary of Biblical Imagery*, ed. Leland Ryken, James C. Wilhoit, and Tremper Longman III (Downers Grove, IL: InterVarstiy Press, 1998), 573.
[37] Beale, *The Temple and the Church's Mission*, 73.
[38] Ibid., 75–76.

This is an important passage of Scripture because it identifies Eden as a temple, the first mountain of God in which he dwelled among men on the earth. Kline says, "Paradise was a sanctuary, a temple-garden. Agreeably, Ezekiel calls it "the garden of God" (28:13;31:8f.) and Isaiah, "the garden of the Lord" (51:3)."[39]

It is interesting that Christian commentators are not the only ones who argue that the garden of Eden was the first temple of God on the earth. There is extra-biblical evidence of understanding the garden as a temple from early Jewish literature. Fesko says:

> Perhaps one of the earliest writings that identify the garden of Eden as a temple comes from the Jewish book of Jubilees (c. 75–50 B.C.): 'And he [Noah] knew that the garden of Eden was the holy of holies and the dwelling of the LORD.'[40]

Beale notes that the Qumran community, an intertestamental group, identified "itself as the 'Temple of Adam…' and 'an Eden of glory [bearing] fruits [of life]'."[41]

Adam was made outside the garden-temple, then placed in it. But what was he supposed to do in or with that temple? His commission was obviously vitally connected to the garden in which God put him, though not limited to it. Remember, he was to fill the earth and subdue it (Genesis 1:28). So, the garden of Eden was not the end; it was only the beginning. Adam was called as an image-bearer of God who was sinless and a representative of others to multiply, fill the earth, and subdue it. His calling was to extend the garden-temple throughout the entire earth. In effect, the whole earth was to be God's special dwelling place with man. Eden was a prototype of something much greater, or, as Dumbrell puts it, "Eden is the representation of what the world is to become…"[42]

Eighth, *Adam was commanded to cultivate and keep the garden in obedience to God*. Genesis 2:15 says, "Then the LORD God took the man and put him into the garden of Eden to cultivate it and keep it." If the garden was a temple, then was Adam a priest who was to offer his work to God? It is of interest to note, when Adam is exiled from the garden due to his sin, Mo-

---

[39] Kline, *Kingdom Prologue*, 48. Oren R. Martin takes the same view of Ezekiel 28 in Oren R. Martin, *Bound for the Promised Land: The land promise in God's redemptive plan* (Downers Grove, IL: InterVarsity Press, 2015), as do many others.

[40] Fesko, *Last Things First*, 74. Beale dates the book of Jubilees at 160 BC. See Beale, *The Temple and the Church's Mission*, 77.

[41] Beale, *The Temple and the Church's Mission*, 78.

[42] Dumbrell, "Genesis 2:1–17: A Foreshadowing of the New Creation," 61.

ses tells us that "God sent him out from the garden of Eden, to cultivate [or "serve"] the ground from which he was taken" (Genesis 3:23; remember that Adam was created outside the garden of Eden). Then, in the next verse, God "stationed the cherubim and the flaming sword which turned every direction to guard [or "keep"] the way to the tree of life" (Genesis 3:24). Notice that Adam was to "cultivate [or "serve"]" the ground and the cherubim were to "guard [or "keep"] the way to the tree of life." These are the same words used together in Genesis 2:15, which says, "Then the LORD God took the man and put him into the garden of Eden to cultivate it and keep it." What does it mean that Adam was to "cultivate and keep" the garden, especially if it was the earth's first temple?

It is very interesting to note that these two words, *cultivate* and *keep*, are used together in other Old Testament texts to refer to the work of priests in connection with Israel's tabernacle and temple (Numbers 3:7–8; 8:25–26; 18:5–6; 1 Chronicles 23:32; Ezekiel 44:14).[43] Listen to Beale again:

> Genesis 2:15 says God placed Adam in the Garden 'to cultivate [i.e., work] it and to keep it.' The two Hebrew words for 'cultivate and keep' are usually translated 'serve and guard [or keep]' elsewhere in the Old Testament. It is true that the Hebrew word usually translated 'cultivate' can refer to an agricultural task when used by itself... When, however, these two words...occur together in the Old Testament..., they refer either to Israelites 'serving' God and 'guarding [keeping]' God's word...or to priests who 'keep' the 'service' (or 'charge') of the tabernacle (see Num. 3:7–8; 8:25–26; 18:5–6; 1 Chr. 23:32; Ezek. 44:14).[44]
>
> ...the writer of Genesis 2 was portraying Adam against the later portrait of Israel's priests, and that he was the archetypical priest who served in and guarded (or 'took care of') God's first temple.[45]

Since the garden of Eden was a temple, Adam was not only the first prophet and human king of the earth, he was its first priest. But Adam sinned. Adam's sin, therefore, got him excommunicated from the first house of God among men on the earth.

Ninth, *Adam was commanded by God not to eat from the tree of the knowledge of good and evil and threatened with death if he did.*

> The LORD God commanded the man, saying, "From any tree of the garden you may eat freely; but from the tree of the knowledge of good and

---

[43] See Beale, *The Temple and the Church's Mission*, 67.
[44] Ibid., 66–67.
[45] Ibid., 68.

evil you shall not eat, for in the day that you eat from it you will surely die." (Genesis 2:16–17)

Adam had the law written on his heart and a specific external, or positive, command from God not to eat of a certain tree. This was Adam's test, a probation. Would he be an obedient priest in God's house? Commenting on this prohibition, Beale says:

> After telling Adam to 'cultivate' and 'guard/keep' in Genesis 2:15, God gives him a specific 'command' in verse 16. The notion of divine 'commanding'…or giving of 'commandments'…not untypically follows the word 'guard/keep'…elsewhere, and in 1 Kings 9:6, when both 'serving' and 'keeping' occur together, the idea of 'commandments to be kept' is in view. The 1 Kings passage is addressed to Solomon and his sons immediately after he had 'finished building the house of the Lord' (1 Kgs. 9:1): if they do 'not *keep* My commandments…and *serve* other gods…I will cut off Israel from the land…and the house [temple]…I will cast out of My sight' (1 Kgs. 9:6–7)… Hence, it follows naturally that after God puts Adam into the Garden for 'cultivating/serving and keeping/guarding' (v. 15) that in the very next verse God would command Adam to keep a commandment: 'and the LORD God commanded the man…' The first 'torah' was that 'From any tree of the Garden you may eat freely; but from the tree of the knowledge of good and evil you shall not eat, for in the day that you eat from it you shall surely die' (Gen. 2:16–17). Accordingly, Adam's disobedience, as Israel's, results in his being cut off from the sacred land of the Garden.[46]

Tenth, *Adam was given a suitable helper to fulfill his mandate from God*. Adam could not fulfill the mandate of Genesis 1:28 alone. He needed a suitable helper: Eve (Genesis 2:18–25).

Eleventh, *Adam was placed in a covenantal relationship with God*. This was argued in Chapter 5.

A sinless image-bearer was called by God to be fruitful and multiply, and fill the earth with others like him. He was to subdue the earth and rule over other creatures, starting in the garden of Eden and going out from there. He was made of body and soul outside the garden. He was put in the garden to begin the task assigned to him as a priest. He was given law to obey and a helper to complement him so he could fulfill his task. He was a son of God. He was a spokesman for God (i.e., a prophet), a priest, and a ruler (i.e., king). As Bavinck says:

> He is the prophet who explains God and proclaims his excellencies; he is the priest who consecrates himself with all that is created to God as a

[46] Beale, *The Temple and the Church's Mission*, 68–69.

holy offering; he is the king who guides and governs all things in rectitude.[47]

He was in covenant with God, but he violated God's covenant. He sinned. He transgressed God's law. He was subsequently cursed, clothed with animal skins, and then exiled from the garden at its eastern edge (Genesis 3:8–24). In essence, Adam got kicked out of God's house. Now he's sinful, a terrible image of God, a covenant breaker, and no longer the keeper of God's garden-temple. What will God do now?

God's Remedy for Adam's Sin

According to Genesis 3:15 (the first promise of Christ), a seed, or offspring, of the woman will come to destroy the effects of the devil's work on the earth. This seed of the woman will be a man—body and soul—an image-bearer of God. Listen to Galatians 4:4: "But when the fullness of the time came, God sent forth His Son, born of a woman..." Hebrews 2:14 says, "since the children share in flesh and blood, He Himself likewise also partook of the same." Colossians 1:15 says, "He is the image of the invisible God." The seed of the woman is the Son of God incarnate.

The seed of the woman is a sinless image-bearer. Hebrews 4:15 says, "For we do not have a high priest who cannot sympathize with our weaknesses, but One who has been tempted in all things as *we are, yet* without sin."

The seed of the woman has authority to rule over all things. Matthew 28:18 says, "And Jesus came up and spoke to them, saying, 'All authority has been given to Me in heaven and on earth.'" Hebrews 1:3 says:

> And He is the radiance of His glory and the exact representation of His nature, and upholds all things by the word of His power. When He had made purification of sins, He sat down at the right hand of the Majesty on high.

The seed of the woman is the last Adam. First Corinthians 15:45 says, "So also it is written, 'The first MAN, Adam, BECAME A LIVING SOUL.' The last Adam *became* a life-giving spirit." The last Adam is the Lord Jesus Christ, the Son of God who became man.

---

[47] Bavinck, *Reformed Dogmatics*, 2:562. Bavinck adds these words: "And in all this he points to One who in a still higher and richer sense is the revelation and image of God, to him who is the only begotten of the Father, and the firstborn of all creatures. Adam, the son of God, was a type of Christ."

The last Adam, unlike the first, was tempted in the wilderness by the devil and did not succumb to temptation. Luke 4:1–2 says:

> Jesus, full of the Holy Spirit, returned from the Jordan and was led around by the Spirit in the wilderness for forty days, being tempted by the devil. And He ate nothing during those days, and when they had ended, He became hungry.

Notice that these verses follow Adam being identified as "the son of God" in Luke 3:38. The first Adam was a failure. He failed to subdue the devil in the garden. The last Adam, the eternal Son of God who became man, did not fail, and thus is the hero to which the Old Testament pointed.

The last Adam is the temple of God. He dwelt among us (John 1:14). Listen to John 2:13–22.

> The Passover of the Jews was near, and Jesus went up to Jerusalem. And He found in the temple those who were selling oxen and sheep and doves, and the money changers seated *at their tables*. And He made a scourge of cords, and drove *them* all out of the temple, with the sheep and the oxen; and He poured out the coins of the money changers and overturned their tables; and to those who were selling the doves He said, "Take these things away; stop making My Father's house a place of business." His disciples remembered that it was written, "ZEAL FOR YOUR HOUSE WILL CONSUME ME." The Jews then said to Him, "What sign do You show us as your authority for doing these things?" Jesus answered them, "Destroy this temple, and in three days I will raise it up." The Jews then said, "It took forty-six years to build this temple, and will You raise it up in three days?" But He was speaking of the temple of His body. So when He was raised from the dead, His disciples remembered that He said this; and they believed the Scripture and the word which Jesus had spoken.

Jesus' claim is that He will build a new temple. Note that after His resurrection, "His disciples remembered that He said this; and they believed the Scripture and the word which Jesus had spoken" (John 2:22). John makes a distinction between "the Scripture and the word which Jesus had spoken." The Scripture refers to the Old Testament. Thus, what John is saying is that the disciples, upon the resurrection of Christ, understood what Jesus said to be in line with the Old Testament. Jesus is the new temple promised in the Old Testament.[48]

---

[48] See Hopkins, *Jesus as the Fulfillment of the Temple in the Gospel of John*.

But our Lord Jesus Christ also creates a new temple called the church:

> Do you not know *that* you are a temple of God and that the Spirit of God dwells in you? If any man destroys the temple of God, God will destroy him, for the temple of God is holy, and that is what you are. (1 Corinthians 3:16–17)

Ephesians 2:21–22 says:

> in whom [i.e., Christ] the whole building, being fitted together, is growing into a holy temple in the Lord, in whom you also are being built together into a dwelling of God in the Spirit.

Paul is speaking about the church. The church is "a holy temple" and "a dwelling of God in the Spirit." It is God's house (1 Timothy 3:15; Hebrews 3:1–6). Our Lord Jesus Christ is also the new temple-builder, the builder of God's house, promised in the Old Testament. Recall one of the promises of the Davidic covenant. David is promised that a descendant "will come forth from you, and I will establish his kingdom. He shall build a house for My name, and I will establish the throne of his kingdom forever" (2 Samuel 7:12b–13). The promise of the covenant is that David will have a descendant with a kingdom, who will build God's house, and whose kingdom shall last forever. In Acts 2:22–36, Peter, utilizing Psalm 16 (Acts 2:25–28), 2 Samuel 7, Psalm 89, and Psalm 132 (Acts 2:30), and Psalm 110 (Acts 2:34–35), proclaims that our Lord Jesus fulfills the covenantal promise given to king David. The New Testament evokes the Davidic covenant in many places, connecting its fulfillment with Christ and the church (Matthew 1:1, 20–23; Mark 11:9–11; Luke 1:26–33; 2:9–11; Acts 2:22–36; 13:22–41; 15:13–18; Romans 1:1–4; 2 Timothy 2:8; Revelation 3:7). Our Lord promised that He would build His church (Matthew 16:18; see Hebrews 3:1–6).

The last Adam was an obedient priest (Hebrews 5:9–10) who also creates a new priesthood for the house of God, which is the church of the living God. First Timothy 3:15 says, "*I write* so that you will know how one ought to conduct himself in the household of God, which is the church of the living God, the pillar and support of the truth." The church is now the house of God built by Christ. First Peter 2:5 says, "you also, as living stones, are being built up as a spiritual house for a holy priesthood, to offer up spiritual sacrifices acceptable to God through Jesus Christ." Christ's church consists of priests offering up spiritual sacrifices.

The last Adam has a bride through whom he works on the earth. Revelation 21:9 says:

Then one of the seven angels who had the seven bowls full of the seven last plagues came and spoke with me, saying, "Come here, I will show you the bride, the wife of the Lamb.

The bride, the wife of the Lamb, is the church. Ephesians 5:31–32 says:

> FOR THIS REASON A MAN SHALL LEAVE HIS FATHER AND MOTHER AND SHALL BE JOINED TO HIS WIFE, AND THE TWO SHALL BECOME ONE FLESH. This mystery is great; but I am speaking with reference to Christ and the church.

The church is the wife of Christ, the human agent through which Christ builds his temple all around the world. Marriage, from the beginning, was a living picture of Christ and the church. Since Adam was a type of Christ, Eve could well be a type of the church—even prior to the entrance of sin. J. V. Fesko calls the church "the second Eve."[49] New Testament commentator Peter T. O'Brien says, "…the church's marriage to Christ is prefigured in Adam and Eve."[50] In O'Brien's conclusion to his discussion of marriage in Ephesians 5, he says, "…it was God's intention from the beginning when he instituted marriage to picture the relationship between Christ and his redeemed people."[51]

The commission by Christ to the apostles contained in Matthew 28:19–20 says:

> Go therefore and make disciples of all the nations, baptizing them in the name of the Father and the Son and the Holy Spirit, teaching them to observe all that I commanded you; and lo, I am with you always, even to the end of the age.

The apostles took this commission and preached the gospel, made disciples, baptized them, then formed them into churches in which they were taught. The apostles were the initial human agents through whom the Spirit of Christ extended the new temple inaugurated by Jesus Christ, who is its cornerstone (Ephesians 2:20; see Luke 20:17 and Psalm 118:22).

Unlike the first Adam who disobeyed and caused death, the last Adam came to obey and to die that others might live. Romans 5:17 says:

> For if by the transgression of the one [i.e., Adam], death reigned through the one, much more those who receive the abundance of grace and of the gift of righteousness will reign in life through the One, Jesus Christ.

---

[49] Fesko, *Last Things First*, 168.
[50] Peter T. O'Brien, *The Letter to the Ephesians*, PNTC (Grand Rapids: William B. Eerdmans Publishing Company, 1999), 435.
[51] Ibid., 438.

Adam failed to reign. Believers in Christ reign with Him now (Ephesians 2:6) and will do so forever.

Unlike the first Adam, the last Adam is the agent through whom many sons are brought to glory, the glory of which Adam fell short (Romans 3:23). Hebrews 2:10 says, "For it was fitting for Him, for whom are all things, and through whom are all things, in bringing many sons to glory, to perfect the author of their salvation through sufferings." This is what Adam failed to do because of his sin. Adam sinned and, thus fell "short of the glory of God" (Romans 3:23). Jesus suffered and then entered into His glory. Whereas Adam's disobedience prohibited him from entering into glory, Christ's life-unto-death-unto-life obedience is the ground upon which His children enter into glory.

Jesus Christ, the eternal Son of God become man, is God's remedy for Adam's failure. Christ takes His seed where Adam failed to take his. Salvation in Christ is better than creation in the image of God and citizenship in the garden of Eden. God does not place believers in Christ back at the starting line in the same position in which Adam found himself in the garden. He grants irrevocable, eternal life based on the doing, dying, and rising of Jesus to all who believe the gospel. The end is the beginning glorified. It is better than the beginning. God in Christ takes all sinners who believe the gospel to his land, his eschatological temple, his paradise—the new heavens and the new earth, wherein dwells only righteousness.

Creation in the Image of God Requires Imitation of Him

Was Adam obligated to imitate God (according to his creaturely capacities) simply because he was created in the image of God? The discussion above answers in the affirmative. To refine the issue even further: Did the fact and act of creation establish imperatival implications for Adam and Eve even without explicit commands recorded in the Genesis narrative? It is clear from Scripture that the fact of creation by God, which necessarily entails a divine act, calls all creatures to praise him. For example, Psalm 33:6–9 says:

> By the word of the LORD the heavens were made, And by the breath of His mouth all their host. He gathers the waters of the sea together as a heap; He lays up the deeps in storehouses. Let all the earth fear the LORD; Let all the inhabitants of the world stand in awe of Him. For He spoke, and it was done; He commanded, and it stood fast.

Notice that "all the earth" is called to "fear the LORD" and "all the inhabitants of the world [are called to] stand in awe of Him." What is the basis for this universal call to fear and awe (i.e., creaturely acts of worship)? Verse 9 is clear: "For He spoke, and it was done; He commanded, and it stood fast." Both the fact of creation and the divine action of causing that which was made to stand fast (something that is true to this day) are grounds upon which universal praise is due to the Creator. In other words, God's initial act of creation warrants praise from all image-bearers, as does God's subsequent act of providence toward that which had been made (i.e., causing it to stand fast). These divine actions with reference to creation which warrant praise from image-bearers did not first demand such when this Psalm was penned. Both creation and creatures in God's image predate the Psalm. If praise of the Creator due to these divine acts is a creaturely obligation after the fall, surely it was an obligation prior to the fall. God's acts in creation are grounds upon which image-bearing creatures are solicited to act in accord with their creaturely capacities in response to Him, and Adam and Eve were such creatures.

Given what has just been argued, a further question becomes appropriate: Is there anything in the manner in which God created that becomes an example for the creature to follow? I am thinking specifically of the fact that God took six days to create, then rested. By the way, it did not take God six days to create, as if He could not have done it in less time. If we consider the fact that God *took* six days to create, does this divine act provide a paradigm for his image-bearers to follow? This was certainly true for old covenant Israel, for the fourth commandment as recorded in Exodus 20:8–11 clearly bases six days of work and one day of Sabbath on God's acts at creation:

> Remember the sabbath day, to keep it holy. Six days you shall labor and do all your work, but the seventh day is a sabbath of the LORD your God; *in it* you shall not do any work, you or your son or your daughter, your male or your female servant or your cattle or your sojourner who stays with you. For in six days the LORD made the heavens and the earth, the sea and all that is in them, and rested on the seventh day; therefore the LORD blessed the sabbath day and made it holy.

Verse 11 clearly bases the Sabbath for Israel on the divine exemplar, but it also bases their six days of work on the same. The LORD's making "the heavens and the earth, the sea and all that is in them" "in six days" is the basis for Israel's six days of "labor" and "work," and the LORD's resting "on the seventh day" is the divine example for Israel to follow. With this understanding of Exodus 20:11, we know where the six-day work-week originated—the divine acts recorded for us in Genesis 1. We also know where the seven-day week came from; it has a creational origin. Many agree with this assessment.⁵²

Harold H. P. Dressler, however, argues otherwise. In his "The Sabbath in the Old Testament," he not only argues that the Sabbath began with Israel, but also that with Israel began the seven-day week. In the summary section of his discussion entitled "The Origin of the Sabbath," he says, "…we suggest that the Sabbath originated with Israel and that with the Sabbath came the seven-day week."⁵³ One of the problems with Dressler's view is that Genesis 29:27 says, "Complete the week of this one, and we will give you the other also for the service which you shall serve with me for another seven years." The word translated "week" is *shabua*, which refers to a heptad or period of seven days. Also, years were accounted for prior to Exodus 16 and 20 (e.g., Genesis 29:27 and Genesis 31:41, which says: "These twenty years I have been in your house; I served you fourteen years for your two daughters and six years for your flock, and you changed my wages ten times."). According to A. H. Konkel in the *New International Dictionary of Old Testament Theology and Exegesis*, "In several instances *šābûaʿ* means a period of seven days: in Gen 29:27–28 it refers to the week of the wedding feast…"⁵⁴ The seven-day week predates ancient Israel.

Since the seven-day week has a creational origin, let it be noted that there is no command in the Genesis narrative for the creature to submit himself to such. The divine example is sufficient to establish his duty. Neither is there a command to "fear the LORD" or "stand in awe of Him," as discussed above. The Creator/creature relationship is sufficient to establish

---

⁵² For discussions on this issue, see Owen, *Works*, 18:308–13, where he discusses the "hebdomadal [i.e., old word meaning weekly] revolution of time" (308). In that discussion, he quotes approvingly Johannes Philoponus, a sixth-century Alexandrian scholar: "Only the great Moses, being divinely inspired, hath delivered unto men the true reason of the septenary [i.e., relating to the number seven] number of the days" (311–12). See also Martin, *The Christian Sabbath*, 36. Martin interacts with Andrew T. Lincoln's comments in *From Sabbath to Lord's Day* on p. 34, n. 3. Lincoln at least seems to implicitly deny that the seven-day week began at creation because he views "the scheme of a creation week [as] a literary device." See Andrew T. Lincoln, "From Sabbath to Lord's Day: A Biblical and Theological Perspective," in *From Sabbath to Lord's Day*, 347. Both Owen and Martin discuss other theories of the inception of the seven-day week, noting that some deny its creational origin.

⁵³ Dressler, "The Sabbath in the Old Testament," in *From Sabbath to Lord's Day*, 24. See Martin, *The Christian Sabbath*, 29–30, n. 14 for brief interaction with Dressler's view.

⁵⁴ See the entry for *shabua* by A. H. Konkel in *New International Dictionary of Old Testament Theology and Exegesis*, 5 vols., gen. ed. Willem A. VanGemeren (Grand Rapids: Zondervan Publishing House, 1997), 4:20–24. The quote is from page 20.

the duty of man. This would mean that the acts of God at creation provide a divine example for his image-bearers to copy their Maker according to their created capacities. Ames says one of the things required of an image is "that it be formed and fashioned to imitate something as a facsimile."[55] Man was made to imitate his Creator according to his created capacities.

Considering the fact that God could have conducted the days of creation in either fewer or more days does make one wonder why he did it the way he did. It seems to me and many others that what God did, he did for man.[56] In other words, the Creator is the exemplar of work and rest. This is where our week originated. The words of Ralph Wardlaw seem appropriate at this juncture:

> It is true that creation occupied a certain portion of time: but not because omnipotence required it. The same word that commanded into existence the successive parts could, with equal ease, by one fiat, have commanded the whole. But there was a design in its being ordered otherwise; and the design related to man. It was to give commencement to such a division of time amongst the inhabitants of the new-formed world, as should connect the finished work of creation with a commemorative day.[57]

As John Murray asserts, "God's mode of operation is the exemplar on the basis of which the sequence for man is patterned."[58]

Not only are the divine acts in the creation week exemplars, the greatest divine redemptive act of the love manifested in the sending of the Son into the world (1 John 4:9) is the basis upon which the apostle John says, "Beloved, if God so loved us, we also ought to love one another" (1 John 4:11). The manifestation of divine love in the sending of the Son carries along with it an "ought" for the people of God. In addition, John bases the believers' duty to "lay down our life for the brethren" (1 John 3:16b) upon the historical act of the Son of God laying "down His life for us…" (1 John

---

[55] Ames, *The Marrow of Theology*, 1.8.66 (105).

[56] For further discussion, see my *Better than the Beginning*, 84–88.

[57] Quoted in Martin, *The Christian Sabbath*, 35, cited as "Ralph Wardlaw, *Discourses on the Sabbath* (Glasgow: Archibald Fullarton & Co., 1832), 14."

[58] John Murray, *Principles of Conduct* (1957; reprint, Grand Rapids: William B. Eerdmans Publishing Company, 1999), 32. Murray's book is highly recommended. Nicholas Bownd's *The True Doctrines of the Sabbath* was published in 1606. In a recent modern-version print of that work, Bownd affirms the divine exemplar view of the creation week, including the rest of God. He also quotes Zanchius to the same end. See Nicholas Bownd, *The True Doctrine of the Sabbath* (Dallas: Naphtali Press and Grand Rapids: Reformation Heritage Books, 2015), 39 and 44.

3:16a). Both the divine acts of creation and redemption, therefore, imply ethical injunctions for man according to his capacities of nature and grace.

Creation in the Image of God and God's Law

Before embarking upon the discussion on the Creator's rest, it may help to review some things discussed in this chapter. Man is God's image, responsible, according to his created capacities, to be like God, by virtue of the act of God in creating him. This is true of those who have come into contact with the Bible and those who have not. Being the image of God and accountable for such predates the writing of the Bible. All men since the fall and apart from divine grace lack true knowledge of God, righteousness, and holiness. All men, however, have the law of God written on their hearts, for which they are accountable and to which they cannot subject themselves (Romans 8:7). Man's inability to subject himself to that law does not excuse him from its righteous and holy demands. Instead, man's inability to subject himself to God's law is part of the reason he is culpable. Not being able to subject himself to God's law implies that he ought to, irrespective of whether he has read the Bible or not. This means the law of God is the standard for all men: Jew, Gentile, lost, saved, Bible-reader, and those without the Bible. God holds men accountable for breaking His law. God's law is universally binding on all men because all men are created in the image of God and are thus accountable to Him.

One of the interesting things about the book of Romans is its understanding of the universal function of the law of God. For example, Romans 3:19–20 says:

> Now we know that whatever the Law says, it speaks to those who are under the Law, so that every mouth may be closed and all the world may become accountable to God; because by the works of the Law no flesh will be justified in His sight; for through the Law *comes* the knowledge of sin.

In the context of these crucial verses, Paul is establishing the fact that all men, both Jews (i.e., people with Holy Scripture at the time Paul wrote) and Greeks (i.e., people without Holy Scripture at the time Paul wrote), are "under sin" (Romans 3:9). In order to do this, Paul quotes from the Old Testament (Romans 3:10–18). In 3:19, Paul bases universal guilt on universal culpability for violations of the law revealed to us in the Old Testament. Both Jews and Greeks are "under sin" because they are guilty of being violators of laws revealed to us in the Old Testament. It is of interest to note that none of the sins listed in 3:10–18 are violations of what are commonly termed ceremonial laws. These sins reflect breaches of law which is common to all men contained *both* in the Old Testament *and* in the hearts of all men (Romans 2:14–15). Romans 1:18–32 (e.g., v. 21 [not glorifying God as God, not being thankful to God, futile thinking]; v. 25 [not worshiping God]; vv. 26–27 [sexual vices]; vv. 29–32 [various vices]) and 2:14–15 are clear that those without the written word of God are not without law altogether. They were, at the time of Paul's writing, without the Old Testament in the main, but not without the basic, fundamental law of the Old Testament. Jews are "under sin" because they have broken God's law. Greeks are "under sin" because they have broken God's law, the Old and New Testaments indicting both groups. Both Jews and Greeks are "under the law"[59] (Romans 3:19) and "under sin" (Romans 3:9) and therefore guilty before God. The only way this can be possible is if the law the Jews were under and the law the Greeks were and are under correspond at least to a degree. Since the Jews had the whole Old Testament and the Greeks had only the law written on their hearts, then the law being referred to here by Paul could mean one thing for Jews and another thing for Greeks, the form being different though the same in substance. W. G. T. Shedd says:

> ὁ νόμος [the law] the written law, primarily, because St. Paul has been speaking, last, of the Jew; yet not the written law exclusively, because the Gentiles are included in πᾶν στόμα [every mouth] and πᾶς ὁ κόσμος [all the world]. The written law contains the unwritten, by implication, and hence may be put for all law, or law generally.... This passage throws light upon the true interpretation of ii. 14, 15; ii. 26, 27.[60]

The law with reference to Jews refers to the whole Mosaic law. The law with reference to Greeks refers to the law written on the heart, the natural law.

This interpretation is strengthened when one considers the language at the end of verse 19: "that every mouth may be stopped, and all the world may become guilty before God." This argues that the law being referred to is a law common to all men. The only law common to all men, and therefore, the law of which all men can be held guilty of in common, is not the Mosaic law simpliciter, since that law is bound with the Mosaic covenant and was for ancient Israel alone. This does not, however, negate the fact that the Jews were more culpable because they possessed more revelation.

---

[59] The phrase is literally 'in the law' (ἐν τῷ νόμῳ). The word 'in' refers to those who are within the sphere of the law's authority.

[60] W. G. T. Shedd, *Commentary on Romans* (Grand Rapids: Baker Book House, 1980), 71.

This understanding of these verses corresponds with what Paul taught in Romans 2:14–15 and 26–27.

This chapter dealt with man created in the image of God. What does Romans 3 have to do with that? Very much, indeed! The reason why Paul could pronounce universal condemnation upon all men is because all men sin; they transgress God's law. This is so even though not all men have read the Bible and not all men are members of the covenant God enacted with ancient Israel through Moses. How can all men be guilty of violating God's law? The answer must be by virtue of being created in the image of God. Creation in the image of God is shared by all. Since that is the case, then all men have come into contact with God's law by virtue of nature, or their created status as image bearers.

This is why, early in the Bible, there are accounts of persons acting in such a way that the writer paints a dark picture of their conduct. For example, consider Cain (Genesis 4:1ff.). According to the apostle John, Cain "was of the evil one and slew his brother" (1 John 3:12). But there are no prohibitions concerning his act in the text of Genesis prior to the recording of his act. Neither are there any recorded commands to love your neighbor as yourself at this point in the biblical narrative. Most people would quickly condemn Cain's act against his brother Abel, and rightly so. But upon what basis would one do so? Someone might say, "Because everyone knows it's wrong to murder." But how does everyone know it's wrong to murder? In fact, does everyone acknowledge this to be the case? Probably not. This does not mean murder can be justified. It simply recognizes that, since the fall, man's soul is deformed, mangled, twisted, and distorted. We often "call evil good and good evil" (Isaiah 5:20). In our unrighteousness, we suppress the truth that is in us and all around us (Romans 1:18ff.). We live in a day when abortion is rampant. Homosexuality and transgenderism are now accepted alternative lifestyles. Does this make these things right in the sight of God? Of course not. But it does indicate one thing I want to mention. Even though men are created in the image of God, they convince themselves against the truth that is in them and all around them that some things that are, in fact, sinful (i.e., lawless acts [1 John 3:4], transgressions of the law of God). Does this mean they do not have the law of God written on their hearts? No. It means that man can, has, and does get to certain points in his experience where he denies the very truths he knows deep down (Romans 1:18ff.).

If this is the case with the sins mentioned above, could it be the case with other laws of God as well, laws written on everyone's heart via nature? If the Israelites could be scolded for not circumcising male infants (Joshua 5:1–8), even though God revealed his will to them through Abraham (Genesis 17) and Moses (Leviticus 12:3) on this very issue (the same goes for the Passover; see 2 Kings 22:21–23), could it not be the case that man does the same with the law written on the heart? It has been proven that there are creaturely actions frowned upon by Moses in the book of Genesis prior to him writing a prohibition concerning that which is frowned upon (see Genesis 4:1ff.). This could only be the case under two possibilities. First, even though Moses did not write about these issues until after the fact, God had spoken these laws to Adam or someone else and told him or them to tell others. This is certainly plausible, though impossible to prove based on the data of Scripture. Second, it could be that those things frowned upon by Moses prior to writing a prohibition concerning them were known by virtue of men being created in the image of God. This case is certainly plausible as well, since we know that by virtue of creation in the image of God man has the law of God written on his heart (Romans 2:14–15). Though that could be the case, we should be careful not to identify the law of God written on the heart from only those things frowned upon by Moses. Moses' account is a selective narrative, not an exhaustive account of all the sins of all men living from creation to the time of his writing. Moses never rebukes non-Jews for theft, yet surely there were thieves in the world beyond Abraham and his descendants.

The next chapter will begin a discussion on the Creator's rest. One of the issues discussed in this chapter will become especially relevant in that discussion. The specific issue involves whether or not the Creator's rest establishes an ordinance for man. It will be argued that just as the Creator's creation week is the divine ordination for man's workweek, the same holds true for the Creator's rest. Many issues will be discussed to seek to prove this assertion. Does the Creator's rest, as a divine act, constitute a divine example for man? Does being created in the image of God imply ethical responsibilities for man that are sometimes solicited from man by divine acts? These important issues will be discussed in the chapters which follow.

9

The Doctrine of the Christian Sabbath
THE BEGINNING AND THE END

The issue of the Sabbath has caused much ink to be spilled in our day, as well as in previous days.[1] There is much confusion on this issue due to not understanding the first revelation of the Creator's rest as found in Genesis 2:1–3. This confusion, in part, occurs because interpreters do not allow other parts of the Bible to explain the function of the Creator's rest. In order to understand the Bible correctly, we have to understand what the Creator's rest means, both for God and man. In order to fully appreciate God's rest, we must allow the Creator to tell us what it means. He does that in various places in the rest of Scripture. The two questions to be focused on in this discussion are: first, what does God's rest mean for God? and second, what does God's rest mean for man?

In this and following chapters, I will argue that understanding the Creator's rest helps us understand the entire Bible—what the Bible is about, what went wrong in human history, how God planned to remedy what went wrong, and where history is heading. In order to fully appreciate God's rest, it will be helpful to notice the Bible's diversity and unity and its beginning and end.

---

[1] Some of the material in this chapter is taken and expanded from my *Better than the Beginning* and is used with permission.

The Bible's Diversity

The Bible is a large book with many diverse parts. There are two testaments—an Old Testament containing 39 books and a New Testament containing 27 books. The Old Testament was written over a period of about 1,500 years by many different authors in cultural and religious circumstances very different from ours. The New Testament was written within the time-frame of one generation, a little over 2,000 years ago. That generation existed in a world quite different from ours as well. The Bible also has different kinds of literature, such as narratives that tell stories of ancient events, people, and places, prophecies that tell of things to come, and epistles, which are letters written by apostles to local churches in the first century. Given these factors, the Bible may appear to be comprised of disconnected books, written by various authors over a long period of time, with no central point, no plot, no story line, and no solution. When studied carefully, however, the Bible's unity becomes clear.

The Bible's Unity

One of the ways the overall unity of the Bible may be seen is by comparing the beginning of the Bible with its end. I have a book on one of my shelves entitled, *The End of the Beginning: Revelation 21–22 and the Old Testament*.[2] The author, William J. Dumbrell, argues that the end is the beginning brought to its intended goal. He argues that the end is actually better than the beginning. James M. Hamilton concurs when he says, "At this restoration [i.e., a new heaven and earth] God will make things better than they were at the beginning."[3] The conclusion helps us understand the introduction better. T. D. Alexander says:

> As is often the case, a story's conclusion provides a good guide to the themes and ideas dominant throughout. By resolving an intricate plot that runs throughout a story, a good denouement[4] sheds light on the entire story.[5]

---

[2] William J. Dumbrell, *The End of the Beginning: Revelation 21–22 and the Old Testament* (Eugene, OR: Wipf and Stock Publishers, 2001; previously published by Baker Book House, 1985).

[3] Hamilton, *What is Biblical Theology?*, 29. Hamilton also states that the "plot [of the Bible] begins with the making of the cosmic temple, which is defiled by sin" (28). This will be discussed below.

[4] A denouement is the final resolution of a plot, as in a drama or novel, a solution, or the end of a story that ties together its various parts.

[5] T. D. Alexander, *From Eden to the New Jerusalem: An Introduction to Biblical*

This is true in a good mystery novel or movie. The plot (or riddle or problem to be solved) is revealed early on and is finally solved at the end, and then everything in between makes sense. As well, there are usually twists in the story that when resolved exceed one's initial thoughts in oftentimes amazing ways. The end ties up the loose ends of the beginning and middle and makes sense of the whole. So it goes with the Bible.

Commenting on the relationship between the beginning and end of the Bible, Alexander says:

> The very strong links between Genesis 1–3 [the first three chapters of the Bible] and Revelation 20–22 [the last three chapters of the Bible] suggest that these passages frame the entire biblical meta-story.[6]

A meta-story is the overarching story that all of the individual parts of a book are serving. What are some of those themes that end up being in both the beginning and the end of the Bible? The next section contains a proposed answer to this question.

Seven Observations Tying the End of the Bible with the Beginning of the Bible

In this section, some themes that occur at the end of the Bible and which find their origin in its beginning will be explored. This will help us see the big picture so as not to lose the forest for the trees. It will also set a proper context for understanding various particulars in the beginning, such as man as the image of God, the covenant of works, the Creator's rest, and even the promise of Genesis 3:15 (which is beyond the scope of this book).

The Devil, Who First Appears in Genesis 3, Ends Up Thrown into the Lake of Fire

Revelation 20:7–10 says:

> When the thousand years are completed, Satan will be released from his prison, and will come out to deceive the nations which are in the four corners of the earth, Gog and Magog, to gather them together for the war; the number of them is like the sand of the seashore. And they came up on the broad plain of the earth and surrounded the camp of the saints and the beloved city, and fire came down from heaven and devoured

---

Theology (Grand Rapids: Kregel Publications, 2009), 10.
[6] Alexander, *From Eden to the New Jerusalem*, 10.

them. And the devil who deceived them was thrown into the lake of fire and brimstone, where the beast and the false prophet are also; and they will be tormented day and night forever and ever.

The Bible has threads within it that deal with the effects of the devil's activity, not only in the garden of Eden, but after man's expulsion from the garden, involving his posterity. There is conflict between the woman's seed and the devil's seed throughout—the people of God and the children of the devil. But this conflict is individualized as well (Genesis 3:15). The seed of the woman conquers the devil.

The First Heavens and First Earth of Genesis 1:1 Become a New Heaven and a New Earth

Revelation 21:1 says, "Then I saw a new heaven and a new earth; for the first heaven and the first earth passed away, and there is no longer *any* sea." Peter tells us that in this new heaven and earth, "…righteousness dwells" (2 Peter 3:13). Remember, God exiled Adam and Eve from the garden because they became unrighteous. The old creation becomes new.

The Tree of Life, First Revealed in Genesis 2, Ends Up on the New Earth

Describing the eternal state, Revelation 22:2 says, "On either side of the river was the tree of life…" Revelation 22:14 adds, "Blessed are those who wash their robes, so that they may have the right to the tree of life, and may enter by the gates into the city." The eschatological city, the new earth, contains the tree of life, which first appears in the Bible in Genesis 2:9.

God Will Dwell Among All the Citizens of the New Earth

Revelation 21:3 says, "And I heard a loud voice from the throne, saying, 'Behold, the tabernacle of God is among men, and He will dwell among them, and they shall be His people, and God Himself will be among them.'" God dwelt in the garden with Adam and Eve, but they were exiled from that first dwelling place of God among men because of their sin. Then God dwelt in Israel's tabernacle and temple. Then God dwelt among men in the person of Jesus Christ, as John tells us in John 1:14, "And the Word became flesh and dwelt among us…" God's dwelling with men on the earth is now experienced by the church of the inaugurated new covenant, the new temple of God, the new house of God, which is "…a dwelling of God in the Spirit" (Ephesians 2:22). But in the new earth, God will dwell

The Beginning and the End

with everyone, not just the church in distinction from the outer world of men. The whole earth will be a special dwelling place of God among men.

There Will No Longer Be Any Death in the New Earth

Revelation 21:4 says, "…there will no longer be any death." Death came when "sin entered into the world" (Romans 5:12), recorded for us in Genesis 3. In the new earth, there will no longer be any death; death will be no more. There will be no death because there will be no sin. There will be no sin because there will only be righteousness and eternal life. The life then enjoyed was earned by the righteousness of Christ and conferred upon others as a gift.

The New Jerusalem Is Described with the Symbolic Language Often Used of Temples

Here is Revelation 21:10–22.

> And he carried me away in the Spirit to a great and high mountain, and showed me the holy city, Jerusalem, coming down out of heaven from God, having the glory of God. Her brilliance was like a very costly stone, as a stone of crystal-clear jasper. It had a great and high wall, with twelve gates, and at the gates twelve angels; and names *were* written on them, which are *the names* of the twelve tribes of the sons of Israel. *There were* three gates on the east and three gates on the north and three gates on the south and three gates on the west. And the wall of the city had twelve foundation stones, and on them *were* the twelve names of the twelve apostles of the Lamb. The one who spoke with me had a gold measuring rod to measure the city, and its gates and its wall. The city is laid out as a square, and its length is as great as the width; and he measured the city with the rod, fifteen hundred miles; its length and width and height are equal. And he measured its wall, seventy-two yards, *according to* human measurements, which are *also* angelic *measurements*. The material of the wall was jasper; and the city was pure gold, like clear glass. The foundation stones of the city wall were adorned with every kind of precious stone. The first foundation stone was jasper; the second, sapphire; the third, chalcedony; the fourth, emerald; the fifth, sardonyx; the sixth, sardius; the seventh, chrysolite; the eighth, beryl; the ninth, topaz; the tenth, chrysoprase; the eleventh, jacinth; the twelfth, amethyst. And the twelve gates were twelve pearls; each one of the gates was a single pearl. And the street of the city was pure gold, like transparent glass. I saw no temple in it, for the Lord God the Almighty and the Lamb are its temple.

Eschatological or new Jerusalem is described as a cubed city of pure gold. The only other golden cube in the Bible is the inner sanctuary of Israel's temple, called the Holy of Holies, the special dwelling place of God with man. Listen to 1 Kings 6:20: "The inner sanctuary *was* twenty cubits in length, twenty cubits in width, and twenty cubits in height, and he overlaid it with pure gold." Also, gold is often linked with the special dwelling place of God among men. Listen to Genesis 2:10–12.

> Now a river flowed out of Eden to water the garden; and from there it divided and became four rivers. The name of the first is Pishon; it flows around the whole land of Havilah, where there is gold. The gold of that land is good; the bdellium and the onyx stone are there.

It is important to note in Revelation 22:1 John was shown "a river of the water of life…flowing from the throne of God and from the Lamb." The entire new Jerusalem appears to be an expanded Holy of Holies—the special dwelling place of God among men. As Beale says, "…the entire creation has become the holy of holies…"[7]

One more observation on rivers in light of Revelation 22:1 may help. Rivers flow downhill. Since the rivers of Eden (Genesis 2:10–12) flowed downhill, this places its location uphill or upon a mountain. Now listen to Revelation 21:10–11a and 22:1: "And he carried me away in the Spirit to a great and high mountain, and showed me the holy city, Jerusalem, coming down out of heaven from God, having the glory of God… Then he showed me a river of the water of life…" The New Jerusalem is pictured as having a river flowing out of it and connected to a high mountain. The special dwelling place of God among men in the end of the Bible depicts a river of life and a high mountain. Where did this type of language and these concepts come from? From the Bible itself. The entry for "Mountain" in the *Dictionary of Biblical Imagery*, quoted in the previous chapter, reads:

> Almost from the beginning of the Bible, mountains are sites of transcendent spiritual experiences, encounters with God or appearances by God. Ezekiel 28:13–15 places the *Garden of Eden on a mountain. *Abraham shows his willingness to sacrifice Isaac and then encounters God on a mountain (Gen 22:1–14). God appears to Moses and speaks from the *burning bush on "Horeb the mountain of God" (Ex 3:1–2 NRSV), and he encounters Elijah on the same site (1 Kings 19:8–18). Most impressive of all is the experience of the Israelites at Mt. *Sinai (Ex 19), which *Moses ascends in a *cloud to meet God.
>
> A similar picture emerges from the NT, where Jesus is associated with mountains. Jesus resorted to mountains to be alone (Jn 6:15), to

---

[7] Beale, *Temple and the Church's Mission*, 370.

*pray (Mt 14:23; Lk 6:12) and to teach his listeners (Mt 5:1; Mk 3:13). It was on a mountain that Jesus refuted Satan's temptation (Mt 4:8; Lk 4:5). He was also transfigured on a mountain (Mt 17:1–8; Mk 9:2–8; Lk 9:28–36), and he ascended into heaven from the Mount of Olives (Acts 1:10–12).[8]

Jesus also designated a mountain in Galilee from which He gave the Great Commission to the Eleven in Matthew 28:16, "But the eleven disciples proceeded to Galilee, to the mountain which Jesus had designated." Jesus is both the tabernacle of God among men (John 1:14) and a temple (John 2:19–22) who builds the new temple (1 Corinthians 3:16–17; Ephesians 2:19–22), which is His body, the church. Hebrews 12:18–24 contrasts Mount Sinai and Mount Zion in the context of the transition from the old covenant to the inaugurated new covenant. God's people have gone from one mountain to another. Surely these mountains are symbols of the old covenant and the new covenant and have their foundation in the first mountain-temple, the garden of Eden.

The Curse That was Inflicted in Genesis 3 Due to Adam's Sin Is No More

Revelation 22:3 says, "There will no longer be any curse; and the throne of God and of the Lamb will be in it, and His bond-servants will serve Him." Because man did not serve God, the curse came upon man and the earth. In the eternal state, "there will no longer be any curse."

As noted above, the Bible ends "[w]ith [a] remarkable vision of God coming to dwell with humanity on a new earth."[9] But the Bible started with God in the midst of His people in the garden of Eden, on a mountain, with precious stones present, with water flowing out of it, and in a context where Adam, the first prophet-priest-king, was supposed to subdue the earth and fill it with other image-bearers who were like him (i.e., sinless sons of God). What happened? Sin happened. Adam sinned as man's federal head and plunged himself and his posterity into a state of misery and death.

These considerations indicate that the end is the beginning brought to a better state of existence. Not only was the beginning brought to its goal, it is brought to its goal not from its created state, but from that state into which the sin of man brought it.

---

[8] "Mountain," in *Dictionary of Biblical Imagery*, 573. The asterisks are original, indicating other entries in the dictionary.

[9] Alexander, *From Eden to the New Jerusalem*, 14.

The riddle to be solved is who brings the sin-stained, cursed creation to its new state of existence, and how? The answer is the seed of the woman (Genesis 3:15), the son of Abraham (Matthew 1:1), the lion of the tribe of Judah (Genesis 49:9; Numbers 24:9; Revelation 5:5), the one from Jacob who shall have dominion (Numbers 24:19; Genesis 1:28; Zechariah 9:9–10). He is the prophet greater than Moses (Deuteronomy 18:15; Acts 3:22, 7:37), one greater than Joshua, the son of David (Matthew 1:1), the child of the virgin (Isaiah 7:14; Micah 5:3;[10] Matthew 1:23), the child born who governs the kingdom of David (Isaiah 9:6–7; Mark 11:10; Luke 1:32–33). He is the branch of the LORD who will build the temple of the LORD and sit and rule on his throne as a priest (Jeremiah 33:14–15; Isaiah 4:2; 11:1–2 [John 1:32 echoes Isaiah 11:2]; 53:2; Jeremiah 23:5–6; Zechariah 6:11–13), the righteous, suffering servant of the LORD (Isaiah 53). He is the embodiment of all that Israel was not (i.e., a faithful son of God). He is the one who went forth for the LORD "to be ruler in Israel," whose "goings forth are from long ago, from the days of eternity" (Micah 5:2), "the Lord, whom you seek, [who] suddenly [came] to His temple; and the messenger of the covenant" (Malachi 3:1; Luke 1:76). He is the one conceived of the Holy Spirit named "Jesus, for He will save His people from their sins" (Matthew 1:21), "'IMMANUEL,' which translated means, "GOD WITH US" (Matthew 1:23, citing or collating Isaiah 7:14; 8:10; and 9:6). He is the Son of God called out of Egypt (Matthew 2:15; Hosea 11:1; Exodus 4:22–23), the one "led up by the Spirit into the wilderness to be tempted by the devil" (Matthew 4:1). He is the one who said, "I will build My church; and the gates of Hades will not overpower it" (Matthew 16:18b), the one who said, "I was watching Satan fall from heaven like lightning" (Luke 10:18) and "Now judgment is upon this world; now the ruler of this world will be cast out" (John 12:31), "the Lamb of God who takes away the sin of the world" (John 1:29), "the Word [who] became flesh" (John 1:14a), "the Son of God" (John 1:34). He is the one who both cleansed the temple of God and claimed to be the temple of God (John 2:16–22; Malachi 3:1), the one who said, "All authority has been given to Me in heaven and on earth. Go therefore…" (Matthew 28:18–19a). He is the one who suffered, then entered into glory according to the Old Testament Scriptures (Luke 24:25–27, 44–46; Acts 26:22–23; 1 Peter 1:10–12), the one who has "all things in subjection under His feet," who is "head over

---

[10] See Rydelnik, *The Messianic Hope*, 161. Commenting on the relationship between Isaiah 7 and Micah 5, he says: "If a plainly messianic passage like Mic 5:2–5 cites Isa 7:13-15, it shows that the earliest interpretation of Isa 7:14 (and no less, an inspired interpretation) recognizes the messianic prophecy of the virgin birth" (161).

all things to the church" (Ephesians 1:22), the church being "a holy temple in the Lord" (Ephesians 1:21), "a dwelling of God in the Spirit" (Ephesians 1:22), and "the household of God" (1 Timothy 3:15; Hebrews 3:1–6). He is the agent through whom "many sons [are brought] to glory" (Hebrews 2:10), who is coming again that those He has called "may gain [His] glory" (2 Thessalonians 3:14), who will usher in "new heavens and a new earth, in which righteousness dwells" (2 Peter 3:13). He is the one who was sent by the Father in "the fullness of the time…born of a woman, born under the Law, so that He might redeem" and "that [the redeemed] might receive the adoption as sons" and the gift of the Spirit (Galatians 4:4–6). In other words, the one who brings the sin-stained, cursed creation to its new state of existence is our Lord Jesus Christ, the skull-crushing seed of the woman, the incarnate Son of God (for us and for our salvation). He is the second man, the last Adam, the Lord of glory, who is coming again to raise the dead, condemn the wicked, and make all things new. He does these things by virtue of His sufferings and glory.

Toward Understanding the Creator's Rest

The connections that were noted between the end of the Bible and its beginning are very instructive for our study at this point. Here are some reasons why those connections are important for understanding the Creator's rest.

First, *the connections between the end of the Bible and its beginning set the broader, big-picture context in order that the details might be easier to understand.* When we know the end of the story, we may better know the beginning and everything in between. For example, at the end of the Bible, the entire new earth is sacred space. God dwells with his people in that place. In the beginning of the Bible, the sacred space was limited to the garden of Eden. In the middle of the Bible, we see altars, a tabernacle, Israel's temple, Christ himself, and then the church as sacred space—where God dwells with man in a special, unique way. All of these things point forward. They are symbolic of God's special dwelling among men on the earth but also mini-glimpses of the future. One day the whole earth will be sacred space where God dwells with men. Stephen G. Dempster says of the Old Testament what is true of the entire Bible, "The goal of the canon is clearly the great house of God, which is as inclusive as the globe."[11] What was proffered in the garden and spoiled by sin is brought to completion and perfection by our Lord Jesus Christ. As Richard B. Gaffin, Jr. asserts, "[R]

---

[11] Stephen G. Dempster, *Dominion and dynasty: A theology of the Hebrew Bible* (Downers Grove, IL: InterVarsity Press, 2003, reprinted 2006), 227.

edemption restores creation from the ravages of sin and perfects it."[12] Redemption is more than the restoration of creation; it is its perfection.

Second, *the connections between the end of the Bible and its beginning put the Creator's rest in the context of completed temple-building.* This will be discussed further below, but for now remember that temples are where God dwells on earth among men. The first temple was the garden of Eden, the first high mountain of the earth, where God dwelled with Adam and Eve. The Creator's rest comes after He made the earth; it comes after He completed the crafting of His temple.

Third, *the connections between the end of the Bible and its beginning instruct us that the Bible goes from that which was not accomplished by the first Adam to what God Himself accomplishes through the last Adam, our Lord Jesus Christ.* In other words, the end is better than the beginning. The Bible goes from old creation to a cursed creation to a new creation via redemption. It goes from a good creation made bad by Adam's disobedience to a new, perfected creation made so by Christ's life-unto-death-unto-life obedience (Romans 5:12–21; 8:16–25), His sufferings and glory.

Fourth, *the connections between the end of the Bible and its beginning help us understand the gospel.* God takes it upon Himself to dwell among men as the man, Christ Jesus. He came to be the hero of redemption, a new creation, to do what Adam failed to do, to be the agent through whom many sons are brought to glory through sinless obedience. Because of sin, the last Adam, the Lord Jesus Christ, came to suffer unto death for the forgiveness of our sins and create a seed, or spiritual children, who one day will inhabit the new earth, enjoying inviolable communion with God. What Adam brought upon us all (i.e., guilt and the condemnation that comes as a result of it), Christ absolves, and what Adam failed to do, Christ does (i.e., many sons are brought to glory through his obedience). God worked, then entered into rest. Adam sinned and thus did not enter into God's rest. Christ worked (i.e., his suffering obedience), then entered into rest (i.e., via his resurrection), all for us and the glory of God. This is the gospel.

Review and Preview

We have seen that the end of the Bible is like the beginning, but much better. God brings creation to a glorious goal—a new heaven and a new earth that will never be tainted by sin. What God originally intended for the earth comes to fruition when all history is brought to its apex, its cli-

---

[12] Richard B. Gaffin, Jr., "The Redemptive-Historical View," in *Biblical Hermeneutics: Five Views*, eds. Stanley E. Porter & Beth W. Stovell (Downers Grove, IL: IVP Academic, 2012), 92.

max, at Christ's second coming (2 Peter 3:10–13). Once the judgment dust is cleared, there will be a new heaven and a new earth in which dwells righteousness. The whole earth will be a special dwelling place of God among men. It will be a temple in which man communes with God. This is the eternal state, the consummated state, the rest of God for man.

This future state of affairs is not plan B. God created Adam as an image-bearer. He entered into covenant with him, giving Adam the responsibility to be fruitful and multiply and fill the earth with others like him. He started this task in the garden of Eden, which, as we have seen, was the earth's first localized temple. Adam was commissioned to expand that Edenic temple to the four corners of the earth. Though Adam sinned not long after he was created and thus failed his assignment, God has taken it upon Himself to ensure that the earth is full of His recognized and adored glory and that that glory is enjoyed by an innumerable host of men and women. This He does through the mighty warrior, our Lord Jesus Christ. Not only that, but God will make the world to come even better than the first world. It will not only be absent of sin; sin will no longer be possible.

We are now considering the Creator's rest. As was argued above, the end of the Bible is the beginning of the Bible glorified. We looked at the bookends of the Bible because understanding that the end is the beginning glorified helps one understand the Creator's rest in Genesis 2:1–3, the seventh day of the earth's history.

The next chapter will consider the Creator's rest recorded for us in Genesis 2:1–3. The following chapters will consider various texts throughout Scripture which reflect on Genesis 2:1–3. The goal is to show that the Creator's rest is not only a divine act symbolizing God's enthronement over the entire creation, but a creational ordinance for man, concentrating initially upon Adam that he be like God, building a temple, then finally resting from temple-building work, thereby entering God's rest—a state of existence qualitatively better than Adam's created state.

10

The Doctrine of the Christian Sabbath
Genesis 2:1–3

In this chapter, we will consider Genesis 2:1–3—its context and its elements. Two other issues will be discussed as well—whether or not the Creator's rest is exclusively proleptic and whether or not the Creator's rest constitutes a creational ordinance from the beginning for man.

The Context of Genesis 2:1–3

Genesis 1 gives us a broad overview of the six days of the creation week. Man takes center stage in 1:26ff. (and then especially in chapter 2:4ff.) as the only creature of God's creative work made in his image. Man is unique. He was created in the image of God and is responsible to be like God according to his creaturely capacities.

Genesis 2:4ff. focuses on man in the image of God and his Edenic vocation. Chapter 2:4ff. takes us back to the sixth day of creation. In 2:7 we are told that "God formed man of dust from the ground, and breathed into his nostrils the breath of life; and man became a living being." God made a garden and placed Adam in that garden to cultivate and keep it. We have seen that this is priestly language. Adam was a priest in the Eden-temple. In the midst of the garden were two sacred trees—the tree of life and the tree of the knowledge of good and evil. These functioned sacramentally, as visible words indicating curse and blessing. Out of Eden flowed a river. Eden was on a mountain, called God's garden and mountain in Ezekiel 28. There were also precious stones in Eden. This is the language that is consistently applied by the Bible to other earthly sanctuaries, including the eternal state as depicted in Revelation 21–22. Many of these things end up being used to describe the new heavens and the new earth. The garden was a limited space on the earth in which Adam was in communion with God as a sinless image-bearer. The garden of Eden was God's special dwelling place on the earth among men. In that sense, it was the first temple on the earth and Adam was this world's first prophet, priest, and king.

In Genesis 3, we are given the chilling news that Adam sinned against God, failing to comply with the covenant imposed upon him. Not only did he not subdue the earth and fill it with others like him, but prior to Eve bearing children, he sinned and brought a curse upon us all (Romans 5), as well as the earth itself (Romans 8). He took and ate of the forbidden tree. Adam never got farther than the garden in his Edenic, covenantal vocation. He sinned in the Eden-paradise and, as a result, was exiled.

In order to understand the Creator's rest, we must have a firm grasp upon the context in which it comes to us. God creates the earth, then rests. He ceases from His creative work and then enters another manner of activity—rest.

The Elements of Genesis 2:1–3

Genesis 2:1–3 reads:

Thus the heavens and the earth were completed, and all their hosts. By the seventh day God completed His work which He had done, and He rested on the seventh day from all His work which He had done. Then God blessed the seventh day and sanctified it, because in it He rested from all His work which God had created and made.

Creation Completed

There is a clear announcement that the work of creation was completed: "Thus the heavens and the earth were completed, and all their hosts. By the seventh day God completed His work which He had done" (Genesis 2:1–2a). God took six days to create (i.e., "His work") and then went from creating to sustaining that which He had created. He went from the work of creation to the work of providence. But remember that God's work of creation entailed the building of a temple. Heaven is His throne and the earth is His footstool (Isaiah 66:1). God built a temple, then God rested.[1]

---

[1] We will explore this in more detail below.

In verses 2 and 3, Moses informs us three times of God's "work." Gordon J. Wenham observes:

> It is the ordinary word for human work (cf. 39:11; Exod 20:9), and it is therefore a little unexpected that the extraordinary divine activity involved in creating heaven and earth should be so described. It may be, as Westermann suggests (1:170), that this word has been deliberately chosen to hint that man should stop his daily work on the seventh day. The phraseology of Exod 40:33, "And Moses finished the work," is particularly close to this verse and suggests that the erection of the tabernacle is being compared to God's creation of the world.[2]

Could it be that the Creator's acts of work and rest suggest that man was to follow this divine pattern? This is at least plausible at this point of the discussion.

God Rested

There is an announcement that, once the work of creation was completed, God rested from that work: "and He rested [Heb. *shabath*] on the seventh day from all His work which He had done" (Genesis 2:2). This rest is not to be thought of as necessary because God had become weary or tired like His creatures do. God does not get exhausted. He does not need to be replenished with divine energy. He simply went from one external work to another. So, what does it mean that God rested? Exodus 31:17 comments on this very text. Moses writes, "for in six days the LORD made heaven and earth, but on the seventh day He ceased [Heb. *shabath*] *from labor*, and was refreshed." Again, it cannot be that resting and being refreshed are necessary because God was tired. Resting and being refreshed are somewhat opposite to working. It will be argued below that since God's work was the work of a master temple-builder, once He finished the work of cosmic temple-building, He went from one activity to another. The earth had become His footstool. He went from *royal work* to *royal rest* as King of the completed creation. He went from making the heavens and the earth, and everything in them, to a position of enthronement over the sphere He created. Let me explain why this is so.

In Genesis 1 and 2, God worked then entered into rest. The work of creation is acknowledged by many as "the making of the cosmic temple."[3]

---

[2] Wenham, *Genesis 1-15*, 35.

[3] Hamilton, *What is Biblical Theology?*, 28. See also James M. Hamilton, Jr., *God's Glory in Salvation through Judgment: A Biblical Theology* (Wheaton, IL: Crossway, 2010), 73, where he says God is "…presented as building for himself a

As Kline says, "The cosmic structure was built as a habitation for the Creator himself. Heaven and earth were erected as a house of God, a palace of the Great King..."[4] This will become clear in the discussion below.

One thing of great importance to see is the pattern of connecting temple completion and rest in the Bible. For instance, consider Psalm 132:7–8 and 13–14:

> Let us go into His dwelling place; Let us worship at His footstool. Arise, O LORD, to Your *resting place* [emphasis added], You and the ark of Your strength. (Psalm 132:7–8)

> For the LORD has chosen Zion; He has desired it for His habitation. "This is My *resting place* [emphasis added] forever; Here I will dwell, for I have desired it. (Psalm 132:13–14)

God's resting place is the temple. There he dwells. Earth is His footstool, and His throne is in heaven.

Israel's temple was a replica of the original creation.[5] Psalm 78:69 indicates this. It says, "And He built His sanctuary like the heights, Like the earth which He has founded forever." Beale comments:

> The psalmist is saying that, in some way, God designed Israel's earthly temple to be comparable to the heavens and to the earth. Similarly, the earlier 'pattern of the tabernacle and the pattern of all its furniture' was made 'after the [heavenly] pattern...which was shown...on the mountain' (Exod. 25:9, 40; cf. Exod. 26:30; 27:8; Num. 8:4; Heb. 8:5; 9:23–24).[6]

Various texts in the Pentateuch and one in Hebrews help illustrate Beale's point:

> According to all that I am going to show you, *as* the pattern of the tabernacle and the pattern of all its furniture, just so you shall construct *it*. (Exodus 25:9)

cosmic temple. In this cosmic temple, he places his image, whose task is to fill the earth and subdue it such that the glory of Yahweh covers the land as the waters cover the sea..." In subsequent discussion, Hamilton cites J. H. Walton, William J. Dumbrell, G. K. Beale, Gordon J. Wenham, and T. Desmond Alexander. These authors affirm that creation is a cosmic temple and the garden of Eden was earth's first localized temple, the earth's first special dwelling place of God among men.

---

[4] Kline, *Kingdom Prologue*, 27.

[5] See the discussions in Beale, *The Temple and the Church's Mission*, 31ff. and the entry for "Temple," in *Dictionary of Biblical Imagery*, 849-51.

[6] Beale, *The Temple and the Church's Mission*, 32.

> See that you make *them* after the pattern for them, which was shown to you on the mountain. (Exodus 25:40)
>
> Then you shall erect the tabernacle according to its plan which you have been shown in the mountain. (Exodus 26:30)
>
> You shall make it hollow with planks; as it was shown to you in the mountain, so they shall make *it*. (Exodus 27:8)
>
> Now this was the workmanship of the lampstand, hammered work of gold; from its base to its flowers it was hammered work; according to the pattern which the LORD had showed Moses, so he made the lampstand. (Numbers 8:4)
>
> ...who serve a copy and shadow of the heavenly things, just as Moses was warned *by God* when he was about to erect the tabernacle; for, "SEE," He says, "THAT YOU MAKE all things ACCORDING TO THE PATTERN WHICH WAS SHOWN YOU ON THE MOUNTAIN." (Hebrews 8:5)

Citing some of the same texts as Beale, the *Dictionary of Biblical Imagery* says:

> ...the temple is an *earthly archetype of the *heavenly reality, just as *Moses constructed the *tabernacle after the heavenly pattern revealed to him on *Sinai (Ex 25:9, 40).[7]
>
> ...the temple also represents the entire cosmos; it is a microcosm of all creation. "He built his sanctuary like the high heavens, like the earth, which he has founded forever" (Ps 78:69 NRSV)....
> Both the temple and the tabernacle embody a theology of creation and God's presence within it. Consequently there are parallels between the *Genesis creation account and the accounts of the building of the tabernacle and the temple....
> As a symbol of pristine creation the temple evokes the *Garden of Eden, or paradise....[8]

Another text worth noting in this discussion is 1 Chronicles 28:2. David connects building a home for the ark and that home as God's footstool:

> Then King David rose to his feet and said, "Listen to me, my brethren and my people; I *had* intended to build a *permanent* [emphasis added] home for the ark of the covenant of the LORD and for the footstool of our God... (1 Chronicles 28:2)

---

[7] *Dictionary of Biblical Imagery*, 849.
[8] Ibid., 850.

David intended to build a temple, which is the place on earth where God dwells with men, a localized footstool for God, who is King over all, the earth being His cosmic footstool. Exodus 20:11 says:

> For in six days the LORD made the heavens and the earth, the sea and all that is in them, and *rested* [emphasis added] on the seventh day; therefore the LORD blessed the sabbath day and made it holy.

Notice the word translated as "rested." It is not the same Hebrew word Moses used in Genesis 2:2. There he used the word *shabath*. Here in Exodus 20:11, he uses a word (i.e., *nuach*) that is built off the same root as the words translated as "resting place" in Psalm 132:8 and 14 and "permanent" in 1 Chronicles 28:2. As Kline says:

> The Scriptures in effect interpret God's Sabbath rest at the completion of his cosmic house as an enthronement when they present the converse of this idea by portraying God's enthronement above the ark in earthly replicas of his cosmic house as a Sabbath rest.... When God's seventh day resting is referred to in the Sabbath commandment in the Decalogue (Exod 20:11), the verbal root of *menuchah*, "rest," the term used for God's temple enthronement in these passages, is employed in the place of the verb *shabath* used in Gen 2:2.[9]

The words of Isaiah 66:1 may help at this point: "Heaven is My throne and the earth is My footstool. Where then is a house you could build for Me? And where is a place that I may rest?" Here heaven and earth are related to each other. Heaven and earth are identified as God's "throne-house."[10]

The Creator's rest indicates the completion of the earth as His cosmic temple and the announcement of His enthronement over it as King. This is a royal rest. Kline says:

> ...this rest of God may be more specifically understood as a royal kind of resting. The royal nature of the rest follows from the royal nature of the work. God created the heaven and the earth to be his cosmic palace and accordingly his resting is an occupying of his palace, a royal session. The dawning of the Sabbath witnesses a new enthronement of Elohim.[11]

To predicate an enthronement of God on the seventh day of creation history is not to deny that the creative activity of God is from the beginning an exercise of an ultimate and absolute sovereignty which he enjoys as an

---

[9] Kline, *Kingdom Prologue*, 35.
[10] Ibid.
[11] Ibid., 34.

original and everlasting prerogative of his very godhood. It is simply saying that creation produced a new theater for the manifestation of God's eternal majesty, and when the heavenly throne and earthly footstool had been prepared, God assumed his rightful royal place in that new sphere.[12]

This being the case, the main event of the week of creation occurred on the seventh day. As noted in previous discussion, the narrative is heading to a climax. Though man in the image of God is the climax of the things created in the first six days, the actions of God in the creation week reach their zenith on the day God rested, the seventh day of earth's first week. John Walton says:

> On the seventh day we finally discover that God has been working to achieve a rest. This seventh day is not a theological appendix to the creation account, just to bring closure now that the main event of creating people has been reported. Rather, it intimates the purpose of creation and of the cosmos. God does not set up the cosmos so that only people will have a place. He also sets up the cosmos to serve as his temple…[13]

This understanding of God's rest puts peculiar importance upon it. It is not a mere postscript; it is an exclamation point. Beale calls the seventh day "God's climactic resting from his creative work."[14]

Seventh Day Blessed and Sanctified

There is an announcement that God blessed the seventh day and sanctified it, as well as a reason annexed to this blessing and sanctification: "Then God blessed the seventh day and sanctified it, because in it He rested from all His work which God had created and made" (Genesis 2:3). This is the only day of the creation week that is said to be "blessed" and "sanctified." It is hereby set apart. It has a unique status and function. God did not do this out of any felt need or in order for Him to become complete. He did this for man, just as He took six days to create for man. The Creator's rest is a teaching tool for man, as are the six days of creation. It not only tells us something about what God did a long time ago (i.e., He built a cosmic temple, then rested), but it is also a symbol of what could and will happen in the future for man. This rest of God is something man

---

[12] Kline, *Kingdom Prologue*, 37.

[13] As quoted in Alexander, *From Eden to the New Jerusalem*, 24, cited as "J. H. Walton, 'Creation', in T. D. Alexander and D. W. Baker (eds.), *Dictionary of Old Testament Pentateuch* (Downers Grove: IVP; Leicester: IVP, 2003), p. 161."

[14] Beale, *A New Testament Biblical Theology*, 777.

will one day enjoy; and this we know because the Bible tells us, as will be seen below.

Many have noted the peculiarity of the seventh day being blessed and sanctified. To what do these terms refer? Dressler asserts that "...it has been argued convincingly that the terms are synonymous in this passage so that the blessing of the seventh day is to be understood "in the sense of 'sanctification,' i.e., separation and election.""[15] Dressler asserts this view and even quotes someone for support, but there is no discussion to prove the assertion and the endnote referring to Helfmyer is only bibliographic. This appears to be the fallacy of argument by assertion. This is an odd way of defending one's view, especially in a volume which was scrutinized by all its contributors ("doctoral or post-doctoral research students") prior to print.[16] Dressler's view, as stated, is less than convincing. Turretin addressed it as follows:

> Objection two: that sanctification and blessing are to be understood with regard to the intention and destination, not with regard to the execution. We answer that he is said to have blessed the day in the same way that he rested upon it. Now he did not rest only in intention because he intended to do it, but really because he ceased from his works.[17]

The Creator "blessed the seventh day." While seeking to prove that the Creator's rest is a mandate for humans, Beale comments:

> ...the Hebrew word for "bless" is normally restricted to living beings in the OT and typically does not apply to something being blessed or sanctified only for God's sake. Accordingly, Gen. 2:3 appears to be directed to humanity as a creational ordinance to regard the seventh day of the week to be "blessed and set apart" by God. This is suggested further by the fact that the only uses of the verb for "bless" in Gen. 1–2 outside of 2:3 refer to God blessing nonhuman animate creation (1:22) or humans (1:28). It is not until Gen. 14:20 that the verb is applied to God ("blessed be God Most High"). Outside of Gen. 2:3, the object of what is "blessed" is never indefinite. Job 42:12 is the only place in the OT where days are "blessed" and the blessing is for humans ("And the LORD blessed the latter days of Job more than his beginning").[18]

---

[15] Dressler, "The Sabbath in the Old Testament," 29. For further interaction with Dressler at this point see Martin, *The Christian Sabbath*, 42, n. 21.

[16] The words in quotes ("doctoral or post-doctoral research students") are those of D. A. Carson. See D. A. Carson, "Preface," in *From Sabbath to Lord's Day*, 11.

[17] Turretin, *Elenctic Theology*, 11.8.8 (2:79-80).

[18] Beale, *A New Testament Biblical Theology*, 778. Beale's observations have been made by many others in the relevant literature.

Commenting on the term "sanctified," Beale observes that the Hebrew form of the word used in Genesis 2:3 "almost always refers to setting apart humans or things for human cultic [i.e., worship] use."[19] He continues:

> However, the only days said to be "set apart" or "holy" in the OT are Sabbaths and various festival days. In every case, the day is clearly "set apart" for humans to observe…. Thus, outside of Gen. 2:3, all other sacred days include humans and, at least implicitly, God, in their purview. Accordingly, Claus Westermann asserts that one should have an "exegetical instinct" that not only is the seventh day solemn to God, but also the day "must in some way or other signify something related to people," because of the "fact that the verb 'to sanctify' expresses a cultic idea [elsewhere in the OT] and cannot be referred to a day destined [only] for God himself."[20]

Beale concludes:

> Thus, the immediate context of Gen. 2:3 and the pattern of uses of "sanctify a day" elsewhere in the OT point to the seventh day being "blessed" and "set apart" for humans to observe and celebrate.[21]

Similar to Beale, commenting on Genesis 2:1–3, Wenham says:

> …this passage…asserts that the Sabbath idea is as old as creation itself. In observing the seventh day as holy, man is imitating his creator's example….
>
> … The seventh day is the very first thing to be hallowed in Scripture, to acquire that special status that properly belongs to God alone. In this

---

[19] Beale, *A New Testament Biblical Theology*, 778.

[20] Ibid., 778-79; brackets original.

[21] Ibid., 779. In Thomas R, Schreiner, "Good-bye and Hello: The Sabbath Command for New Covenant Believers," in *Progressive Covenantalism: Charting a Course between Dispensational and Covenant Theologies*, ed. Stephen J. Wellum and Brent E. Parker (Nashville: B&H Academic, 2016), he provides push-back to Beale's treatment, though he does not interact with the specifics of Beale's discussion of the terms *blessed* and *sanctified*, except to casually dismiss it as irrelevant to believers today. Schreiner says: "Greg Beale, on the other hand, supports Sabbath keeping from the creation narrative by observing that the blessing of the seventh day and making it holy is for the sake of human beings. Even if this is the case, it does not follow that the seventh day applies to new covenant believers in the same way it applied to Israel…" (161). On the one hand, I believe this is the case. On the other, neither Beale nor anyone else I have ever read on this issue argues from a creational ordinance of the Sabbath to "the seventh day appl[ying] to new covenant believers in the same way it applied to Israel…"

way Genesis emphasizes the sacredness of the Sabbath. Coupled with the threefold reference to God resting from all his work on that day, these verses give the clearest of hints of how man created in the divine image should conduct himself on the seventh day.[22]

Considering the use of the terms *blessed* and *sanctified* elsewhere sheds needed light on their intended meaning in the context of Genesis 2. The divine blessing and sanctification of the seventh day is a service to man, these divine acts being for man's benefit and imitation. Wenham concludes:

> Finally, as the creator rested on the seventh day from all his work, so Genesis 2:1–3 implies man should also take a break from his labors. If the other parts of creation were designed for man's benefit, so too was the Sabbath.[23]

A Proleptic Rest in Genesis 2?

Some have understood the Creator's rest as proleptic; that is, as establishing a pattern for man to follow, but not imposed as such until much later in man's history (i.e., Exodus 16 and 20). This view is not new. In the early seventeenth century, Bownd acknowledges a form of this view and interacts with it.[24] Likewise, Owen interacts with this view in at least two places in his treatise on a day of sacred rest.[25] Owen recognized that some viewed Genesis 2:3 as "a prolepsis."[26] The Creator's rest in Genesis 2:3 represents something to be instituted for man in the future. Between the Creator's initial rest and that future institution, there is no Sabbath day for anyone (and no seven-day week, according to some). One form of the proleptic view Owen addresses sees the sanctification of the seventh day occurring at Sinai. Owen seeks to state this view as follows:

> And so the sense of the words must be, that "God rested on the seventh day from all his work which he had made;" that is, the next day after the finishing of the works of creation: wherefore, two thousand four hundred years after, "God blessed the seventh day, and sanctified it,"—not that seventh day whereon he rested, with them that succeeded in the like

---

[22] Wenham, *Genesis 1-15*, 36.
[23] Ibid., 38.
[24] Bownd, *The True Doctrine of the Sabbath*, 44.
[25] Owen, *Works*, 18:294 and 299-300.
[26] Ibid., 18:294. Owen carefully distinguished between various forms of the proleptic view.

revolution of time, but a seventh day that fell out so long after, which was not blessed nor sanctified before!²⁷

Owen's discussion is quite fascinating. It reveals that the proleptic view is not new and has been discussed before. At one point in his discussion, Owen says, "I know not well how men learned and sober can offer more hardship unto a text than is put upon this before us by this interpretation."²⁸

Similar to Owen, Turretin discusses the institution of the Sabbath before the promulgation of the law via Moses. He offers six arguments in favor of a creational institution. The arguments are as follows: from Genesis 2:3; from Exodus 16:23, 25; from Exodus 20:8; from Hebrews 4:3–4; from the religion of the fathers; and from traces of a Sabbath among Gentiles.²⁹ While discussing his first argument, he says:

> This is said proleptically by Moses to show the equity, not the beginning of the command; so that God may be said to have sanctified this day, not when he ceased from his works, but when he gave the manna or when he delivered the law by Moses. We answer that although the Scriptures sometimes use a prolepsis, we are never to have recourse to it unless driven by necessity. But here there is no necessity for a prolepsis and many reasons stand in the way of its adoption. First, as God is said to have rested from his works on the seventh day properly and historically (not proleptically), so also to have blessed and sanctified it. These things are proposed in the same connection and ought to be understood concerning the same seventh day of creation; not of another similar day (which also the thrice repeated demonstrative article *h* indicates). Second, on the supposition of a prolepsis, the sense of the words of Moses will be: God, after the six days' work was finished, rested on the seventh day; therefore after the lapse of two thousand four hundred and fifty-three years, he blessed a similar day and sanctified it to sacred use. Everyone sees this to be harsh and forced. Third, no solid reason can be adduced why Moses in a simple narration of history or of events (two thousand years before they occurred) determined to insert something which took place only in his own time. It would plainly tend to obscure rather than explain the history he was composing, not even the slightest intimation of such a prolepsis being introduced.³⁰

---

²⁷ Owen, *Works*, 18:300.

²⁸ Ibid.. See Ames, *The Marrow of Theology*, 3.15.9 (288-89), where he also refutes the view he calls "a prolepsis or anticipation."

²⁹ Turretin, *Elenctic Theology*, 11.8.6-18 (2:79-83).

³⁰ Ibid., 11.8.7 (2:79).

In the seventeenth century after Owen and Turretin, John Bunyan and Benjamin Keach held a version of the proleptic view of God's rest.[31] Both men were combating seventh-day Baptists in the late seventeenth century. Both affirmed that time to worship God is moral and perpetual, being written on man's heart via creation. But neither affirmed that God required obedience to this moral law in terms of a day of worship until the Sabbath was instituted with Israel. This seems quite odd. If a law is moral, it is perpetual. They are to be commended for acknowledging time to worship God as moral and advocating a Sabbath under the inaugurated new covenant (i.e., the Lord's Day). I cannot, however, understand how one can affirm a moral law from creation but delay the revelation of a positive law to apply the moral law until Israel.

Recently, Robert P. Martin discussed the proleptic view. He interacted with a chapter in *From Sabbath to Lord's Day* (edited by Carson, referenced above). Dressler claims that both the Sabbath and the seven-day week came with Israel, first instituted by God according to Exodus 16 and then put in the form of a command in Exodus 20. He views Genesis 2:3 as proleptic. He says, "…we interpret this in terms of an eschatological, proleptic sign indicating some future rest."[32] This is said with reference to the divine acts of sanctifying and blessing. What is that future rest? Concluding his discussion about the inauguration of the Sabbath for Israel, he says:

> Genesis 2 does not teach a "creation ordinance" in our opinion; the institution of the Sabbath for the people of Israel, however, was based on the creation account and became a sign of God's redemptive goal for mankind.[33]

Dressler views the Creator's rest as a sign of the future, becoming "a sign of God's *redemptive* [emphasis added] goal for mankind" when it was instituted for Israel. This would mean that the Sabbath for Israel is broader than a sign of the Mosaic covenant. In his conclusion, he mentions that "as a sign of the [Mosaic] covenant it was to last as long as that covenant."[34]

---

[31] See John Bunyan, "Questions about the Nature and Perpetuity of the Seventh-Day Sabbath," in *The Works of John Bunyan*, Volume Two (Edinburgh: The Banner of Truth Trust, 1991), 359-85 and Benjamin Keach, *The Jewish Sabbath Abrogated: or, the Saturday Sabbatarians confuted* (London: John Marshall, 1700). Keach's view, sadly, is not in accord with the 2LCF, which he subscribed in 1689.

[32] Dressler, "The Sabbath in the Old Testament," 29. By proleptic, I understand Dressler to mean an anticipation or representation of something yet future. This seems to be Schreiner's view as well. See the discussion below.

[33] Dressler, "The Sabbath in the Old Testament," 30.

[34] Ibid., 34.

The last sentence of his discussion ends with these words: "...Israel... looked forward with joy and anticipation to the coming of the final Rest."[35]

I appreciate the acknowledgement that the Sabbath has an eschatological goal in mind, but Dressler merely asserts such without proof. Also, his view seems to entail that the Creator's rest takes on eschatological significance in view of or because of the fall into sin and its institution for Israel. Dressler was quoted above as saying, "...we interpret this in terms of an eschatological, proleptic sign indicating some future rest."[36] The "some future rest" is "God's redemptive goal for mankind." It has been mentioned above that the Creator's rest has eschatological significance prior to and quite apart from the fall into sin. It is first a creational goal for man. It becomes a redemptive goal due to the entrance of sin, but its primal function precedes the need for redemption. It is protologically eschatological at its inception. It was the symbol and type of a quality of life man could have entered via obedience but did not. This will be further discussed when Hebrews 4 is considered, which ties together God's rest, Israel's rest, the Sabbath rest that remains for the people of God, Christ's entrance into rest, and the fully-consummated eschatological rest.

Thomas Schreiner holds a view similar to Dressler's. He suggests "that the seventh day [i.e., of creation] bears a symbolic significance."[37] He says, "The OT Sabbath points forward to the eschatological Sabbath rest..."[38] He makes this statement as well:

> The seventh day of creation, then, is not necessarily tied to any particular day of the week: it points to, as Hebrews teaches (4:1–11), *and especially in light of the fall*, the eschatological rest that believers now enjoy in Christ and will enjoy in fullness in the new creation.[39]

Notice the words, "especially in light of the fall." This is similar to Dressler's statement above. A little later in Schreiner's discussion, he says:

> Hence, the Sabbath [i.e., for Israel under the Mosaic covenant] points back to the rest lost in creation and forward to the rest that will ultimately be enjoyed in Jesus Christ.[40]

---

[35] Dressler, "The Sabbath in the Old Testament," 35. In earlier discussion, he asks, "...is it [i.e., the Sabbath] rather an Israelite institution based on the heavenly pattern and eschatological in its ultimate purpose and goal?" (27).

[36] Dressler, "The Sabbath in the Old Testament," 29.

[37] Schreiner, "Good-bye and Hello," 161.

[38] Ibid., 160.

[39] Ibid., 161; emphasis added.

[40] Ibid., 165.

> The Sabbath rest [i.e., for Israel under the Mosaic covenant] points back to creation rest and is consummated in our rest in Christ.[41]

While commenting on Hebrews 4, he says:

> The author pulls in God's creation rest in 4:3–4, indicating that the rest promised to believers transcends residence in the land. The Sabbath points back to the rest of creation *which was lost in the fall* and is ultimately fulfilled in the new creation, as Hebrews argues.[42]

> The Sabbath points backward to the rest of creation *lost in the fall* and forward to the heavenly rest which belongs to those who believe in Christ.[43]

> To sum up, the letter to the Hebrews teaches that God's seventh-day rest points to the eschatological rest believers will enjoy in the heavenly city—a rest *provided at creation, lost in the fall*, and *restored in Jesus Christ*.[44]

As with Dressler, the acknowledgement that the Sabbath has an eschatological goal in mind is appreciated. Schreiner's view, however, seems, at least at various points, to entail that the Creator's rest takes on eschatological significance in view of or because of the fall into sin and its institution for Israel. As argued above (and below), the Creator's rest possesses eschatological significance for man prior to and apart from the fall into sin. Though sin makes redemption necessary if man is to enjoy the Creator's rest, this rest was not something Adam *had* and *lost*. It was proffered to him, but never attained by him.

The exclusively proleptic view of Genesis 2:3 (in whatever form in which it might be presented) does not take into account various factors that lead to viewing the Creator's rest as both paradigmatic for man and proleptic, or, better stated, a symbol and type of eschatological rest prior to the fall into sin.

This is a good point in the discussion to offer arguments in favor of viewing the Creator's rest in Genesis 2:3 as *both* a creational ordinance for man from the beginning *and* as a symbol and type of things to come for man, also from the beginning. Before doing so, it is necessary to distinguish between symbols and types.[45]

A symbol portrays a fact or reality that presently exists. A type is prospective. Perhaps Geerhardus Vos' discussion of the fourth commandment

---

[41] Schreiner, "Good-bye and Hello," 170.
[42] Ibid., 181; emphasis added.
[43] Ibid., 182; emphasis added.
[44] Ibid., 186; emphasis added.
[45] See my discussion of Vos on symbols and types in *The Family Tree*, 207-12.

can help at this juncture.⁴⁶ In his *Biblical Theology*, the fourth commandment gets much more comment from Vos than the others.⁴⁷ One of the reasons is due to its origin and modified applicability throughout redemptive history. He says:

> It must be remembered that the Sabbath, though a world-aged observance, has passed through the various phases of the development of redemption, remaining the same in essence but modified as to its form, as the new state of affairs at each point might require. The Sabbath is not only the most venerable, it is likewise the most living of all the sacramental realities of our religion. It has faithfully accompanied the people of God on their march through the ages.⁴⁸

Another reason for the fourth commandment getting more discussion is due to the principle underlying it: "man must copy God in his course of life."⁴⁹ God's rest is prototypical of man's. "It stands for consummation of a work accomplished and the joy and satisfaction attendant upon it."⁵⁰ This is not only the duty of man individually, but that of the entire race throughout its history.

Probably the greatest reason why Vos gives so much attention to the fourth commandment is due to the transcovenantal, eschatological function of the Sabbath. James T. Dennison comments, "…the fourth precept is an idealizing of a transhistorical and eschatological paradigm."⁵¹ Vos says:

> Before all other important things, therefore, the Sabbath is an expression of the eschatological principle on which the life of humanity has been

---

⁴⁶ The brief discussion of Vos is taken and expanded with permission from my *The Family Tree*, 205-07.

⁴⁷ Vos only discusses the first four commandments. He does so because the last six refer to man's relationship with man; the first four deal with man's relationship with God. The last six commandments, according to Vos, ought to be discussed in a course on Ethics. See Vos, *Biblical Theology*, 134 and James T. Dennison, "Vos on the Sabbath: A Close Reading," *Kerux* 2.1 (May 1987): 61-70, esp. 61-62.

⁴⁸ Vos, *Biblical Theology*, 139. Vos acknowledges emphatically that we have been released from any typical elements subsequently connected to the Sabbath in the OT "but not from the Sabbath as instituted at Creation. In light of this we must interpret certain New Testament statements such as Romans 14.5, 6; Galatians 4.10, 11; Colossians 2.16, 17" (143).

⁴⁹ Vos, *Biblical Theology*, 139.

⁵⁰ Ibid., 140.

⁵¹ Dennison, "Vos on the Sabbath," 62.

constructed. There is to be to the world-process a finale, as there was an overture, and these two belong inseparably together. To give up the one means to give up the other, and to give up either means to abandon the fundamental scheme of Biblical history. Even among Jewish teachers this profound meaning of the Sabbath was not entirely unknown. One of them, being asked what the world to come would be like, answered that it would resemble the Sabbath. In the law, it is true, this thought is not developed further than is done in the primordial statement about God's resting on the seventh day and hallowing it. For the rest, the institution, after having been re-enforced in the Decalogue, is left to speak for itself, as is the case with most institutions of the law. The Epistle to the Hebrews has given us a philosophy of the Sabbath on the largest of scales, partly in dependence on Psa. 95 [*Heb.* 3, 4].[52]

Recall the fact that, for Vos, the Sabbath principle "was true before, and apart from, redemption."[53] The weekly Sabbath is symbolic and typical of "the eschatological structure of history."[54] Life is not aimless; it has a goal beyond it. The successful probation of the covenant of works would have brought the sacramental Sabbath "into the reality it typified, and the entire subsequent course of the history of the race would have been radically different."[55] The theocracy is a typical and "temporary 'mirror' of an eschatological and permanent state, i.e., holiness to the Lord in the arena of the perfect and eternal Sabbath."[56] "[T]he Sabbath principle and the theocratic era both contain and point to something beyond themselves—a heavenly theocracy and an everlasting Sabbath rest."[57] The theocracy functions as a recapitulation of the symbolic and typological pre-redemptive revelation and the covenant of works in the garden of Eden. The Christian Lord's Day, the first day of the week,[58] is both a looking back to the resurrection as the accomplishment of redemption (i.e., "[t]he new exodus in the eschatological lamb of God")[59] and "a sign looking forward to the final eschatological rest."[60] "Weekly sabbatizing is a mirror imaging of eschatological sabbatizing."[61] Though the theocracy was a temporary institution,

---

[52] Vos, *Biblical Theology*, 140.
[53] Ibid.
[54] Ibid.
[55] Ibid.
[56] Dennison, "Vos on the Sabbath," 62.
[57] Ibid.
[58] See Dennison, "Vos on the Sabbath," 67 for a discussion on the change of the day.
[59] Dennison, "Vos on the Sabbath," 62.
[60] Vos, *Biblical Theology*, 141.
[61] Dennison, "Vos on the Sabbath," 64.

its antitype being the church (ultimately in glory), the weekly Sabbath remains with the people of God until its antitype, the eternal state, comes in its fullness.[62] "Our weekly Sabbath now is a reflection of our resurrection union with him who has entered perfectly into his rest—and waits to welcome us to a consummate everlasting Sabbath."[63]

A careful reading of Vos sees him grounding the symbolic and eschatological functions of the Sabbath as beginning with the Creator's rest. The Sabbath principle is pre-redemptive revelation for Vos, something revealed to man as such. A merely proleptic function of the Creator's rest does not give proper place to how the rest of the Bible understands it.

The Creator's Rest as Creational Ordinance for Man

That the Creator's rest establishes a creational ordinance for man from the beginning has been mentioned in the discussion above. The section below will not present the arguments already given. Instead, it will summarize some of those and mention a few others. I will also mention two more in the conclusion to this chapter and explain why these were not developed. Taken cumulatively, I think the case for the Sabbath as a creational ordinance for man from creation is cogent, logical, and, of course, the teaching of the Bible.

God's acts of creation and rest in the context of temple-building and man's vocation as image-bearer argue for the Sabbath as a creational ordinance.

We have noted that divine acts at creation are grounds upon which creaturely response is mandated by Scripture, whether or not one has read it. God is the divine exemplar; man is His image-bearer, made to be like Him according to his created capacities and vocation. As God made a cosmic temple, then sat enthroned over it, so man was to extend the local temple of Eden, then finally enter into a state of enthronement. In light of this, the sufferings and glory of Christ indicate His obedience on our behalf and the reward of enthronement enjoyed by our Lord in His resurrected state now in heaven and to be enjoyed fully and participated in by His children in the age to come on the perfected earth.

---

[62] Dennison, "Vos on the Sabbath," 62-63, 66.
[63] Ibid., 68.

Genesis 2:1–3

God's creational provision for the accounting of time in terms of days and years, including periodic festivals, argues for the seven-day week, and thus a Sabbath day for man as a creational ordinance.

In a previous chapter, mention was made of the days of creation as paradigmatic for man's week. In Genesis 1, a creational provision for the accounting of time on the earth was infused into the created realm. Genesis 1:14–19 says:

> Then God said, "Let there be lights in the expanse of the heavens to separate the day from the night, and let them be for signs and for seasons and for days and years; and let them be for lights in the expanse of the heavens to give light on the earth"; and it was so. God made the two great lights, the greater light to govern the day, and the lesser light to govern the night; *He made* the stars also. God placed them in the expanse of the heavens to give light on the earth, and to govern the day and the night, and to separate the light from the darkness; and God saw that it was good. There was evening and there was morning, a fourth day.

Commenting on Genesis 1:14–19, Wenham says:

> The creation of the sun, moon, and stars is described in much greater length than anything save the creation of man. The description is also quite repetitive. The fullness of the description suggests that the creation of the heavenly bodies held a special significance for the author…[64]

On day four, the Creator infused into the realm of creation the means by which day and night are to be separated (Genesis 1:14, 18) and governed (Genesis 1:16, 18). Psalm 136, evoking God's acts at creation, indicates that the Creator "made the heavens with skill" (Psalm 136:5a), "spread out the earth above the waters" (Psalm 136:6a), "made *the* great lights" (Psalm 136:7a), made "[t]he sun to rule by day" (Psalm 136:8a) and "[t]he moon and stars to rule by night" (Psalm 136:9a). These provisions are coeval with creation. They are the divine means by which humans are to account for temporal divisions, "for days and years" (Genesis 1:14), for "day" and "night" (Genesis 1:16).

Of special interest is the clause in Genesis 1:14, "and let them be for signs and for seasons." The Holman Christian Standard Bible translates this as "They will serve as signs for festivals." The New International Version has "let them serve as signs to mark seasons." The variety in translation

---

[64] Wenham, *Genesis 1-15*, 21.

is interesting to note. This indicates that the translators wrestled with the exact nuances indicated by the terms used. In a 2003 article in the *Tyndale Bulletin*, David J. Rudolph argues for the translation "festivals" or "festivals and seasons."[65] He supports the plausibility of his translation on various factors: modern English and non-English translations,[66] lexicons and theological dictionaries,[67] commentaries,[68] and "recent studies on Israel's calendar."[69] The bulk of his article surveys usage distribution in the Torah. His focus is on the word *moed*, translated "seasons" (NASB and NIV) and "festivals" (HCSB) in Genesis 1:14. He sums up his survey of usage distribution as follows:

> To sum up, out of 224 occurrences of [*moed*] in the Hebrew Bible, 197 are singular and twenty-seven are plural (including Gn. 1:14). Table 3 indicates that of the twenty-six plural forms subsequent to the creation account, twenty-two mean 'festivals'. This demonstrates that the plural form of [*moed*] eighty-five percent of the time means 'festivals' in the Hebrew Bible. The figure rises to one hundred percent in the Torah, the literary background of Genesis 1:14. Moreover, when all the exact lexical forms of [*moed*] in Genesis 1:14 are extracted from Table 3 and evaluated, the 'festivals' rendering occurs one hundred percent of the time.[70]

Rudolph also notes the immediate literary context within which Genesis 1:14 occurs. It contains priestly language and "places strong emphasis on order and separation."[71] The priestly language is seen in the fourth day's provision of "lights." "[A]ll other occurrences of [this term] in the Torah refer to lamps in the [tent of meeting] (Ex. 25:6; 27:20; 35:8, 14, 28; 39:37; Lv. 24:2; Nu. 4:9, 16)."[72] The term "lamp" is used "as a metonymy for sun and moon (Gn. 1:14, 15, 16 [3x])."[73] Rudolph concludes: "…the writer of Genesis 1 uses this cultic imagery to depict the sun and moon as being like 'sacred lamps in the sanctuary of the universe'."[74]

---

[65] David J. Rudolph, "Festivals in Genesis 1:14," *Tyndale Bulletin* 54.2 (2003): 23-40.
[66] Ibid., 23-24.
[67] Ibid., 24.
[68] Ibid., 24-25.
[69] Ibid., 25-26.
[70] Ibid., 31.
[71] Ibid., 33.
[72] Ibid., 32. Wenham, *Genesis 1-15*, says: "'light, lamp' is always used in the Pentateuch to designate the sanctuary lamp in the tabernacle…" (22).
[73] Rudolph, "Festivals in Genesis," 32.
[74] Ibid. Rudolph is quoting another scholar.

The emphasis on order and separation is seen in various ways in Genesis 1.

> God divides his creation into distinct spheres. Light is separated from darkness, day from night, waters above from waters below, earth from seas, plants from trees, birds from fish, cattle from wild animals, and male from female. The verb...(to separate) occurs five times in Genesis 1 (vv. 4, 6, 7, 14, 18). Notably, two out of the five references are to the fourth day of creation; one reference is in Genesis 1:14.
>
> Viewed against the backdrop of *havdil* [i.e., separation] imagery, the string of plural nouns...in Genesis 1:14 may arguably be a division of two types of time: *sacred time* (signs and festivals) and *ordinary time* (days and years).[75]

Commenting on Genesis 1:14, Gordon J. Wenham says, "What is clear is the importance attached to the heavenly bodies' role in determining the seasons, in particular in fixing the days of cultic celebration. This is their chief function."[76] This function is creational, prior to both the fall into sin and Israel's later calendar.

What does all of this have to do with our discussion? There is a creational provision for accounting both ordinary time and sacred time, for days and years, and for festivals in the midst of days and years. These were to occur on a regular basis, the sun and moon being signs which indicate the passing of one day to another. The seventh day should not be forgotten in this creational sequence and qualitative distinction of time. As Randolph says, "Analogous to such a qualitative time distinction is the relationship between the first six days of creation and the seventh day."[77] Relying on Rudolph's work, Beale says:

> Since we have seen that the notion of "sanctify" elsewhere in the OT often is related to setting apart people, things, and certainly days as holy for cultic purposes, it is natural to see that God's sanctifying of the seventh day in Gen. 2:3 is one of those festival days included in Gen. 1:14, which is part of the temporal divisions within which Gen. 1:14 says humans are to live.[78]

Since Genesis 1:14 establishes qualitative time distinctions, the seventh day is the first occurrence of such. It is a day qualitatively distinct from days one through six; on it God rested.

---

[75] Rudolph, "Festivals in Genesis," 33.
[76] Wenham, *Genesis 1–15*, 23.
[77] Rudolph, "Festivals in Genesis," 33.
[78] Beale, *A New Testament Biblical Theology*, 780.

One more factor is important to consider. Rudolph asserted, "…the writer of Genesis 1 uses this cultic imagery to depict the sun and moon as being like 'sacred lamps in the sanctuary of the universe'."[79] If this is the case, and I think the evidence above supports this view, this comports with viewing the heavens and the earth as God's cosmic temple. It also ties in with Adam's identity and vocation. As God worked in creation unto consummation, so Adam was to do the same according to his creaturely capacity and calling. As Beale asserts:

> …just as God subdued and ruled over the chaos at the inception of creation, so Adam was to subdue and rule over the earth [and] just as God created and filled the earth, so was Adam to "be fruitful and multiply and fill the earth."[80]

Just as God entered into his rest from his creative work, so Adam was to do the same according to his creaturely capacity and vocation. Adam, by virtue of his obedience in accord with the covenant imposed upon him, was to work then enter God's rest. Beale says:

> Just as God had achieved heavenly rest after [creating] and constructing the beginning of his creational temple, so Adam presumably would achieve unending rest after…extending the boundaries of the glorious Eden temple around the entire earth.[81]

As Owen says, "for herein [the covenant of works] rest with God was proposed unto him as the end or reward of his own works…"[82] We could add this as well: though Adam failed as a public person to work and then enter God's rest on behalf of others, Christ as a public person successfully worked, then entered rest on behalf of others. The rest God proffered to Adam was attained by Christ, indicated by the reward of resurrection.

The separation of days mentioned above is reflected in the subsequent narrative in Genesis. After the fall into sin, days, weeks, and years are mentioned (e.g., Genesis 5:3–32). Moses notes that after a period of days, cultic acts were conducted. In Genesis 4:3, we read, "So it came about in the

---

[79] Rudolph, "Festivals in Genesis," 32.
[80] Beale, *A New Testament Biblical Theology*, 776.
[81] Ibid., 40.
[82] Owen, *Works*, 18:338. Owen's treatment of "A Day of Sacred Rest" argues in many places for an eschatological function of God's rest from the beginning. He views God's rest as proffering to Adam a quality of life to be obtained via obedience.

course of time that Cain brought an offering to the LORD of the fruit of the ground." No commands for such are mentioned prior to this event. Cain and Abel brought offerings to the LORD without a command recorded by Moses and, literally, "at the end of days." This act of worship occurs after a non-specified period of days after the fall into sin. Somehow, they knew that God required offerings and, quite plausibly, they knew these were to be offered at specific times (Genesis 1:14). As well, Moses wrote of this event that predated him, most likely either by the testimony of others passed down to him or by direct revelation from God. In either case, offerings were made "at the end of days" quite early in the post-fall narrative. The concept of days does not seem to be an introduction of anything new in man's experience, nor does the concept of offerings "at the end of days." If Genesis 1:14 indicates a creational provision for both days, years, and festivals (i.e., acts of worship on a given day or days), then the almost casual mention of offerings "at the end of days" makes sense.[83]

God's making man in His image, with the law written on his heart, argues for the Sabbath as a creational ordinance.

God's acts were divine exemplars for image-bearing man to follow. As the divine exemplar, God gives divine examples, which become positive laws seeking to draw out of man what he knows intuitively (i.e., that time is to be taken to do something other than work). Man cannot work every moment of his life on the earth. But how is he to regulate his time? Owen argues that the works of God directed Adam in his innocence. He states that "the innate light of nature…[was] directed by the works of God…to be one day in seven."[84]

> This was it [i.e., the light of nature within unfallen man] to learn, and this it did learn, from God's creating the world in six days, and resting on the seventh; for God affirms everywhere that because he did so, therefore it was the duty of man to labour on six days, as his occasions do require, and to rest on the seventh. This, therefore, they were taught by those works and rest of God, or it could not be proposed as the reason of their suitable practice; and for this end did God so work and rest.[85]

In this case, the works of God establish positive law.

---

[83] See Martin, *The Christian Sabbath*, 63–65 for discussion on Genesis 4:3–4.
[84] Owen, *Works*, 18:408.
[85] Ibid.

The acts of God at creation gave concrete, revelatory grounds for the innate light of nature in man to objectify what was subjectively part of his created status. As man's unfallen reason encountered the order of creation (i.e., divine revelation), he came to realize that "the law of nature, [required] that in general a proportion of time, by God's appointment, be set apart for the worship of God" (2LCF 22.7a). The proportion of time appointed by God was "one day in seven…from the beginning of the world" (2LCF 22.7). Owen's words may be of help at this juncture.

> …for it is vain to imagine that the world was made in six days, and those closed with a day of rest, without an especial respect unto the obedience of rational creatures, seeing absolutely with respect unto God himself neither of them was necessary. And what he intended to teach them thereby, it was their duty to inquire and know. Hereby, then, man in general was taught obedience and working before he entered into rest; for being created in the image of God, he was to conform himself unto God. As God wrought before he rested, so was he to work before his rest, his condition rendering that working in him obedience, as it was in God an effect of sovereignty. And by the rest of God, or his satisfaction and complacency in what he had made and done, he was instructed to seek rest with God, or to enter into that rest of God, by his compliance with the ends intended.[86]

God's creational institution and perpetuity of marriage is analogous to God's creational institution and perpetuity of the Sabbath.

It was argued in Chapter 8 that marriage, from the beginning, was designed by God to be a type of Christ and His church. Marriage, as a divine creational institution, continues until Christ returns. It is not abrogated by His first coming. So, just as the creational ordinance of marriage is an agelong divine institution pointing to Christ and His church, so similarly with the Creator's rest and a Sabbath day for man. A Sabbath day for man is a creational ordinance pointing to eschatological rest. As a type of the ultimate rest to be enjoyed in Christ, the earthly symbol remains as a Sabbath rest, or a Sabbath-keeping, for the people of God (Hebrews 4:9–10).[87]

---

[86] Owen, *Works*, 18:343–44.
[87] Hebrews 4:9–10 will be discussed in Chapter 13. Thanks to Andrew Lindsey for helping with this section. John Owen also presents an argument concerning a day of sacred rest and marriage as creational institutions. See Owen, *Works*, 18:345.

God's subsequent comments in His written word concerning Genesis 2:1–3 argue for the Sabbath as a creational ordinance.

The use of *blessed* and *sanctified* was discussed above. The uses noted above outside of Genesis 2 are verbal echoes of the Genesis text. There are, however, various types of uses of Genesis 2:1–3 in other passages. Three such passages will be noted especially and discussed in subsequent chapters (Exodus 20:8–11; Mark 2:27–28; and Hebrews 4). What will be argued is that subsequent texts ground the Sabbath (i.e., one day in seven as a day of sacred rest) in creation, assume it to be an age-long ordinance, and incorporate it into the days of the inaugurated new covenant.

Christ's work as a temple-builder who entered His rest at the resurrection argues for the Sabbath as a creational and new-creational ordinance.

Since this will be discussed in a subsequent chapter, brief comment will have to suffice. That Christ is a temple-builder has already been discussed. What will be shown in a subsequent chapter is that Christ worked, then entered into rest via the resurrection. He rose from the dead on the first day of the week, the inauguration of a new creation. Only Christ enjoys God's rest in both body and soul presently,[88] though even that has a future aspect to it in the new heavens and new earth. Since God's rest from the beginning was proffered to Adam as head of the human race and to be obtained by his obedience, Christ as the head of a new race obtained rest through His obedience for those He represented. God's rest for man, however, is not enjoyed in its fullness until the age to come arrives in its fullness. Since God's rest points to that rest and since it always has been a symbol and type of an eschatological state of existence, the day Christ entered that rest symbolizes and points to the same eschatological state of existence. This is why the first day of the week is given a technical name (i.e., the Lord's Day) after Christ's resurrection. Since His resurrection is seen as the inauguration of a new creation, along with this new creation comes a new Sabbath day. Like the old Sabbath day, it looks back to its basis (i.e., the new-creational work of Christ) and forward to its terminus (i.e., the rest of God in the eschaton). Owen says:

---

[88] The cases of Enoch and Elijah are intriguing. Either they are an exception or, more likely, they will experience final glorification at the second coming of our Lord.

...there is an *instructive resemblance* between the works of the one sort and of the other. So the rest of God after the works of the old creation is answered by the rest of the Son of God upon his laying the foundation of the new heavens and new earth in his resurrection.[89]

Conclusion

There are at least two more arguments for the Creator's rest as a creational ordinance: *God's institution of Israel as His corporate son, recapitulating Adam, argues for the Sabbath as a creational ordinance* and *God's institution of Israel as a covenant nation, typological of Christ and the church, argues for the Sabbath as a creational ordinance.* These arguments are beyond the scope of this book.

Genesis 2:1–3 is an important passage in any discussion of the Sabbath. Assuming the exposition above, it establishes a creational ordinance for man and proffers a quality of life to Adam upon his obedience that he failed to attain. It is just this quality of life that our Lord attains via His obedience, the divine approval of such witnessed by His resurrection.

The next chapter will discuss Exodus 16, Exodus 20, and Old Testament prophecy as it relates to the Sabbath under the inaugurated new covenant.

---

[89] Owen, *Works*, 18:379. The words "*instructive resemblance*" are italicized in the original. This is due to the fact that Owen did not view the Creator's rest of Genesis 2 as prefiguring "as in a shadow" a *redemptive* reality. He says: "But that Sabbath originally, and in its whole nature, should be a free institution, to prefigure and as in a shadow to represent any thing spiritual or mystical, afterwards to be introduced, is not nor can be proved. It was, indeed, originally a moral pledge of God's rest and of our interest therein, according to the tenor of the covenant of works; which things belong unto our relation unto God by virtue of the law of our creation" (379). Owen, like Vos (see above), views the Creator's rest as pre-redemptive revelation, a protologically eschatological state of blessedness to be entered into by virtue of obedience to the covenant of works. I think they are right to do so.

11

The Doctrine of the Christian Sabbath
EXODUS AND THE PROPHETS

Exodus 16 and 20 and Old Testament prophecy, as it relates to the Sabbath under the inaugurated new covenant, are important issues when discussing the Creator's rest and a Sabbath for man. In the discussion in this chapter and the two following, I will attempt to build on the previous discussion, showing that what has been established is further developed by the rest of the Bible.[1] As well, I will interact with NCT and those who hold similar views at various points in the discussion.

Exodus 16

Exodus 16 is an important passage in this discussion because it is the first time in the Old Testament the word *Sabbath* is used (Exodus 16:23) and also due to the specific redemptive-historical context in which this Sabbath occurs (i.e., Israel in the wilderness before Sinai).

> Now on the sixth day they gathered twice as much bread, two omers for each one. When all the leaders of the congregation came and told Moses,

---

[1] There are many other issues related to the Sabbath that could have been addressed and which warrant discussion, but they are beyond the scope of this book. For a recent treatment of all the relevant texts in this discussion, I recommend Martin, *The Christian Sabbath*. For an older work that I think does the best job in relating the Creator's rest to the subsequent theology of the Bible, I highly recommend Owen, *Works*, 18:261–460.

then he said to them, "This is what the LORD meant: Tomorrow is a sabbath observance, a holy sabbath to the LORD. Bake what you will bake and boil what you will boil, and all that is left over put aside to be kept until morning." So they put it aside until morning, as Moses had ordered, and it did not become foul nor was there any worm in it. Moses said, "Eat it today, for today is a sabbath to the LORD; today you will not find it in the field. Six days you shall gather it, but on the seventh day, *the* sabbath, there will be none." (Exodus 16:22–26)

This passage indicates that the Sabbath goes back at least to the events recorded in Exodus 16. Like other of the Ten Commandments, the Sabbath command gets some press prior to Exodus 20. In Exodus 16, prior to the promulgation of the Decalogue and the inauguration of the Mosaic covenant, Israel obeyed the Sabbath law by resting "on the seventh day" (Exodus 16:30). God indicted some Israelites, however, for not keeping the Sabbath commandment with these words: "How long do you [plural] refuse to keep My commandments and My instructions [or 'laws'; Heb. *torah*]? See, the LORD has given you the sabbath…" (Exodus 16:28–29). That this is not a new, unknown institution seems to be indicated by the words of Exodus 16:23, "This is what the LORD meant: Tomorrow is a sabbath observance, a holy sabbath to the LORD." The NASB is the only major English translation that translates the Hebrew *dabar* as "meant." It is normally translated at this point as "said" or "commanded." Taking it as "meant" does not necessarily rule out that God had said or commanded these very words (or something close to them) at some point prior to the events narrated in Exodus 16. It is clear that God had previously spoken and instituted a Sabbath for which ancient Israel was accountable prior to the inauguration of the Mosaic covenant.

There are some difficulties that need to be discussed. At first glance, one might take Exodus 16:23 to be epexegetical of Exodus 16:5, which says, "On the sixth day, when they prepare what they bring in, it will be twice as much as they gather daily." There are a few problems with this view. Exodus 16:4–5 are words spoken by the LORD to Moses: "Then the LORD said to Moses…" (Exodus 16:4a). As a result of this, we are told in Exodus 16:6–7 that Moses and Aaron spoke to the sons of Israel. Exodus 16:23 continues the narrative, "Bake what you will bake and boil what you will boil…" Nothing is said of either baking or boiling in the entire episode until this point. In Exodus 16:27 we are told that "on the seventh day… some of the people went out to gather." Then we read:

Then the LORD said to Moses, "How long do you refuse to keep My commandments and My instructions? See, the LORD has given you the sabbath; therefore He gives you bread for two days on the sixth day. Remain every man in his place; let no man go out of his place on the seventh day." So the people rested on the seventh day. (Exodus 16:28–30)

As noted above, the pronoun "you" is plural. That these words were intended to be for the people is clear from their response, indicated by Exodus 16:30, which says, "So the people rested on the seventh day." The question posed, "How long do you refuse to keep My commandments and My instructions?" refers specifically to violations of the Sabbath.

Notice carefully what Moses records in Exodus 16:28, "How long do you refuse to keep My commandments…?" Interacting with Dressler on this passage, who argues that Exodus 16 is the first institution of a Sabbath day for anyone and the beginning of the seven-day week for Israel, Martin says:

> …the stated purpose of this incident [i.e., Exodus 16] was the moral testing of the people—as the Lord says, "that I may test them, whether they will walk in my law, or not" (16:4). And when some failed this test, so that the Lord complains to Moses about those who gathered manna on the Sabbath [Exodus 16:28], his words imply that this incident is indicative of a long-standing pattern of violating his commands in such matters. He says, "How long do you refuse to keep my commandments and my laws?" (16:28). If, as Dressler suggests, the Sabbath law has just been instituted…, we would expect different words, such as, "Why do you refuse to keep my new commandment?" The expression "how long"… seems out of place if this is the first Sabbath in history. Is "how long do you refuse" the language of rebuke for first-time transgression?[2]

The violation of God's law seems to be a recurrent phenomenon. Matthew Poole says on Exodus 16:28, "He signifies that this was an old disease in them, to disobey God's precepts, and to pollute his sabbaths."[3]

Turning back to Exodus 16:23, Poole says, *"This is that which the Lord had said;* either to Moses by inspiration, or to the former patriarchs…"[4] Though we are not told when or to whom the LORD had spoken about

---

[2] Martin, *The Christian Sabbath*, 71. Martin treats Exodus 16 on pp. 65–72. His discussion interacts with Dressler on several fronts. See Schreiner, "Good-bye and Hello," 166, where he takes a view similar to Dressler. Schreiner does not discuss Exodus 16:28. Wells, *The Christian and the Sabbath*, does not discuss Exodus 16, except one mention of 16:29 while discussing a Sabbath's day journey (105).

[3] Matthew Poole, *Commentary on the Holy Bible*, 3 vols. (1683; reprint, London: The Banner of Truth Trust, 1968), 1:151.

[4] Ibid., 1:151.

the Sabbath, the explicit language used (i.e., "a sabbath observance, a holy sabbath") implies that it predates Exodus 16. Let me further explain why this is the case.

It is important to take into account Exodus 16:4–5, where Moses writes:

> Then the LORD said to Moses, "Behold, I will rain bread from heaven for you; and the people shall go out and gather a day's portion every day, that I may test them, whether or not they will walk in My instruction. On the sixth day, when they prepare what they bring in, it will be twice as much as they gather daily."

Owen's perceptive comments on this text are worth hearing:

> Here is no mention of the Sabbath, nor any reason given why they should gather a double portion on the sixth day. This command, therefore, must needs have seemed somewhat strange unto them, if they had before no notion at all of a seventh day's sacred rest.[5]

For these reasons, it is best to understand Exodus 16 as assuming that the institution of the Sabbath predated the events recorded there. The Sabbath commandment or law is not uniquely and exclusively an ordinance of the Mosaic covenant. According to Exodus 16, it is one of the Lord's "commandments" and "laws." These "commandments and laws" were already in place, not only before Sinai, but prior to this episode in the wilderness between Egypt and Sinai.[6]

This understanding of the Sabbath as predating the wilderness generation is not new, nor does it find its first expression in the seventeenth

---

[5] Owen, *Works*, 18:393.

[6] Genesis 18:19 is of interest at this point. There we read, "For I have chosen him, so that he may command his children and his household after him to keep the way of the LORD by doing righteousness and justice, so that the LORD may bring upon Abraham what He has spoken about him." Abraham was chosen, in part, to command others to "keep the way of the LORD by doing righteousness and justice." This implies there was a "way of the LORD" in place in some form. See the discussion in Ross, *From the Finger of God*, 78. Ross argues that the term 'way' often refers to the Decalogue. He views Genesis 18:19 as a "narrative anticipation of the Decalogue" (79). He closes his brief discussion on this text as follows: "Abraham lived in accord with the Decalogue... He did not need the Decalogue to know what God expected of him, confirming that, according to the Pentateuch, knowledge of its content predated its delivery" (79). This discussion occurs under the heading "General Examples of the Decalogue's Antecedence" (74–79).

century.⁷ Owen argues that some ancient Jewish scholars held it. He says:

> Some of their most famous masters are otherwise minded [i.e., that the Sabbath originated somewhere in the wilderness]; for they both judge that the Sabbath was instituted in paradise, and that the law of it was equally obligatory unto all nations in the world. Of this mind are Maimonides, Aben Ezra, Abarbanel, and others; for they expressly refer the revelation of the Sabbath unto the sanctification and benediction of the first seventh day, Gen. ii. 3. The Targum on the title of Ps. xcii. ascribes that psalm to Adam, as spoken by him on the Sabbath day; whence Austin esteemed this rather the general opinion of the Jews, Tractat. in Johan. And Manasseh Ben Israel, lib. de Creat. Problem. 8, proves out of sundry of their own authors that the Sabbath was given unto and observed by the patriarchs, before the coming of the people into the wilderness. In particular, that it was so by Abraham, Jacob, and Joseph, he confirms by testimonies out of the Scripture not to be despised.⁸

Understanding a Sabbath for man as predating both Sinai and the wilderness generation has a long history.

Some argue that silence on the Sabbath in the book of Genesis and up to Exodus 16 implies it was not instituted in any sense until the wilderness generation. Schreiner, for example, argues this way. He says:

> Some are surprised to learn that the Sabbath is not mentioned in the creation narrative (Gen 2:1—3), but silence regarding the Sabbath in Genesis 2:1–3 explains why nothing is said about the patriarchs (Abraham, Isaac, and Jacob) keeping Sabbath. Nor is there any evidence that Israel kept the Sabbath before they were liberated from Egypt.⁹
>
> …if the Sabbath were truly a creation ordinance, it should have been required for the patriarchs, but we have already seen it was not mandated. Instead, the Sabbath was instituted when Israel was constituted as a nation, and it was not authorized for Israel until after the exodus (Exodus 16).¹⁰

It has been argued that this is not the case from the Creator's rest, other related issues, and Exodus 16 itself. When it comes to arguing from silence,

---

⁷ See Bownd, *The True Doctrine of the Sabbath*, 42–43, for evidence that the sixteenth-century theologian Zanchius held this view. See Ames, *The Marrow of Theology*, 2.15.10 (289) and Turretin, *Elenctic Theology*, 11.13.2 (2:80) for the same view in the seventeenth century.

⁸ Owen, *Works*, 18:291–92.

⁹ Schreiner, "Good-bye and Hello," 160.

¹⁰ Ibid., 168.

it is often the case that it proves too much. For example, if one argued from the silence in the book of Genesis concerning loving our neighbor to the conclusion that this requirement was not known or not binding on anyone until explicitly revealed in Leviticus 19:18 ("…you shall love your neighbor as yourself…"), this would prove too much. The argument would look like this: If loving our neighbor were truly a creational requirement, it should have been required for the patriarchs, but we have already seen that it was not mandated. Instead, loving our neighbor was instituted when Israel was constituted a nation, and it was not authorized for Israel until after the Exodus (Leviticus 19:18). Does anyone want to argue this way? I do not think so. Also, the relative silence concerning monogamy as the will of God from creation in the early chapters of Genesis onward does not prove that monogamous marriage was not a creational institution. Schreiner is correct when he says, "Jesus argues from creation for the notion that marriage must be between one man and one woman…"[11]

Both Ames and Turretin, among others, dealt with the argument from silence long ago. Ames says:

> 10. There is no record in the history of Genesis that the first patriarchs held to the observance of the seventh day as holy—but this is no hindrance. First, all and everything observed by them for fifteen hundred years neither could nor ought to have been set down in particular in so short a history as that found in Genesis. Thus, though the law of the sabbath was delivered by Moses, no mention is made of its observance in the Book of Judges and other histories. Second, even if it is granted that the observance of this day was for the most part neglected, this would in no way cast doubt on its first institution. Polygamy of the same age no more demonstrates that the sacred laws of wedlock were not instituted at the time of the very first marriage.[12]

---

[11] Schreiner, "Good-bye and Hello," 168. Reisinger devotes a whole chapter to polygamy, divorce, and adultery in his *Continuity and Discontinuity*, 83–102. The chapter is entitled, "Raising the Standards of Conduct." Among other things, he seeks to prove (contra John Murray) that monogamy is an illustration of the standard being raised under the inaugurated new covenant. In his closing paragraph to that chapter, he says, "I believe that the plain texts of Scripture show that Jesus changed the law concerning divorce and remarriage and polygamy" (102). This seems to be something different from what Schreiner argues. "Commands rooted in creation still apply today" ("Good-bye and Hello," 168).

[12] Ames, *The Marrow of Theology*, 2.15.10 (289).

Similar to Ames, Turretin says:

> XVIII. Although in the life of the patriarchs no express mention is made of a Sabbath kept by them, it does not follow that it was not at all known or observed by them. Theirs is a compendious narrative in which it is not necessary that all things pertaining to them should be found. It was sufficient for the Holy Spirit to touch upon those things which bore upon his purpose (namely, to confirm the promises made to them concerning the blessed seed, and to weave together their genealogy to exhibit the truth of history). So no mention is made of the Sabbath observed in the time of the Judges and of Samuel. But the inference would be false that it was not observed.[13]

The argument from silence on this issue does not stand.

Having considered Exodus 16, the next major passage to consider is Exodus 20, the promulgation of the Decalogue via Moses to old covenant Israel.

Exodus 20

> Remember the sabbath day, to keep it holy. Six days you shall labor and do all your work, but the seventh day is a sabbath of the LORD your God; in it you shall not do any work, you or your son or your daughter, your male or your female servant or your cattle or your sojourner who stays with you. For in six days the LORD made the heavens and the earth, the sea and all that is in them, and rested on the seventh day; therefore the LORD blessed the sabbath day and made it holy. (Exodus 20:8–11)

Here the Sabbath for Israel finds its basis in creation and the divine exemplar—God. It is of interest to note verses 8 and 11. "Remember the sabbath day, to keep it holy" (Exodus 20:8) and "For in six days the LORD made the heavens and the earth, the sea and all that is in them, and rested on the seventh day; therefore the LORD blessed the sabbath day and made it holy" (Exodus 20:11). When did God bless the Sabbath day and make it holy? When he "rested on the seventh day." A day consecrated by God for man did not begin at Sinai or with the wilderness generation. A day of sacred rest for man predates both Sinai and Israel as God's old covenant nation. It is not unique or exclusive to Israel, though it takes on a temporary status for Israel.[14] It is from the beginning. The Sabbath day derives its

---

[13] Turretin, *Elenctic Theology*, 11.13.18 (2:83).

[14] See Owen, *Works*, 18:385–403, on "OF THE JUDAICAL SABBATH." There are many other places in Owen's essay where he identifies and discusses unique redemptive-historical issues related to the Sabbath under the Mosaic covenant.

existence from God at the end of the creation week. It has meaning prior to its status as an ordinance for ancient Israel. Its consecration as a sacred day of rest dates to what is revealed to us in Genesis 2, not Exodus 20 (or Exodus 16).

Let's consider four further observations which overlap at points with the discussion above but advance the argument as well. First, consider that the language of this text implies that the Sabbath was not to be instituted for the first time, but respected as an already known institution. "Remember the Sabbath" assumes its previous existence. Tom Wells, however, argues that this interpretation is debatable. He says:

> The Hebrew word for "remember" occurs three times in Exodus. Chapter 32:13 looks back to the days of Abraham. This one in 20:8 is debatable. The instance in 13:3 is a command to remember the Passover, given on the day the Passover began. So "remember" settles nothing. Many scholars have recognized this. Dr. Clowney has written, "We do not know whether the Sabbath law was known in some form by God's people before he revealed it to them through Moses at Sinai."[15]

As we have seen, Exodus 16 gives explicit evidence that the Sabbath predates Sinai. Though *remember* can have an exclusively future referent, it seems a bit clumsy to take that meaning here since Israel already knew of the Sabbath institution. This same word is used 27 times in the Pentateuch. A survey of usage seems to indicate that most uses, by far, have a backward referent. When Moses informs us of the reason or basis for the Sabbath in Exodus 20, interestingly, he goes back to Genesis 2. He does not go back to the events of Exodus 16, which he could have done very easily. Plausibly, *remember* could mean to recall (a backward referent) or "don't forget" (a future referent). Either way, an exclusively future referent seems strained and unnecessary.

Second, consider the obvious parallels between Exodus 20:8–11 and Genesis 2:2–3. Exodus 20 echoes Genesis 2. Genesis 2:2–3 says:

> By the seventh day God completed His work which He had done, and He rested on the seventh day from all His work which He had done.

---

[15] Wells, *The Christian and the Sabbath*, 30. Clowney is cited as "Clowney, 53." There is no bibliographic information given prior to this quote of Clowney. The "Bibliography of Referenced Materials" at the end of the book includes this: "Clowney, Edmund P., *How Jesus Transforms the Ten Commandments*, Phillipsburg, NJ: P&R, 2007." I assume the quote is from this book by Clowney. It is apparent that Clowney overlooked Exodus 16. Contrary to his claim, we do, in fact, know with certainty that the Sabbath was known prior to Sinai.

> Then God blessed the seventh day and sanctified it, because in it He rested from all His work which God had created and made.

The Sabbath is a day that is to be kept holy (i.e., set apart from other normal days of labor). The reason for this is stated in Exodus 20:11, "For in six days the LORD made the heavens and the earth, the sea, and all that is in them, and rested the seventh day. Therefore the LORD blessed the Sabbath day and hallowed it." Moses records that God bases Sabbath-keeping for Israel on God's work/rest cycle at creation. Just as God worked six days and then rested, so Israel under the Mosaic covenant is told to work six days, then rest. As argued above, this is not the institution of the seven-day week. It is the incorporation of the work/rest cycle established by the divine acts of creation and rest in the beginning to Israel under the Mosaic covenant. Though the Sabbath takes on unique covenantal and typological purposes with Israel and the Mosaic covenant, it is not a new or unique institution exclusively.

Third, consider that Exodus 20:11 refers both to God's rest and man's Sabbath. John Frame says:

> It is important to ask, What Sabbath does Exodus 20:11 refer to? Does "Sabbath" here refer to God's rest after creating the world or to man's own Sabbath rest? It must refer to both. The first sentence of Exodus 20:11 refers to God's own rest, but "Sabbath" in the second sentence must refer to the "Sabbath" of verse 8, the weekly Sabbath that God requires of Israel. Exodus 20:11 sees an identity between these. It teaches that when God took his own rest from his creative labors and rested on the seventh day, which he hallowed and blessed, he also hallowed and blessed a human Sabbath, a Sabbath for man (Mark 2:27). In other words, when God blessed his own Sabbath rest in Genesis 2:3, he blessed it as a model for human imitation. So Israel is to keep the Sabbath, because in Genesis 2:2–3 God hallowed and blessed man's Sabbath as well as his own.[16]

Owen says that "in the decalogue…[it is] 'the day of the Sabbath,' or God's rest and ours."[17] This is why the Sabbath is called God's day elsewhere. He instituted it and owns it (Isaiah 58:13, "My holy day"). Also, this is why it is said to be something made for man (Mark 2:27, "the Sabbath was made for man"). The Sabbath is God's because of His example and institution. The Sabbath is for man because God made it for him. Surely "the everlasting God, the LORD, the Creator of the ends of the earth, neither faints nor is weary" (Isaiah 40:28). God did not make the Sabbath for Himself be-

---

[16] John M. Frame, *The Doctrine of the Christian Life* (Phillipsburg, NJ: P&R Publishing, 2008), 532–33.
[17] Owen, *Works*, 18:278.

cause He was tired and needed rest. He made it for man; and His example at creation is imperatival for man. The fourth commandment as recorded in Exodus 20, then, is the incorporation of a creational institution into Israel's covenantal life.

Fourth, consider that the basis of the fourth commandment is grounded in creation and God's example of working six days and resting. Here is where Moses does what Jesus and Paul do later (see Matthew 19:1–8 and 1 Timothy 2:12–14); he bases ethics on creation. The ethical implications of God's example in working six days and then resting transcends covenants and cultures. Though it is clear from Exodus 20:1–2 and Deuteronomy 5:6, 15 that God is speaking to the Jews as a nation brought "out of the land of Egypt, out of the house of bondage," it is also true that the basis for the fourth commandment in Exodus 20 is creation, not Israel's covenant alone. In other words, God is applying a creational ordinance to a specific redemptive-historical situation, just as He applies the creational ordinances of labor and marriage/procreation in the same redemptive-historical situation (Exodus 20:9, 4th commandment—labor; 20:12, 5th commandment—marriage/procreation; 20:14, 7th commandment—marriage/procreation). Paul applies a creational ordinance to a unique redemptive-historical situation—the new covenant church (1 Timothy 2:12–14). Both the old covenant and the new covenant incorporate aspects of creational ordinances into their ethical schemes. The common ground between them is the fact and function of creation and the Creator/creature relationship.

Before discussing Old Testament prophecy and the Sabbath, it is interesting to consider the fact that the basis for the fourth commandment in Deuteronomy 5:15 is not creation, but the exodus:

> Six days you shall labor and do all your work, but the seventh day is a sabbath of the LORD your God; *in it* you shall not do any work, you or your son or your daughter or your male servant or your female servant or your ox or your donkey or any of your cattle or your sojourner who stays with you, so that your male servant and your female servant may rest as well as you. You shall remember that you were a slave in the land of Egypt, and the LORD your God brought you out of there by a mighty hand and by an outstretched arm; therefore the LORD your God commanded you to observe the sabbath day. (Deuteronomy 5:13–15)

This means that under the Mosaic covenant there was a two-fold basis for the seventh-day Sabbath—creation and redemption, both divine acts. Since this will be discussed below, I will leave the observation alone for now.

Old Testament Prophecy and the Sabbath of the Inaugurated New Covenant

The Old Testament prophesies both the perpetuity and an abrogation of the Sabbath under the inaugurated new covenant era. The best way to account for this is understanding the Sabbath principle as transcending covenants and finding its basis and function before the fall into sin, something that has been discussed above. Let's consider the evidence for the perpetuity and abrogation of the Sabbath under the inaugurated new covenant.

The Old Testament Prophesies a Sabbath for the Inaugurated New Covenant Era

The Old Testament prophesies a Sabbath connected to the inaugurated new covenant in at least two places. The first is Jeremiah 31:33, which implies a Sabbath under the new covenant because the law being referred to is the same law God wrote on stone tablets. I want to focus, however, on an explicit text concerning the Sabbath in Old Testament prophecy, not an implicit one, though I think it is a valid argument. Those interested in my exegesis of Jeremiah 31:33 can read my *RBTR* article, "The Old Testament Theology of the Sabbath—Creation, Old Covenant and Old Testament Prophecy" (cited above). My understanding of this text is not novel. It has a long history.[18]

A second, explicit text is Isaiah 56:1-8.

> Thus says the LORD, "Preserve justice and do righteousness, for My salvation is about to come and My righteousness to be revealed. How blessed is the man who does this, and the son of man who takes hold of it; Who keeps from profaning the sabbath, and keeps his hand from doing any evil." Let not the foreigner who has joined himself to the LORD say, "The LORD will surely separate me from His people." Nor let the eunuch say, "Behold, I am a dry tree." For thus says the LORD, "To the eunuchs who keep My sabbaths, and choose what pleases Me, and hold fast My covenant, to them I will give in My house and within My walls a memorial, and a name better than that of sons and daughters; I will give them an everlasting name which will not be cut off. Also the foreigners who join themselves to the LORD, to minister to Him, and to love the name of the LORD, to be His servants, every one who keeps from profaning the

---

[18] See Barcellos, "John Owen and New Covenant Theology," 331–37, where it is shown that John Owen, Herman Witsius, Francis Turretin, and Thomas Boston held this view.

sabbath and holds fast My covenant; Even those I will bring to My holy mountain and make them joyful in My house of prayer. Their burnt offerings and their sacrifices will be acceptable on My altar; For My house will be called a house of prayer for all the peoples." The Lord GOD, who gathers the dispersed of Israel, declares, "Yet *others* I will gather to them, to those *already* gathered."

Several observations will assist us in understanding how this passage explicitly prophesies the perpetuity and continuation of a Sabbath under the inaugurated new covenant. First, the section of the book of Isaiah starting at chapter 40 and ending with chapter 66 is pointing forward to the days of the Messiah, and in some places to the eternal state. This section includes language pointing forward to the time primarily between the two comings of Christ, the interadventual days of the inaugurated new covenant. It is understood this way by the New Testament in several places (e.g., Matthew 3:3; 8:16, 17; 12:15–21; and Acts 13:34).

Second, Isaiah 56:1–8 speaks prophetically of a day in redemptive history in which God will save Gentiles (see vv. 7 and 8). The language of "all nations" in verse 7 reminds us of the promise given to Abraham concerning God blessing all nations through his seed (see Genesis 12:3 and Galatians 3:8, 16), who is our Lord Jesus Christ. This Abrahamic promise is pursued by the Great Commission of Matthew 28:18–20. Isaiah is speaking about the days of the inaugurated new covenant.

Third, in several New Testament texts, the language of Isaiah 56:1–8 (and the broader context) is applied to the days between Christ's first and second comings in the motif of fulfillment (e.g., Matthew 21:12–13; Acts 8:26–40; Ephesians 2:19; and 1 Timothy 3:15). Compare Matthew 21:13, "My house shall be called a house of prayer," with Isaiah 56:7, "For My house shall be called a house of prayer for all nations." This anticipates the inclusion of Gentiles in the house of God, a common New Testament phenomenon. Compare Acts 8:26–40 (notice a eunuch was reading from Isaiah) with Isaiah 56:3–5, which says:

> Let not the foreigner who has joined himself to the LORD say, "The LORD will surely separate me from His people." Nor let the eunuch say, "Behold, I am a dry tree." For thus says the LORD, "To the eunuchs who keep My sabbaths, and choose what pleases Me, and hold fast My covenant, to them I will give in My house and within My walls a memorial, and a name better than that of sons and daughters; I will give them an everlasting name which will not be cut off."

The Mosaic covenant placed restrictions on eunuchs. Deuteronomy 23:1 says, "He who is emasculated by crushing or mutilation shall not enter the assembly of the LORD." Isaiah is prophesying about a day in redemptive history when those restrictions no longer apply.

In Ephesians 2:19, the church is called the "household of God," and in 1 Timothy 3:15, it is called "the house of God." The context of 1 Timothy 3:15 includes 2:1–7, where Paul outlines regulations for church prayer. Now listen to Isaiah 56:7, which says:

> Even them [i.e., the foreigners (Gentiles) of v. 6a] I will bring to My holy mountain, and make them joyful in My house of prayer. Their burnt offerings and their sacrifices *will be* accepted on My altar; for My house shall be called a house of prayer for all nations.

The New Testament sees Isaiah's prophecy as fulfilled under the inaugurated new covenant. However, the privileges, responsibilities, and the people of God foretold there (Isaiah 56) are transformed to fit the redemptive-historical conditions brought in by the inaugurated new covenant. The *people of God* are transformed (i.e., from a typical people of God to believing Jews and Gentiles); *the house of God* is transformed (i.e., from a geographic people and temple to a worldwide church); the *burnt offerings, sacrifices,* and *altar* are transformed (i.e., from old covenant priestly acts to our bodies presented as living and holy sacrifices, sacrifices of praise to God, and offering up spiritual sacrifices); and *the Sabbath* is transformed (i.e., from the seventh day to the first day, reflecting the inauguration of a new creation via the resurrection of Christ). Isaiah, as with other Old Testament prophets, accommodates his prophecy to the language of the old covenant people, but its New Testament fulfillment specifies exactly what his prophecy looks like in the motif of fulfillment. Jeremiah does this with the promise of the new covenant. What was promised to "the house of Israel" and "the house of Judah" (Jeremiah 31:31) is fulfilled in the Jew-Gentile church, the inaugurated new covenant people of God, the transformed, eschatological Israel of Old Testament prophecy.

NCT author Tom Wells discusses Old Testament prophecy and the Sabbath (e.g., Isaiah 56:2–5).[19] He notes that some Reformed theologians who believe in an abiding Sabbath day under the inaugurated new covenant era maintain that Old Testament prophecy about the Sabbath has to be understood as the prophets utilizing old covenant forms of worship (i.e., Sabbath, new moons, incense, sacrifices, etc.). These old covenant

---

[19] Wells, *The Christian and the Sabbath*, 35–40. Schreiner does not discuss the Sabbath and OT prophecy in "Good-bye and Hello," which is understandable since he states the following, with which I agree: "In a short essay the complex issues on this matter cannot be handled in detail" (159). Similarly, Owen does not discuss Isaiah 56 in his treatment of the subject.

forms of worship are used to describe worship under the inaugurated new covenant, so they are not intended to be understood literally. He says:

> Here in the judgment of the men I have cited, they [old covenant forms of worship in new covenant prophecies] stand for New Covenant realities that would replace the Old Covenant customs in the gospel era.[20]

Though I think these men are right, I do not think this necessarily means these texts do not teach that an abiding Sabbath day is to be rendered under the inaugurated new covenant. In other words, the prophets utilize old covenant language, but prophesy a transformed Sabbath to be kept under the new covenant, a day of sacred rest that reflects the redemptive-historical era in which it is to be rendered. The Old Testament prophesies not the mere *replacement* of old covenant forms, but their *transformation by fulfillment*. As noted above, the *people of God* are transformed; *the house of God* is transformed; the *burnt offerings, sacrifices*, and *altar* are transformed; and *the Sabbath* is transformed—all to fit the conditions brought in by virtue of the sufferings and glory of Christ.

With these considerations before us, between the two advents of Christ, when the old covenant law restricting eunuchs no longer restricts them, and when the nations (i.e., Gentiles) are becoming the Lord's and frequenting His house, which is His church, a Sabbath (see Isaiah 56:2, 4, 6) remains for the people of God (Hebrews 4:9). Isaiah is speaking prophetically of Sabbath-keeping during the era of the inaugurated new covenant. The English Puritan John Bunyan, commenting on Isaiah 56, said, "Also it follows from hence, that the sabbath that has a promise annexed to the keeping of it, is rather that which the Lord Jesus shall give to the churches of the Gentiles."[21] Bunyan sees Isaiah 56 speaking prophetically of that which is given to the church by Christ. I think he is right.

The essence of the Sabbath (i.e., a day to be kept holy to the Lord) transcends covenantal bounds. Its roots are in creation, not the Mosaic covenant exclusively. It transcends covenants and cultures because the ethics of creation are trans-covenantal and trans-cultural. The Sabbath day is an application of God's moral law. Time set apart for special service to God is written on our hearts.

---

[20] Wells, *The Christian and the Sabbath*, 39.

[21] Bunyan, *The Works of John Bunyan*, 2:361. See Jonathan Edwards, *The Works of Jonathan Edwards*, Volume Two, revised and corrected by Edward Hickman (1834; reprint, Edinburgh and Carlisle, PA: The Banner of Truth Trust, 1992), 96, for the same understanding of Isaiah 56.

The Old Testament Prophesies the Abrogation and Cessation of Ancient Israel's Sabbaths

The Old Testament clearly prophesies the abrogation and cessation of ancient Israel's Sabbaths. It does so in Hosea 2:11, which says, "I will also cause all her mirth to cease, her feast days, her New Moons, her Sabbaths—all her appointed feasts." Several observations support this view. First, Hosea's prophecy is dealing with the days of the inaugurated new covenant. The phrase "in that day" (vv. 16, 18, 21) is used prophetically of inaugurated new covenant days in Isaiah 22:20–22, which also mentions the Lord's servant, a type of Christ (cf. Revelation 3:7). Isaiah says:

> Then it will come about in that day, that I will summon My servant Eliakim the son of Hilkiah, and I will clothe him with your tunic and tie your sash securely about him. I will entrust him with your authority, and he will become a father to the inhabitants of Jerusalem and to the house of Judah. Then I will set the key of the house of David on his shoulder, when he opens no one will shut, when he shuts no one will open.

Revelation 3:7, echoing Isaiah 22:22, says:

> And to the angel of the church in Philadelphia write, "These things says He who is holy, He who is true, He who has the key of David, He who opens and no one shuts, and shuts and no one opens."

The phrase, "in that day," refers to the days of Christ—the days of the inaugurated new covenant. Paul references Hosea 1:10 and 2:23 in Romans 9:25, applying them to first-century Christians. "As He says also in Hosea: 'I will call them My people, who were not My people, and her beloved, who was not beloved'" (Romans 9:25). Peter references Hosea 1:9–10 and 2:23 in 1 Peter 2:10 and applies them to first-century Christians as well. He says, "who once were not a people but are now the people of God, who had not obtained mercy but now have obtained mercy" (1 Peter 2:10). Hosea is clearly speaking of the days of the inaugurated new covenant. According to the New Testament usage of Hosea, he is speaking of the time in redemptive history when God will bring Gentiles into a religious relationship with Jews. Much of the New Testament deals with this very issue.

Second, Hosea 2:11 clearly prophesies the abrogation of old covenant Israel's Sabbaths, along with "all her appointed feasts." Hosea uses a triad of terms ("feast days, New Moons, Sabbaths") that is used in many places in the Old Testament (1 Chronicles 23:31; 2 Chronicles 2:4; 31:3; Nehemiah 10:33; and Isaiah 1:13–14). Clearly, he is speaking of the abrogation of old covenant laws. When the old covenant goes, Israel's "feast days, New Moons, Sabbaths," and "all her appointed feasts" go with it.

Third, the New Testament confirms this understanding of Hosea 2:11. It uses this triad of terms in Colossians 2:16, which says, "So let no one judge you in food or in drink, or regarding a festival or a new moon or Sabbaths." In the context, Paul is combating those who were attempting to impose old covenant laws on first-century believers after the inauguration of the new covenant. So Colossians 2:16 is clear New Testament language that sees Hosea's prophecy as fulfilled. It is of interest to note that Paul uses the plural for Sabbath in Colossians 2:16 (σαββάτων). (Note: The old covenant had weekly and non-weekly Sabbaths [e.g., Exodus 20:8–11 and 23:10–11; Leviticus 23:24, 32, 39 and 25:4]). It is not too difficult to assume that Paul had the Old Testament triad in mind and Hosea's prophecy while penning these words. The New Testament announces the abrogation of the old covenant in many places. For instance, 2 Corinthians 3:7–18; Galatians 3–4; Ephesians 2:14–16; and Hebrews 8–10 (see esp. 8:6–7, 13; 9:9–10, 15; 10:1, 15–18) are clear that the old covenant has been abrogated.

The old covenant and all its ceremonies are obsolete and have vanished away (Hebrews 8:13). Taking these passages and Colossians 2:16 together, they clearly teach that when the old covenant goes, the triad of Colossians 2:16 goes as well. In other words, the Sabbath *as given to the people of Israel under the Mosaic covenant* has been abolished. Owen's words are to the point: "To say that the Sabbath as given unto the Jews is not abolished, is to introduce the whole system of Mosaical ordinances, which stand on the same bottom with it."[22]

The Old Testament prophesies a Sabbath for the inaugurated new covenant era while at the same time announcing the end of old covenant Sabbaths. According to the Old Testament, when the old Sabbaths go, a Sabbath yet abides. Thus, a new Sabbath must be instituted. What this Sabbath looks like, in terms of reflecting the redemptive-historical circumstances in which it is to occur, must await further revelation. This further revelation we now possess in our New Testament, to which we will turn in the next three chapters.

Conclusion

We have discussed three issues: Exodus 16, Exodus 20, and Old Testament prophecy and the Sabbath under the inaugurated new covenant. There is evidence in Exodus 16 that the concept of a Sabbath day predates

[22] Owen, *Works*, 18:393.

the wilderness generation. Exodus 20 provides evidence that the Sabbath predates Sinai and the inauguration of the Mosaic covenant. In Exodus 20, God incorporates creational institutions (i.e., Sabbath, labor, marriage) into Israel's covenantal life. Of interest to note prior to examining the New Testament is that Israel's covenantal Sabbath has a twofold basis—creation and redemption. The prophets assume the Sabbath of the Mosaic covenant in their writings. With reference to the future, they predict the abolition of Israel's "feast days, New Moons, [and] Sabbaths" under the inaugurated new covenant. They also hold out the prospect of a Sabbath in the Messianic era. Though they utilize old covenant forms of worship to depict the worship of the new covenant people of God in the future, just what these forms look like awaits further revelation in the motif of fulfillment, which we have in the New Testament.

12

The Doctrine of the Christian Sabbath
NEW TESTAMENT FULFILLMENT

As we enter the New Testament, we must not attempt a *tabula rasa* (i.e., clean slate) approach hermeneutically or theologically. The New Testament assumes the Old, and it interprets the events of the sufferings and glory of Christ and their implications in light of it. In the survey on the doctrine of the Sabbath below, we will consider the Sabbath in the Gospels and the first day of the week in the New Testament.

The Gospels and the Sabbath

A few comments on the genre and interpretation of the Gospels may be helpful at this point. The Gospels contain narrative accounts of various aspects of our Lord's earthly ministry. He served in a very distinct redemptive-historical context, and the Gospel authors each had theological purposes for choosing what they narrated and that upon which they commented. We must remind ourselves that Old Testament and New Testament narratives do just that—they narrate, telling us what happened, though with theological purpose and sometimes with commentary on the events narrated.[1] It must be granted that some of the teachings of Christ

---

[1] This is not to suggest that OT narratives and the Gospels are one and the same genre on every level. Whether the Gospels are seen as theological biographies, covenantal treaty documents, or a complex of various genres, the presence of narrative is still true.

in the Gospels are perpetually binding and not to be left on the shelf of narrated history. I say *some* because Christ commanded things to individuals that are not meant to bind others perpetually (e.g., Matthew 26:36, "Sit here while I go over there and pray."). But to demand a distinct type of teaching in order to justify ethics (e.g., demanding that Jesus say, "The fourth commandment is binding during the days of the inaugurated new covenant.") and then claim that the Gospel passages do not contain that type of teaching is simply a wrongheaded, constricting hermeneutical procedure. NCT author Tom Wells does something like this. Let's examine his theory.

In Chapter 3 of his *The Christian and the Sabbath*, Wells combs the Gospels for teaching related to the Sabbath. He makes this assertion: *"There is not one syllable of positive teaching by the Lord Jesus peculiar to the Sabbath in any Gospel passage."*[2] What he means by "positive teaching" is "teaching that tells Christians or Jews what they must do, or not do on any Sabbath."[3] What he means by "peculiar to the Sabbath" is "teaching that is true for the Sabbath that is not also true for every other day of the year."[4] In Wells' thinking, this would mean that if the Gospels do not contain teaching that either commands or forbids specific activities on the Sabbath, or commands or forbids things for any other day, then it was never Jesus' intention "to command anyone to keep a Sabbath."[5] Do you feel the pressure of these twin pillars? If there is no *"positive teaching…peculiar to the Sabbath,"* Jesus was not commanding Sabbath observance. I find these constricting hermeneutical hedges both interesting and wrongheaded. It is as if Wells sets up for us in advance what kind of teaching on the Sabbath must be present in order to justify any kind of Sabbath observance for Christians or Jews from the lips of our Lord. Wells knows, as does any casual reader of the Gospels, that the Sabbath command was something already in place at the time of Christ's earthly ministry. Jesus simply assumes its validity. Wells also knows, as does any casual reader of the Gospels, that Christ sought to correct the faulty understanding and practice of some first-century Jews concerning the Sabbath. The Sabbath was already an ancient institution, predating Jesus and His contemporaries, but it had been abused. Requiring Jesus to present us with *"positive teaching…peculiar to the Sabbath"* seems to exclude any other type of teaching, such as the type that might lead us to the conclusion that the Sabbath transcends the old

---

[2] Wells, *The Christian and the Sabbath*, 42; emphasis original.
[3] Ibid., 42.
[4] Ibid.
[5] Ibid., 47.

covenant and has ethical implications that reach into the era of the inaugurated new covenant. No such constrictions should be imposed on any texts.

Let's assume Wells' argument, however. Jesus' teaching was not for the purpose of identifying what Christians or Jews can or can't do on the Sabbath or Lord's Day.[6] Jesus' teaching on the Sabbath did not command or forbid anything either commanded or forbidden on any other day. Does that prove that there is no Sabbath or Lord's Day for the Christian to obey? Assuming the validity of Wells' hypothesis, all it would prove is what it asserts—nothing more and nothing less. Jesus was correcting the faulty teaching of His day on the Sabbath that added to and took from the word of God, commanding and forbidding things God did not. Jesus advocated a return to Sabbath-keeping as it had been revealed by God. As we shall see, however, our Lord's words concerning the Sabbath do much more than correct the faulty thinking of some of His contemporaries.

What if there are other grounds for considering Christ's teachings on the Sabbath as applicable to Christians? A much better approach would be to read the Gospels looking for teaching related to prior and subsequent revelation, and then to determine ethical perpetuity based on how Christ's teaching is related to its broader, canonical-ethical/redemptive-historical context. The Gospels are full of allusions to and echoes of previous revelation. Also, the events narrated for us in the Gospels set the stage for further revelation, which explains both the redemptive acts and words of Jesus Christ (John 14:26; 16:13–15). We must never interpret the Gospels as an end in themselves. Two passages in the Gospels are especially instructive in light of this—Matthew 12:1–14 and Mark 2:27–28.

Matthew 12:1–14

> At that time Jesus went through the grainfields on the Sabbath, and His disciples became hungry and began to pick the heads *of grain* and eat. But when the Pharisees saw *this*, they said to Him, "Look, Your disciples do what is not lawful to do on a Sabbath." But He said to them, "Have you not read what David did when he became hungry, he and his companions, how he entered the house of God, and they ate the consecrated bread, which was not lawful for him to eat nor for those with him, but for the priests alone? Or have you not read in the Law, that on the Sabbath the priests in the temple break the Sabbath and are innocent? But I say to you that something greater than the temple is here. But if you had known what this means, 'I DESIRE COMPASSION, AND NOT A SACRIFICE,' you would not have condemned the innocent. For the Son of Man is Lord of the Sabbath." Departing from there, He went into their synagogue. And

---

[6] See Wells, *The Christian and the Sabbath*, 45.

a man *was there* whose hand was withered. And they questioned Jesus, asking, "Is it lawful to heal on the Sabbath?"—so that they might accuse Him. And He said to them, "What man is there among you who has a sheep, and if it falls into a pit on the Sabbath, will he not take hold of it and lift it out? How much more valuable then is a man than a sheep! So then, it is lawful to do good on the Sabbath." Then He said to the man, "Stretch out your hand!" He stretched it out, and it was restored to normal, like the other. But the Pharisees went out and conspired against Him, *as to* how they might destroy Him.

In Matthew 12, we are told that "Jesus went through the grainfields on the Sabbath, and His disciples became hungry and began to pick the heads of grain and eat" (Matthew 12:1). The Pharisees replied, "Look, Your disciples do what is not lawful to do on a Sabbath" (Matthew 12:2). Jesus then offers two examples from the Old Testament: "…David…and those who were with him" (Matthew 12:3) and "the priests in the temple" (Matthew 12:5).[7] Concerning the priests, He says, "Or have you not read in the law that on the Sabbath the priests in the temple profane the Sabbath, and are blameless?" (Matthew 12:5). The Pharisees' assumptions logically implied that whatever the priests were doing, it was a violation of the Sabbath, and that David and Christ's disciples were also profaning the Sabbath. But Jesus says the priests "…are blameless" (Matthew 12:5). Then he quotes Hosea 6:6, saying, "But if you had known what this means, 'I DESIRE COMPASSION, AND NOT A SACRIFICE,' you would not have condemned the guiltless" (Matthew 12:7).[8] He pronounces His disciples "guiltless" by referencing two Old Testament examples.

Commenting on the account recorded in Matthew 12, D. A. Carson says:

> This does not mean that Jesus here actually breaks the sabbath or overrides it, at least as far as Torah is concerned, but it does mean He claims authority to do so… In the apparent conflict between what Jesus and His disciples did and the Sabbath regulations, Jesus claimed the authority to supersede the sabbath without guilt. It is not a matter of comparing Jesus' actions with those of the priests, nor is it likely that this is an explicit reference to Jesus as High Priest. Rather, it is a question of contrasting His authority with the authority of the priests.[9]

---

[7] Notice that Jesus is referring to previous revelation.

[8] Here is another reference to previous revelation.

[9] Carson, "Jesus and the Sabbath in the Four Gospels," in *From Sabbath to Lord's Day*, 67.

It is difficult to determine whether or not Carson is asserting that Jesus is claiming authority to break the Sabbath or not. His words could be understood that way. What is clear, however, is that the claim "It is not a matter of comparing Jesus' actions with those of the priests" seems to be a very strained reading of the passage. This comparison is, in fact, exactly what Jesus did. He consulted previous revelation to proclaim His disciples guiltless. Rather than this being a mere display of Jesus' authority to change the law or His authority over others, it is an illustration of His submission to and compliance with the Old Testament as it stood.

Schreiner holds a similar view to Carson. Discussing this Gospel account, he says:

> What is the fundamental point of the account? It does not seem to be legal, where Jesus appeals to the OT to demonstrate that he and the disciples are innocent. Instead, the main truth of the story is Christological. Jesus is the new and final David, the King promised according to the covenant with David. Hence, those who belong to him have a right to eat on the Sabbath.[10]

Jesus did, in fact, appeal "to the OT to demonstrate that he and his disciples are innocent." Though not denying its Christological thrust, it is at least an appeal to previous revelation to justify the conduct of His disciples. The way Jesus argues would give Pharisees the right to "pick the heads *of grain* and eat" on the Sabbath as well, provided that they were under the same conditions in which His disciples found themselves.

In the next section of Matthew 12, the Pharisees ask, "Is it lawful to heal on the Sabbath?" (Matthew 12:10). Jesus concludes in verse 12, "Therefore it is lawful to do good on the Sabbath." This clearly teaches that healing on the Sabbath was lawful, as was preserving the life of sheep (vv. 10–12). His disciples ate because eating is necessary to sustain human life, and what they did was not a violation of God's law. All of these actions, according to Christ, were lawful on the Sabbath according to Old Testament revelation. They did not become lawful due to His pronouncement. Jesus was correcting faulty thinking about the Sabbath by consulting prior revelation and interpreting and applying it correctly. As Roger T. Beckwith says:

> …our Lord was not opening a new category of permitted actions. He was simply extending an existing category from cases where life was in danger to other cases also, so as to cover all acts of healing, and acts of mercy in general. As he pointed out, his hearers were accustomed to

---

[10] Schreiner, "Good-bye and Hello," 172.

show mercy to animals on the sabbath, so how much more ought they to do the same to men? (Matt. 12:11f.; Luke 13:15f.; 14:5). Consistency required that they should treat men in the same merciful manner.[11]

Someone might want to offer Matthew 12 as an example of Jesus abrogating the Sabbath in all senses (see Mark 2:23–28 and Luke 6:1–11). They might claim that Jesus advocates Sabbath-breaking, thereby proving that He was abolishing it. But does this text (and others) bear this weight? Did Jesus, in fact, advocate Sabbath-breaking during His earthly ministry? We have just examined Matthew 12:1–14 and seen Christ justifying works of necessity and mercy, and concluding in verse 12, "Therefore it is lawful to do good on the Sabbath." The "good" in the context of Matthew 12 involved not only what His disciples did and what He did, but what David and those with him and the old covenant priests did. The supposed violation of the Sabbath in this passage (and others) is actually an upholding of the Sabbath in accordance with Old Testament revelation. Jesus never advocated Sabbath-breaking during His earthly ministry. His teaching and actions reflect existing Sabbath law.

Those who offer this objection may claim that, when Jesus says "But I say to you that something greater than the temple is here" (Matthew 12:6) and "For the Son of Man is Lord of the Sabbath" (Matthew 12:8), He is claiming authority to abolish the Sabbath as He abolished the temple. In one sense, Christ did abolish the Sabbath. He abolished it in its various functions under the old covenant. Also, in one sense, Christ abolished the temple. He did not, however, abolish the temple in all senses. His church is now God's temple, where spiritual sacrifices are offered (Ephesians 2:19–22; 1 Peter 2:4–5). What does Jesus mean when he says, "But I say to you that something greater than the temple is here" (Matthew 12:6) and "For the Son of Man is Lord of the Sabbath" (Matthew 12:8; cf. Mark. 2:28)? Fairbairn offers this explanation:

> The Temple, He had said, has claims of service, which it was no proper desecration of the Sabbath, but the reverse, to satisfy; and 'a greater than the Temple was there.' 'The Temple yields to Christ, the Sabbath yields to the Temple, therefore the Sabbath yields to Christ'—so the sentiment is syllogistically expressed by Bengel; but yields, it must be observed, in both cases alike, only for the performance of works not antagonistic, but homogeneous, to its nature.... He is Lord of the Sabbath, and, as such,

---

[11] Roger T. Beckwith and Wilfrid Stott, *This is the Day: The Biblical Doctrine of the Christian Sunday in its Jewish and Early Christian Setting* (London: Marshall, Morgan & Scott, 1978), 24. Beckwith wrote Part I of the book and Stott wrote Part II.

has a right to order everything concerning it, so as to make it, in the fullest sense, a day of blessing for man—a right, therefore, if He should see fit, to transfer its observance from the last day of the week to the first, that it might be associated with the consummation of His redemptive work, and to make it, in accordance with the impulsive life and energy thereby brought in, more than in the past, a day of active and hallowed employment for the good of men.[12]

Just as the temple yields to Christ and is transformed to fit the redemptive-historical circumstances brought in by His sufferings and glory, so the Sabbath yields to Christ and is transformed to fit the same redemptive-historical circumstances. The inaugurated new covenant has both a temple and a Sabbath. This connects Christ's teaching on the temple and the Sabbath with subsequent revelation.

Instead of Matthew 12 proving that Christ abolished the Sabbath in all senses, it actually argues that He upheld it and sought to correct the Pharisees' faulty interpretation of Sabbath law as it then stood. Fairbairn says, "Jesus grasped, as usual, the real spirit of the institution; for we are to remember, He is explaining the law of the Sabbath as it then stood, not superseding it by another."[13] Christ upheld the Sabbath and cleared it of Pharisaic encumbrances, but also set the stage for further revelation about it.

The objection stated above assumes that the Sabbath in all senses was temporary, old covenant ceremonial law. Old covenant ceremonial laws are temporary positive laws for old covenant Israel and were a shadow of things to come (e.g., Colossians 2:16–17; Hebrews 10:1). They were all abrogated by the coming of Christ and the inauguration of the new covenant (2 Corinthians 3:7–18; Galatians 3–4; Ephesians 2:14–16; Colossians 2:16; and Hebrews 8–10 [see esp. 8:6–7, 13; 9:9–10, 15; 10:1, 9, 15–18]). If the Sabbath is old covenant ceremonial law in all senses (or absolutely), then it has been abrogated in all senses. But the Sabbath is not old covenant ceremonial law in all senses, as we have seen (see Genesis 2; Exodus 16 and 20; and Isaiah 56; see also Mark 2:27 and Hebrews 4:9–10 and the discussions below). If Jesus considered it as absolutely ceremonial, exclusive to the Mosaic covenant alone, one would think he would treat it like he did other such temporary institutions. Beckwith comments:

> But if Jesus regarded the sabbath as *purely* ceremonial and *purely* temporary, it is remarkable that he gives so much attention to it in his teaching,

---

[13] Patrick Fairbairn, *The Revelation of Law in Scripture* (Phillipsburg, NJ: P&R Publishing Company, 1996), 238.
[13] Ibid., 237.

> and also that in all he teaches about it he never mentions its temporary character. This is even more remarkable when one remembers that he emphasizes the temporary character of other parts of the Old Testament ceremonial—the laws of purity in Mark 7:14–23 and Luke 11:39–41, and the temple (with its sacrifices) in Mark 13:2 and John 4:21. By contrast,...he seems...to speak of the sabbath as one of the unchanging ordinances for all mankind.[14]

Jesus neither abrogated the Sabbath in all senses in His earthly ministry nor did He predict its soon demise in all senses. He upheld it and gave evidence that it would continue under His lordship as the Son of Man.

A detailed examination of all the passages in the Gospels where Christ discusses the issue of the Sabbath will show that He never predicted its absolute abolition, nor did He ever profane it. In fact, He could not profane it, nor advocate its profanation by others, without sinning. He was born under the law, not to profane it but to keep it (Galatians 4:4–5). If Christ violated the Sabbath, then He sinned and would not be a suitable Savior for others. Instead, He advocated works of necessity (Matthew 12:1–8; Mark 2:23–28; Luke 6:1–5), mercy (Matthew 12:9–14; Mark 3:1–6; Luke 4:31–41; 6:6–11; 13:10–17; 14:1–6; John 5:8–10; 7:23; 9:13–16), and piety (Matthew 12:9; Mark 6:2; Luke 4:16; 6:6; John 7:22–23) on the Sabbath by His teaching and example. Also, by His use of the Old Testament (as seen above), Jesus demonstrated that His attitude toward and conduct on the Sabbath was consistent with lawful Sabbath-keeping. In other words, He did not demonstrate His authority by abrogating or changing what had already been sanctioned as lawful Sabbath-keeping. He did not use His authority in order to supersede existing law to fit His particular needs. Our Lord never violated the Sabbath, advocated its violation by others, or prophesied its absolute demise.

Mark 2:27–28

> Jesus said to them, "The Sabbath was made for man, and not man for the Sabbath. "So the Son of Man is Lord even of the Sabbath."

Here Jesus asserts that "[t]he Sabbath was made for man, and not man for the Sabbath." Man came first, then Sabbath. He does not say that the Sabbath was made for the Jews, but for man. The making of the Sabbath happened in the same time frame of the making of man, not the making

---

[14] Beckwith and Stott, *This is the Day*, 26; emphasis original.

of the nation of Israel. Sabbath predates Israel. God instituted a Sabbath for man the day after He made him, man's first full day of life on the earth. The Sabbath is not as old as the Jews; it is as old as mankind (or at least one day younger). Here are some further reflections on this text.

Jesus here draws from creation a moral principle that is germane to mankind as a whole. "And He said to them, 'The Sabbath was made for man, and not man for the Sabbath. Therefore the Son of Man is also Lord of the Sabbath.'" First, note that both man and the Sabbath are said to have been made. The verb used (*ginomai*) means "to become" or "to be." It is the same verb used in John 1:3, where it is translated "made," and where it refers to the creation of all things through the Word. What Jesus is saying in Mark 2:27 is that, in the past, both man and the Sabbath came into being (i.e., "were made"). That this basically dual creation (man and Sabbath) is described by one verb suggests that man and the Sabbath were made at the same approximate time. It would be exegetically clumsy to separate the making of man and the making of the Sabbath by thousands of years by placing the Sabbath's institution after Israel's deliverance from Egypt. Since we know that man was created (i.e., "came into being") according to the Genesis 1–2 account, Christ would have us conclude that the Sabbath, as He refers to it here, was made at the same time. This corresponds with what we saw in previous discussions. That our Lord is evoking the Genesis account is admitted by others. For example, the entry for σάββατον (*sabbaton* ["sabbath"]) in the *New International Dictionary of New Testament Theology and Exegesis* says, "…it would seem that there is at least an indirect ref. to the account of Gen 2:1–2…"[15] Immediately after these words, we are told to confer "J. Jeremias, *New Testament Theology: The Proclamation of Jesus* [1971], 208."[16] Jesus' words in Mark 2:27 evoke previous revelation.

Second, both *Sabbath* and *man* are singular and articular in the Greek text, though we need to be careful not to make too much of either case. It is interesting that Jesus did not say, "The Sabbath was made for the Jews" or "The Sabbaths were made for the Jews."[17] He said "the Sabbath" was made for "the man." "The man" refers either to Adam as the head of the human race or, most likely, to mankind. Either way, Christ goes back to the creation account and sees both man and the Sabbath being made then.

---

[15] Wilfrid Stott, "σάββατον," in *New International Dictionary of New Testament Theology and Exegesis*, Second Edition, rev. ed. Moisés Silva (Grand Rapids: Zondervan, 2014), 4:226.

[16] Stott, "σάββατον," in *NIDNTTE*, 4:226.

[17] The Jews under the old covenant had both a weekly Sabbath and other, non-weekly Sabbaths.

D. A. Carson admits that "[t]he number of writers who reason thus is staggering."[18] The word "thus" refers to those who take Mark 2:27 "to mean that God established the seventh day for man and not man for the day, but then go on to see secondary support for a creation ordinance."[19] Carson understands Mark 2:27 as an aphorism. He says, "The word 'man' is used neither to limit the reference to Jews, nor to extend it to all mankind; that question is not considered."[20] If Beckwith is right, however, there is good reason why our Lord's use of the term *man* is extending the Sabbath to all mankind. As Owen did in the seventeenth century, Beckwith argues persuasively that some intertestamental Jews held the Sabbath to be a creational institution for all mankind.[21] It is clear from the evidence he presents that there was a strand of thought in Hellenistic Judaism that extended an original creational Sabbath to all mankind. Jesus was addressing Palestinian Jews, however. According to Beckwith, "Palestinian Judaism… regarded [the Sabbath] as a Mosaic ordinance for Israel alone."[22] Extending the Sabbath to mankind in Mark 2:27, Jesus' words are a further correction of the faulty views of the Pharisees. Not only did they add to the word of God, thus assuming Jesus and His disciples violated Sabbath law, they took away from it by viewing the Sabbath for Israel alone. Jesus' words were a rebuke to those in charge of interpreting God's law.

In context, Christ not only corrects the Pharisees for misunderstanding the Sabbath (Mark 2:23–24), but He also in effect rebukes their narrow-minded approach to it. Jesus teaches us that the Sabbath is not unique to the Jews. God caused it to come into being when He caused Adam and all mankind through Him to come into being, for His glory and their good. According to Christ, the Sabbath is as old as man, not merely as old as the Jews.

Third, the Sabbath is said to have been "made for man, and not man for the Sabbath." Jesus says, "the Sabbath was made *for* man." It was not made for God. God does not need a Sabbath. We do. It was made by God for our good. Also, man was not made "for the Sabbath." Man existed first. His needs existed before the Sabbath did. The Sabbath came into being to serve man's needs to be like God (according to man's creaturely capacity) and to enjoy Him forever. We don't serve the Sabbath; it serves us.

---

[18] Carson, "Jesus and the Sabbath in the Four Gospels," 89, n. 54.
[19] Ibid., 65.
[20] Ibid.
[21] See Beckwith and Stott, *This is the Day*, 8–11. The pertinent section heading is: "The Primeval Sabbath in Hellenistic Judaism."
[22] See Ibid., 17–21. The pertinent section heading is: "The Mosaic Sabbath in Palestinian Judaism."

Fourth, Christ puts His stamp of Messianic lordship on the Sabbath that was made at creation and for man. "Therefore the Son of Man is also Lord of the Sabbath" (Mark 2:28). This provides us with the expectation that the Sabbath will abide in some sense under His lordship and will take on characteristics appropriate to this lordship under the inaugurated new covenant (see Revelation 1:10). Carson, commenting on this statement by our Lord, says:

> Within such a framework the fact that Jesus is Lord of the Sabbath becomes the more significant, for the very concept of Sabbath begins to undergo transformation. That Jesus Christ is Lord of the Sabbath is not only a messianic claim of grand proportions, but it raises the possibility of a future change or reinterpretation of the Sabbath, in precisely the same way that His professed superiority over the Temple raises certain possibilities about ritual law. No details of that nature are spelled out here, but the verse arouses expectations.[23]

This is an astute observation with which I agree. Though Carson obviously takes these aroused expectations of Sabbath "transformation," "change," and "reinterpretation" in a different direction than I do, it is important to affirm what he asserts here. One problem with Carson's view, however, is that, as was shown in the previous chapter, Sabbath transformation is not novel to Jesus. It is predicted in the Old Testament.

John Murray's comments on Jesus as Lord of the Sabbath are very helpful:

> What the Lord is affirming is that the Sabbath has its place within the sphere of his messianic lordship and that he exercises lordship over the Sabbath because the Sabbath was made for man. Since he is Lord of the Sabbath it is his to guard it against those distortions and perversions with which Pharisaism had surrounded it and by which its truly beneficent purpose has been defeated. But he is also its Lord to guard and vindicate its permanent place within that messianic lordship which he exercises over all things—he is Lord of the Sabbath, too. And he is Lord of it, not for the purpose of depriving men of that inestimable benefit which the Sabbath bestows, but for the purpose of bringing to the fullest realization on behalf of men that beneficent design for which the Sabbath was instituted. If the Sabbath was made for man, and if Jesus is the Son of man to save man, surely the lordship which he exercises to that end is not to deprive man of that which was made for his good, but to seal to man that which the Sabbath institution involves. Jesus is Lord

---

[23] Carson, "Jesus and the Sabbath in the Four Gospels," 66. Schreiner says similar things to Carson in Schreiner, "Good-bye and Hello," 172 and 73.

of the Sabbath—we dare not tamper with his authority and we dare not misconstrue the intent of his words.[24]

It is clear from the text in Daniel, from which the phrase "Son of Man" comes, that it refers to Christ, our Mediator, in the posture of enthronement immediately following His ascension into glory, and is a title appropriate for Him during the days in which He is given a kingdom and the nations become His. Jesus' words in Mark 2:28 evoke previous revelation.

> I kept looking in the night visions, and behold, with the clouds of heaven one like a Son of Man was coming, and He came up to the Ancient of Days and was presented before Him. And to Him was given dominion, glory and a kingdom, that all the peoples, nations and *men of every* language might serve Him. His dominion is an everlasting dominion which will not pass away; and His kingdom is one which will not be destroyed. (Daniel 7:13–14)

In other words, as the Son of Man, Christ governs the Sabbath during the whole interadventual period (i.e., which include the days of the inaugurated new covenant). Christ's lordship over the Sabbath also implies His deity. The Sabbath is God's (Isaiah 56:4; 58:13). Since as Son of Man Christ is Lord of the Sabbath, and since this title is His during the days of the inaugurated new covenant, we should not be shocked if the Sabbath bears unique characteristics of His lordship under the new covenant. Recall the words of Fairbairn:

> He is Lord of the Sabbath, and, as such, has a right to order everything concerning it, so as to make it, in the fullest sense, a day of blessing for man—a right, therefore, if He should see fit, to transfer its observance from the last day of the week to the first, that it might be associated with the consummation of His redemptive work, and to make it, in accordance with the impulsive life and energy thereby brought in, more than in the past, a day of active and hallowed employment for the good of men.[25]

Jesus (Matthew 19), Paul (1 Timothy 2), and Moses (Exodus 20) argue in a similar fashion to Mark 2. They go back to the creation account for the basis of ethics in terms of marriage, divorce, male/female roles in the church, and Sabbath. They apply the same reasoning, though to different issues. If the basis for their arguments is creation, and if creation transcends covenants and cultures, how can we not conclude that what they are

---

[24] John Murray, *Collected Writings of John Murray* (Edinburgh: The Banner of Truth Trust, 1976), 1:208.
[25] Fairbairn, *Revelation of Law*, 238.

arguing applies to all men at all times, at least in some senses? Though the application may vary given differing redemptive-historical situations, the principle itself abides, and the reason it abides is due to creation's ethical implications drawn out by the Bible itself.

Tom Wells has a somewhat lengthy discussion of Mark 2:27–28.[26] He opens his discussion with these words:

> There is no command in these verses, but an argument for Sabbath keeping has been drawn from each of them. The argument is twofold. First, if God at creation made the Sabbath a blessing for mankind, He certainly did not do so only to abolish it later. Second, when the Lord Jesus announces Himself as Lord of the Sabbath, it seems unlikely to suppose that He intended to exercise His Lordship over it by doing away with it.[27]

Interacting with the argument for the Sabbath as a creational ordinance and assuming its validity while arguing against it, Wells says:

> The first argument implies the impossibility of God later abolishing anything that He made for mankind's benefit at the creation. But is this sound reasoning? It may be true or it may be false, but it is certainly not obvious. Where is it written that if God once made something a blessing for mankind at large that He would never suspend it?
>
> Didn't God make the Garden of Eden for the blessing of mankind? Yes, though at the time Adam was the whole of mankind. But He shortly withdrew that garden from his use. How many wonderful fruits did man forfeit forever by eating from the tree of the knowledge of good and evil and by forfeiting his own life in the garden? It is hard to imagine how great that number might be.
>
> Didn't God make the birds and animals that are now extinct for the good of mankind? Despite that fact, we do not enjoy them today either as food or objects of delight. Note also that as far as food was concerned, God kept Israel from the use of many kinds of animals for over one thousand years. Yet He made them for the good of mankind.[28]

I have already interacted with Wells' argument against creational ordinances so I will be brief in responding to these statements. No one, as far as I know, who argues for creational ordinances does so without identifying what those are, and none that I have read argue that the garden of Eden, wonderful fruits of various kinds, birds, animals, or food are included in their lists. Wells' arguments are *non sequiturs*. Though his conclusion may

---

[26] See Wells, *The Christian and the Sabbath*, 48–57.
[27] Ibid., 49.
[28] Ibid.

follow from his premise, his argument is invalid because he loaded his premise with faulty freight. He makes creational ordinances equivalent to things made "for the good of mankind." This type of reasoning puts words into the mouths of others. It might have a certain powerful rhetorical effect about it, but it does not interact with others on a truthful basis.

Both Matthew 12:1–14 and Mark 2:27–28 contain trans-covenantal principles relating to the Sabbath. Works of mercy and necessity are lawful on the Sabbath, linking Jesus' teaching with revelation given prior to His earthly ministry (i.e., the Old Testament). Jesus as Son of Man is Lord of the Sabbath, linking the Sabbath and its Lord with future revelation (i.e., the New Testament). Jesus' teaching on the Sabbath leaves us with the expectation that He will execute His lordship over the Sabbath in the future, during the interadventual days of the inaugurated new covenant. His teaching on the Sabbath is related to antecedent revelation (explicitly) and subsequent revelation (implicitly). It establishes a basis for the basic perpetuity of the Sabbath institution, and yet in such a way as to expect changes in application due to the redemptive-historical shift that takes place by virtue of His entrance into glory. These expected changes are not novel to Jesus; they reflect the expectations revealed to us in the Old Testament.

The First Day of the Week in the New Testament

It is good to remember the uniqueness of the first day of the week in the New Testament. The concept of a unique day of the week is not novel to the New Testament. What is novel is the uniqueness of the *first* day of the week. In order to show that the first day is unique in the New Testament, why it is so, and what implications for Christians are entailed in light of it, the following will be examined: 1) the fact that Christ rose from the dead on the first day; 2) the prominence of the first day immediately subsequent to our Lord's resurrection; 3) that the New Testament Christians met on the first day; and 4) identifying the reason for such first-day meetings. This will display that the uniqueness of the first day of the week in the New Testament is rooted in the epoch-changing, redemptive-historical event of the resurrection of our Lord Jesus Christ. This will also set the stage for a discussion of Hebrews 4:9–10 and Revelation 1:10 in the next two chapters.

Conservative biblical scholars admit the first-day resurrection of our Lord. The prominence of the first day of the week immediately after our Lord's resurrection is an indisputable phenomenon in the New Testament, as is the fact that the early Christians met on the first day of the week. The debate comes when seeking to determine the reason for and the implications of first-day meetings of the church. If the reason is mere convenience, then there is nothing significant in the resurrection of Christ in terms of directing orthopraxy or conduct with respect to public church worship on the first day of the week. If the reason is redemptive-historical, however, there is a theological basis for first-day church meetings that transcends the first century and ought to shape our conduct. If the reason is convenience, then anyone who mandates a particular day for churches to gather and conduct public worship has violated the law of Christ. If the reason is redemptive-historical, and therefore theological, then first-day church meetings for worship are rooted in the act of Christ and we should expect the apostles and writers of the New Testament to reflect this. These are important issues through which we need to think carefully. We will come back to the issue of the basis for first-day meetings in the discussion below.

Christ Rose from the Dead on the First Day of the Week

The New Testament is clear: the Lord Christ rose from the dead on the first day of the week. The first day is the day "after the Sabbath…the first *day* of the week" (Matthew 28:1; see Luke 24:1; John 20:1, 19), "when the Sabbath was over" (Mark 16:1). Several passages testify of Christ's first-day resurrection (Matthew 28:1–8; Mark 16:1–11; Luke 24:1–12; John 20:1–23). Jesus rose from the dead early on the first day of the week (Mark 16:2, 9). Five times the Gospels mention this fact (Matthew 28:1; Mark 16:1; Luke 24:1; John 20:1, 19). Sam Waldron comments on this unique phenomenon, suggesting a reason why.

> Is this five-fold re-occurrence of the phrase "the first day of the week" merely an interesting detail or is it of religious significance? The singular importance of this repeated reference to the first day of the week may be seen by asking the question, How many times are days of the week mentioned by their number in the New Testament? The answer is not once. The third day after Christ's death is mentioned. The Lord's Day is also mentioned. The preparation day for the Sabbath is mentioned. Yet, there is no other reference to a day of the week by its number in the entire New Testament. This being the case it is difficult to think that the mention of "the first day of the week" five times by the evangelists is incidental. We are constrained to think that it has religious significance. But what is that significance? It appears to be recorded to show the origin of the church's practice of observing the first day. There is no other natural explanation of this peculiar insistence on the "first day of the week" in the resurrection account.[29]

---

[29] Samuel E. Waldron, *Lectures on the Lord's Day*, unpublished. These lectures have been recently published as Sam Waldron, *The Lord's Day: Its Presuppositions, Proofs, Precedents, and Practice* (Pensacola: Chapel Library, 2017).

Most conservative biblical scholars agree that the New Testament church met on the first day of the week because Christ rose from the dead on that day. What Waldron is asking is how should we understand the repeated phenomena of the Gospels mentioning the fact of Christ's first-day resurrection? Is it merely historical accounting with no theological and practical entailments? Or could it be that the accounting of redemptive history in the Gospels lays a basis for theological and practical significance which awaits further revelation for its explanation? Let's explore this a bit before continuing the discussion. It is very important to consider.

We have seen that historical acts of God subsequently recorded for us in narrative accounts often have their significance teased out in later revelation. Could this be the case with Christ's resurrection? If this is the case (and I think it is), we should not demand or even expect the gospel accounts to draw out the theological and practical implications of the resurrection of our Lord for the church of the inaugurated new covenant. The Gospels record the redemptive-historical acts of God in the sufferings and glory of Christ. It is left up to later divine revelation to draw out the implications of these redemptive-historical acts. We have this in the apostles and the other books of the New Testament (i.e., Acts–Revelation). The theological and practical implications of Christ's first-day resurrection are not left up to us to interpret on our own. God has acted in Christ's sufferings and glory recorded for us in the Gospels. God also interprets those acts through His divinely-ordained agents, drawing out the implications for us in the rest of the New Testament. As Michael J. Kruger says:

> God did not simply perform redemptive acts and then leave the announcement and promulgation of those redemptive acts to chance or to random movements of human history. Instead, God established the authority structure of his apostolate to be the foundation of his church for generations to come.[30]

One interesting aspect of the book of Acts and the Epistles is that there are points at which it may be observed that the early Christians did certain things that are assumed to be already in practice prior to the written record concerning the practice. For example, in 1 Corinthians 10:21, Paul writes about "the cup of the Lord" and "the table of the Lord." Then in 1 Corinthians 11:20 he reduces those phrases to the phrase "the Lord's Supper." In 1 Corinthians 11:23–25, he recounts the words of the first institution of the Supper by our Lord. It is obvious that the Corinthians did

---

[30] Michael J. Kruger, *Canon Revisited: Establishing the Origins and Authority of the New Testament Books* (Wheaton, IL: Crossway, 2012), 174–75.

not first partake of the Lord's Supper after Paul wrote 1 Corinthians. He wrote to them to correct their thinking and practice, not to institute something never before practiced. In other words, the Corinthians knew about the Lord's Supper and were in fact abusing it prior to Paul writing to them about it. This indicates that the practice of the Lord's Supper predates Paul's corrective concerning it. In 1 Corinthians 11:23, Paul says, "For I received from the Lord that which I also delivered to you…" This pertains to the Lord's Supper. Paul had already delivered to the Corinthians the words of institution and their practical significance for the Corinthian church. Interestingly, in 1 Corinthians 11:2, Paul says, "Now I praise you because you remember me in everything and hold firmly to the traditions, just as I delivered them to you." In context, it seems inescapable that one of those apostolic traditions is the Lord's Supper. This is an instance where what is recorded for us in the Gospels (i.e., our Lord's words of institution) is brought by an apostle to a local church along with theological and practical implications.

When did Paul first bring the theological and practical implications of the institution of the Supper by our Lord to the Corinthians? The answer is he did so prior to writing 1 Corinthians, and he did so in the form of authoritative apostolic tradition.[31] Paul does not say, however, "By the way, I am an apostle. The traditions I delivered to you as a church are the theological and practical implications of the redemptive-historical acts of God in Christ. Just as the events recorded for us in the Pentateuch form the historical and theological basis for the rest of the Old Testament and are the source from which the writers of the Old Testament draw out theological and practical inferences for the people of God, so it goes with the events connected to our Lord's sufferings and glory and the church of the inaugurated new covenant." Though he does not say this, it is the best way to account for what took place in the first century. The Lord's Supper did not start with Paul. It was instituted by our Lord and put into practice by other apostles prior to Paul's conversion, and even prior to the writing of any New Testament books. When was it first called "the Lord's Supper"? Though we cannot pinpoint an exact date, we know that it at least predates the writing of 1 Corinthians. Most likely, it goes back either to our Lord himself prior to His ascension or to the apostles prior to Paul. Why do I assert this?

Recall that the eleven were addressed by our Lord after His resurrection. The event to which I am referring is recorded for us in Luke 24:44–49.

---

[31] See the compelling discussion on apostolic tradition in Kruger, *Canon Revisited*, 174–94.

> Now He said to them, "These are My words which I spoke to you while I was still with you, that all things which are written about Me in the Law of Moses and the Prophets and the Psalms must be fulfilled." Then He opened their minds to understand the Scriptures, and He said to them, "Thus it is written, that the Christ would suffer and rise again from the dead the third day, and that repentance for forgiveness of sins would be proclaimed in His name to all the nations, beginning from Jerusalem. You are witnesses of these things. And behold, I am sending forth the promise of My Father upon you; but you are to stay in the city until you are clothed with power from on high." (Luke 24:44–49)

Our Lord could have instructed them about the Lord's Supper and called it such at this time (or before), though we cannot know for certain.

The Book of Acts (written by Luke) informs us of other post-resurrection appearances by our Lord to the apostles. We read in Acts 1:1–4 the following:

> The first account I composed, Theophilus, about all that Jesus began to do and teach, until the day when He was taken up *to heaven*, after He had by the Holy Spirit given orders to the apostles whom He had chosen. To these He also presented Himself alive after His suffering, by many convincing proofs, appearing to them over *a period of* forty days and speaking of the things concerning the kingdom of God. Gathering them together, He commanded them not to leave Jerusalem, but to wait for what the Father had promised, "Which," *He said*, "you heard of from Me…" (Acts 1:1–4)

The "first account" (v. 1) refers to the gospel of Luke. The words "all that Jesus began to do and teach" imply the book of Acts concerns what Jesus *continued* to do and teach after His resurrection. Alan J. Thompson says:

> Luke tells Theophilus in the first verse in Acts that his first book was all about what Jesus began to do and teach. The implication of these opening words in Acts is that he is now going to write about all that Jesus *continues* to do and teach.[32]

Thompson adds, "Acts 1:1 indicates that the book is going to be about what Jesus is continuing to do and teach; therefore, the 'Acts of the Risen Lord Jesus' would be a better title."[33] Before Christ's ascension, He "had

---

[32] Alan J. Thompson, *The Acts of the Risen Lord Jesus: Luke's account of God's unfolding plan*, New Studies in Biblical Theology (Downers Gove, IL: InterVarsity Press, 2011), 48; emphasis original. Thompson's book is highly recommended.
[33] Ibid., 49.

given orders to the apostles..." He appeared "to them over *a period of* forty days and" spoke "of the things concerning the kingdom of God." He also reminded them of what Luke records for us in Luke 24 (see Acts 1:4). They were to wait in Jerusalem for Pentecost, at which time they would receive a special pneumatic endowment, equipping them for apostolic ministry while Christ was in heaven.

Now notice what Luke records in Acts 6:2–4.

> So the twelve summoned the congregation of the disciples and said, "It is not desirable for us to neglect the word of God in order to serve tables. Therefore, brethren, select from among you seven men of good reputation, full of the Spirit and of wisdom, whom we may put in charge of this task. But we will devote ourselves to prayer and to the ministry of the word."

The "ministry of the word" most likely refers to the message preached, the things proclaimed by the apostles. This is, in fact, the ministry of the word of God. This is confirmed for us in 1 Thessalonians 2:13.

> For this reason we also constantly thank God that when you received the word of God which you heard from us, you accepted *it* not *as* the word of men, but *for* what it really is, the word of God, which also performs its work in you who believe.

Kruger comments on this text as follows:

> Paul emphasizes that the apostolic message borne by the apostles was to be received as the authoritative word of God... Although this message was certainly passed along orally by the apostles, it is clear that Paul expected his written letters to bear the same weight as his words spoken in the Thessalonians' presence. Second Thessalonians 2:15 says, "Stand firm and hold to the traditions that you were taught by us, *either by our spoken word or by our letter.*" It is difficult to imagine that the Thessalonians would have understood Paul's letters in any other way than as the authoritative apostolic message that demanded their submission and obedience.[34]

The apostles realized their message was God's message in light of the sufferings and glory of our Lord. It was God's message through them, something communicated by Christ in them by virtue of the promise and ministry of the Spirit. Our Lord had prepared them to expect this.

---

[34] Kruger, *Canon Revisited*, 186–87; emphasis original.

New Testament Fulfillment

The following words by the Lord to the disciples prior to His death and resurrection apply to them in a unique way as apostles.

> These things I have spoken to you while abiding with you. But the Helper, the Holy Spirit, whom the Father will send in My name, He will teach you all things, and bring to your remembrance all that I said to you. (John 14:25–26)

> When the Helper comes, whom I will send to you from the Father, *that is* the Spirit of truth who proceeds from the Father, He will testify about Me, and you *will* testify also, because you have been with Me from the beginning. (John 15:26–27)

> But when He, the Spirit of truth, comes, He will guide you into all the truth; for He will not speak on His own initiative, but whatever He hears, He will speak; and He will disclose to you what is to come. He will glorify Me, for He will take of Mine and will disclose *it* to you. All things that the Father has are Mine; therefore I said that He takes of Mine and will disclose *it* to you. (John 16:13–15)

These promises set the background for the apostolic ministry. The apostolic ministry includes both speaking and writing on behalf of Christ in fulfillment of these very words.

The apostles have left the church with what has been termed *apostolic tradition*. These apostolic traditions were first spoken by the apostles and then written for us in the New Testament. This means that some things done by the early churches prior to the writing of the New Testament were based on the authoritative spoken word of the apostles (e.g., the Lord's Supper in Corinth [1 Corinthians 10 and 11]; the presence and function of teachers of the word in Galatia [Galatians 6:6]; the presence and function of overseers and deacons in Philippi [Philippians 1:1]; and the presence and function of laborers who oversee and instruct in Thessalonica [1 Thessalonians 5:12–13]). It is important to note, as Kruger asserts, the authoritative tradition that the New Testament speaks of is not human tradition or ecclesiastical tradition, but apostolic tradition.[35] It is also important to realize that what was first spoken was subsequently written and canonized. As Kruger acknowledges:

> Although this apostolic tradition was initially delivered orally as the apostles preached, taught, and visited churches (2 Thess. 2:15), it very soon began to be preserved and passed along in written form. Of course,

---

[35] See Kruger, *Canon Revisited*, 177. As understood and explained by Kruger, apostolic tradition is categorically different from Roman Catholic tradition.

this transition did not happen all at once—oral apostolic tradition and written apostolic tradition would have existed side by side for a period of time.[36]

In sum, the New Testament documents can be understood as the written expression of the authoritative, foundational, and eyewitness tradition delivered by the apostles of Jesus Christ.[37]

Oral apostolic tradition is assumed and further explicated by written apostolic tradition.

What does the discussion above about apostolic tradition have to do with the fact that Christ rose from the dead on the first day of the week? The resurrection of our Lord is not left as a self-interpreting act of God. Its theological and practical implications were brought to the early church by the apostles via both oral and written apostolic tradition. Though we do not necessarily possess the oral apostolic tradition in the exact words in which it was first delivered, the written assumes the oral and builds upon it. This being the case, if the New Testament indicates that the church met on the first day for public worship (i.e., practice), that it did so due to the first-day resurrection of our Lord (i.e., redemptive-historical basis), and that this practice was approved by an apostle or apostles (i.e., authoritative approval), is it too difficult to conclude that first-day meetings of the church for worship were also ordained by Christ through the apostles (i.e., dominical and apostolic sanction)? Just as the book of Acts and the Epistles do not command the Lord's Supper to be instituted, neither do they command the churches to meet on the first day of the week. Just as the Lord's Supper is assumed by the Epistles, so the Lord's Day is assumed. The churches addressed in the New Testament, *and the things they practiced*, existed prior to letters being written to them. As we shall see in our discussion of 1 Corinthians 16:1–2, first-day church meetings at Corinth are assumed to be in place, just as the Lord's Supper is assumed to be in place, and both prior to the writing of 1 Corinthians. The importance of the discussion on apostolic tradition will become more evident in the discussion below.

The Prominence of the First Day Immediately Subsequent to Christ's Resurrection

Notice the prominence of the first day immediately subsequent to Christ's resurrection.

---

[36] Kruger, *Canon Revisited*, 179.
[37] Ibid., 181.

New Testament Fulfillment

Now after the Sabbath, as it began to dawn toward the first *day* of the week, Mary Magdalene and the other Mary came to look at the grave. (Matthew 28:1)

The angel said to the women, "Do not be afraid; for I know that you are looking for Jesus who has been crucified. He is not here, for He has risen, just as He said. Come, see the place where He was lying. (Matthew 28:5–6)

And behold, Jesus met them and greeted them. And they came up and took hold of His feet and worshiped Him. Then Jesus said to them, "Do not be afraid; go and take word to My brethren to leave for Galilee, and there they will see Me." (Matthew 28:9–10)

Now when he rose early in the first day of the week, he appeared first to Mary Magdalene. (Mark 16:9)

After that, he appeared in another form to two of them as they walked and went into the country. (Mark 16:12)

Afterward he appeared to the eleven as they sat at the table (Mark 16:14)

Now on the first day of the week, very early in the morning, they, and certain other women with them, came to the tomb bringing the spices which they had prepared. But they found the stone rolled away from the tomb. (Luke 24:1–2)

Now behold, two of them were traveling that same day to a village called Emmaus, which was seven miles from Jerusalem. And they talked together of all these things which had happened. So it was, while they conversed and reasoned, that Jesus himself drew near and went with them. (Luke 24:13–15)

Now as they said these things, Jesus himself stood in the midst of them, and said to them, "Peace to you." (Luke 24:36)

These post-resurrection appearances of Christ all happened on the first day of the week. How can we best account for this? Waldron comments on this phenomenon:

(1) We note first the phrase in John 20:26, "eight days later". Since the Jews counted inclusively, this eighth day was the first day of the week. John is careful to include these details of time because they point to his Lord's Day theology (Rev. 1:10). In fact, four of the eight New Testament references to the first or Lord's Day are in the Johannine literature of the New Testament (John 20:1,19,26; Rev. 1:10). John 20:26 increases

strikingly in its significance when it is compared with John 21:14. There the appearance beside the Sea of Tiberias is said to be "the third time that Jesus was manifested to His disciples." This statement is, of course, problematic and must be qualified in some fashion. Whatever its specific meaning, it clearly marks the post-resurrection appearances of Jesus of John 20:19, 20:26, and 21:1 as unique and distinct. There were no intervening appearances of like character. Probably the meaning is that Jesus between these three appearances did not appear to a large group of disciples (Apostles). This means, of course, that between the first and eighth days of John 20 there were no like appearances to the disciples. This fact must have had a psychological effect upon the gathered disciples which would have clearly marked the first day of the week as of special significance for their resurrected Lord.

(2) Acts 2:1f. is also significant because the day of Pentecost occurred upon the first day of the week (Lev. 23:15–21). Pentecost, it is interesting to note was a day upon which no laborious work was to be done. Thus, it was in a sense a Sabbath. At any rate, the two constitutive events of the New Covenant and New Creation (the resurrection of Christ and the Pentecostal giving of the Spirit) both occurred on the first day of the week. Surely the disciples of Christ could not have overlooked or failed to ponder these facts.[38]

The New Testament notes recurring first days after the resurrection of Christ. These post-resurrection and pre-ascension appearances seem to assume something peculiar about the first day of the week. Though these observations of themselves do not prove that the first day of the week is the Christian sacred day for church worship, taken together with the many other issues we have discussed and will discuss below, they indicate that something is unique about the first day of the week *even after Christ rose from the dead*. Ascertaining what that unique quality is demands further revelation.

First-Day Corporate Meetings in the New Testament

Notice the phenomenon of first-day corporate meetings in the New Testament. Acts 2:1 indicates that the Jerusalem disciples were assembled on the day of Pentecost, the first day of the week. "When the day of Pentecost had come, they were all together in one place."

Acts 20:7 says, "Now on the first day of the week, when the disciples came together to break bread, Paul, ready to depart the next day, spoke to

---

[38] Waldron, *Lord's Day*.

them and continued his message until midnight." Here Luke tells us that the disciples in Troas met "on the first day of the week" with no comment on the reason why. This is not a command to meet on the first day of the week. It does, however, appear to assume a practice already in place. As Owen says, "This [i.e., gathering on the first day] they did without any extraordinary warning or calling together…"[39] It is not the institution of first-day meetings; it is a record of one such. On this day, the disciples conducted activities with special religious significance. Some understand the breaking of bread as the Lord's Supper. Paul spoke to them, surely teaching them apostolic doctrine (i.e., authoritative oral apostolic tradition). They met on the first day of the week and had fellowship around spiritual matters. This text echoes aspects of the conduct of the early church, as recorded in Acts 2:42, "And they continued steadfastly in the apostles' doctrine and fellowship, in the breaking of bread, and in prayers." It is also of interest to note that Paul was in a hurry to get to Jerusalem (Acts 20:16), yet he stayed seven days in Troas (Acts 20:6) and did not leave until the day after the one described in 20:7. He left on Monday. Commenting on Acts 20:7, Martin notes:

> …it seems that this incident occurred on the day that the churches ordinarily gathered for worship, for the way that Luke includes a reference to the church meeting "on the first day of the week," *i.e.*, with no further explanation, indicates that this was, as Owen says, "that which was in common observance amongst all the disciples of Christ."[40]

The reference to the first day of the week in Acts 20:7 seems to be something early readers of Acts would not need explained to them. Though the basis for meeting on that day as opposed to another day is not stated, putting the various pieces of evidence provided for us in the New Testament together, it is not a leap in the dark to assume they met on that day due to the theological and practical implications for the church of our Lord's resurrection.

In 1 Corinthians 16:1–2, we read:

> Now concerning the collection for the saints, as I directed the churches of Galatia, so do you also. On the first day of every week each one of you is to put aside and save, as he may prosper, so that no collections be made when I come.

---

[39] Owen, *Works*, 18:423.
[40] Martin, *The Christian Sabbath*, 278. The quote from Owen is cited as "John Owen, *Hebrews*, 2:423."

Here the Corinthians are told to do something that Paul had ordered the churches of Galatia to do. Though the fact that the specific apostolic injunction has to do with a first-century need is agreed upon by all, Paul's mention of "the first day of every week" is what is of interest to our discussion. Paul does not order first-day meetings in Corinth in this text; he assumes that's when they meet, and he assumes that they meet every week. Earlier in 1 Corinthians, Paul discusses the meeting of the Corinthian church in the context of the Lord's Supper:

> But in giving this instruction, I do not praise you, because you come together not for the better but for the worse. For, in the first place, when you come together as a church, I hear that divisions exist among you; and in part I believe it. For there must also be factions among you, so that those who are approved may become evident among you. Therefore when you meet together, it is not to eat the Lord's Supper, for in your eating each one takes his own supper first; and one is hungry and another is drunk. What! Do you not have houses in which to eat and drink? Or do you despise the church of God and shame those who have nothing? What shall I say to you? Shall I praise you? In this I will not praise you. (1 Corinthians 11:17–22)

Paul distinguishes between the gathered church, the house of God, and their own homes in verses 17 ("you [plural] come together"), 18 ("when you [plural] come together as a church"), 20 ("when you [plural] meet together"), and 22 ("Do you [plural] not have houses in which to eat and drink?"). He specifically mentions coming together for the purpose of partaking of the Lord's Supper (v. 20), though they had so trampled upon it that their practice had ceased being what they intended it to be. Upon what day of the week did the Corinthians "come together as a church"? Though Chapter 11 does not tell us, we do have 1 Corinthians 16:1–2 and other considerations from the New Testament that lead us to the conclusion they came "together as a church" every first day of the week.

Some want to argue what Paul is requiring in 1 Corinthians 16 is a private putting aside and saving,[41] but if that were his intent, they would have to take a collection when he came. This, in fact, is what he does not want. Martin's words are to the point:

> He is not saying, as is often suggested, that each one should lay aside his contributions privately at home, for then, any day of the week would do

---

[41] Wells, *The Christian and the Sabbath*, 95, commenting on 1 Corinthians 16:1–2, says: "Is Paul speaking of an activity that was to take place in church meetings here? Probably not."

as well as another and a final collection still would need to be made. In specifying the first day of the week, Paul makes it clear that he is speaking of an activity that will take place at the time of their public assemblies. And he assumes that this will take place on the same day as in the churches of Galatia.[42]

It is no small matter for the apostle Paul to give orders to the churches concerning first-day meetings. Apostolic authority is binding for all churches. When Paul gave orders to the churches, his orders were the orders of Christ Himself. John 16:13–14 (referenced above) contain a promise from Christ of inspired truth to complete the revelation of the Father's will. This promise refers to the apostolate. Ephesians 2:20 says that the church was "built on the foundation of the apostles and prophets." First Corinthians 4:17 says:

> For this reason I have sent to you Timothy, who is my beloved and faithful child in the Lord, and he will remind you of my ways which are in Christ, just as I teach everywhere in every church.

What Paul taught "everywhere in every church" was binding on the Corinthians. In 1 Corinthians 7:17, Paul says, "Only, as the Lord has assigned to each one, as God has called each, in this manner let him walk. And so I direct in all the churches." Paul had authority to ordain the same things in all the churches. First Corinthians 11:2 says, "Now I praise you because you remember me in everything and hold firmly to the traditions, just as I delivered them to you." Apostolic traditions were binding on the Corinthians (see 2 Thessalonians 2:15).

So for Paul to give orders to the churches means that whatever he ordered was binding on them (and subsequent churches). Apostolic authority carried with it the authority of Christ Himself. The apostles were the revelatory agents through whom Christ completed the will of His Father. As the saying goes, the apostle of the man is as the man himself. First-day meetings of the church for worship, then, are the will of Christ for His churches, revealed through His apostles.

It is of interest to note something that goes on in the New Testament that relates to our discussion. Paul's words in 1 Corinthians 16 imply that it is the will of our Lord that churches gather on the first day of the week. As Paul told us, what he ordered for the Corinthians he had also ordered for the Galatian churches, which assumes they met on the first day of the week as well. According to Acts 20:7 and the other relevant factors noted

---

[42] Martin, *The Christian Sabbath*, 281–82. See Owen, *Works*, 18:424.

above, first-day meetings for acts of public worship by the churches was the New Testament norm.

Assuming that first-day meetings were based on the day of Christ's resurrection and that such meetings were apostolically sanctioned, it is interesting to consider the practice in light of the probability that 1 Corinthians was written prior to the letters to the Romans and Colossians. If one takes Romans 14:5–6, Galatians 4:9–10, and Colossians 2:16–17 as the negation of all special days pertaining to Christians and churches, this would seem to contradict the assumption of 1 Corinthians 16 and other parts of the New Testament. The words of William Ames are worth pondering at this point:

> …in the practice of the churches at the time of the apostles, when mention is made of the observance of the first day, Acts 20:7; 1 Cor. 16:2, it is not remembered as some recent ordinance but as something long since accepted by the disciples of Christ…. [I]n all things the apostles delivered to the churches what they had received from Christ, 1 Cor. 11:23…. [T]his institution could have been deferred not more than one week after the death of Christ if God's own law of one sanctified day per week were to remain firm… The placing of the holy sabbath of the Jews on the seventh day was abrogated by the death of Christ…. [I]t was also most appropriate that the day of worship in the New Testament should be ordained by him who ordained the worship itself and from whom all blessing and grace is to be expected in worship.[43]

Assuming what Ames says is the case (and I think it is), how can Romans 14, Galatians 4, and Colossians 2 refer to the Lord's Day? Ames comments on these texts as follows:

> First, in all these passages the observance of some day for religious use by the action of Christ is no more condemned or denied than the choice of certain meat for religious use by the action of the same Christ. But no Christian would reasonably conclude from those passages that the choice of bread and wine for religious use in the Lord's Supper is either unlawful or not ordained by Christ. Nothing, therefore, can be drawn from these passages against the observance of the Lord's Day on the authority of Christ. Second, the Apostle in Rom. 14 expressly speaks of the judgment about certain days which then produced offense among Christians; but the observance of the Lord's Day which the Apostle himself teaches had already taken place in all the churches (1 Cor. 16:1, 2) and could not be the occasion of offense. Third, it is most probable that the Apostle in this passage is treating of a dispute about choosing of days to

---

[43] Ames, *The Marrow of Theology*, 2.15.30 (295).

eat or to refuse certain meats, for the question is put in Rom. 14:2 about meats only and in verses 5 and 6 the related problem of duty is discussed; and in the remainder of the chapter he considers only meats, making no mention of days. Fourth, in the Galatians passage the discussion relates only to the observance of days, months, and years as an aspect of bondage to weak and beggarly elemental spirits (4:9). But it was far from the Apostle's mind and altogether strange to the Christian faith to consider any commandment of the decalogue or any ordinance of Christ in such a vein. Fifth, in Col. 2 the sabbaths mentioned are specially and expressly described as new moons and ceremonial shadows of things to come in Christ. But the sabbath commanded in the decalogue and our Lord's Day are of another nature entirely, as has been shown.[44]

Whether or not readers agree with every element of Ames' arguments is not the point. The point being made is that prior to the writing of Romans and Colossians, holy drink and food (i.e., the Lord's Supper), and a holy day (i.e., the Lord's Day) were already in place. Whatever particular issues each passage is addressing, they cannot teach against the bread and wine and the sanctity of the first day of the week.

A further dilemma for those who think Romans 14, Galatians 4, and Colossians 2 deny the sanctity of the Lord's Day needs mention at this time. If the Lord's Day, the first day of the week, has not been sanctioned by our Lord Himself through the apostles for churches to gather for public worship, who determines when churches ought to gather for such? If one says it is up to each church, does each church then have the authority to discipline one of its own for preferring another day and rarely attending their own church's meetings for worship? Would this not be a violation of the interpretation of Romans 14, Galatians 4, and Colossians 2 that those who advocate against the sanctity of the first day take? It seems to me it would. If the words "Each person must be fully convinced in his own mind" refer to the Lord's Day, the first day of the week, as well as all other days, how could a church discipline any of its members for forsaking the assembly of the saints, let alone encourage them to assemble on a stated day? Romans 14 cannot be a universal law against all holy days, just as it cannot be a universal law against all holy food and drink, and neither can Galatians 4 or Colossians 2. If they were, the Lord's Supper could just as well be observed by using tacos and beer.

First day of the week meetings in the New Testament were sanctioned by Christ through His apostles. These meetings for worship are not to be placed in the category of *adiaphora*, something indifferent or outside the law of Christ. This is not an issue of Christian liberty, left up to each

---

[44] Ames, *The Marrow of Theology*, 2.15.32 (297).

individual soul to determine what's best for them. It is the will of Christ revealed to us in the New Testament in various ways to be practiced by His churches until He comes again.

The Reason for First-Day Meetings in the New Testament

Finally, consider the reason for first-day meetings in the New Testament. Though it does not state the reason in explicit terms, the New Testament does present enough evidence to provide an answer. The reason for first-day meetings can be none other than the fact and implications of Christ's first-day resurrection. The resurrection—the pivotal, epoch-changing event in redemptive history—becomes the redemptive-historical and theological basis for first-day meetings in the New Testament. It is seen as an epoch-changing event—the beginning of the new creation. It is also seen as the day in which Christ ceased from His redemptive labors (Hebrews 4:9–10).

Schreiner admits that the day of Christ's resurrection is unique, saying, "Even by stating that it [i.e., the resurrection of Christ] was the first day of the week, the authors assign a special significance to that day."[45] He then appears to acknowledge that subsequent first days of the week were viewed in a unique way:

> We also see hints elsewhere in the NT that the church gathered for worship on the Lord's Day, the first day of the week (Acts 20:7; 1 Cor 16:2; cf. Rev 1:10). Such a practice is most naturally linked to Sunday being the day on which the Lord rose from the dead, though no explicit link is made between the two.[46]

Schreiner identifies church gatherings "for worship on the Lord's Day, the first day of the week…[as] a practice…most naturally linked to Sunday being the day on which the Lord rose from the dead."

Wells makes a similar statement, though with a degree of hesitation not evident in Schreiner:

> I have argued that the meeting day of the early church was not fixed by apostolic authority, but by convenience. Nevertheless there *might* have been a natural preference for the first day of the week. Why? Because our Lord rose from the dead on that day.[47]

---

[45] Schreiner, "Good-bye and Hello," 186.
[46] Ibid., 186–87.
[47] Wells, *The Christian and the Sabbath*, 95; emphasis added.

Both Schreiner and Wells claim the connection between first-day church meetings and the resurrection of our Lord is a natural one, though Wells does so reluctantly. If one is reminded that the resurrection is a redemptive-historical act of God in Christ, a better word to use to indicate the connection is "theological" instead of "natural." In other words, the practical implication of the resurrection of our Lord in terms of church gatherings for worship finds its basis in a redemptive-historical reality. It appears Schreiner would agree with this. I do not think Wells does, however. He claims that first-day meetings were "fixed…by convenience." Earlier in his discussion of 1 Corinthians 16:1–2, he says, "If, however, we ask why Paul said, 'On the first day of every week?' there is a good chance that he chose that day because the Christians met on that day."[48] The question we are asking and seeking to answer is *why* they met on the first day. Wells says it was out of convenience, though he does not argue his case cogently. Then he suggests, "there might have been a natural preference for the first day of the week." If there is a redemptive-historical reason for first-day meetings, however, it is a theologically revealed basis and does not and cannot change, whether convenient for us or not. If the early Christians met on the basis of convenience, would it not have been less threatening to their well-being to meet on the last day of the week (especially Jewish believers) so as not to draw unwanted and potentially adverse attention to themselves? As will be argued below, the reason for first-day meetings of the church is not based on the mere natural connection between the resurrection of our Lord and first-day meetings. It is, in fact, very redemptive-historical, theological, and even Christological.

It is important to recognize that the resurrection is an epoch-changing event. The resurrection is seen as the beginning of the new creation. Believers are united to Christ in his death, burial, and resurrection through faith.

> Or do you not know that all of us who have been baptized into Christ Jesus have been baptized into His death? Therefore we have been buried with Him through baptism into death, so that as Christ was raised from the dead through the glory of the Father, so we too might walk in newness of life. For if we have become united with *Him* in the likeness of His death, certainly we shall also be *in the likeness* of His resurrection, knowing this, that our old self was crucified with *Him*, in order that our body of sin might be done away with, so that we would no longer be slaves to sin. (Romans 6:3–6)

> and in Him you were also circumcised with a circumcision made without hands, in the removal of the body of the flesh by the circumcision

---

[48] Wells, *The Christian and the Sabbath*, 95.

of Christ; having been buried with Him in baptism, in which you were also raised up with Him through faith in the working of God, who raised Him from the dead. (Colossians 2:11–12)

Union with Christ brings believers into the orbit of redemptive privilege. They may know "the power of His resurrection" (Philippians 3:10) because they are united to Him through faith. God "made us alive together with Christ…and raised us up with Him, and seated us with Him in heavenly *places* in Christ Jesus" (Ephesians 2:5–6). Being in Christ makes believers citizens of heaven (Philippians 3:20).

Union with Christ also involves existence in two ages at once—this age (the old creation) and the age to come (the new creation). The age to come is the age of the resurrection.

> Jesus said to them, "The sons of this age marry and are given in marriage, but those who are considered worthy to attain to that age and the resurrection from the dead, neither marry nor are given in marriage; for they cannot even die anymore, because they are like angels, and are sons of God, being sons of the resurrection. (Luke 20:34–36)

Christ's resurrection is the first bodily resurrection of the age to come because it was "the firstfruits" (1 Corinthians 15:20).

> But now Christ has been raised from the dead, the first fruits of those who are asleep. For since by a man *came* death, by a man also *came* the resurrection of the dead. For as in Adam all die, so also in Christ all will be made alive. But each in his own order: Christ the first fruits, after that those who are Christ's at His coming. (1 Corinthians 15:20–23)

Christ's resurrection was the first of similar resurrections to come. Being "the firstfruits," it is not totally other than that which follows. It is different in time, but it is part of the same resurrection. It is part of the same harvest, just the first of the much greater harvest to come. Gaffin, commenting on "firstfruits," says:

> The word is not simply an indication of temporal priority. Rather it brings into view Christ's resurrection as the "firstfruits" of the resurrection-harvest, the initial portion of the whole. His resurrection is the representative beginning of the resurrection of believers. In other words, the term seems deliberately chosen to make evident the organic connection between the two resurrections. In the context, Paul's "thesis" over against his opponents is that the resurrection of Jesus has the bodily resurrection of "those who sleep" as its necessary consequence. His resurrection is not simply a guarantee; it is a pledge in the sense that it is the actual begin-

ning of the general event. In fact, on the basis of this verse it can be said that Paul views the two resurrections not so much as two events but as two episodes of the same event.[49]

Christ's resurrection is the most powerful sign of the presence of the age to come. His resurrected body took on qualities it did not possess prior to the resurrection (Romans 1:4). It was an age-to-come body, existing in this age for a brief time on the earth and now in heaven. In Christ's resurrection, then, we see the age to come eclipsing this age. This is why Paul says, "Therefore, if anyone *is* in Christ, *he is* a new creation; old things have passed away; behold, all things have become new" (2 Corinthians 5:17, NKJV). This is not only true of personal renovation, but also a state of existence in the new creation brought in by Christ. In Galatians 6:15, Paul says, "For neither is circumcision anything, nor uncircumcision, but a new creation."

The age to come has eclipsed this age in the resurrection of Christ. Hebrews 6:5 says that some "have tasted the good word of God and the powers of the age to come." Waldron says, "The great realities of the age to come have in some sense broken into and become operative in this age."[50] Waldron's further comments are helpful at this point:

> The New Testament teaches, therefore, that there is a new creation in Christ (Gal. 6:15; 2 Cor. 5:17; Eph. 2:10). The idea of new creation is frequently associated with Christ's resurrection (cf. Eph. 2:10 with 2:5,7; Eph. 4:24; Col. 3:10 with Rom. 6:1–6; Col. 1:15–18). By union with Christ in His death, the old man is destroyed. By union with Christ in His resurrection, the new man is created. When He rose again He became the firstborn of God's new creation. As He was the beginning of the old creation, so He is now the beginning of the new (Rev. 3:14). Thus, the memorial of Christ's resurrection is of necessity a memorial of the new creation. Thus, the Lord's Day like the Sabbath and unlike any other religious observance points to both creation and redemption.[51]

Christ's resurrection is the apex of all of God's redemptive work on the earth. It is an epoch-changing event. It ushers in the first phase of the new creation, the last Adam's entrance into glory. In one sense, it affects everything. But how does it affect the Sabbath under the inaugurated new

---

[49] Richard B. Gaffin, Jr., *Resurrection and Redemption* (Phillipsburg, NJ: Presbyterian and Reformed Publishing, 1987), 34–35.

[50] Samuel E. Waldron, *The End Times Made Simple* (Amityville, NY: Calvary Press, 2003), 49.

[51] Waldron, *Lord's Day*.

covenant? That it is the redemptive-historical, theological, and Christological basis for first-day church meetings seems clear. But does it mark the end of all Sabbaths for the people of God? Or does it function as the first creation did in relation to the first Sabbath? Does it function as the basis for the change of the Sabbath from the seventh to the first day because it is the day Christ ceased from His redemptive work, as God rested from His creative work? Surely, no greater, more unique event could be asked for to change the day of sacred rest for the people of God.

13

The Doctrine of the Christian Sabbath
Hebrews 4:9–10

This chapter will address Hebrews 4:9–10 and the next will address Revelation 1:10. The case for a Sabbath day to be observed under the inaugurated new covenant does not depend on one or two texts of Scripture. It is an extensive argument, requiring careful exegesis, biblical-theological synthesis, and interaction with those who advocate the doctrine and those who deny it. Hebrews 4 is a passage that has been used to support the case for a day of sacred rest for the people of God under the inaugurated new covenant. Revelation 1:10 has given the church an inscripturated name for the first day of the week, reflective of Christ's resurrection and lordship. The discussion of these two texts is a fitting conclusion to our study of the doctrine of the Christian Sabbath.

Hebrews 4:9–10 and the Sabbath

> So there remains a Sabbath rest for the people of God. For the one who has entered His rest has himself also rested from his works, as God did from His.

Hebrews 4 contains the best passage in the New Testament indicating the redemptive-historical and Christological basis for the shift of a Sabbath day from the last day of the week to the first day of the week. I do not, however, think the case for a Sabbath day to be kept under the new covenant relies solely on this passage. As we have seen, the argument for a Christian Sabbath is quite extensive. It is a scriptural argument; that is, it takes into account the entire Bible exegetically, redemptive-historically, and systematically.

Admittedly, good men disagree as to what is going on in this text as it relates to the Sabbath. For example, some see Hebrews 4:9–10 referring to the future alone, denying any present Sabbath day.[1] Others see an already/not-yet motif here, viewing the "Sabbath rest" as the believer's rest in Christ.[2] Some see the "Sabbath rest" as wholly future, though advocating the Lord's Day as the Christian Sabbath on other grounds.[3] Still others view this text as advocating a day of sacred rest for the people of God under the inaugurated new covenant—the day of Christ's resurrection, the Lord's Day.[4] This last view is the one I will argue below.

This will not be an exhaustive treatment of the passage. As readers will soon become aware, I think the essence of John Owen's view of this passage is worthy of following. In my judgment, Owen accounts for various aspects of the passage in a way that makes the best sense of the author's overall argument in this section (3:1–4:13). In the discussion on this passage, we will consider the following: 1) the context of Hebrews 4:9–10; 2) the exposition of Hebrews 4:9–10; and 3) the implications of Hebrews 4:9–10.

---

[1] E.g., Peter T. O'Brien, *The Letter to the Hebrews*, The Pillar New Testament Commentary (Grand Rapids: Wm. B. Eerdmans Publishing Co., 2010), 164–66, 170–71.

[2] E.g., Thomas R. Schreiner, *Commentary on Hebrews*, Biblical Theology for Christian Proclamation (Nashville: B&H Publishing Group, 2015), 144 and "Good-Bye and Hello," 181–86.

[3] E.g., Richard B. Gaffin, Jr., "A Sabbath Rest Still Awaits the People of God," in *Pressing Toward the Mark: Essays Commemorating Fifty Years of the Orthodox of the Presbyterian Church*, ed. Charles G. Dennison (Willows Grove, PA: Orthodox Presbyterian Church, 1985), 46.

[4] E.g., John Owen; Edwards, *Works*, 2:97–98; Daniel Wilson, *The Lord's Day* (London: The Lord's Day Observance Society, 1988), 106, n. 1; Robert L. Dabney, *Discussions of Robert L. Dabney*, Volume 1 (1891; reprint, Edinburgh and Carlisle, PA: The Banner of Truth Trust, 1982) 535, n. 1; Walter J. Chantry, *Call the Sabbath a Delight* (Edinburgh; Carlisle, PA: The Banner of Truth Trust, 1991), 86–96; Joseph A. Pipa, *The Lord's Day* (Ross-shire, Great Britain: Christian Focus, 1997), 111–29; and most recently Martin, *The Christian Sabbath*, 249–63.

The Context of Hebrews 4:9–10

Richard B. Gaffin, Jr. sees the motif of the church as a wilderness community dominating the context of Hebrew 4:9–10.[5] This influences his understanding of Hebrews 4:10. Commenting on that verse, he says:

> In a word, the works of 4:10 are *desert*-works, the works of believers in the present wilderness, that is, *non*-rest situation, looking toward the future, hoped-for promised rest. They are the wilderness-works of the church on the way between exodus from Egypt/redemption…and Canaan/rest.[6]

Though wilderness is *a* motif in the context, beginning at 3:7 the author mentions the concept of rest using Psalm 95 (and Genesis 2:2) to frame his discussion through 4:11. Though the wilderness motif is present, the mention and development of rest at 3:7–4:11 must not be minimized.[7] It is good to be reminded that the conclusion in 4:9 is "So there remains a Sabbath rest for the people of God." That which remains is assumed to be related to the previous discussion, which is infused with the motif of rest. In fact, in light of Hebrews 3:1–6 and the first word of 3:7, "Therefore," entering into rest is connected to Christ being "over His house—whose house we [i.e., believers] are, if we hold fast our confidence and the boast of our hope firm until the end" (Hebrews 3:6). Owen helps make the connection in these words:

> The illative, "wherefore," as was first observed, denotes both the deduction of the ensuing exhortation from the preceding discourse, and the application of it unto the particular duty which he enters upon, verse 12. "Wherefore;" that is, 'Seeing the Lord Christ, who is the author of the gospel, is in his legatine [i.e., authorized by a legate] or prophetical office preferred far above Moses in the work of the house of God, as being the son and lord over that house as his own, wherein Moses was a servant only, let us consider what duty is incumbent on us, especially how careful and watchful we ought to be that we be not by any means diverted or turned aside from that obedience which he requires, and which on all accounts is due unto him.'[8]

---

[5] Gaffin, "A Sabbath Rest Still Awaits the People of God," 42–46.

[6] Ibid., 45; emphasis original.

[7] See Nicholas J. Moore, "Jesus as 'The One who Entered his Rest': The Christological Reading of Hebrews 4:10," *Journal for the Study of the New Testament*, 2014, Vol. 36(4): 385–86, 397.

[8] Owen, *Works*, 20:18. In context, when Owen says 'prophetical office,' he is referring to Christ as "the Apostle…of our confession" (Hebrews 3:1).

To what duty, incumbent upon believers, is Owen referring? Several texts in the context answer this question:

> Take care, brethren, that there not be in any one of you an evil, unbelieving heart that falls away from the living God. But encourage one another day after day, as long as it is *still* called "Today," so that none of you will be hardened by the deceitfulness of sin. (Hebrews 3:12–13)

> Therefore, let us fear if, while a promise remains of entering His rest, any one of you may seem to have come short of it. (Hebrews 4:1)

> Therefore let us be diligent to enter that rest, so that no one will fall, through *following* the same example of disobedience. (Hebrews 4:11)

Though Hebrews 4:9 is not an explicit exhortation to duty, it is a conclusion to previous discussion and contains an implicit duty.

What follows in Hebrews 3:7ff. is dependent upon what was stated in 3:1–6, which says:

> Therefore, holy brethren, partakers of a heavenly calling, consider Jesus, the Apostle and High Priest of our confession; He was faithful to Him who appointed Him, as Moses also was in all His house. For He has been counted worthy of more glory than Moses, by just so much as the builder of the house has more honor than the house. For every house is built by someone, but the builder of all things is God. Now Moses was faithful in all His house as a servant, for a testimony of those things which were to be spoken later; but Christ *was faithful* as a Son over His house—whose house we are, if we hold fast our confidence and the boast of our hope firm until the end.

Owen summarizes the importance of 3:1–6 in these words:

> The proposition is this, that "Christ was counted worthy of more glory than Moses." The first proof of this proposition lies in these words of verse 3, "Inasmuch as he who hath built the house hath more honour than the house;" and this he further confirms or illustrates, verse 4, "For every house is builded of some; but he that built all things is God;" the latter expressly in verses 5, 6, of which afterwards.
>
> As for the manner of arguing here used by the apostle, it is educed from the foregoing verses. In the comparison made between Christ and Moses, he allowed Moses to be faithful, proving it by the testimony of God himself, who had said he was "faithful in all his house" [see Num. 12:7]. The church or people of God being in that testimony called "The house of God," and that by God himself, the apostle takes advantage of the metaphor to express the dignity of Christ in his relation to the

church under that expression of "The house of God;"... And a double relation unto this house doth he ascribe unto him, which are the principal relations that attend any house whatever. The first is of a builder, whence he takes his first argument, verses 3, 4; the other is of an owner, inhabiter, and possessor, whence he takes his second, verses 5, 6....

In his first argument, verse 3, the proposition only is expressed, the assumption is included, and the conclusion left unto an obvious inference; for plainly the apostle reasons syllogistically in this case.

The proposition is this, "He that buildeth the house hath more honour than the house."

The assumption included is, "But Christ built the house, and Moses was only of the house, or a part of it: and therefore he had more glory than Moses."

... The proposition of the argument in these verses [i.e., 5 and 6] is, 'A son over his own house is of more honour than a servant in the house of another.' This is only supposed.

The assumption is expressed, "But Christ is a son over his own house; Moses was only a servant in another's house:" whence the conclusion is plain and evident.

... In the confirmation of the first argument [i.e., Christ is worthy of more glory than Moses] the fourth verse is inserted, "For every house is builded of some; but he that built all things is God."[9]

In his essay on a day of sacred rest, Owen says that the writer in Hebrews 3:3–4

expressly asserts the Son to be God, and shows the analogy that is between the creation of all things and the building of the church,—that is, *the works of the old and new creation*. As, then, God wrought in the

---

[9] Owen, *Works*, 19:532–33. Schreiner points out many of the same things as Owen. "Still, Jesus deserves greater honor than Moses, for Moses is a member of the house (the people of God), but Jesus is the builder of the house (v.3)" (Schreiner, *Hebrews*, 113). "Indeed, Moses was faithful in God's house as well. 'House' in this context refers to the people of God. As a member of God's people Moses was faithful. In that sense he anticipated the greater ministry of Jesus.... Moses and Jesus are not on the same level.... Jesus as 'the builder'...of the house warrants more honor than Moses as a member of the house" (Schreiner, *Hebrews*, 115). "Verses 5–6 contrast Moses and Christ. Moses was a faithful servant in the house, functioning as a prelude and anticipation of Christ as the faithful Son. Hebrews again underscores that Moses was not the builder of the house; i.e., Moses did not establish the people of God. Instead, he was a member of the people of God...." (Schreiner, *Hebrews*, 117).

creation of all, so Christ, who is God, wrought in the setting up of this new church-state.[10]

It is important to note the words "the works of the old and new creation." Owen views the finished work of Christ as the establishment of the new creation. This motif will show up in our ensuing discussion.

Hebrews 3:5 says, "Now Moses was faithful in all His house as a servant, for a testimony of those things which were to be spoken later." Owen comments:

> In his ministry he was a testimony, or by what he did in the service of the house he gave testimony. Whereunto? To the things that were afterwards to be spoken, namely, in the fulness of time, the appointed season, by the Messiah,—that is, the things of the gospel. And this, indeed, was the proper end of all that Moses did or ordered in the house of God.
>
> This is the importance of the words, and this was the true and proper end of the whole ministry of Moses, wherein his faithfulness was tried and manifested. He ordered all things by God's direction in the typical worship of the house, so as that it might be a pledge and testimony of what God would afterward reveal and exhibit in the gospel…[11]

Moses paved the way for Christ. As Schreiner says:

> The readers should not turn back to Moses the faithful servant, for Moses himself spoke of a coming day. Moses himself looked forward to the arrival of the faithful Son, and the readers should remain loyal to the Son. In this sense Moses functions as the type of the one to come, Jesus.[12]

Christ as the cornerstone of the church (Ephesians 2:20) established the new temple of God via His work on the earth, and now a rest connected to that finished work and related to previous rests is pressed upon the Hebrews. In Hebrews 3:1–6, the author is arguing from Moses to Christ as the greater faithful servant of God over His own house (Hebrews 3:2–6) and to a rest to be entered (4:1, 6, 8, 9–11). The redemptive-historical institution of Christ's house, therefore, entails a rest to be entered. It is a

---

[10] Owen, *Works*, 18:416; emphasis added. See Owen, *Works*, 18:418 for another reference to Hebrews 3:3–4 as implying the deity of Christ. Schreiner argues similarly to Owen at this point: "On the one hand Jesus as a human being and as the high priest is faithful to God. On the other hand, as the divine son he is the builder of the house—the Creator of all! … Jesus is the divine Builder of the house" (Schreiner, *Hebrews*, 116–17).

[11] Owen, *Works*, 19:559.

[12] Schreiner, *Hebrews*, 118.

work of God that has practical implications for the people of God in their service for God.

In Hebrews 3:7–4:11, divine rests are presented by the author to induce perseverance in the readers' profession of faith in Christ. Owen identifies three divine rests in the passage. These rests are all founded upon a great work of God, are identified as divine rests, are the grounds upon which man is invited into God's rest, and include a sign or emblem of that rest via a day of rest. The first divine rest pertains to creation and man under the law of nature. The second rest pertains to the people of God under the law of institutions. The third rest pertains to the people of God under the Messiah.[13]

We will now identify the first two divine rests in the passage. What is important about Owen's view of these divine rests is the way he describes them and the way he connects them to Hebrews 4:9–10, which will be noted later. After quoting Owen extensively, I will offer brief comments. I will also show that some of the insights made by Owen have been made by others. What are the first two divine rests in the context? First, in the words of Owen:

> He considers the church and the state of it under *the law of nature*, before the entrance of sin. And herein he shows first that there was a rest of God in it; for saith he, "The works were finished from the foundation of the world.... And God did rest the seventh day from all his works," verses 3, 4. As the foundation of all, he layeth down first the works of God; for the church, and every peculiar state of the church, is founded in the work, some especial work of God, and not merely in a law or command. "The works," saith he, "were finished from the foundation of the world." ... This work of God, as hath been proved, Exerc. iii., was the foundation of the church in the state of nature, and gave unto it the entire law of its obedience.
>
> On this work, and the completing of it ensued the rest of God himself: Verse 4, "God did rest the seventh day from all his works." This rest of God, and the refreshment he took in his works, as comprising the law and covenant of our obedience, have been explained already.
>
> But this alone doth not confirm, nor indeed come near, the purpose or argument of the apostle: for he is to speak of such a rest of God as men might enter into, as was a foundation of rest unto them, or otherwise his discourse is not concerned in it; whereupon, by a citation of the words of Moses from Gen. ii. 2, he tells us that this rest of God was on the seventh day, which God accordingly blessed and sanctified to be a day of rest unto man. So that in this state of the church there were three

---

[13] Owen, *Works*, 18:413–16. Owen's discussion reflects a redemptive-historical reading of Scripture terminating upon Christ and His kingdom.

things considerable:—(1.) The rest of God himself in his works, wherein the foundation of the church was laid; (2.) A rest proposed unto man to enter into with God, wherein lay the duty of the church; and (3.) A day of rest, the seventh day, as a remembrance of the one and a means and pledge of the other. And herewith we principally confirm our judgment on the Sabbath's beginning with the world; for without this supposition the mentioning of God's work and his rest no way belonged to the purpose of our apostle. For he discourseth only of such rests as men might enter into and have a pledge of; and there was no such thing from the foundation of the world, unless the Sabbath was then revealed. Nor is it absolutely the work and rest of God, but the obedience of men and their duty with respect unto them, which he considers; and this could not be, unless the rest of God was proposed unto men to enter into from the foundation of the world.[14]

The first divine rest came as a result of a divine work (i.e., creation). It included a rest proposed to man to be entered via obedience and it had added to it a weekly pledge, the seventh day. This rest reflects man under the covenant of works, which has been discussed in previous chapters of this book.

The second rest in Hebrews 4 is described by Owen as follows:

The apostle considers the church under the law of institutions; and herein he presenteth the rest of the land of Canaan, wherein also the three distinct rests before mentioned do occur:—(1.) There was in it a rest of God. This gives denomination to the whole. He still calls it his rest: "If they shall enter into my rest." And the prayer about it was, "Arise, O Lord, into thy rest, thou and the ark of thy strength," or the pledge of his presence and power. And this rest also ensued upon his work; for God wrought about it works great and mighty, and only ceased from them when they were finished. And this work of his answered in its greatness unto the work of creation, whereunto it is compared by himself: Isa. li. 15, 16, "I am the Lord thy God, that divided the sea, whose waves roared: The Lord of hosts is his name. And I have put my words in thy mouth, and I have covered thee in the shadow of mine hand, that I may plant the heavens, and lay the foundation of the earth, and say unto Zion, Thou art my people." The dividing of the sea, whose waves roared, is put by a synecdoche for the whole work of God in preparing a way for the church-state of that people in the land of Canaan. And this he compares to the work of creation, in planting the heavens, and laying the foundations of the earth; for although these words are but a metaphorical expression of the political and church state of that people, yet there is an evident allusion in them unto the original creation of all things. This was the work of God, upon the finishing whereof he entered into his rest, in the

---

[14] Owen, *Works*, 18:413–14; emphasis original.

satisfaction and complacency that he had therein; for after the erection of his worship in the land of Canaan, he says of it, "This is my rest, and here will I dwell [Psalm 132:14]."

God being thus entered into his rest, in like manner as formerly two things ensue thereon:—(2.) That the people are invited and encouraged to enter into the rest of God. This the apostle treats concerning in this and the foregoing chapter. And this their entrance into rest, was their coming by faith and obedience into a participation of the worship of God wherein he rested, as a means and pledge of their everlasting rest in him. And although some of them came short hereof, by reason of their unbelief, yet others entered into it under the conduct of Joshua. (3.) Both these, his own rest and the rest of the people, God expressed by appointing a day of rest. This he did, that it might be a token, sign, and pledge, not now, as given to the people absolutely, of his first rest at the creation, but of his present rest in his instituted worship, and to be a means, in the solemn observation of that worship, to further their entrance into his rest eternally. Hence had the seventh day a peculiar institution among that people, whereby it was made to them a sign and token that he was their God, and that they were his people. And here lies the Judaical Sabbath in our fourth Exercitation.

It is true, this day was the same in order of the days with that before observed, namely, the seventh day of the week; but it was now re-established upon new considerations, and unto new ends and purposes. The time of the change of the day was not yet come; for this work was but preparatory for a greater. And the covenant whereunto the seventh day was originally annexed being not yet to be abolished, that day was not to be yet changed, nor another to be substituted in the room of it. Hence this day came now to fall under a double consideration,—first, As it was such a *proportion of time* as was requisite unto the worship of God, and appointed as a pledge of his rest in his covenant; secondly, As it received a new institution, with superadded ends and significations, as a *token and pledge of God's rest* in the law of institutions, and the worship erected therein.[15]

Notice how Owen views the rest of Canaan grounded upon a divine work that is reflective of the original creation. He bases this on a text in Isaiah:

> "For I am the LORD your God, who stirs up the sea and its waves roar (the LORD of hosts is His name). I have put My words in your mouth and have covered you with the shadow of My hand, to establish the heavens, to found the earth, and to say to Zion, 'You are My people.'" (Isaiah 51:15–16)

---

[15] Owen, *Works*, 18:414–15; emphasis original.

Canaan is viewed as a new Eden. Israel is God's corporate son, a new son of God (Exodus 4:22–23) with a new rest (Psalm 132:14) in the promised land. God's people are now in a new place, with a new rest, based on a new divine creational work, along with a new divine rest.

Viewing Canaan as a recapitulation of Eden is not unique to Owen. For example, Oren R. Martin, while discussing the book of Exodus, says:

> Furthermore, the multiplication of a people and movement towards inhabiting a place to live under God's blessing is rooted in his original blessing on humanity. The promises to Israel to plant them in the land are reiterations of a former promise. This connection is forcefully illustrated in Exodus 15:17:
>
>> You will bring them in and plant them on your own mountain, the place, O LORD, which you have made for your abode, the sanctuary, O LORD, which your hands have established.
>
> At the end of the song sung by Israel after crossing the Red Sea, 'the establishment of Israel in the land of Canaan is pictured as the planting of a tree in a *mountain sanctuary*, exactly the picture of Eden presented in Genesis 2 and Ezekiel 28.'[16] Through their redemption, then, Israel inherits the role of Adam in a new Eden-like land and are the means by which God will fulfill his worldwide purposes.[17]

In subsequent discussion, Martin says:

> Through the miraculous act of the exodus (ch. 14), an event pregnant with creational overtones, God delivers his people through the chaotic waters of judgment and brings them out as a new creation, free from foreign rule.[18]

While discussing the book of Deuteronomy, Martin says:

> …the land is described as a new paradise.[19] That is, the description of the land holds out promise of a return to an Eden-like bliss.[20]

---

[16] Martin footnotes the citation of this quote as follows: "Gentry and Wellum 2012: 227; emphasis original."

[17] Martin, *Bound for the Promised Land*, 78. The formatting of Exodus 15:17 is original. See Dempster, *Dominion and dynasty*, 102–03, where he discusses creational echoes in the book of Exodus.

[18] Martin, *Bound for the Promised Land*, 80. See Owen, *Works*, 18:414–15, quoted above.

[19] Martin lists the following texts in a footnote: Deuteronomy 6:3; 11:9; 26:9, 15; 27:3; 31:20.

[20] Martin, *Bound for the Promised Land*, 83.

… Deuteronomy contains numerous references to the creational mandate given to Adam.[21]

…recurring themes of 'life' and the 'prolonging of days' allude back to Eden and the life Adam enjoyed before the fall.[22]

…inheritance and rest become important aspects of the promise of land.[23]

Finally, Deuteronomy 12:9–11 pulls together the thematic threads of inheritance and rest.… That is, rest provides the opportunity for Israel to worship in the place God has chosen to dwell with his covenant people. On this note, Alexander rightly points out that it is impossible to consider the concept of rest without noting its association with the Sabbath. Despite differences in wording, the Decalogue in both Exodus and Deuteronomy associate these two concepts. Whereas Exodus 20:11 contains an explicit connection between the divine institution of the Sabbath and the seventh day of creation, Deuteronomy highlights God's deliverance of the Israelites from the Egyptians (e.g., Deut. 5:15). As a result, Alexander suggests that the deliverance of the Israelites from Egyptian bondage and subsequent settlement in the Promised Land were viewed as in some manner paralleling God's rest following the completion of his creative activity. This textual connection indicates that the rest offered in the land may be tied to the rest of God in creation prior to the fall.[24]

Martin's insights correspond to Owen's. In fact, many contemporary authors make connections between Eden and Canaan.[25] Israel is God's son in a new Eden-like place, given a task, and a weekly Sabbath based on divine acts. Just as Adam, the protological and typological son of God, was placed in Eden, given a task, and had a weekly Sabbath day founded on the divine rest, so Israel, the redemptive-historical and typological son of God (Exodus 4:22–23) was placed in Canaan, given a task, and had a weekly Sabbath day founded on the creational rest of God (Exodus 20) and the redemptive work of God (Deuteronomy 5). This implies that Israel ought to be viewed as a corporate Adam.[26]

---

[21] Martin, *Bound for the Promised Land*, 84.
[22] Ibid.
[23] Ibid., 85.
[24] Ibid., 85–86. Martin is referring to T. Desmond Alexander. Commenting on the book of Deuteronomy, Dempster says: "Divine presence and holy land echo the lost glory of Eden" (Dempster, *Dominion and dynasty*, 118).
[25] E.g., Alexander, Beale, Dempster, Dumbrell, Fesko, and Hamilton.
[26] See the discussion in Beale, *The Temple and the Church's Mission*, 118–21.

Owen also views the rest of Canaan as a preparation for a greater work. Many others have seen the pattern of divine works preparing the people of God for greater works in the future. Francis Foulkes, for example, shows that the writers of the Old Testament viewed the past acts of God as the basis for future, greater acts of God ultimately pointing to Christ and His kingdom.[27] As Oren Martin says, "…God's past dealings with his people serve as patterns, or types, for his future dealings with his people."[28] Israel (as with Adam) functions as a type of something greater to come—the people of God under the inaugurated new covenant. Commenting on Hebrews 4:9, Schreiner says this of Israel:

> Another typological connection should be made explicit. The writer refers here to "the people of God"… The rest given to Israel was a rest for a particular people in a specific location. But just as the rest points forward to a rest that embraces the whole creation, the new creation, the heavenly city, so Israel functions as a type for the new people of God, the church of Jesus Christ. The new people of God is not restricted to Israel but consists of Jewish and Gentile believers scattered throughout the world.[29]

Owen draws this conclusion from these two divine rests:

> So both these states of the church had these three things distinctly;—a rest of God in his works, for their foundation; a rest in obedience and worship, for man to enter into; and a day of rest, as a pledge and token of both the others.[30]

The common features of these rests are: 1) a divine rest after a divine work; 2) a rest to be entered in terms of man's obedience and worship in light of the divine work/rest; and 3) a day of rest as a pledge and token of the divine rest and of man's entrance into it. These rests function, in part, as foreshadowings of a better rest to come for the people of God.

Having mentioned the two previous divine rests, Hebrews 4:9 announces that "there remains a Sabbath rest for the people of God." Does this relate to previous rests? If so, how? Is this rest related to a divine work? If previous rests had an eschatological element to them, does this one? And who is the someone who has entered his rest in 4:10? The answers to these and other questions will be pursued below.

---

[27] See Francis Foulkes, "The Acts of God: A Study of the Basis of Typology," in *The Right Doctrine from the Wrong Texts?*, 342–71.
[28] Martin, *Bound for the Promised Land*, 25.
[29] Schreiner, *Hebrews*, 144.
[30] Owen, *Works*, 18:415.

The Exposition of Hebrews 4:9–10

Here is an outline of these two verses as I understand the syntax:

I. The conclusion to previous discussion (v. 9)

    A. Its indicator: ἄρα ("so")

    B. Its essence: ἀπολείπεται…("there remains…")

        1. The fact that something remains: ἀπολείπεται ("there remains")

        2. The identity of what remains: σαββατισμὸς ("a Sabbath rest")

        3. The party for whom it remains: τῷ λαῷ τοῦ θεοῦ ("for the people of God")

II. The basis for the conclusion (v. 10)

    A. Its indicator: γὰρ ("For")

    B. Its precondition: ὁ εἰσελθὼν εἰς τὴν κατάπαυσιν αὐτοῦ ("the one who has entered His rest")

    C. Its statement: καὶ αὐτὸς κατέπαυσεν…("has himself also rested…")

        1. The essence of it—someone has rested from his works: καὶ αὐτὸς κατέπαυσεν ἀπὸ τῶν ἔργων αὐτοῦ ("has himself also rested from his works")

        2. The correspondent to it—this rest corresponds to God's rest at creation: ὥσπερ ἀπὸ τῶν ἰδίων ὁ θεός ("as God did from His")

The exposition below will follow the syntactical outline above.

First, note that verse 9 is a conclusion to previous discussion. This is recognized by the commentators. For example, Schreiner says, "The word 'therefore' (ἄρα) signals that a conclusion is drawn from the preceding verses."[31] Upon what specifically is this conclusion based? Two themes seem to be picked up by Hebrews 4:9 (and v. 10) from the preceding discussion—the concept of remaining (Hebrews 4:1 and 6) and the concept

---

[31] Schreiner, *Hebrews*, 143.

of rest (Hebrews 3:11, 18, 19 [implied]; 4:1, 3, 4, 5, 6 [implied], and 8). As will be noted below, however, a new word for *rest* is brought into the discussion at Hebrews 4:9 (i.e., "Sabbath rest" [σαββατισμὸς (*sabbatismos*)]). Schreiner notes, "The threads of the preceding verses are picked up here and the author draws a conclusion about the nature of the rest God promised."[32] Owen, commenting on the particle "therefore" (ἄρα [*ara*]), says:

> ...the common note of inferring a conclusion from any argument... Hereby, therefore, he would mind the Hebrews to attend both to what he was about to assert, and to the dependence of it on the former testimonies and arguments that he had pleaded and vindicated.[33]

That Hebrews 4:9–10 are connected to the previous discussion is vital to keep in mind as we work our way through those verses. Hebrews 4:9 is an inference based on the previous discussion. It is not another way of saying what had already been said. It is not tautological. It finds as its basis the previous rests of God and the practical inferences for the people of God, but it is not a repetition of what had been said in different words.

Notice the essence of the conclusion: "There remains a Sabbath rest for the people of God." There are three views on Hebrews 4:9. First, the "Sabbath rest" is wholly future. Second, it is an already/not-yet soteric reality experienced by believers in Christ. Third, it is "a Sabbath rest" for the people of God in terms of a day of sacred rest to be kept, reflective of the finished work of Christ, the Lord of the Sabbath, though involving a symbolic and typological element.

The verb translated "there remains" is used in Hebrews 4:1, 6, and 9. In 4:1, it appears as a participle (καταλειπομένης [*kataleipomenēs*]): "while a promise remains of entering His rest…" At 4:1, it is compounded with the preposition κατά (*kata*). In 4:6 and 4:9, it appears in its present passive indicative verbal form (ἀπολείπεται [*apoleipetai*]). Here it is compounded with ἀπό (*apo*). This compound form occurs seven times in the New Testament. The present passive verbal form, however, is used only three times—Hebrews 4:6, 9, and 10:26. Hebrews 4:6 says, "Therefore, since *it remains* for some to enter it" (emphasis added). And Hebrews 4:9 reads, "So *there remains* a Sabbath rest for the people of God" (emphasis added). This word occurs in the same form in Hebrews 10:26, where we read, "For if we go on sinning willfully after receiving the knowledge of the truth, there no longer *remains* a sacrifice for sins" (emphasis added).

The question that pertains to our discussion is whether or not "there remains" of Hebrews 4:9 refers to something exclusively future, to an al-

---

[32] Schreiner, *Hebrews*, 143.
[33] Owen, *Works*, 20:325.

ready/not-yet soteric experience of believers, or to the present. That it refers to the present, though symbolic and typological of the future eschatological rest as well, is the best understanding for at least three reasons. First, notice the use and meaning of the word translated "there remains" in the same form elsewhere in Hebrews. In the two previous uses in Hebrews 4 (vv. 1 and 6), it refers to the (then) here and now, and both times it is connected to a rest which is both now and future, an already/not-yet rest of God, ultimately in Christ, though experienced by believers of all ages.[34] This is so because of Hebrews 4:3a, which says, "For we who have believed enter that rest."[35] The use in Hebrews 10:26 seems to refer to both the present and the future. The second and third reasons for taking "there remains" as referring to the present, though with symbolic and typological significance, pertain to what "a Sabbath rest" means and the interpretation of Hebrews 4:10. These will be discussed below.

That which "remains" is "a Sabbath rest." The noun "a Sabbath rest" (σαββατισμὸς [*sabbatismos*]) is used only here in the Bible. Various cognate forms of it are used in the Septuagint (LXX) in at least four places (Exodus 16:30; Levitcus 23:32; 26:34; 2 Chronicles 36:21). Each use in the LXX, when referring to men, refers to Sabbath-keeping in terms of an activity in the (then) here and now. Lincoln admits this, when he says, "In each of these places the term denotes the observance or celebration of the Sabbath."[36] This can be seen especially in Exodus 16:30, Leviticus 23:32, and 26:35.

> So the people rested (LXX: ἐσαββάτισεν [*esabbatisen*]; a verb) on the seventh day. (Exodus 16:30)

> It is to be a sabbath (LXX: σάββατα [*sabbata*]; a noun) of complete rest (LXX: σαββάτων [*sabbatōn*]; a noun) to you, and you shall humble your souls; on the ninth of the month at evening, from evening until evening you shall keep (LXX: σαββατιεῖτε [*sabbatieite*]; a verb) your sabbath (LXX: τὰ σάββατα ὑμῶν [*ta sabbata hymōn*]; a noun). (Leviticus 23:32)

---

[34] Cf. Schreiner, *Hebrews*, 135; Philip Edgcumbe Hughes, *A Commentary on the Epistle to the Hebrews* (1990; reprint, Grand Rapids: Wm. B. Eerdmans Publishing Company, 1977), 155–56 and 159–60; and Andrew T. Lincoln, "Sabbath, Rest, and Eschatology in the New Testament," in *From Sabbath to Lord's Day*, 206, 207, 210, 211, and 212.

[35] Cf. Lincoln, "Sabbath, Rest, and Eschatology in the New Testament," 206, where he says, "Hence also the fact that those who by faith already enter rest (4:3) need at the same time to be exhorted to strive to enter that rest (4:11)."

[36] Ibid., 213.

All the days of *its* [i.e., the land's] desolation it will observe the rest (LXX: σαββατιεῖ [*sabbatiei*]; a verb) which it did not observe (LXX: ἐσαββάτισεν [*esabbatisen*]; a verb) on your sabbaths (LXX: τοῖς σαββάτοις ὑμῶν[*tois sabbatois hymōn*]; a noun), while you were living on it. (Leviticus 26:34–35)

Something interesting occurs in the LXX version of Leviticus 23:32a. The LXX text reads as follows: σάββατα σαββάτων ἔσται ὑμῖν (*sabbata sabbatōn estai hymin*). The NASB translates this verse: "It is to be a sabbath of complete rest to you." The word σάββατα in the LXX complements the verb "to be" (ἔσται). The word σαββάτων ("of complete rest") modifies σάββατα. Both nouns clearly refer to an activity, a Sabbath-keeping to be rendered by those addressed in the passage. In Leviticus 23:32b of the LXX, a verb is followed by its direct object as follows: σαββατιεῖτε τὰ σάββατα ὑμῶν (*sabbatieite ta sabbata hymōn* ["you shall keep your sabbath"]). Here a Sabbath for the people of God to keep is pressed upon them, explicitly by verbs and implicitly by nouns. Also, in each case the word *Sabbath* is the same used by Moses in Genesis 2:2, "and He *rested* on the seventh day" (emphasis added). Pertinent to our discussion as well is the fact that God's creational rest in the LXX of Exodus 20:11 is referred to with the verb κατέπαυσεν (*katepausen*), the same word translated "rest" in Hebrews 3 and 4. In the LXX, the Creator's rest implies a Sabbath day to be kept for creatures. Hebrews 3 and 4 seem to follow this Septuagintal pattern (see the discussion on divine rests above and the exposition of Hebrews 4:10 below).

Robert P. Martin has an excellent discussion on the word translated "a Sabbath rest" (σαββατισμὸς [*sabbatismos*]). In the context of interacting with Andrew T. Lincoln, Martin says:

> It is interesting that Lincoln acknowledges that "in each of these places [i.e., the LXX texts cited above] the term denotes the observance or celebration of the Sabbath," *i.e.*, not *a Sabbath rest* as a *state* to be entered into but *a Sabbath-keeping* as a *practice* to be observed. This, of course, corresponds to the word's morphology, for the suffix -μὸς indicates an *action* and not just a *state*. This at least suggests that if the writer of Hebrews meant only "a Sabbath rest," *i.e.*, "a Sabbath state" to be entered into, he would have used the term σάββατον ("Sabbath") or continued to use κατάπαυσιν ("rest"), for he already had established the referent of κατάπαυσιν as God's own Sabbath rest which is to be entered into by faith (*cf.,* 4:1, 3–4, 11). Thus σαββατισμὸς suggests a Sabbath action, *i.e.*, "a Sabbath-keeping," although the idea of a "a Sabbath state" is not necessarily excluded because of the overarching theme of the larger context.[37]

[37] Martin, *The Christian Sabbath*, 251–52.

Throughout the passage thus far, the word translated "rest" is κατάπαυσις (*katapausis*). This word is also used in Hebrews 4:10–11. The shift from *katapausis* to *sabbatismos* at Hebrews 4:9 is deliberate.[38] But why the change? Joseph A. Pipa suggests the following:

> The uniqueness of the word suggests a deliberate, theological purpose. He selects or coins *sabbatismos* because, in addition to referring to spiritual rest, it suggests as well an observance of that rest by a 'Sabbath-keeping'. Because the promised rest lies ahead for the New Covenant people, they are to strive to enter the future rest. Yet as they do so, they anticipate it by continuing to keep the Sabbath.[39]

Notice that Pipa includes "spiritual rest" in his understanding of the word *sabbatismos*. This is an important observation, also made by Martin above (i.e., "the idea of 'a Sabbath state' is not necessarily excluded because of the overarching theme of the larger context").

Though many commentators take *sabbatismos* as either salvation rest in Christ (now and in the future) or exclusively eschatological rest, its use here in light of the flow of the contextual argument and its LXX usages suggest a different meaning. The LXX use has already been noted. In the context of Hebrews 4:9–10, the divine rests referred to have at least three things in common: 1) a divine rest after a divine work; 2) a rest to be entered in terms of man's obedience and worship in light of the divine work/rest; and 3) a day of rest as a pledge and token of the divine work/rest and of man's entrance into it. Each divine rest as given to the people of God (i.e., at creation and Canaan) had an abiding rest day remaining once the rest was instituted. If the other two divine rests included rest-keeping in the form of a Sabbath day, it is not without warrant to expect future divine rests (assuming they occur) to include the same. I am suggesting Hebrews 4:9–10 indicates just such a rest.

The party for whom "a Sabbath rest" remains is "the people of God." The people of God in this context refers to the church under the inaugurated new covenant, which obviously includes the recipients of the book of Hebrews. Christians are called the people of God elsewhere in the New Testament. First Peter 2:10 mentions those "who once were not a people but are now the people of God" (see Romans 9:25 and Hosea 1:10 and 2:23). The people of the inaugurated new covenant have a Sabbath day to keep. But why does there remain a Sabbath-keeping for the people of the

---

[38] See Lincoln, "Sabbath, Rest, and Eschatology in the New Testament," 213, where he admits this.

[39] Pipa, *The Lord's Day*, 117.

inaugurated new covenant? Because a new divine rest has been inaugurated and the not-yet eternal rest of God in the eternal state is yet future. So, as the old Sabbath looked both back to creation and forward to an eternal rest, so the inaugurated new covenant's Sabbath looks back to the inauguration of the new creation (i.e., Christ's resurrection on the first day) and forward to the eternal rest of God. The "Sabbath rest" of Hebrews 4:9 is for "the people of God" under the inaugurated new covenant.

The rests prior to Hebrews 4:9 referred to divine rests into which people entered and remained on the earth, though symbolic and typological of eschatological rest. The conclusion being drawn is that the people of God under the inaugurated new covenant have "a Sabbath rest" which remains, a divine rest instituted by the Son of God, the Lord of the Sabbath. This becomes clear in Hebrews 4:10.

In Hebrews 4:10, the author accounts for the remaining "Sabbath rest for the people of God." This is indicated by the conjunction γὰρ (*gar* ["For"]). Owen comments on the function of γὰρ (*gar* ["For"]).

> The conjunction γὰρ, "for," which introduceth this assertion, manifests that the apostle in these words gives an account whence it is that there is a new sabbatism remaining for the people of God. He had proved before that there could be no such rest but what was founded in the works of God, and his rest that ensued thereon. Such a foundation therefore, he saith, this new rest must have; and it hath it.[40]

Understanding the function of γὰρ (*gar* ["For"]) is very important in order to account for how verse 10 relates to verse 9. Lincoln seems to ignore it while discussing Hebrews 4:9–10.[41] Jonathan Edwards' comments are helpful and to the point:

> When it is said, "There remaineth a rest to the people of God;" in the original, it is *sabbatism*, or *the keeping of a sabbath*: and this reason is given for it, "For he that entered into his rest, he also hath ceased from his own works, as God did from his."[42]

The participial clause "the one who has entered His rest" functions as the precondition for the main clause of Hebrews 4:10 (see the outline above). In other words, because someone has entered into his rest and also rested from his works, "there remains a Sabbath rest for the people of

---

[40] Owen, *Works*, 20:332.
[41] See Lincoln, "Sabbath, Rest, and Eschatology in the New Testament," 212–14.
[42] Edwards, *Works*, 2:98.

God." As will be shown below, though the grammar and syntax argues for this understanding of the text, the way most explain the clause does not make sense.

The identity of this someone who has entered into his rest is debated. A common view is that it refers to believers.[43] Taken as referring to believers, the subsequent words "has himself also rested from his works" (the basis for the conclusion in v. 9; see the outline above) refers to the same believers. In other words, some understand this to mean that when believers have entered their or God's rest (v. 10), they will have entered the "Sabbath rest" that remained for them to enter while still on the earth. In other words, taking "Sabbath rest" as wholly future, it could read this way: "There remains a personal rest in the future, a personal Sabbath rest for the future, when individual believers enter their rest, that is, when they cease from their works as believers."[44] Or it could be stated this way for the already/not-yet view of 4:9: "There remains a Sabbath rest for believers, a Sabbath rest that we taste of in the present, to be fully enjoyed when believers have ceased from their earthly works."[45] Either way, verse 10 would seem to be saying that there is a future rest until we rest in the future. This view does not make sense in light of the grammar and syntax of verses 9 and 10 and the contextual argument. The common view makes verse 10 tautological or epexegetical of verse 9. There remains a future, full rest until we rest in the future fully? The grammar and syntax of verse 10 argue otherwise.

As indicated above, the conjunction γὰρ (*gar* ["For"]) introduces us to the basis for the conclusion stated in verse 9. The conclusion stated in verse 9 is: "So there remains a Sabbath rest for the people of God." The basis for this conclusion is: "For the one who has entered His rest has himself also rested from his works, as God did from His." There remains, in the here and now (see above), a Sabbath rest for the people of God under the inaugurated new covenant *because* someone has entered his rest, ceasing from his works. Who is this someone who has entered his rest, if it does not refer to believers?

There is another view of Hebrews 4:10 which makes more sense of its relation to verse 9, the context, and the flow of argumentation. In brief, this view maintains that Christ is the one who has entered (in the past) his rest.

---

[43] E.g. Hughes, Gaffin, O'Brien, Schreiner, Lincoln. This is not a novel view. It has adherents, for example, in the English Puritan era as well.

[44] See Hughes, *Hebrews*, 161–62 and O'Brien, *Hebrews* 171–72. Gaffin, "A Sabbath Rest Still Awaits the People of God," 45, says, "A parallel is drawn, with some deliberateness, between believers and God; *their* resting is to *their* works, as God's resting is to his works" (emphasis added).

[45] See Schreiner, *Hebrews*, 144–46.

Assuming this interpretation for now, verses 9 and 10 would be saying, "There is a remaining Sabbath day to be kept under the inaugurated new covenant for the present people of God on the earth because Christ, who is God, has entered His rest via His first-day resurrection, ceasing from the work of redemption, a new creation, just as God rested from His works of the old creation." This is Owen's view, and that of many others, and I think it is correct.

In a 2014 article, Nicholas J. Moore shows that some before and many after John Owen understand Hebrews 4:10 as a Christological referent. Moore notes that though William Gouge takes Hebrews 4:10 to refer to believers, he was aware of the Christological view held by others. Gouge's work was published posthumously in 1655. Owen's work on this text was published in 1674. Moore also lists the following as adherents to a Christological view: Ebrard, 1850; Vanhoye, 1963; Andriessen and Lenglet, 1971; Sabourin, 1973; and deSilva, 2000.[46] As noted above, there are others who hold the Christological view, such as: John Gill, 1809; Daniel Wilson, 1827; Jonathan Edwards, 1834; Henry Alford, 1857; Robert L. Dabney, 1891; Walter J. Chantry, 1991; Joseph A. Pipa, 1997; and Robert P. Martin, 2015.[47] Though a view ought not to be taken simply because others have taken it, it is important to acknowledge that Owen's view is not unique to him. The major issue is not who holds what; it is the identity of the person or persons in the clauses: "the one who has entered His rest" and "has himself also rested from his works." The Christological reference makes the best sense of the verse, its relation to verse 9, and the overall flow of the argument (see below).

Before continuing, it may help to notice several translations of Hebrews 4:10. This will display the fact that various interpretive nuances are evidenced in these translations.

> For he that is entered into his rest, he also hath ceased from his own works, as God *did* from his. (Hebrews 4:10, KJV, 1611)

> For he that is entered into his rest hath himself also rested from his works, as God did from his. (Hebrews 4:10, ERV, 1885)

> For he that is entered into his rest hath himself also rested from his works, as God did from his. (Hebrews 4:10, ASV, 1901)

> For he who has entered His rest has himself also ceased from his works as God *did* from His. (Hebrews 4:10, NKJV, 1982)

[46] Moore, "Jesus as 'The One who Entered his Rest,'" 386.

[47] Gill and Alford deny Hebrews 4:9 teaches a Sabbath day to be observed under the inaugurated new covenant.

for anyone who enters God's rest also rests from his own work, just as God did from his. (Hebrews 4:10, NIV, 1984)

for those who enter God's rest also cease from their labors as God did from his. (Hebrews 4:10, NRSV, 1989)

For the one who has entered His rest has himself also rested from his works, as God did from His (Hebrews 4:10, NASB Updated, 1995).

For the person who has entered His rest has rested from his own works, just as God did from His (Hebrews 4:10, CSB, 2004).

for whoever has entered God's rest has also rested from his works as God did from his (Hebrews 4:10 ESV, 2007 update).

The first clause in the Greek text of Hebrews 4:10 reads, ὁ γὰρ εἰσελθὼν εἰς τὴν κατάπαυσιν αὐτοῦ (*ho gar eiselthōn eis tēn katapausin autou* ["For the one who has entered His rest"]). The word for *God* is not in the clause, yet the NKJV, NIV, NRSV, NASB, CSB, and ESV either insert the word "God's" or capitalize the pronoun "His." This clearly tilts readers in a certain interpretive direction. According to this reading, the "rest" someone has entered is "God's" creational rest, which is implied in the last clause of the verse (i.e., "as God did from His" [i.e., as God rested from His works]). The second clause of 4:10 reads, καὶ αὐτὸς κατέπαυσεν ἀπὸ τῶν ἔργων αὐτοῦ (*kai autos katepausen apo tōn ergōn autou* ["has himself also rested from his works"])." Notice that the second use of the pronoun *autou* ("his") refers to the person "who has entered His rest." The first referent of *autou* is taken to be God, the second to be the person or persons who have rested from works. Though this is certainly plausible, I think there is a better way to understand the pronouns. Both refer to the same person. The "one who has entered His rest has himself also rested from his works." I take both pronouns as referring to Christ. The reasons for this should be clear in the ensuing discussion.

An important interpretive question has to do with the time reference in the initial dependent clause and the independent clause which follows it. The two options are either a future time referent or a past time referent. If taken as referring to believers, there are three views. For the future rest view of Gaffin and O'Brien, it puts the time referent at death, when believers cease working on the earth. For the already/not-yet view of Schreiner,

---

[48] Though Schreiner advocates an already/not-yet motif in Hebrews 4:9, he seems to locate Hebrews 4:10 exclusively in the future. See Schreiner, *Hebrews* 144–46.

it would seem to put the time referent both in the past and the future.[48] For the already/not-yet view of Lincoln, it puts the time referent in the past, when believers came to faith in Christ and ceased their sinful works, but also has a future referent.[49] It is best to take the time referent for both clauses as past, the reasons for which will be shown below.

Who is the author referring to in verse 10, when he says, "For *the one who has* entered His rest" (emphasis added)? As noted, some refer this to the believer who has "rested from his works" (Hebrews 4:10b). But this interpretation would compare God's ceasing from His work of creation and being refreshed by it (Genesis 1:31, "Then God saw everything that he had made, and indeed it was very good" and Exodus 31:17, "and on the seventh day he rested and was refreshed") with the believer's ceasing from his unrighteous works of sin and resting in God's salvation rest in Christ or the wilderness works of believers which are mixed, the rest being experienced in the intermediate or eternal state. When God ceased from His work of creation, it was not because it was bad or mixed, but because it was "very good." He was refreshed; that is, He approved what He had done. God's ceasing from His work of creation and His subsequent rest does not compare with the believer's ceasing from sinful works and taking rest in God or ceasing from wilderness works then entering the intermediate or eternal state. Believers don't cease from their work and call it "very good." They are not "refreshed" as they look back at their sinful works or their mixed wilderness works; they don't approve them (or at least not all of them). This kind of rest finds no parallel with God's rest. Owen comments:

> But now, if those mentioned be the works here intended, men cannot so rest from them as God did from his; but they cease from them with a detestation of them as far as they are sinful, and joy for their deliverance from them as far as they are sorrowful. Now, this is not to rest as God rested. Again, when are men supposed to rest from these works? It cannot be in this world, for here we rest not at all from temptations, sufferings, and sorrows; and for that mortification of sin of which we attain unto, we are to fight continually, "resisting even unto blood." It must therefore be in heaven that they so rest; and this is affirmed accordingly.[50]

The text presents a parallel between "the one who has entered His rest" and "has himself rested from his works" and God, who ceased from His work of creation. This cannot apply to believers. It destroys the parallel. The writer is speaking of an individual ("the one who…himself…his") who has entered his rest. Owen says:

---

[49] See Lincoln, "Sabbath, Rest, and Eschatology in the New Testament," 213.
[50] Owen, *Works*, 20:332.

> A single person is here expressed; on whose account the things mentioned are asserted. And of this change of phrase there can no reason be given, but only to signify the introduction of a singular person.[51]

To maintain the parallel, it must be an individual "who has entered His rest" and "rested from his works, as God did from His." The only individual who can fit this parallel is Jesus Christ, who entered His rest as our representative and "rested from his works" of redemption/re-creation when He rose from the dead. Owen says:

> There is a direct parallel in the whole verse between the works of the old creation and those of the new, which the apostle is openly comparing together. 1. For the authors of them: Of the one it is said to be God, —"As God did from his;" that is, the Creator: of the other, "He,"…; 'who is that of whom we speak,' saith our apostle, 'verse 13,'—for in these words he makes also a transition to the person of Christ… 2. The works of the one and the other are expressed. The works of the Creator are,… "his works;" "his own works," the works of the old creation. And there are the works of him of whom he speaks,…, "his works;" those which he wrought in like manner as God did his own at the beginning—that is, the work of building his church. For these works must answer each other, and have the same respect unto their authors or workers. They must be good and complete in their kind, and such as rest and refreshment may be taken in as well as upon. To compare the sins of the sufferings of men with the works of God, our apostle did not intend. 3. There is the rest of the one and the other. And these must also have their proportion to one another. Now God rested from his own works of creation,—(1.) By *ceasing from creating*, only continuing all things by his power in their order, and propagating them to his glory. (2.) By his respect unto them or *refreshment* in them, as those which set forth his praise and satisfied his glorious design. And so also must he rest who is here spoken of. (1.) He must cease from working in the like kind. He must suffer no more, die no more, but only continue the work of his grace, in the preservation of the new creature, and orderly increase and propagation of it by the Spirit. (2.) In his delight and satisfaction which he taketh in his works, which Jesus Christ hath to the utmost. "He sees of the travail of his soul, and is satisfied," and is in possession of that "glory which was set before him" whilst he was at his work.[52]

Taking both clauses as referring to Christ is the better option for these reasons: first, the first clause is best understood as a reference to an indi-

---

[51] Owen, *Works*, 20:333.
[52] Ibid., 20:333–34.

vidual; second, the past tense referents in the two clauses; third, the previous rests are divine; fourth, the comparison with God's rest; fifth, it makes better sense of the conjunction "For"; and sixth, the overall flow of the contextual argument. Since most of these have been discussed above, let's consider the first clause as a reference to an individual and the time referent of both clauses. These will be considered together.

In both clauses, the word "rest" is used. The first clause uses a noun form (κατάπαυσιν [*katapausin*]) and the second a verb form (κατέπαυσεν [*katepausen*]). This verbal form occurs in Hebrews 4:4 and 4:8. Hebrews 4:4 reads, "For He has said somewhere concerning the seventh *day*: 'AND GOD RESTED [κατάπαυσιν (*katapausin*)] ON THE SEVENTH DAY FROM ALL HIS WORKS'." Hebrews 4:8 reads, "For if Joshua had given them rest [κατάπαυσιν (*katapausin*)], He would not have spoken of another day after that." Both uses clearly refer to past events.

Another issue concerns the participle of the first clause (ὁ εἰσελθὼν [*ho eiselthōn*]), translated "the one who has entered." When does this one enter his rest? The participle is aorist active, which does not in itself tell us when this action occurred. The participial clause occurs prior to the main verb in the Greek text. It is dependent upon the aorist active verb of the main clause (κατέπαυσεν [*katepausen*]), and "any temporal reference is relative to the action of the main verb."[53] Moore's discussion of participles preceding main verbs is helpful at this point:

> As a general but not universal rule, participles preceding the main verb tend to be antecedent to the action of that verb, whereas those following the main verb tend to be concurrent or subsequent; additionally, aorist participles tend to precede the main verb, and present participles tend to follow it (Fanning 1990: 407; Porter 1989: 380–81; 1994: 188). These considerations suggest that we would expect ὁ εἰσελθὼν ["the one who has entered"], which is both aorist and prior to the main verb, to be antecedent to the action of the main verb; examination of the verse confirms this expectation: the action of entering rest is logically prior to the state of resting from works.[54]

Moore analyzed all the substantival aorist participles (i.e., participles that function as nouns as in Hebrews 4:10a) in the book of Hebrews.[55]

---

[53] Moore, "Jesus as 'The One who Entered his Rest,'" 388.

[54] Ibid.

[55] Moore lists all the substantival aorist participles in Moore, "Jesus as 'The One who Entered his Rest,'" 389, n. 19. They are as follows: for plurals, 2:1, 3; 3:16 (2x), 17, 18; 4:2, 3, 6; 6:4–5 (4x), 18; 11:31; 12:19; and for singulars, 3:2, 3, 4; 4:10; 5:5; 9:16, 17; 10:23, 28, 29 (3x), 30; 11:11, 17; and 13:20.

This is an important interpretive consideration, especially since the clause "the one who has entered" can refer to a number of people or anyone who thus enters rest. Moore says:

> The letter contains 33 substantival aorist participles, of which 17 are plural and 16 are singular (including the one in question here). All of the plural instances refer to a group of people who did something in the past; similarly, 11 of the singular instances refer unambiguously to the past. Of the five remaining participles, one is the case in question, leaving four to account for. In Heb. 3.3 and 4 ὁ κατασκευάσας [*ho kataskeuasas* ("the builder")] occurs twice—first referring generically to 'the builder of the house', and, on the second occasion, referring to God, 'the builder of everything'. In the case of God, it is clear that this refers to past action: God is 'the one who prepared/built everything'; but also in the case of the nonspecific 'builder', who is a builder because he or she has built a house—and indeed it is precisely the relationship to the house that is in view in 3.3. A similar argument obtains for the remaining participle [τοῦ διαθεμένου (*tou diathemenou*)], which comes twice, in Heb. 9.16 and 17. Although one might translate this as 'the testator', a person can be a testator only if he or she has made a will at some point in the past. Thus all substantival aorist participles in Hebrews refer either explicitly or implicitly to the past, a consistent feature of the letter's style, which means that a gnomic sense [i.e., not limiting action in the past, present, or future] for ὁ εἰσελθὼν ["the one who has entered"] in Heb. 4.10 is not impossible but would be at least unusual. Grammatical considerations are not decisive for or against either interpretation, but they do give reason to favour a past sense.[56]

This gives a sufficient background for Owen's claim above:

> A single person is here expressed; on whose account the things mentioned are asserted. And of this change of phrase there can no reason be given, but only to signify the introduction of a singular person.[57]

The "change of phrase" refers to going from "We who believe" and "the people of God" to the singular participle, "He that is entered."[58]

Taking the referent to past actions of Christ in both cases (the participle and the main verb) makes sense for other reasons as well. As Moore says, and as mentioned above:

> The presence of the particle ["For"] leads us to expect v. 10 to give the

---

[56] Moore, "Jesus as 'The One who Entered his Rest,'" 389.
[57] Owen, *Works*, 20:333.
[58] See Owen, *Works*, 18:418 and 20:333.

reason or cause for v. 9. On the usual reading of v. 10, however, it does not give grounds for v. 9 but rather introduces a clarification or explication of the σαββατισμὸς. ...

On the christological reading of v. 10, then, the ["For"] has it full force: '*for* the one who entered his rest (i.e., Jesus) has also rested from his works'. That is, it is because Jesus has completed his salvific work that rest remains open for the people of God. ...[59]

Also, the comparison in 4:10 is between our Lord as Mediator and God as Creator. This gives credence to the fact that the work of the old and new creations is that to which the author is referring. Moore agrees when he says:

...the statement juxtaposes the creative work of God with the salvific work of Christ... This, then, enables us to identify the 'works' with confidence, something which defenders of the standard reading are unable to do. There is a careful patterning: each party enters rest only after the completion of his specific and deeply important tasks, a parallel which becomes less exact if ["the one who entered"] refers to believers.[60]

Once Christ's work was accomplished He entered His rest, and we must remember that Christ is God. Just as previous divine rests came after divine works, so with our Lord's rest. There is a new covenant Sabbath rest, the foundation of which is the great redemptive work of Christ. Both the initial rest of God and the rest of Canaan are creational (see above) and so is this one. This interpretation would paraphrase Hebrews 4:9–10 as follows: "There remains a Sabbath-keeping for the people of God under the inaugurated new covenant in terms of a day of rest symbolizing the rest won for us by Christ and typifying the eternal rest of God to be enjoyed in the eternal state because Christ has rested from His works of accomplishing redemption and inaugurating a new creation via His resurrection."

Just as God entered His rest on the seventh day at creation, thus instituting the Sabbath day by positive example (and a pledge of glory to come), so Christ entered His rest on the first day, the day He rose from the dead, the day His new-creative/redemptive work was accomplished, thus instituting the Sabbath day for the new covenant people of God by positive example. Owen says:

Therefore did the Lord Christ enter into his rest, after he had finished and ceased from his works, 'on the morning of the first day of the week,'

---

[59] Moore, "Jesus as 'The One who Entered his Rest,'" 390–91.
[60] Ibid., 393.

when he rose from the dead, the foundation of the new creation being laid and perfected.[61]

Though the interpretation of Hebrews 4:9–10 offered above appears to be the minority view in current literature, when many discuss the sufferings and glory of our Lord, they often do so utilizing such language as redemption accomplished via the foundation of the new creation by the work and resurrection of Christ. When the question is asked, "When did our Lord enter rest?" many reply, "At His resurrection." Why did He enter His rest at the resurrection? Because His work of redemption was finished. In fact, Christian hymnody reflects the theology of Hebrews 4:9–10 as offered above. There seems to be a theological intuition reflecting this view in older hymn-writers. Two such examples make this clear. Notice the creational and new-creational motifs in both of these hymns, as well as Edenic, redemptive-historical, and eschatological emphases. The first hymn was written by Christopher Wordsworth in 1862 and the second by William Walsham How in 1871. Both men were Anglicans.

1. O day of rest and gladness,
O day of joy and light,
O balm of care and sadness,
Most beautiful, most bright;
On thee the high and lowly,
Through ages joined in tune,
Sing Holy, Holy, Holy,
To the great God Triune,

2. On thee, at the creation,
The light first had its birth;
On thee, for our salvation,
Christ rose from depths of earth;
On thee our Lord, victorious,
The Spirit sent from heav'n;
And thus on thee, most glorious,
A triple light was giv'n.

3. Thou art a port protected
From storms that round us rise;
A garden intersected
With streams of Paradise;
Thou art a cooling fountain
In life's dry, dreary sand;

---

[61] Owen, *Works*, 20:335.

From thee, like Pisgah's mountain,
We view the promised land.

4. Today on weary nations
The heav'nly manna falls;
To holy convocations
The silver trumpet calls,
Where gospel light is glowing
With pure and radiant beams,
And living water flowing
With soul-refreshing streams.

5. New graces ever gaining
From this our day of rest,
We reach the rest remaining
To spirits of the blest.
To Holy Ghost be praises,
To Father and to Son;
The church her voice upraises
To thee, blest Three in One.[62]

1. This day at thy creating word
First o'er the earth the light was poured:
O Lord, this day upon us shine
And fill our souls with light divine.

2. This day the Lord for sinners slain
In might victorious rose again:
O Jesus, may we raised be
From death of sin to life in thee!

3. This day the Holy Spirit came
With fiery tongues of cloven flame:
O Spirit, fill our hearts this day
With grace to hear and grace to pray.

4. O day of light and life and grace,
From earthly toil sweet resting place,
Thy hallowed hours, blest gift of love,
Give we again to God above.

---

[62] Christopher Wordsworth, "O Day of Rest and Gladness," in *Trinity Hymnal—Baptist Edition*, #321.

> 5. All praise to God the Father be,
> All praise, eternal Son, to thee,
> Whom, with the Spirit, we adore
> For ever and for evermore.[63]

The Implications of Hebrews 4:9–10

Assuming the exposition above, several implications follow. First, there is a present Sabbath rest, a Sabbath-keeping, for the people of God under the inaugurated new covenant. This is what the Old Testament prophesied and what the gospel accounts lead us to expect.

Second, the present Sabbath rest is for the people of God to enter into and remain in. This is why the recipients of Hebrews were exhorted to persevere in it, for it includes gospel or evangelical worship, not only union with Christ and the individual benefits of that union. This Sabbath rest is for the people of God as such.

Third, the present Sabbath rest is founded on the work of Christ in the accomplishment of redemption, the foundation of the new creation. That work is the foundation upon which salvation rest is offered to man (and always has been since the fall), which rest is inclusive of a day of rest that is symbolic of and typifying a future, eschatological rest.

Fourth, this Sabbath rest is reflective of the fact that our Lord entered His rest, via His first-day resurrection, for us and for our salvation. He entered glory, the eschatological state, proffered in Eden and typified in Canaan but attained only by our Lord. The inaugurated new covenant's Sabbath day reflects redemptive-historical conditions brought in by the sufferings and glory of our Lord, as the Old Testament predicted He would and the Gospels confirmed He did.

Finally, this remaining Sabbath rest corresponds to the original creational rest of God. As with many divine acts, earlier acts of God often typify later, greater acts of God, which are both similar and dissimilar to His previous acts. Just as God at creation and in Canaan, so also with our Lord. God, the Creator and Redeemer, worked, then rested, and God, the Mediator, worked, then rested. Just as the Creator's acts were both divine exemplars, imperatival for man, so also with the acts of the Mediator, our Lord Jesus Christ.

---

[63] William Walsham How, "This Day at Thy Creating Word," in *Trinity Hymnal—Baptist Edition*, #324.

14

The Doctrine of the Christian Sabbath
Revelation 1:10

Revelation 1:10 says, "I was in the Spirit on the Lord's day." It identifies the name of the sacred day for the inaugurated new covenant and further confirms its change from the seventh day to the first day of the week. We will consider the following in an attempt to prove this: 1) the context of Revelation 1:10; 2) the translation of the phrase "the Lord's day;" 3) the grammatical relations of "the Lord's day" in the New Testament; 4) the theological-covenantal parallels of "the Lord's day"; and 5) the parallels between "the Lord's day" and God's authority and the Sabbath under the old covenant.

The Context of Revelation 1:10

Note the context of Revelation 1:10. John had a vision of the resurrected, ascended, and reigning Christ. In verse 5, John identifies our Lord Jesus Christ as "the faithful witness, the firstborn of the dead, and the ruler of the kings of the earth." The three phrases in this verse are an allusion to Psalm 89:27 and 37 (i.e., the Davidic covenant; see 2 Samuel 7).[1] The words "the firstborn of the dead" not only evoke Psalm 89, but Colossians

---

[1] See G. K. Beale, *The Book of Revelation*, The New International Greek Testament Commentary (Grand Rapids: William B. Eerdmans Publishing Company, 1999), 190–91. See also Beale and Carson, CNTUOT, 1089.

1:18 as well. This is a reference to Christ's resurrection, which constitutes the inauguration of the new creation.

John identifies believers in Christ under the inaugurated new covenant as "a kingdom, priests to His [i.e., Christ's] God and Father" (Revelation 1:6; the NKJV translates this "kings and priests"; see 1 Peter 2:9, "a royal priesthood" and Ephesians 2:6, "seated us with Him…"). As was discussed above, the concept of man as king and priest under God finds its historical origin in Adam. Revelation 1:6 also evokes old covenant Israel according to Exodus 19:6a, "and you shall be to Me a kingdom of priests and a holy nation" (Exodus 19:6). John identifies believers in Christ under the inaugurated new covenant as kings and priests, offices at which both Adam and Israel failed and for which they were exiled. This status has been conferred upon believers by Christ based on His work for them. This means the Mediator's kingdom is populated by kings and priests who function as such.[2] This is important in order to highlight the use of the Old Testament in John's Revelation. This means John utilized the Old Testament to interpret and apply the sufferings and glory of Christ to the church. It is also of interest to note, in light of previous discussion, that the primary tasks of priests are connected to temple service.

In verse 7, John says:

> BEHOLD, HE IS COMING WITH THE CLOUDS, and every eye will see Him, even those who pierced Him; and all the tribes of the earth will mourn over Him. So it is to be. Amen. (Revelation 1:7)

This verse contains two brief citations from the Old Testament—Daniel 7:13 and Zechariah 12:10.[3] Our Lord references these two texts together in Matthew 24:30, attributing their eschatological fulfillment to Himself: "And then the sign of the Son of Man will appear in the sky, and then all the tribes of the earth will mourn, and they will see the SON OF MAN COMING ON THE CLOUDS OF THE SKY with power and great glory" (Matthew 24:30). John acknowledges Christ's resurrection and coming in these verses (i.e., Revelation 1:5 and 7). This implies that He has ascended.

In 1:9–11, John says:

> I, John, your brother and fellow partaker in the tribulation and kingdom and perseverance *which are* in Jesus, was on the island called Patmos because of the word of God and the testimony of Jesus. I was in the Spirit

---

[2] See the discussion in Beale, *Revelation* 192–96, on Revelation 1:6, esp. the section concerning Christ installing "saints to function *in the present* as kings and priests" (194ff.; emphasis original). See also, Beale and Carson, *CNTUOT*, 1090.

[3] See Beale and Carson, *CNTUOT*, 1090–91.

on the Lord's day, and I heard behind me a loud voice like *the sound* of a trumpet, saying, "Write in a book what you see, and send *it* to the seven churches: to Ephesus and to Smyrna and to Pergamum and to Thyatira and to Sardis and to Philadelphia and to Laodicea."

John is commissioned to write what he witnessed to the churches. He acknowledges Christ as both a Davidic figure and Son of Man, evoking Old Testament teaching about the Messiah to come in a manner consistent with other New Testament texts (e.g., Matthew 12:8; 24:30 and Mark 2:28). John understands Jesus to be the Davidic Son of Man spoken of in the Old Testament, as do other figures of the New Testament.

The book of Revelation was written to "seven churches that are in Asia" (Revelation 1:4). Coming from an apostle of Christ, it would have been read to those churches while conducting public worship, which took place on Sunday.[4] Kruger's assessment of the early practice of reading in public worship services is important to consider:

> The practice of reading canonical books in worship—though visible only in seed form in the books of the New Testament—is more explicitly affirmed as commonplace by the time of Justin Martyr in the middle of the second century.
>
> And on the day called Sunday, all who live in cities or in the country gather together to one place, and the memoires of the apostles or the writings of the prophets are read…[5]

John's use of "on the Lord's day" occurred at least 35 to 40 years after the resurrection of our Lord. This shows that by that time the phrase did not refer exclusively to a day in the past; it was a particular day of the week contemporary with John and his audience. When the letter was read to the churches the phrase "on the Lord's day" had been in use for some time. The readers would have heard the book read on a Sunday and knew what John meant by "on the Lord's day."

---

[4] See the discussion under the heading "Public Reading of Canonical Books," in Kruger, *Canon Revisited*, 209–10.

[5] Kruger, *Canon Revisited*, 210. Justin is cited as "*1 Apol.* 67.3." Later Kruger says this of Justin: "As for Revelation, he affirms its apostolic character and even refers to it as one of 'our writings'" (228).

The Translation of the Phrase "the Lord's Day"

Note the translation of the particular phrase under consideration—"the Lord's day." It is not translated "the day of the Lord," as in 2 Peter 3:10, because it is a different construction and uses a different word for "Lord." Second Peter 3:10 reads, ἡμέρα κυρίου (*hēmera kyriou* ["the day of the Lord"]). The word κυρίου (*kyriou* ["of the Lord"]) is a genitive masculine singular noun. It comes from κύριος (*kyrios*), a noun meaning "Lord." In the context of 2 Peter 3, "the day of the Lord" likely refers to the eschatological day of the Lord, "the day of God, because of which the heavens will be destroyed by burning" (2 Peter 3:12). Peter is referring to the last day judgment, the day of the general resurrection (see John 5:28–29 and 6:40).

Revelation 1:10, however, reads τῇ κυριακῇ ἡμέρᾳ (*tē kyriakē hēmera* ["the Lord's day"]). The word κυριακῇ (*kyriakē*), translated "Lord's," is a dative feminine singular adjective, agreeing in case and gender with the noun it modifies (i.e., ἡμέρα [*hēmera*; "day"]). It comes from κυριακός (*kyriakos*), an adjective meaning "belonging to the Lord."[6] "Lord's" is an adjective attributing a quality to the noun it modifies (i.e., "day"). The Lord's Day, therefore, is a day belonging to Jesus Christ as Lord. The word κυριακῇ (*kyriakē* ["Lord's"]) is used twice in the New Testament—here in Revelation 1:10 and in 1 Corinthians 11:20.

What about the use of κυριακῇ (*kyriakē* ["Lord's"]) outside the New Testament? According to Beale, it "is never used of the 'Day of the Lord' in the LXX, NT, or early fathers."[7] Beale also says that "the phrase is clearly and consistently used of Sunday from the second half of the second century on."[8] Its reference to Sunday in extra-biblical literature, however, probably dates to the first century. In *The Didache* (i.e., *The Teaching*), we find a use of the word κυριακός (*kyriakos*) in a very strategic context for our discussion. *The Didache* is an early church teaching manual. It was compiled, most likely, over several decades (beginning in the first century) and completed sometime late in the first century. Michael W. Holmes says:

> A remarkably wide range of dates, extending from before AD 50 to the third century or later, has been proposed for this document. Dating *The Didache* is made difficult by a lack of hard evidence and by its composite

---

[6] H. Bietenhard, "Lord," in *The New International Dictionary of New Testament Theology*, ed. Colin Brown (Grand Rapids: Zondervan Publishing House, 1986), 2:518.

[7] Beale, *Revelation*, 203.

[8] Ibid., Beale later denies any reference to the Sabbath in Revelation 1:10, though without elaboration.

character. Thus the date when the anonymous author or authors compiled this document on the basis of earlier materials must be differentiated from the time represented by the materials so utilized. *The Didache* may have been put into its present form as late as 150, though a date considerably closer to the end of the first century seems more probable. The materials from which it was composed reflect the state of the church at an even earlier time. The relative simplicity of the prayers, the continuing concern to differentiate Christian practice from Jewish rituals (8.1), and in particular the form of church structure—note the twofold structure of bishops and deacons (cf. Phil. 1:1) and the continued existence of traveling apostles and prophets alongside a resident ministry—reflect a time closer to that of Paul and James (who died in the 60s) than Ignatius (who died sometime after 110).[9]

If Holmes is right, *The Didache* reflects Christian thought and practice prior to the writing of at least some of the New Testament books, including John's Revelation. Holmes asserts that the final product reflects "the state of the church at an even earlier time." This is important because in *The Didache* 14.1, we read, "On the Lord's own day gather together and break bread and give thanks."[10] The Greek text reads: Κατὰ κυριακὴν δὲ κυρίου (literally, "And according to the Lord's of the Lord"). Κυριακὴν (*Kyriakēn* ["the Lord's"]) is the same word (an adjective) used in 1 Corinthians 11:20 of the Lord's Supper and Revelation 1:10 of the Lord's Day. Holmes' translation above assumes an ellipsis, supplying "day" to complete the thought. It appears that *The Didache* is connecting the Lord's Day with the Lord's Supper. Also, *The Didache* clearly refers to a gathering of the church. The word translated by Holmes as "gather together" is συνάγω (*synagō*). Paul uses the same participial form of this word in 1 Corinthians 5:4 in the context of the church gathered. Our Lord uses a form of the same word in the context of teaching which concerns church discipline in Matthew 18:20. *The Didache* 14.1 refers to a gathering of the church on the Lord's Day to partake of the Lord's Supper.

It seems evident that *The Didache* makes a theological connection between a weekly Lord's Day and a weekly Lord's Supper. It could be that both phrases either predate or closely correspond to the use of these phrases by Paul (1 Corinthians 11:20) and John (Revelation 1:10). This gives evidence to something mentioned above. Some technical terms and

---

[9] Michael W. Holmes, Editor and Translator, *The Apostolic Fathers: Greek Texts and English Translations*, third edition (Grand Rapids: Baker Academic, 2007), 337. Kruger dates *The Didache* to c. AD 100. See Kruger, *Canon Revisited*, 212.

[10] Holmes, *The Apostolic Fathers*, 365.

phrases utilized by the New Testament were extant prior to being incorporated into it. *The Didache*, most likely, reflects technical nomenclature that predates John's writing. This means that John did not invent the phrase "the Lord's day." The phrase was in use prior to his writing and may go back (at least) to the middle decades of the first century.

In both of its New Testament uses κυριακός (*kyriakos* ["Lord's"]) refers to something belonging to the Lord Jesus. Here in Revelation 1:10, therefore, John is referring to a day that belongs to the Lord as resurrected and ascended. The Lord's Day is a day which belongs peculiarly to Christ as the resurrected Lord who is now in heaven (i.e., the Son of Man, who is also Lord of the Sabbath). This use of the phrase and its intended meaning does not give the appearance of being novel to John, as was noted with Paul and the phrase "the Lord's Supper" in Chapter 13. In other words, John did not coin the phrase while writing. If this were not the case, his readers might not have known what he meant. Instead, it appears to be used because it was known and in use prior to being inscripturated by John. Owen's words are to the point:

> …he did not surprise the churches with a new name, but denoted to them the time of his visions by the name of the day, which was well known unto them. And there is no solid reason why it should be so called, but that it owes its pre-eminence and observation unto his [i.e., Christ's] institution and authority.[11]

Just as the Supper is called "the Lord's" due to being instituted by our Lord, so it is with the first day of the week. Both phrases, and their technical meanings, predate their use by the New Testament. The most plausible accounting of these phrases is that they were used because their use and meaning were already established and well-known. When John said, "I was in the Spirit on the Lord's day," his initial readers knew he was referring to the first day of the week, on which churches met for public worship. They met on the first day of the week due to the epoch-changing, redemptive-historical act of God in Christ—the resurrection of the Son of Man, the Lord of the Sabbath.

The Grammatical Relations of "the Lord's Day" in the New Testament

Note the grammatical relations the phrase "the Lord's day" has in the New Testament. The closest grammatical parallel is found in 1 Corinthians

---

[11] Owen, *Works*, 18:424.

11:20. As stated above, the word *kyriakē* (an adjective meaning "belonging to the Lord") is used twice in the New Testament (1 Corinthians 11:20 and Revelation 1:10). In 1 Corinthians 11:20, we read, "Therefore when you meet together, it is not to eat the Lord's Supper." That "when you meet together" refers to a formal gathering of the church is clear from 1 Corinthians 11:18, "…when you come together as a church…" The word "Lord's" in 1 Corinthians 11:20 is an accusative neuter singular adjective, agreeing in case and gender with the noun it modifies (i.e., "Supper"). It is a form of the same adjective John uses in Revelation 1:10. The Lord's Supper is a supper which belongs to the Lord Jesus in a peculiar manner. He instituted it and regulates it through the apostolic deposit of truth we have in the New Testament (1 Corinthians 11:23ff.; Matthew 26:26ff.). It is a sacramental and memorial meal commemorating and proclaiming His death (1 Corinthians 10:16; 11:24–26).[12] Though all suppers come from the Lord, not all suppers are "the Lord's." And though all days come from the Lord, not all days are "the Lord's." There is both a distinction of suppers (i.e., food and drink) and a distinction of days in the New Testament.[13] Just as the Lord's Supper has peculiar religious significance for Christians, so does the Lord's Day. All suppers are not alike; neither are all days alike. There is only one "Lord's Supper" and only one "Lord's day." Both the Lord's Supper and the Lord's Day belong to Jesus Christ in a unique manner, and both get their technical, inscripturated names after He rises from the dead and ascends into heaven.

The Theological-Covenantal Parallels of "the Lord's Day"

Note the theological-covenantal parallels that the phrase "the Lord's day" has in conjunction with "the Lord's Supper" and the old covenant. The old covenant had a memorial day and a memorial meal. The memorial day was the old covenant's weekly Sabbath. It commemorated both creation

---

[12] For my treatment of the Supper as more than a memorial ordinance, see Richard C. Barcellos, *The Lord's Supper as a Means of Grace: More than a Memory* (Fearn, Ross-shire, Scotland: Christian Focus Publications, Mentor Imprint, 2013).

[13] There is also a distinction made between the "houses" of believers and the house of God, the church. See 1 Corinthians 11:22, "What! Do you not have houses in which to eat and drink? Or do you despise the church of God…?" The Corinthians had trivialized the Supper such that it was not, in fact, the Lord's Supper in which they were partaking (see 1 Corinthians 11:20). Their "houses" are distinguished from "the church of God" (i.e., the assembly of the saints for public worship). The church is "the household of God" (1 Timothy 3:15), the Son's house (see Hebrews 3:1–6).

(Exodus 20:11) and redemption (Deuteronomy 5:15). The weekly Sabbath was God's because He instituted it by His example of resting after the work of creation and he regulated it (Genesis 2:2–3; Exodus 20:8–11; 31:13, "my Sabbath"; Isaiah 58:13, "the Sabbath…my holy day…the holy day of the LORD"). So the Lord's Day, the first day of the week, is Christ's day. It is His because He instituted it at least by the act of His resurrection, which was the day He "entered His rest" and "also rested from his works as God did from His" (Hebrews 4:10). This is why the Lord's Day is termed by many as the Christian Sabbath. It is a Sabbath because it is a day of sacred rest. It is Christian because it was instituted by Christ and regulated by Him through the apostles. The Lord's Day bears the marks of Christ's lordship, reflecting His redemptive work and the inauguration of the new creation by His resurrection.

The memorial meal of the old covenant was the Passover. The Passover was instituted prior to the inauguration of the old covenant (Exodus 12) and was incorporated into and legislated by the old covenant Scriptures (Exodus 34:25; Leviticus 9; Deuteronomy 16). The same is true of the old covenant's Sabbath (Genesis 2:3; Exodus 16 and 20). Interestingly, the Lord's Supper was instituted prior to the inauguration of the new covenant (Matthew 26:26–29; Mark 14:22–25; Luke 22:14–20) and incorporated into and legislated by the new covenant Scriptures (1 Corinthians 10 and 11). The Passover was a memorial meal, reminding the ancient Israelites of God's deliverance of them from Egyptian bondage (Exodus 12; 34:25; Leviticus 9; Deuteronomy 16). The Lord's Supper has a similar function; it looks back to our Lord's death.

Just as the old covenant's Passover was a memorial meal commemorating redemption, and just as the old covenant's weekly Sabbath commemorated both creation and redemption, so the new covenant's Lord's Supper commemorates redemption (i.e., Christ's death) and the new covenant's Lord's Day commemorates creation (i.e., new creation) and redemption. Murray says:

> The two pivotal events in this accomplishment [i.e., of redemption] are the death and resurrection of Christ and the two memorial ordinances of the New Testament institution are the Lord's supper and the Lord's day, the one memorializing Jesus' death and the other his resurrection.[14]

For those who understand the old covenant people of God as typological of Christ and His church, these theological-covenantal parallels should not be surprising.

---

[14] Murray, *Romans*, 258.

The Parallels Between "the Lord's Day" and God's Authority and the Sabbath Under the Old Covenant

Note the parallel that the phrase "the Lord's day" has with God's authority and the Sabbath under the old covenant. We have seen the Old Testament call the Sabbath God's (Exodus 20:8–11; 31:13, "my Sabbath"; Isaiah 58:13, "the Sabbath…my holy day…the holy day of the LORD"). It was His due to example, institution, and legislation. We have also seen Christ claim to be Lord of the Sabbath, that lordship being exercised during the entirety of the interadvental days of the new covenant (Mark 2:28). In Revelation 1:10, one day is marked out as belonging peculiarly to Christ as the resurrected Lord. Just as the old covenant's Sabbath was God's due to creation and redemption, so the new covenant's Sabbath, the Lord's Day, is Christ's due to creation and redemption. Also, just as the old covenant's Sabbath was God's due to example, institution, and legislation, so the new covenant's Sabbath is Christ's due to example, institution, and legislation.

Christ's lordship is connected to His resurrection in many places in the New Testament:

> And so, because he was a prophet and knew that GOD HAD SWORN TO HIM WITH AN OATH TO SEAT *one* OF HIS DESCENDANTS ON HIS THRONE, he looked ahead and spoke of the resurrection of the Christ, that HE WAS NEITHER ABANDONED TO HADES, NOR DID His flesh SUFFER DECAY. This Jesus God raised up again, to which we are all witnesses. Therefore having been exalted to the right hand of God, and having received from the Father the promise of the Holy Spirit, He has poured forth this which you both see and hear. For it was not David who ascended into heaven, but he himself says: "THE LORD SAID TO MY LORD, 'SIT AT MY RIGHT HAND, UNTIL I MAKE YOUR ENEMIES A FOOTSTOOL FOR YOUR FEET.'" Therefore let all the house of Israel know for certain that God has made Him both Lord and Christ—this Jesus whom you crucified. (Acts 2:30–36)

> Paul, a bond-servant of Christ Jesus, called *as* an apostle, set apart for the gospel of God, which He promised beforehand through His prophets in the holy Scriptures, concerning His Son, who was born of a descendant of David according to the flesh, who was declared the Son of God with power by the resurrection from the dead, according to the Spirit of holiness, Jesus Christ our Lord (Romans 1:1–4)

> Have this attitude in yourselves which was also in Christ Jesus, who, although He existed in the form of God, did not regard equality with God a thing to be grasped, but emptied Himself, taking the form of a bond-servant, *and* being made in the likeness of men. Being found in appear-

ance as a man, He humbled Himself by becoming obedient to the point of death, even death on a cross. For this reason also, God highly exalted Him, and bestowed on Him the name which is above every name, so that at the name of Jesus EVERY KNEE WILL BOW, of those who are in heaven and on earth and under the earth, and that every tongue will confess that Jesus Christ is Lord, to the glory of God the Father. (Philippians 2:5–11)

As we have seen, the resurrection is the redemptive-historical basis for first-day meetings by the New Testament Christians. These connections between Christ's lordship and resurrection support our observations above that the Lord's Day, the first day of the week, is, therefore, His day, possessing religious significance for Christians.

Conclusion

The Lord's Day, according to Revelation 1:10 and the informing theology of other pertinent portions of Scripture, refers to the first day of the week—our Sunday. It is the Mediator's day in the same way the seventh day from creation to the resurrection was the Creator's day. It is Christ's because of His lordship as the resurrected Son of Man (Matthew 12:8; Mark 2:28; Revelation 1:5). It is the fulfillment of Old Testament prophecy (Isaiah 56:1–8; Jeremiah 31:33). It is commemorative of the new creation and the accomplishment of soteriological redemption (Hebrews 4:9–10). His resurrection, which signifies the presence of the new creation, inaugurates a new sacred day for the people of God. It looks back to the resurrection of Christ as the foundation of the new creation and forward to the age of the full resurrection harvest and the fullness of the Spirit, the consummation of the eschatological strand of Scripture that began in the garden of Eden.

Conclusion

I began this book with these words:

> This book, in one sense, concentrates on hermeneutics and theological method. I contend that NCT gets the covenant of works and the Sabbath wrong because it gets the garden of Eden wrong, and it gets the garden of Eden wrong because it gets crucial aspects of hermeneutics wrong.

It should be obvious by now to readers that the issue behind the issues is hermeneutics and the manner by which one formulates doctrinal tenets. I have contended that NCT is in need of reexamining its method of interpretation with the goal of applying its basic principles more consistently. This was shown through a positive presentation of the covenant of works and the Sabbath. The challenge now for NCT adherents and those who hold similar views is to revisit hermeneutical principles and ask whether or not they are being consistently applied and if adjustment is necessary.

The doctrines of the covenant of works and the Sabbath were used to illustrate some weaknesses I see in NCT and others who hold some of their tenets. It is encouraging that some NCT adherents are applying proper hermeneutical principles to the garden of Eden and defending a covenantal arrangement between God and Adam. This is a move in the right direction. My hope is that more NCT writers will follow their lead and reflect further on this covenant. With NCT's commitment to be Christocentric in the interpretive process, understanding the Edenic covenant of works and analyzing Christ as the antitype of Adam will produce rich dividends.

The Sabbath, however, is another issue. NCT has yet to apply their basic hermeneutical principles consistently to this question. With NCT's tendency to apply a Christ-centered hermeneutic, it is hoped that its adherents will rethink many texts and their relation to each other in light of the study presented in this book. Adam was under the law of works. His obedience would have earned him and those he represented the reward of life. Though Adam failed to obey and enter rest as a result of his obedience, our Lord faithfully carried out His vocation, evidenced by His resurrection. The Sabbath, from the beginning, had an eschatological focus which was attained by our Lord for us and for our salvation. Its function with old covenant Israel had various aspects, but its ultimate purpose was to symbolize and point to the state of glory, a state of existence to which Adam failed to attain but which was attained by our Lord. The Lord's Day is a celebration of the fact that our Lord Jesus entered rest and, as a result, believers in Christ will receive the fullness of rest in the age to come.

I will not recapitulate the arguments of the book in this conclusion. There are, however, some issues worth recalling in order to highlight their importance. Understanding the garden of Eden is important in order to understand the Bible correctly. It sets the context for understanding man's identity and vocation, the Creator's rest as it relates to man, the fall, the first gospel promise of Genesis 3:15, the unfolding of that promise throughout the Old Testament, the relation of the biblical covenants to that promise, ancient Israel's vocation, and, most importantly, the vocation of our Lord and Savior Jesus Christ. The first Adam was a son of God who was a prophet, priest, and king. He failed his task as assigned to him by the Creator. He did not enter the rest of God proffered to him which was predicated upon obedience to the stipulations imposed upon him. Israel, the corporate son, failed its task as well, though God's purpose for Israel did not fail. The Messiah was to come through Israel and did. Old covenant Israel typified aspects of the person, work, people, and kingdom of the Messiah. The failures of Adam and Israel establish the context for a proper understanding of the sufferings and glory of our Lord Jesus Christ. Our Lord is both the last Adam and faithful Israel.

Many typological parallels between Adam and Christ were discussed above. Adam was the earth's first son of God, and Israel was God's corporate and typological son. Parallels between Adam in the garden and Israel in the land of promise were mentioned as well. Putting all the pieces together would indicate that Israel is a recapitulation of Adam in the garden on a corporate and typological level. Like Adam, Israel was God's son in God's place under God's rule[1] and like Adam, they broke covenant with

---

[1] I am borrowing from Graeme Goldsworthy.

God and were exiled—Adam from the garden and Israel from the holy land. Adam was God's protological and prototypical son, Israel was God's corporate and typological son, and our Lord is the eschatological and antitypical Son. Our Lord recapitulates various aspects of Adam's history and Israel's history, providing what the types never did. This argues that the Bible from the outset is a book about Christ.

I have argued that both the covenant of works and the Sabbath have much to do with our Lord Jesus Christ. The violation of the covenant of works by the first Adam is the reason there is a last Adam. The fact that Adam sinned and did not enter the Creator's rest is also related to the vocation of our Lord. The sin of Adam and his failure to take his seed to glory is why the Son of God became incarnate, suffered, died, was buried, and entered into glory. Everything in the Bible since the fall into sin is a preparation for the fullness of time, when "God sent forth His Son" (Galatians 4:4–5). Through ancient Israel, God prepared the world for the incarnation, sufferings, and glory of our Lord. This makes the scope of the Bible to be our Lord, promised in the Old Testament and revealed in the New Testament.

I have sought to present the views of others fairly and to interact with those views on exegetical, biblical-theological, systematic, and historical grounds. Though on one level NCT is a relatively new school of thought, many of its tenets have been proposed prior to our day and its objections to the views of others have been dealt with by many before us. My hope is that this contribution to the issues discussed will be received and pondered by my readers so they might come to know our Lord and His work for us in a deeper, more biblically faithful manner and, in light of that, love and serve Him more faithfully. *Soli Deo gloria!*

Appendix

New Covenant Theology:
Description, Definition, Defense,
Tom Wells and Fred Zaspel
(Frederick, MD: New Covenant Media, 2002),
reviewed by Richard C. Barcellos

Tom Wells and Fred Zaspel are to be commended for their work entitled *New Covenant Theology: Description, Definition, Defense (NCT)*. It is a very irenic and well-documented presentation of New Covenant Theology. I am thankful to the authors for providing us with a book that advances the important discussion among Calvinistic Baptists regarding the law and the covenants.

While reading *NCT*, I learned some new things and was reminded of other noteworthy facts about New Covenant Theology. Not all New Covenant Theology adherents equate the Decalogue with the old covenant. John Reisinger held this view for many years. It formed the main thesis of his influential *Tablets of Stone*. Reisinger has made it known recently on his website that he no longer holds this view. I also learned that I misrepresented Fred Zaspel in my book *In Defense of the Decalogue* (*NCT*, 188, n. 263). I stand corrected and regret this careless, though unintentional, misrepresentation. I was reminded that New Covenant Theology relies heavily on a certain understanding of Matthew 5:17–48, especially v. 17. Finally, I learned some new things about New Covenant Theology and its perspective on the nature of moral law. I will limit my critique to the following issues: *NCT* and Matthew 5:17–48; *NCT* and moral law; and *NCT* and *In Defense of the Decalogue (IDOTD)*.

Fred Zaspel discusses what appears to be the exegetical lynchpin of *NCT* in Chapters 5–8. His discussion surrounds what Douglas J. Moo (on the back cover) calls "the pivotal Matthew 5:17–20." Zaspel himself acknowledges this:

> Indeed, the whole NT theology of law grows out of this pivotal statement of Jesus. It is of "primary importance in trying to understand Jesus' attitude to the law" [quoting D. A. Carson] and, consequently, in developing a consistent theology of law and its relation to the Christian. (*NCT*, 78)

NCT bases its subsequent exegetical and theological discussion on Zaspel's interpretation of Matthew 5:17–20, which is dependent upon D. A. Carson. Greg Welty has written a critical analysis of their view entitled, "Eschatological Fulfillment and the Confirmation of Mosaic Law (A Response to D. A. Carson and Fred Zaspel on Matthew 5:17–48)." It is available on the Internet at: www.ccir.ed.ac.uk/~jad/welty/carson.htm.

Welty demonstrates that their interpretation of πληρόω (fulfill, Matthew 5:17) is implausible and that the subsequent application of this concept to the antitheses of Matthew 5:21–48 is contradictory. Welty argues, and I think persuasively, that Carson's interpretation of πληρόω is a novelty in Matthean usage. Carson claims that Jesus' ethical teaching fulfills what is foreshadowed in Moses' law. Welty acknowledges that several times πληρόω refers to Christ's person or actions fulfilling OT prophecy, but he also demonstrates that πληρόω never refers to OT laws being fulfilled by Jesus' teaching or, as Welty states it, "laws fulfilling laws."

Zaspel's thesis revolves around the meaning of one word, πληρόω. He claims that it is "the key word to the entire discussion" (*NCT*, 111). The "entire discussion," in the context of Zaspel's statement, refers to Matthew 5:21–48 as well. Putting such stock in the meaning of one word is hermeneutically dangerous and may be theologically disastrous. If Zaspel's interpretation of πληρόω is found wanting, then suspicion must be cast upon the validity of *NCT*'s main arguments, since so much of its subsequent discussion relies on the meaning of this word.

Zaspel says, "With all the press Matthew gives to this word (*pleroo*), the question of definition becomes greatly simplified" (*NCT*, 111). What follows in the book are eight pages dedicated to defining this one word. He concludes that πληρόω means that "Jesus came to bring about what Moses' law anticipated" (*NCT*, 118). "Just as Moses' law advanced the law which God had 'written on the heart' of man at creation, so also in Jesus' teaching that advance is brought to full completion" (*NCT*, 118). It is of interest to note that no exegesis is provided for this claim. Zaspel does footnote one of his pamphlets at this point. This understanding of the advancement of law throughout redemptive history, however, is such a crucial and pivotal element of *NCT*'s view of the law that making a passing reference to this leaves the critical reader wondering. Where does the Bible teach that Moses' law advanced the law that God had written on the heart of man at creation, in the sense intended by Zaspel? Could this have come from the authors' view of πληρόω infused back into the OT? For the record, Reformed theology teaches that the law written on the heart at creation was advanced by the law written on stones at Sinai in *clarity* and *perspicuity*, though not in *essence* and *spirituality*. It is the same law revealed in a different manner. The advance is not one of *quality* but of *clarity* due to the presence of sin in man's heart. Is this not what Jesus is doing in Matthew 5:17–48? He is making clear what had become obscure through the sinful teachings of the Pharisees.

NCT's understanding of πληρόω may be labeled the *eschatological advance* view. "It is not that Moses is set aside so much as he is 'fulfilled' by the advance Jesus gave him" (*NCT*, 87). This concept of eschatological advance is then applied to the antitheses of Matthew 5:21–48. As Zaspel examines the antitheses, he finds several nuances of eschatological advance: Matthew 5:21–22, "some sort of advance…extension or addition" (*NCT*, 105); Matthew 5:27–28, "advance of some sort" (*NCT*, 105); Matthew 5:31–32, "another advance…a tightening…an abrogation" (*NCT*, 106); Matthew 5:33–34, "obsolete" (*NCT*, 106); Matthew 5:38–39, "while Jesus may not formally repeal the lex [law], he very severely restricts its use" (*NCT*, 107); Matthew 5:43–44, "Jesus extends the law's requirement. Simply put, Jesus demands more than Moses" (*NCT*, 107). Zaspel claims that the view which understands Jesus as correcting Pharisaic casuistry does not fit the evidence (*NCT*, 108). According to Zaspel, the antitheses are not contrasting Pharisaic teaching with the law of Moses, but rather contrasting the law of Moses, on the main, with the law of Christ, thus illustrating his understanding of πληρόω. Zaspel closes his discussion of the antitheses with these words:

> …it seems that Jesus, 1) claims an authority that is superior to that of Moses; and 2) exercises that authority by taking the law of Moses in whatever direction he sees fit. In some cases, he leaves the particular command intact (#1 and 2). In other cases he extends the teaching of the command as originally given or advances it in some other way (#1, 2, 3?, 6). In still other cases he seems to rescind the original legislation (#3, 4) or at least restrict it (#5). (*NCT*, 108)

In ethical contexts, πληρόω refers to obeying and upholding the law as stated (cf. Romans 8:3; 13:8–10). Nowhere in the rest of the NT do we see the phenomenon of eschatological advance as necessitated by Zaspel's interpretation. If the law of Christ is all the commands of the NT plus those things in the OT "that are moral laws in light of the NT" (*NCT*, 75), as Wells claims, and if the law of Christ was anticipated by and advanced beyond the law of Moses, then why don't we see this phenomenon in the rest of the NT? Indeed, what we see is direct quotations of the very law that is supposedly advanced, and that without qualification (cf. Ephesians 6:2–3; James 2:8–11). It appears that *NCT* confuses moral law with positive law (see below).

Zaspel's understanding of πληρόω in Matthew 5:17 is a novelty in Matthean usage, complicates the antitheses unnecessarily, and does not find support in other NT ethical contexts where the word is used to refer to the law and its new covenant fulfillment.

While discussing moral law, Wells says, "Whatever is moral binds all men at all times" (*NCT*, 176, n. 253). With this I agree. On the next page, however, he says, "We must not, then, make Christ look and sound very much like Moses in his approach to moral law" (*NCT*, 177). I find this difficult, if not impossible, to reconcile with his previous assertion about the universality of moral law. Wells defines moral law as follows:

> Moral law is the law that has its source in the unchanging moral character of God with the result that it is intrinsically right and therefore binds all men of every era and land to whom it comes. (*NCT*, 162)

Wells adds, "moral law is found wherever there is a revelation of the moral character of God" (*NCT*, 162). But then he asks, "Is the revelation of God's character progressive?" (*NCT*, 162). He proceeds to base moral law on the progressive nature of special revelation. Since God reveals His character progressively in the Bible, moral law is revealed progressively. In other words, he argues for a dynamic concept of moral law. Indeed, he even claims that we will not know *the* moral law until the eternal state (*NCT*, 164, 166). Is this not a bit speculative? Reformed theology, however, bases its understanding of moral law on creation *imago Dei*. When God made Adam, He made him to be like Himself, to reflect His communicable attributes. Creation *imago Dei* involves having the law of God written on the heart (Romans 1, 2). It is that law which is based on God's character. In another place, Wells says that "all law from God came with moral force" (*NCT*, 164). He appears to base moral law upon God's will *and* His unchanging character. He makes no distinction between positive law and moral law. Positive law includes any laws added to the natural law (i.e., law of creation or moral law) due to the entrance of sin. It is based on God's will and is man's possession via special revelation (i.e., Scripture). Moral law is based on creation *imago Dei* and on God's unchanging nature and is man's possession via general revelation and, due to the entrance of sin, Scripture. Positive law is dynamic throughout redemptive history; moral law is static. Wells appears to infuse Zaspel's understanding of πληρόω into his discussion of moral law. This has detrimental implications for the identity of the law written on the heart (i.e., natural law), the basis of the covenant of works, the perpetuity of moral law, the Sabbath, the active obedience of Christ, and the imputation of righteousness.

In the Preface, the authors state that "the occasion that prompted this volume was the publication of a book containing a friendly but serious attack on NCT" (*NCT*, 1). They are referring of course to my book. Though they chose not to interact with it on all fronts, something for which I do not fault them, I was happy to see that they devoted specific interaction in Chapters 11 and 12. I was rather perplexed, however, that they did not deal with Jeremiah 31:31–34 and my exposition of it in any depth. Wells makes a somewhat cavalier dismissal of my interpretation and then makes a very confusing statement. He says, "Barcellos argues at length that the law in Jeremiah 31:33 is the Decalogue (pp. 16–24). I suspect that this is too constricting and that the law there is the full Mosaic law" (*NCT*, 170, n. 246). I would expect him to say that my view is too constricting, but I would not expect him to imply that Jeremiah meant that God would write *the full Mosaic law* on the hearts of new covenant saints. This appears to contradict the main thesis of Zaspel's argument from Matthew 5:17, unless of course one reads Zaspel's argument back into Jeremiah. This seems a bit hermeneutically strained.

Jeremiah 31:31–34 and its corroborating New Testament witnesses are foundational to the issues at stake. The text in Jeremiah discusses both the new covenant and the law. For this reason, we should expect this text to get more exegetical attention in a book entitled *New Covenant Theology*. In fact, the pivotal biblical passage of the entire book, Matthew 5:17–48, though it discusses law, does not discuss the new covenant, at least explicitly. In hermeneutics, it is always safest to start with the explicit words of Scripture pertaining to the issues at stake. *NCT's* theological methodology leaves room for improvement at this point since it is established upon shaky hermeneutical and exegetical grounds.

While discussing my exposition of Matthew 5:17–20, Wells says:

> I suspect our author shows here that he has confused the NCT position with some views of classical Dispensationalism…. Barcellos, however, must not attribute these things to NCT as he seems to do by repeating the words "this view" throughout pages 62–63. (*NCT*, 200)

For the record, I was intending older Dispensationalism by the phrase "this view."

While discussing my exposition of 1 Timothy 1:8–11, Wells points out several observations and disagreements (*NCT*, 190–99). The reader is encouraged to read my article in the *Reformed Baptist Theological Review* I:1 (January 2004). It has been considerably edited and expanded since the publication of the book.

In an appendix, "John Bunyan on the Creation Sabbath," Zaspel provides an extended quote from Bunyan (*NCT*, 293–294). No explanation is provided concerning what is being argued by this quotation. He prefaces Bunyan's words with these: "Bunyan responded more thoroughly." What we are not informed of is the context and reason why Bunyan says what he does. The quote in question comes under this heading: "Whether the seventh day Sabbath, as to man's keeping of it holy, was ever made known to, or imposed by, a positive precept upon him until the time of Moses? which from Adam was about two thousand years" (John Bunyan, *The Works of John Bunyan* [Carlisle, PA: The Banner of Truth Trust, 1991], 2:363). The full title of Bunyan's treatise is "Questions about the Nature and Perpetuity of the Seventh-Day Sabbath and Proof that the First Day of the Week is the True Christian Sabbath" (Ibid., 2:359). In *IDOTD*, I attempted to show that Bunyan was arguing against the perpetuity of the *seventh-day* Sabbath from creation to consummation (*IDOTD*, 100–107). Ample references from Bunyan were provided to prove that he did not believe the seventh-day Sabbath was moral but that "a Sabbath for holy worship is moral" (Bunyan, *Works*, 2:361). Elsewhere, Bunyan says, "it is evident that the substance of the ten commandments was given to Adam and his posterity" (Bunyan, *Works*, 1:499). It is very evident Bunyan held that the Sabbath as moral law predated the tablets of stone but that the *seventh-day* Sabbath began with the positive laws attending the Old Covenant. It is unclear to me what Zaspel was seeking to prove by this appendix. If he was attempting to prove that Bunyan did not believe that the *seventh-day* Sabbath predated Moses, then I agree with him. If he was attempting to prove that Bunyan did not believe the Sabbath is moral law and rooted in creation, then I disagree with him.

While reading *NCT*, I was reminded that the issue of the Sabbath is not the only thing upon which we differ. New Covenant Theology adherents often tout this as the only difference between us. Reading *NCT* convinced me that, though we differ on the Sabbath, our differences cut much deeper than this subject alone. Those differences are exegetical, theological, and historical. It is improper, therefore, for those on either side of this issue to claim that the Sabbath is the only issue dividing us.

I would like to close on a positive note. Through various circumstances, I have come to know Tom Wells on a personal level and consider him to be a dear, highly esteemed brother in the Lord. We have had several friendly, challenging, and edifying email exchanges and phone conversations. I am sure that this would be true of many other New Covenant Theology adherents and trust that this review will be taken as constructive criticism from a differing friend and brother.

Indices

Index of Scripture References

Old Testament

Genesis 1—138, 174, 176
Genesis 1–2—36, 158, 163
Genesis 1–3—23, 25, 32, 55, 59, 66, 147
Genesis 1:1—114, 115, 148
Genesis 1:1–12—59
Genesis 1:2—119
Genesis 1:3—116
Genesis 1:4—175
Genesis 1:6—116, 175
Genesis 1:7—175
Genesis 1:9—116
Genesis 1:11—116
Genesis 1:14—59, 116, 173, 174, 175, 177
Genesis 1:14–16—174
Genesis 1:14–19—173
Genesis 1:16—173
Genesis 1:16–18—59
Genesis 1:18—173, 175
Genesis 1:20—116
Genesis 1:20–22—59
Genesis 1:22—163
Genesis 1:24—116
Genesis 1:24–29—59
Genesis 1:26–27—114, 118, 121
Genesis 1:26—45, 103, 104, 114, 116, 119, 120
Genesis 1:26ff—89, 156
Genesis 1:27—18, 60, 103, 119, 120
Genesis 1:28—104, 127, 130, 132, 152, 163
Genesis 1:31—59, 252
Genesis 2—20, 27, 54, 148, 165, 167, 179, 180n, 188, 204, 240
Genesis 2–3—64, 128
Genesis 2:1–2—157, 206
Genesis 2:1–3—78, 88, 89, 90, 91, 145, 155, 156, 157, 164, 165, 179, 180, 185
Genesis 2:2—112, 158, 161, 233, 237, 246
Genesis 2:2–3—59, 87, 107, 107n, 188, 188–189, 189, 267
Genesis 2:3—162, 163, 164, 165, 166, 167, 169, 175, 185, 189, 267
Genesis 2:4—59, 60, 116
Genesis 2:4–5—59
Genesis 2:4ff—58, 59, 66, 77, 156
Genesis 2:7—60, 103, 115, 127, 156
Genesis 2:7–8—44, 60, 116
Genesis 2:7–9—59
Genesis 2:8—60, 128
Genesis 2:9—148
Genesis 2:10–12—150
Genesis 2:15—44, 60, 128, 130, 131, 132
Genesis 2:15–16—59

Genesis 2:15–25—116
Genesis 2:16—132
Genesis 2:16–17—43, 45, 46, 60, 104, 131–132, 132
Genesis 2:17—64, 69, 104
Genesis 2:18–19—59
Genesis 2:18–25—132
Genesis 2:21–22—59
Genesis 3—24, 149, 151, 157
Genesis 3:6—103
Genesis 3:8—128
Genesis 3:8–24—133
Genesis 3:8ff—69
Genesis 3:13–19—124
Genesis 3:15—10, 17, 17n, 18, 124, 124n, 133, 147, 148, 152, 271
Genesis 3:17–19—88
Genesis 3:22ff—71n
Genesis 3:23—124, 130–131
Genesis 3:24—131
Genesis 4:1—61n
Genesis 4:1ff—143, 144
Genesis 4:3—176
Genesis 4:3–4—177n
Genesis 4:3–5—61n
Genesis 4:17—55
Genesis 5—116
Genesis 5:1–2—116, 120
Genesis 5:3–32—176
Genesis 6—53
Genesis 6–9—56
Genesis 6:18—32, 33
Genesis 8:20—61n
Genesis 8:22—56
Genesis 9—116
Genesis 9:1–17—61n
Genesis 9:6—116, 120
Genesis 9:9–10—56
Genesis 9:13—56
Genesis 9:15–16—56
Genesis 12:3—192

Genesis 14:20—163
Genesis 17—143
Genesis 18:19—184n
Genesis 22:1–14—150
Genesis 29:27—139
Genesis 29:27–28—139
Genesis 31:41—139
Genesis 49:9—152

Exodus 3:1–2—150
Exodus 4:22–23—63, 152, 240, 241
Exodus 12—267
Exodus 13:3—188
Exodus 14—240
Exodus 15:17—129, 240, 240n
Exodus 16—86, 139, 165, 167, 180, 181, 182, 183, 183n, 184, 185, 187, 188, 188n, 196, 204, 267
Exodus 16:1—86
Exodus 16:4—182, 183
Exodus 16:4–5—182, 184
Exodus 16:5—182
Exodus 16:6–7—182
Exodus 16:22–26—181–182
Exodus 16:23—166, 181, 182, 183
Exodus 16:25—166
Exodus 16:27—182
Exodus 16:28—183, 183n
Exodus 16:28–29—182
Exodus 16:28–30—182–183
Exodus 16:29—183n
Exodus 16:30—182, 245
Exodus 19—150
Exodus 19:5–6—64
Exodus 19:6—261
Exodus 20—103, 139, 165, 167, 180, 181, 182, 187, 188, 190, 196, 197, 204, 209, 241, 267
Exodus 20:1–2—190
Exodus 20:8—82, 100, 166, 187, 188
Exodus 20:8–11—138, 179, 187, 188, 196, 267, 268

Index of Scripture References

Exodus 20:8ff—90
Exodus 20:9—158, 190
Exodus 23:10–11—196
Exodus 20:11—138, 161, 187, 189, 241, 246, 267
Exodus 20:12—190
Exodus 20:14—190
Exodus 25:6—174
Exodus 25:9—159, 160
Exodus 25:40—159, 160
Exodus 26:30—159, 160
Exodus 27:8—159, 160
Exodus 27:20—174
Exodus 31—85
Exodus 31:12–18—85
Exodus 31:13—267, 268
Exodus 31:15–17—84
Exodus 31:17—158, 252
Exodus 32:13—188
Exodus 34:25—267
Exodus 35:8—174
Exodus 35:14—174
Exodus 35:28—174
Exodus 39:37—174
Exodus 40:33—158

Leviticus 9—267
Leviticus 12:3—143
Leviticus 19:18—186
Leviticus 19:19—87
Leviticus 21:23—129
Leviticus 23:15–21—220
Leviticus 23:24—196
Leviticus 23:32—196, 245, 246
Leviticus 23:39—196
Leviticus 24:2—174
Leviticus 25:4—196
Leviticus 26:12—128
Leviticus 26:34—245
Leviticus 26:34–35—246
Leviticus 26:35—245

Numbers 3:7–8—131
Numbers 4:9—174
Numbers 4:16—174
Numbers 8:4—159, 160
Numbers 8:25–26—131
Numbers 12:7—234
Numbers 18:5–6—131
Numbers 24:9—152
Numbers 24:19—152

Deuteronomy 5—103, 241
Deuteronomy 5:6—190
Deuteronomy 5:13–15—190
Deuteronomy 5:15—190, 241, 267
Deuteronomy 6:3—240n
Deuteronomy 11:9—240n
Deuteronomy 12:9–11—241
Deuteronomy 16—267
Deuteronomy 18:15—152
Deuteronomy 23:1—192
Deuteronomy 23:14—128
Deuteronomy 26:9—240n
Deuteronomy 26:15—240n
Deuteronomy 27:3—240n
Deuteronomy 31:20—240n

Joshua 5:1–8—143

2 Samuel 7—65, 66, 135, 260
2 Samuel 7:6–7—128
2 Samuel 7:8–17—65
2 Samuel 7:12–13—135
2 Samuel 23—65
2 Samuel 23:1—65
2 Samuel 23:1–7—65
2 Samuel 23:5—65, 66

1 Kings 9:1—132
1 Kings 9:6—132
1 Kings 9:6–7—132
1 Kings 19:8–18—150

2 Kings 22:21–23—144

1 Chronicles 23:21—195
1 Chronicles 23:32—131
1 Chronicles 28:2—160, 161

2 Chronicles 2:4—195
2 Chronicles 31:3—195
2 Chronicles 36:21—245

Nehemiah 10:33—195–196

Job 31:33—63
Job 33:4—119
Job 42:12—163

Psalm 16—36, 39, 135
Psalm 16:8–11—54
Psalm 33:6—90, 119
Psalm 33:6–9—137
Psalm 33:8—90
Psalm 33:9—90, 138
Psalm 78:69—159, 160
Psalm 89—65, 135, 260
Psalm 89:3—66
Psalm 89:3–4—65
Psalm 89:27—260
Psalm 89:37—260
Psalm 92—185
Psalm 95—171, 233
Psalm 103:24—113
Psalm 110—135
Psalm 118:22—136
Psalm 132—135
Psalm 132:7–8—159
Psalm 132:8—161
Psalm 132:13–14—159
Psalm 132:14—161, 239, 240
Psalm 136—173
Psalm 136:5—173
Psalm 136:6—173
Psalm 136:7—173
Psalm 136:8—173
Psalm 136:9—173

Ecclesiastes 7:29—45, 103, 121, 121n, 124

Isaiah 1:13–14—196
Isaiah 4:2—152
Isaiah 5:20—143
Isaiah 7—152n
Isaiah 7:13–15—152n
Isaiah 7:14—152, 152n
Isaiah 8:10—152
Isaiah 9:6—152
Isaiah 9:6–7—152
Isaiah 11:1–2—152
Isaiah 11:2—152
Isaiah 22:20–22—195
Isaiah 22:22—195
Isaiah 24:5—66
Isaiah 24:5–6—61, 77
Isaiah 40:28—189
Isaiah 45:18—127
Isaiah 51:3—130
Isaiah 51:15–16—238, 239
Isaiah 53—152
Isaiah 53:2—152
Isaiah 56—193, 193n, 194, 194n, 204
Isaiah 56:1–8—191, 191–192, 269
Isaiah 56:2—194
Isaiah 56:2–5—193
Isaiah 56:3–5—192
Isaiah 56:4—194, 209
Isaiah 56:6—194
Isaiah 56:7—192, 193
Isaiah 58:13—189, 209, 267, 268
Isaiah 66:1—157, 161

Jeremiah 23:5–6—152
Jeremiah 31:31—193
Jeremiah 31:31–34—277
Jeremiah 31:33—106, 191, 269, 277
Jeremiah 33:14–15—152
Jeremiah 33:20—56
Jeremiah 33:25—56

Index of Scripture References

Jeremiah 51:51—129

Ezekiel 7:24—129
Ezekiel 28—129, 156, 240
Ezekiel 28:11–19—128, 129
Ezekiel 28:13—129, 130
Ezekiel 28:13–14—128, 129
Ezekiel 28:13–15—150
Ezekiel 28:14—129
Ezekiel 28:16—128, 129
Ezekiel 28:18—128
Ezekiel 31:8ff—130
Ezekiel 40:32—129
Ezekiel 43:12—129
Ezekiel 44:14—131

Daniel 7:13—261
Daniel 7:13–14—209

Hosea 1:9–10—195
Hosea 1:10—195, 247
Hosea 2:11—195, 196
Hosea 2:16—195
Hosea 2:18—195
Hosea 2:21—195
Hosea 2:23—195, 247
Hosea 6:6—201
Hosea 6:7—108n, 32, 32n, 33, 62, 62n, 63, 64n, 66, 77
Hosea 11:1—152

Micah 5—152n
Micah 5:2—152
Micah 5:2–5—152n
Micah 5:3—152

Zechariah 6:11–13—152
Zechariah 9:9–10—152
Zechariah 12:10—261

Malachi 3:1—152

New Testament

Matthew 1:1—135, 152
Matthew 1:20–23—135
Matthew 1:21—152
Matthew 1:23—152
Matthew 2:15—152
Matthew 3:3—192
Matthew 4:1—152
Matthew 4:8—151
Matthew 5—16
Matthew 5:1—151
Matthew 5:17–20—15, 15–16, 16, 274, 277
Matthew 5:17–48—273, 274, 275, 277
Matthew 5:17—85, 274, 276, 277
Matthew 5:21–22—275
Matthew 5:21–48—274, 275
Matthew 5:27–28—275
Matthew 5:31–32—275
Matthew 5:33–34—275
Matthew 5:38–39—275
Matthew 5:43–44—275
Matthew 8:16–17—192
Matthew 11:28–30—85
Matthew 12—201, 202, 203, 204
Matthew 12:1–14—200, 203, 211
Matthew 12:1–8—205
Matthew 12:1—201
Matthew 12:10–12—202
Matthew 12:10—202
Matthew 12:11ff—203
Matthew 12:12—202
Matthew 12:15–21—192
Matthew 12:2—201
Matthew 12:3—201
Matthew 12:5—201
Matthew 12:6—203
Matthew 12:7—201
Matthew 12:8—203, 262, 269

Matthew 12:9—205
Matthew 12:9–14—205
Matthew 14:23—151
Matthew 16:18—135, 152
Matthew 17:1–8—151
Matthew 19—88, 209
Matthew 19:1–8—190
Matthew 19:17—69
Matthew 21:12–13—192
Matthew 21:13—192
Matthew 22:36–40—18
Matthew 24:30—261, 262
Matthew 26:26–29—267
Matthew 26:26ff—266
Matthew 26:36—199
Matthew 28:1—212, 219
Matthew 28:1–8—212
Matthew 28:5–6—219
Matthew 28:5–10—219
Matthew 28:16—151
Matthew 28:18—133
Matthew 28:18–19—152
Matthew 28:18–20—192
Matthew 28:19–20—136

Mark 2—209
Mark 2:23–24—207
Mark 2:23–28—203, 205
Mark 2:27—90, 189, 204, 206, 207
Mark 2:27–28—179, 200, 205, 210, 211
Mark 2:28—90, 203, 208, 209, 262, 268, 269
Mark 3:1–6—205
Mark 3:13—151
Mark 6:2—205
Mark 7:14–23—205
Mark 9:2–8—151
Mark 11:9–11—135
Mark 11:10—152
Mark 12:1–14—200–201

Mark 13:2—205
Mark 14:22–25—267
Mark 16:1—212
Mark 16:1–11—212
Mark 16:2—212
Mark 16:9—212, 219
Mark 16:12—219
Mark 16:14—219

Luke 1:26–33—135
Luke 1:32–33—152
Luke 1:76—152
Luke 2:9–11—135
Luke 3—55
Luke 3:38—55, 63, 68, 128, 134
Luke 4:1–2—134
Luke 4:5—151
Luke 4:16—205
Luke 4:31–41—205
Luke 6:1–5—205
Luke 6:1–11—203
Luke 6:6—205
Luke 6:6–11—205
Luke 6:12—151
Luke 9:28–36—151
Luke 10:18—152
Luke 11:39–41—205
Luke 13:10–17—205
Luke 13:15ff—203
Luke 14:1–6—205
Luke 14:5—203
Luke 17:10—43n
Luke 20:17—136
Luke 20:34–36—228
Luke 22:14–20—267
Luke 24—216
Luke 24:1—212
Luke 24:1–2—219
Luke 24:1–12—212
Luke 24:14–15—219
Luke 24:25–27—152

Index of Scripture References

Luke 24:26—74
Luke 24:26–27—26
Luke 24:27—17
Luke 24:36—219
Luke 24:44–46—152
Luke 24:44–49—214, 215
Luke 24:45–46—26
Luke 24:46—74, 77

John 1:3—119, 206
John 1:14—116, 134, 148, 151, 152
John 1:29—152
John 1:32—152
John 1:34—152
John 2:13–22—134
John 2:16–22—152
John 2:19–22—151
John 2:22—134
John 3:16—117
John 4:21—205
John 5:8–10—205
John 5:28–29—263
John 6:15—151
John 6:40—263
John 6:44—123
John 7:22–23—205
John 7:23—205
John 7:39—18
John 9:13–16—205
John 12:31—152
John 14:25–26—217
John 14:26—200
John 15:26–27—217
John 16:13–14—223
John 16:13–15—200, 217
John 17:3—67
John 17:21–22—18
John 20—220
John 20:1—212, 219
John 20:1–23—212
John 20:19—212, 219, 220

John 20:26—219, 220
John 21:1—220
John 21:14—220

Acts 1:1—215
Acts 1:1–4—215
Acts 1:4—216
Acts 1:4–5—18
Acts 1:10–12—151
Acts 2—54
Acts 2:1—220
Acts 2:1ff—220
Acts 2:22–31—54
Acts 2:22–36—135
Acts 2:25–28—135
Acts 2:30—135
Acts 2:30–36—268
Acts 2:31—36, 39
Acts 2:34–35—135
Acts 2:36—75
Acts 2:42—221
Acts 3:22—152
Acts 6:2–4—216
Acts 7:37—152
Acts 8:26–40—192
Acts 13:22–41—135
Acts 13:34—192
Acts 15:13–18—135
Acts 20:6—221
Acts 20:7—100, 220, 221, 223, 224, 226
Acts 20:16—221
Acts 26:19–23—74, 77
Acts 26:22–23—152

Romans 1–2—89, 276
Romans 1:1–4—75, 135, 268
Romans 1:4—75, 229
Romans 1:18—104
Romans 1:18–32—123, 142
Romans 1:18ff—143
Romans 1:19ff—126

Romans 1:21—142
Romans 2—123
Romans 2:14–15—18, 46, 103, 122, 123n, 142, 143, 144
Romans 2:14ff—123
Romans 2:26–27—142, 143
Romans 3—143
Romans 3:9—141
Romans 3:9–12—123
Romans 3:10–18—141
Romans 3:19—141, 142
Romans 3:19–20—141
Romans 3:23—70, 72, 77, 124, 137
Romans 5—55, 157
Romans 5:1–2—73
Romans 5:2—73
Romans 5:12—149
Romans 5:12–19—17, 32, 126
Romans 5:12–21—66, 124, 154
Romans 5:12ff—68, 69
Romans 5:14—55, 63, 67, 68, 77
Romans 5:17—66, 67, 77, 136
Romans 5:19—66, 77
Romans 5:21—67, 68, 77
Romans 6:1–6—229
Romans 6:3–6—227
Romans 7:10—69
Romans 8—157
Romans 8:3—276
Romans 8:7—123, 141
Romans 8:16–25—154
Romans 8:18—73
Romans 8:30—73
Romans 9—15
Romans 9:25—195, 247
Romans 11:36—123
Romans 13:8–10—18, 276
Romans 14—83n, 85, 92, 110, 224, 225
Romans 14:2—225
Romans 14:5—82, 85, 93, 97

Romans 14:5–6—91, 92, 170, 224

1 Corinthians 3:16–17—135, 151
1 Corinthians 4:17—223
1 Corinthians 5:4—264
1 Corinthians 5:7—105
1 Corinthians 7:7–8—88
1 Corinthians 7:17—223
1 Corinthians 9:8–10—105
1 Corinthians 9:20–21—18
1 Corinthians 10–11—217, 267
1 Corinthians 10:16—266
1 Corinthians 10:21—213
1 Corinthians 11:2—214
1 Corinthians 11:7—120
1 Corinthians 11:12—223
1 Corinthians 11:17–22—222
1 Corinthians 11:18—266
1 Corinthians 11:20—213, 263, 264, 265–266, 266, 266n
1 Corinthians 11:22—266n
1 Corinthians 11:23—214, 224
1 Corinthians 11:23–25—213
1 Corinthians 11:23ff—266
1 Corinthians 11:24–26—266
1 Corinthians 12:13—18
1 Corinthians 15—55
1 Corinthians 15:20—228
1 Corinthians 15:20–23—228
1 Corinthians 15:22—55, 68, 69
1 Corinthians 15:45—75–76, 133
1 Corinthians 16—223, 224
1 Corinthians 16:1–2—100, 218, 221, 222, 222n, 224, 227
1 Corinthians 16:2—224, 226

2 Corinthians 1:20—17
2 Corinthians 3:7–18—196, 204
2 Corinthians 3:18—76
2 Corinthians 5:17—122, 229

Galatians 3–4—196, 204

Index of Scripture References

Galatians 3:8—192
Galatians 3:16—125, 192
Galatians 4— 83n, 92, 110, 224, 225
Galatians 4:4—117, 133
Galatians 4:4–5—125, 205, 272
Galatians 4:4–6—153
Galatians 4:8–11—82, 83
Galatians 4:9—225
Galatians 4:9–10—224
Galatians 4:9–11—85
Galatians 4:10—93
Galatians 4:10–11—91, 170
Galatians 6:2—18
Galatians 6:6—217
Galatians 6:15—229

Ephesians 1:4—76
Ephesians 1:11—18
Ephesians 1:20–23—75
Ephesians 1:21—153
Ephesians 1:22—153
Ephesians 2:1–3—123
Ephesians 2:5—229
Ephesians 2:5–6—228
Ephesians 2:6—137, 261
Ephesians 2:7—229
Ephesians 2:10—229
Ephesians 2:12—17, 17n
Ephesians 2:14—105
Ephesians 2:14–16—196, 204
Ephesians 2:16—105
Ephesians 2:19—192, 193
Ephesians 2:19–21—18
Ephesians 2:19–22—151, 203
Ephesians 2:20—136, 223, 236
Ephesians 2:21–22—135
Ephesians 2:22—148
Ephesians 3:11—18
Ephesians 4—123
Ephesians 4:17–19—123
Ephesians 4:24—89, 122, 229

Ephesians 5—136
Ephesians 5:31–32—136
Ephesians 6:2–3—276

Philippians 1:1—217, 264
Philippians 2:5–8—117
Philippians 2:5–11—268–269
Philippians 2:6–9—75
Philippians 2:9—76
Philippians 2:9–11—75
Philippians 3:10—228
Philippians 3:20—228
Philippians 3:21—76

Colossians 1:15—133
Colossians 1:15–18—229
Colossians 1:16—119
Colossians 1:18—18, 260–261
Colossians 1:24—18
Colossians 1:26–27—18
Colossians 2—83n, 92, 110, 224, 225
Colossians 2:11–12—227–228
Colossians 2:14—105
Colossians 2:16—86n, 91, 92, 93, 196, 204
Colossians 2:16–17—82, 85, 93, 97, 105, 170, 204, 224
Colossians 2:17—93, 94, 105
Colossians 3—123
Colossians 3:10—89, 121, 229

1 Thessalonians 2:13—216
1 Thessalonians 5:12–13—217

2 Thessalonians 2:14—72n, 76
2 Thessalonians 2:15—216, 217, 223
2 Thessalonians 3:14—153

1 Timothy 1:8–11—278
1 Timothy 2—209
1 Timothy 2:1–7—193
1 Timothy 2:11ff—90
1 Timothy 2:12–14—190

1 Timothy 3:5—135
1 Timothy 3:15—135, 153, 192, 193, 266n
1 Timothy 3:16—117

2 Timothy 1:9—18
2 Timothy 2:8—135
2 Timothy 2:10—73

Hebrews 1:1–2—119
Hebrews 1:3—133
Hebrews 2:1—254n
Hebrews 2:3—254n
Hebrews 2:10— 70, 72n, 76, 84, 137, 153
Hebrews 2:10–18—125
Hebrews 2:14—133
Hebrews 2:14–18—117
Hebrews 3–4—171, 246
Hebrews 3:1–6—135, 153, 233, 234, 236, 266n
Hebrews 3:1–4:13—232
Hebrews 3:2–4—254n
Hebrews 3:2–6—236
Hebrews 3:3–4—235, 236n, 255
Hebrews 3:5—236
Hebrews 3:6—233
Hebrews 3:7—233
Hebrews 3:7–4:11—83, 233, 237
Hebrews 3:7ff—234
Hebrews 3:11—243
Hebrews 3:12–13—234
Hebrews 3:16–18—254n
Hebrews 3:18–19—244
Hebrews 4—85, 169, 179, 231, 238
Hebrews 4:1—234, 236, 243, 244, 245, 246n
Hebrews 4:1–11—168
Hebrews 4:2–3—254n
Hebrews 4:3—93, 245
Hebrews 4:3–4—166, 169, 246n
Hebrews 4:3–6—244

Hebrews 4:4—90, 254
Hebrews 4:6—236, 243, 244, 245, 254n
Hebrews 4:8—236, 244, 254
Hebrews 4:9—84, 90, 194, 233, 234, 242, 244, 247, 248, 249, 250n, 251n
Hebrews 4:10–11—247
Hebrews 4:9–10—178, 178n, 204, 211, 226, 231, 232, 233, 237, 243, 244, 247, 248, 256, 257, 259, 269
Hebrews 4:9–11—236
Hebrews 4:10—233, 242, 245, 246, 248, 249, 250, 251, 251n, 252, 254, 254n, 255, 256, 267
Hebrews 4:11—233, 234, 246n
Hebrews 4:15—77, 133
Hebrews 5:5—254n
Hebrews 5:9–10—135
Hebrews 6:4–5—254n
Hebrews 6:5—229
Hebrews 6:18—254n
Hebrews 7:12—18
Hebrews 8–10—196, 204
Hebrews 8:5—159, 160
Hebrews 8:6—18
Hebrews 8:6–7—196, 204
Hebrews 8:13—196, 204
Hebrews 9:9–10—196, 204
Hebrews 9:15—196, 204
Hebrews 9:16–17—254n, 255
Hebrews 9:23–24—159
Hebrews 10:1—94, 105, 196, 204
Hebrews 10:4—67
Hebrews 10:5–10—117
Hebrews 10:9—204
Hebrews 10:11–14—67
Hebrews 10:15–18—196, 204
Hebrews 10:23—254n
Hebrews 10:26—244, 245
Hebrews 10:28–30—254n
Hebrews 11:11—254n
Hebrews 11:17—254n

Index of Scripture References

Hebrews 11:31—254n
Hebrews 11:39–40—18
Hebrews 12:18–24—151
Hebrews 12:19—254n
Hebrews 13:20—254n

James 2:8—18
James 2:8–11—276
James 3:9—89, 120

1 Peter 1:10–12—74, 77, 152
1 Peter 1:12—24n
1 Peter 2:4–5—203
1 Peter 2:5—135
1 Peter 2:9—261
1 Peter 2:10—195, 247
1 Peter 3:21–22—75

2 Peter 1:3—122
2 Peter 3—263
2 Peter 3:10—263
2 Peter 3:10–13—155
2 Peter 3:12—263
2 Peter 3:13—148, 153

1 John 2:2—15
1 John 3:4—143
1 John 3:8—125
1 John 3:12—143
1 John 3:16—140–141
1 John 4:9—140
1 John 4:11—140
1 John 5:3—18

Revelation 1:4—262
Revelation 1:5—260, 261, 269
Revelation 1:6—261, 261n
Revelation 1:7—261
Revelation 1:9–11—261, 261–262
Revelation 1:10—90, 100, 208, 211, 219, 226, 231, 260, 263, 263n, 264, 265, 266, 268 Revelation 2:7—71n
Revelation 3:7—135, 195

Revelation 3:14—229
Revelation 5:5—152
Revelation 12:9—24
Revelation 20–22—147
Revelation 20:2—24
Revelation 20:7–10—147–148
Revelation 21–22—157
Revelation 21:1—148
Revelation 21:3—148
Revelation 21:9—135, 136
Revelation 21:10—129
Revelation 21:10–11—150
Revelation 21:10–22—149
Revelation 21:14—149
Revelation 22:1—150
Revelation 22:2—148
Revelation 22:3—151
Revelation 22:14—148

Index of Names and Subjects

à Brakel, Wilhelmus, 63
Abrahamic covenant, 57, 125, 184, 185, 188, 192
Adam, 9–11, 17, 18, 20, 31–34, 36, 38, 40, 43–48, 50, 52, 55–64, 66–72, 74–78, 89, 98, 104, 108n, 110–114, 116, 120, 122–128, 130–138, 144, 148, 151, 153–155, 156, 157, 169, 176, 177, 179, 180, 185, 206, 207, 210, 228, 229, 240–242, 261, 270–272, 276, 278
Alexander, T. D., 146–147, 151n, 159n, 162n, 241
Allen, Michael, 35n
Ames, William, 26, 115–116, 123, 140, 166n, 185–187
analogy of faith, 22–25
analogy of Scripture, 22
antitype, 67–69, 84, 114, 172, 270
antitypical, 70, 272
ascended, 151, 260, 261, 265, 268
ascension, 75, 209, 214, 215, 220
Barcellos, Richard C., 13n, 15, 21n, 25n, 35n, 39n, 41n, 45n, 47n, 51n, 53n, 73n, 88n, 92n, 95n, 106n, 112n, 123n, 124n, 191n, 266n, 273, 277

Bavinck, Herman, 68, 120n, 123n, 132, 133n
Beale, G. K., 68n, 112, 128–132, 127n, 150, 159, 160, 162–164, 175, 176, 241n, 260n, 261n, 263
Beckwith, Roger T., 202, 203n, 204, 205n, 207
Beeke, Joel R., 45n
biblical theology, 9–12, 39
biblical-theological, 109, 111, 231, 272
biblicism/biblicist, 35, 36
Bownd, Nicholas, 140n, 165, 185n
Bunyan, John, 167, 194, 278
Burgess, Anthony, 25n, 47, 67
Canaan, 93, 233, 238–243, 247, 256, 259
Carson, D. A., 111n, 163n, 167, 201, 202, 207, 208, 260n, 261n, 274
ceremonial law, 105, 106, 142, 204
Chantry, Walter J., 232n, 250
Christian Sabbath, 99–101, 107–109, 110, 111, 231, 232, 267, *See also* Sabbath.
Christological, 58, 202, 227, 230, 231, 250, 256
Christology, 10, 12

civil law, 105, 106
condescension, 41–43, 47–50, 70, 72, 117, 118
covenant, 10, 11, 17, 18, 19, 20, 31–34, 35, 40–52, 53, 55–57, 60–66, 71, 76–78, 81, 105, 133, 135, 143, 152, 155, 157, 176, 180, 190–192, 194, 197, 209, 237, 239, 241, 260, 266, 267, 271, 273. *See also* covenant of works; old covenant; new covenant; covenantal; divine covenant; Mosaic covenant.
covenant of works, 5, 9–12, 19, 20, 21n, 27, 31–36, 38–43, 45, 48–52, 53, 55–61, 63, 66, 67–72, 77, 87, 94n, 95, 98, 108n, 111–113, 147, 171, 176, 238, 270, 272, 277
covenantal, 11, 16–18, 19, 20, 34, 35, 41n, 43, 44, 46, 47n, 48, 57, 59, 60, 66, 68, 77, 81, 98, 106, 132, 135, 157, 164, 170, 189, 190, 194, 197, 198n, 211, 260, 266, 267, 270
Coxe, Nehemiah, 20, 21, 25n, 26, 46n, 47, 49, 51, 56, 57, 71, 94n, 124n
creation, 9–12, 31, 32, 33n, 36, 41, 44–48, 50, 51, 58–60, 69, 70, 71n, 76–78, 81, 84, 87–90, 98, 100, 101, 104–108, 111, 113n 114–116, 118–124, 126, 127, 137–141, 143, 144, 148, 150, 152–155, 156–169, 172–180, 185–191, 193, 194, 197, 206–211, 220, 226–230, 235–243, 247, 248, 250, 252, 256, 257, 259, 261, 266–269, 274–278
creational, 43, 66, 84, 89, 138, 139, 155, 156, 163, 164n, 166, 168, 169, 172, 173, 175–180, 186, 190, 197, 207, 210, 211, 240, 241, 246, 251, 256, 257, 259
creation *ex nihilo*, 115
Creator, 9, 10, 20, 27, 41–44, 46n, 50, 59, 60, 61n, 84, 87, 98, 102, 103, 111–113, 118, 119, 123, 138–141, 144, 145, 147, 153–156, 157–159, 161–165, 167–169, 172, 173, 178, 180, 181, 185, 189, 190, 236n, 246, 253, 256, 259, 269, 271, 272
Creator/creature, 42, 43, 139, 190
creature, 41–44, 45n, 47, 50, 56, 61n, 98, 103, 104, 112, 114, 116, 120, 122, 123, 125–127, 132, 133n, 137–139, 144, 156, 172, 176, 178, 190, 207, 246, 253
Currid, John D., 60n
Dabney, Robert L., 232n, 250
Dempster, Stephen G., 153, 240m, 241n
Denault, Pascal, 20, 49
Didache, 263–265
Dispensationalism, 19, 277, 278
divine covenant, 36, 56, 57, 78
Dumbrell, William J., 9, 10, 130, 146, 159n, 241n
Eden, 9, 19, 27, 31, 33, 38, 44, 47, 52, 55, 61, 62, 64, 71, 72, 94n, 98, 124, 127–132, 137, 148, 150, 151, 153–155, 156, 157, 159n, 160, 171, 172, 176, 210, 240, 241, 259, 269, 270, 271
Edenic, 31, 59, 60, 66, 77, 88, 112, 124, 126, 156, 157, 257, 270
Edwards, Jonathan, 124n, 194n, 232n, 248, 250
Egypt, 152, 184, 185, 190, 206, 233, 241, 267
eschatological, 9, 17, 38, 57, 70, 71n, 72, 83, 84, 97, 112, 113, 114, 137, 148, 150, 167–172, 176n, 178–179, 180n, 193, 242, 245, 247, 248, 257, 259, 261, 263, 269, 271, 272, 274–276

Index of Names and Subjects

eschatology, 10, 12, 19, 59, 70–72, 81, 85, 113

eternal life, 41, 67–72, 74, 117, 137, 149

Eve, 10, 61n, 89, 116, 122–124, 127, 128, 132, 136–138, 148, 157

exaltation, 73–77

exile, 124, 130, 133, 148, 157, 261, 272

federal, 25, 38, 51, 57, 68, 151

Fesko, J. V., 59, 62n, 63, 118n, 119, 120n, 130, 136, 241n

Frame, John M., 189

Gaffin, Richard B., 153, 154n, 228, 229n, 232m, 233, 249n, 251

garden, 9, 10, 19, 21n, 27, 31–35, 38–40, 44, 46, 47, 52, 53, 55, 56, 58, 60–62, 70–72, 78, 88, 98, 104, 124, 127–134, 137, 148, 150, 151, 153–157, 160, 171, 210, 257, 269, 270–272

Gill, John, 73, 250

glory of God, 9, 26, 70, 72–74, 76, 77, 120, 124, 137, 149, 150, 154, 269

Hamilton, James M., 68n, 146, 158n, 159n, 241n

hermeneutical, 6, 10, 19–21, 23, 26, 36, 40, 58, 68n, 77, 91, 111, 198, 199, 270, 271, 274, 277

hermeneutics, 5, 9, 10, 12, 13, 14, 17, 19–28, 39, 40, 58, 270, 277

Hodge, A. A., 43n, 44

Hodge, Charles, 73

Holmes, Michael W., 263, 264

humiliation, 48, 75, 76

image of God, 12, 43, 45, 60, 98, 103, 114, 118–126, 133, 137, 141, 143, 144, 147, 156, 162, 178

imago Dei, 90, 121, 276, 277

immortal, 45n, 103

immutable, 70

incarnate, 26, 51, 74–76, 133, 153, 272

incarnation, 98, 113, 272

interadvental, 84, 85, 192, 209, 211, 268

Israel, 10, 17, 54, 60, 63–65, 77, 81, 83, 86, 89, 94, 105, 106, 108, 110, 111, 128, 129, 131, 132, 138, 139, 142, 143, 148–150, 152, 153, 159, 164n, 167–169, 174, 175, 180, 181–183, 185–190, 192, 193, 195–197, 204, 206, 207, 210, 240–242, 261, 268, 271, 272

Israelites, 57, 89, 90, 131, 143, 150, 168n, 182, 241, 267

Johnson, Dennis E., 23

judicial law, 105

justice, 56, 77, 127, 184n, 191

justification, 6, 48, 73, 74, 126, 141, 203

Kaiser, Jr., Walter C., 22–24

Keach, Benjamin, 167

Kelly, Douglas F., 116, 119n, 120n

Kline, Meredith G., 66, 126, 130, 159, 161, 162n

king, 98, 118, 127, 131–133, 135

Kruger, Michael J., 213, 214n, 216, 217, 218n, 262, 264n

last Adam, 9, 48, 57, 70, 75–77, 114, 126, 133–137, 153, 154, 229, 271, 272

law of God, 16, 18, 20, 35, 46, 71, 95, 101, 103, 104, 108, 122, 123, 141, 143, 144, 276

law of Moses, 17, 95, 215, 275, 276

law of nature, 10, 99, 100, 101, 102, 104, 107, 178, 237

Lehrer, Steve, 34, 36n, 81n, 86, 87

Lincoln, Andrew T., 139n, 245, 246, 247n, 248, 249, 252

Long, Gary D., 14, 16–18, 31–35, 36n, 77, 84

Lord's Day, 81, 97, 99–101, 108, 167, 171, 179, 200, 212, 218, 219, 224–226, 229, 232, 260, 262–269, 271

Lord's Supper, 104, 105, 213–215, 217, 218, 221, 222, 224, 225, 264–267

LXX, *See* Septuagint.

Martin, Oren R., 130n, 240–242

Martin, Robert P., 111n, 139n, 140n, 163n, 167, 177n, 181n, 183, 221–223, 232n, 246, 247, 250

marriage, 44, 88, 136, 178, 186, 190, 197, 209, 228

mediator, 41, 68, 75, 84, 103, 106, 209, 256, 259, 261, 269

Messiah, 74, 105, 106, 192, 236, 237, 262, 271

Messianic, 24n, 75, 124n, 152, 197, 208

Moo, Douglas J., 16, 73n, 75n, 274

moral law, 35, 94n, 95, 96n, 102–106, 123n, 167

Mosaic covenant, 64, 71n, 81, 83–86, 97, 103, 110, 111, 142, 167–169, 182, 184, 187n, 189, 190, 192, 194, 196, 197, 204

Mosaic law, 87, 102, 106, 142, 274, 277

Moses, 17, 54, 55, 58–62, 64, 66, 67, 71n, 74, 77, 83, 87, 89, 94n, 95, 105, 118–120, 126, 130, 131, 139n, 143, 144, 150, 152, 158, 160, 161, 166, 176, 177, 181–184, 186–190, 209, 215, 233–237, 246, 274–276, 278

Mount Sinai, 81, 86, 102, 103, 105, 106, 113, 150, 151, 160, 165, 181, 184, 185, 187, 188, 197, 275

Muller, Richard A., 22, 25n, 47n, 62, 96, 102, 106, 108

Murray, John, 70, 72n, 73n, 75, 76, 140, 186n, 208, 209n, 267

mutable, 70, 78

natural law, 94, 102–106, 142, 276, 277

new covenant, 10, 18, 20, 27, 57, 81–87, 91, 92, 94n, 97, 103, 106, 108, 110, 111, 148, 151, 164n, 167, 179, 180, 181, 186n, 190–197, 199, 200, 204, 208, 209, 211, 213, 214, 220, 229, 230, 231, 232, 242, 247–250, 256, 259, 260, 261, 267, 268, 276, 277

New Covenant Theology (NCT), 5, 6, 9–11, 13–18, 19, 20, 21n, 26–28, 31–37, 38, 58, 77, 78, 81–83, 85, 86, 94–98, 99, 107, 181, 199, 270–272, 273–279

new creation, 12, 88, 106, 122, 130, 154, 168, 169, 179, 193, 220, 226–229, 235, 236, 240, 242, 248, 250, 256, 257, 259, 261, 267, 269

New Testament, 11, 16, 17, 21, 26, 56, 57, 59, 67, 71, 75, 81–83, 85, 96, 97, 104, 107, 111, 116, 135, 136, 142, 146, 170n, 192, 193, 195–198, 211–214, 217–226, 229, 231, 244, 247, 260, 262–269, 272, 277

old covenant, 10, 17, 83, 85–87, 94n, 97, 105, 110, 138, 151, 187, 190, 191, 193–197, 200, 203, 204, 206n, 260, 261, 266–268, 271, 273, 278

old creation, 148, 154, 180, 228, 229, 250, 253

Old Testament, 16, 17, 21, 23n, 55, 57, 66, 67, 74, 88, 104, 105, 108, 111, 131, 134, 135, 141, 142, 146,

Index of Names and Subjects

152, 153, 180, 181, 190, 193–196, 198, 201, 202, 203, 205, 208, 211, 214, 242, 259, 261, 262, 268, 269, 271, 272

ordinance, 61, 84, 88, 89, 94, 105, 112, 144, 155, 156, 163, 164n, 167, 169, 172, 173, 177–180, 184, 185, 188, 190, 196, 205, 207, 210, 211, 224, 225, 266n, 267

Owen, John, 20n, 21, 25n, 26, 39n, 45n, 46n, 47n, 51n, 56n, 57n, 71n, 72, 76, 91–94, 95n, 110, 112, 118, 139n, 165–167, 176–179, 180n, 181n, 184n, 185, 187n, 189n, 191n, 193n, 196, 207, 221, 223n, 232–241, 242n, 244, 248, 250, 252, 253, 255, 256, 257n, 265

paradise, 44, 45, 64, 130, 137, 157, 160, 185, 240, 257

Particular Baptist, 20, 39, 40, 49, 52

Passover, 134, 144, 188, 267

patristic, 62, 111n

Perkins, William, 123n

Pipa, Joseph A., 232n, 247, 250

Poole, Matthew, 120n, 183

positive law, 46n, 47, 60, 104, 105, 108, 167, 177, 204, 276–278

Poythress, Vern S., 19, 22n, 26n

Presbyterian, 11, 49

priest, 98, 117, 125, 130–133, 151, 152, 156, 157, 200–203, 234, 236n, 261, 271

priestly, 156, 174, 193

probation, 71, 113, 132, 171

Progressive Covenantalism, 11

proleptic, 156, 165–169, 172

prophet, 24n, 26, 54, 58, 61–64, 74, 75, 77, 98, 127, 129, 131, 132, 148, 151, 152, 157, 181, 192–195, 197, 215, 233, 262, 264, 268, 271

protological, 70, 72, 114, 168, 180n, 241, 272

protology, 12, 72, 113

Puritan, 107, 194, 249n

redemption, 9, 17, 23n, 51, 63, 88, 105, 112, 114, 125, 136, 141, 153, 154, 168–171, 190, 197, 229, 233, 240, 250, 235, 256, 257, 259, 267–269

redemptive-historical, 15, 51n, 58, 88, 103, 106, 107 111, 181, 187n, 190, 193, 194, 196, 198, 200, 204, 210–214, 218, 226, 227, 230–232, 236, 237n, 241, 257, 259, 265, 269

Reformed, 21, 25, 27, 32–34, 36, 39n, 44n, 45n, 51, 71, 96, 101, 107, 108, 113, 123, 193, 275, 276, 278

Reisinger, John G., 14–16, 33–35, 85, 86, 94n, 95, 96, 186n, 273

Renihan, James M., 20, 25, 35, 41, 45, 49, 51n

resurrection, 36, 54, 58, 74–77, 81, 83–86, 97, 99–101, 106, 107, 134, 154, 171, 172, 176, 179, 180, 193, 211–215, 217–221, 224, 226–229, 231, 232, 248, 250, 256, 257, 259, 261–263, 265, 267–269, 271

Sabbath, 5, 9–12, 20, 27, 44, 81–269, 270, 271, 277, 278. *See also* Christian Sabbath.

sanctification, 87, 101, 117, 125, 157, 162–167, 175, 179, 185, 189, 224, 237

sanctuary, 128, 130, 150, 159, 160, 174, 176, 240

Savoy Declaration (SD), 6, 20, 25, 39, 40, 41, 44, 46, 48, 51, 52, 60

scope of Scripture, 25–27

Second London Confession of Faith of 1677/89 (2LCF), 6, 15n, 19–22,

25, 27, 28, 31, 35, 36, 38, 40–52, 60, 70, 77, 95, 98–101, 103–107, 108n, 121n, 122, 124n, 167n, 178

Septuagint (LXX), 124n, 245–247, 263

Schreiner, Thomas R., 82, 96, 97, 164n, 168, 169, 183n, 185, 186, 193n, 202, 208n, 226, 227, 232n, 235n, 236, 242–244, 245n, 249n, 251

Shaw, Robert, 43n, 44, 69

Shedd, W. G. T., 142

Sinai, *See* Mount Sinai.

sola Scriptura, 26

Son of Man, 128, 191, 200, 203, 205, 206, 208, 209, 211, 261, 262, 265, 269

suffer, 54, 74, 76, 77, 105, 117, 125, 137, 152, 154, 215, 252, 253, 268, 272

sufferings and glory, 59, 75, 98, 111, 113, 152–154, 172, 194, 198, 204, 213, 214, 216, 257, 259, 261, 271, 272

Swain, Scott R., 35n

temple, 74, 98, 112, 128–137, 146n, 148–162, 172, 176, 179, 193, 200, 201, 203–205, 208, 236, 261

temporal, 173, 175, 228, 254

theological method, 9, 12, 39n, 270, 277

Thompson, Alan J., 215

Trinitarian, 119

Trinity, 96, 119

Trueman, Carl R., 96n

Turretin, Francis, 63n, 102n, 103n, 104n, 115, 123n, 163, 166, 167, 185n, 186, 187, 191n

type, 55, 58, 59, 67–69, 72, 77, 83, 84, 93, 112–115, 126, 130, 133n, 136, 160, 168, 169, 172, 178, 179, 195, 236, 242, 270, 272

typological, 171, 180, 189, 241, 242, 244, 245, 248, 267, 271, 272

typology, 67, 68n, 93

unconditional, 46n

union, 18, 172, 228, 229, 259

Vanhoozer, Kevin J., 68n

voluntary condescension, 41–43, 47, 48, 50

Vos, Geerhardus, 39n, 70, 71n, 112, 113, 169–172, 180n

Waldron, Samuel E., 95, 212, 213, 219, 220n, 229

Ward, Rowland S., 44n, 45n, 63n, 108

Warfield, Benjamin B., 62–64

Watson, Thomas, 123n

Wells, Tom, 5, 14–16, 82, 87–95, 183n, 188, 193, 194n, 199, 200, 210, 222n, 226, 227, 273, 276–279

Wenham, Gordon J., 9, 158, 159n, 164, 165, 173, 174n, 175

Westminster Confession of Faith (WCF), 6, 20, 25, 40, 41, 43n, 44, 46, 48, 51, 52, 60, 72, 95, 101, 102, 107n

Westminster Standards, 11, 20, 28, 108n

White, A. Blake, 14n, 16, 17n, 32–35, 77, 82–84

wilderness, 86, 134, 152, 181, 184, 185, 187, 197, 233, 252

Witsius, Herman, 62, 63n, 71, 72, 124n, 191n

Young, Edward J., 61

Zaspel, Fred, 5, 14–16, 85, 95, 273–278

Bibliography

Books

a' Brakel, Wilhelmus. *The Christian's Reasonable Service*, 4 vols. Grand Rapids: Reformation Heritage Books, 1992, Third printing 1999.

Alexander, T. D. *From Eden to the New Jerusalem: An Introduction to Biblical Theology*. Grand Rapids: Kregel Publications, 2009.

Allen, Michael and Scott R. Swain. *Reformed Catholicity: The Promise of Retrieval for Theology and Biblical Interpretation*. Grand Rapids: Baker Academic, 2015.

Ames, William. *The Marrow of Theology*. Durham, NC: The Labyrinth Press, 1983.

Baines, Ronald S., Richard C. Barcellos, and James P. Butler, editors. *By Common Confession: Essays in Honor of James M. Renihan*. Palmdale, CA: RBAP, 2015.

Barcellos, Richard C. *Better than the Beginning: Creation in Biblical Perspective*. Palmdale, CA: RBAP, 2013.

_____. *In Defense of the Decalogue: A Critique of New Covenant Theology*. Enumclaw, WA: WinePress Publishing, 2001.

_____. *The Family Tree of Reformed Biblical Theology: Geerhardus Vos and John Owen — Their Methods of and Contributions to the Articulation of Redemptive History*. Owensboro, KY: RBAP, 2010.

_____. *The Lord's Supper as a Means of Grace: More than a Memory*. Fearn, Ross-shire, Scotland: Christian Focus Publications, Mentor Imprint, 2013.

Barcellos, Richard C., editor. *Recovering a Covenantal Heritage: Essays in Baptist Covenant Theology*. Palmdale, CA: RBAP, 2014.

_____. *Southern California Reformed Baptist Pastors' Conference Papers*, Volume I (2012). Palmdale, CA: RBAP, 2012.

Bavinck, Herman. *Reformed Dogmatics*, vol. 2. John Bolt, general editor and John Vriend, translator. Grand Rapids: Baker Academic, 2004, Third printing, July 2008.

Beale, G. K. *A New Testament Biblical Theology: The Unfolding of the Old Testament in the New*. Grand Rapids: Baker Academic, 2011.

_____. *Handbook on the New Testament Use of the Old Testament: Exegesis and Interpretation*. Grand Rapids: Baker Academic, 2012.

_____. *The Book of Revelation*, The New International Greek Testament Commentary. Grand Rapids: William B. Eerdmans Publishing Company, 1999.

_____. *The Temple and the Church's Mission: A biblical theology of the dwelling place of God*. Downers Grove, IL: InterVarsity Press, 2004.

Beale, G. K., editor. *The Right Doctrine from the Wrong Texts? Essays on the Use of the Old Testament in the New*. Grand Rapids: Baker Books, 1994.

Beckwith, Roger T. and Wilfrid Stott. *This is the Day: The Biblical Doctrine of the Christian Sunday in its Jewish and Early Christian Setting*. London: Marshall, Morgan & Scott, 1978.

Beeke, Joel R. & Mark Jones. *A Puritan Theology: Doctrine for Life*. Grand Rapids: Reformation Heritage Books, 2012.

Blowers, Paul M. *Drama of the Divine Economy: Creator and Creation in Early Christian Theology and Piety*. Oxford: Oxford University Press, 2012.

Bownd, Nicholas. *The True Doctrine of the Sabbath*. Dallas: Naphtali Press and Grand Rapids: Reformation Heritage Books, 2015.

Brown, Colin, editor. *The New International Dictionary of New Testament Theology*, vol. 2. Grand Rapids: Zondervan Publishing House, 1986.

Brown, Michael G. and Zach Keele. *Sacred Bond: Covenant Theology Explored.* Grandville, MI: Reformed Fellowship, Inc., 2012.

Bunyan, John. *The Works of John Bunyan*, Volume Two. Edinburgh: The Banner of Truth Trust, 1991.

Carson, D. A. *From Sabbath to Lord's Day: A Biblical, Historical, and Theological Investigation*. Reprint ed., Eugene, OR: Wipf and Stock Publishers, 1999.

Casselli, Stephen J. *Divine Rule Maintained: Anthony Burgess, Covenant Theology, and the Place of the Law in Reformed Scholasticism*. Grand Rapids: Reformation Heritage Books, 2016.

Chantry, Walter J. *Call the Sabbath a Delight*. Edinburgh and Carlisle, PA: The Banner of Truth Trust, 1991.

Coxe, Nehemiah and John Owen. *Covenant Theology From Adam to Christ*. Ronald D. Miller, James M. Renihan, and Francisco Orozco, editors. Palmdale, CA: Reformed Baptist Academic Press, 2005.

Currid, John D. *A Study Commentary on Genesis*, Volume 1: *Genesis 1:1–25:18*. Darlington, UK: Evangelical Press, 2003.

Dabney, Robert L. *Discussions of Robert L. Dabney*, Volume 1. 1891; reprint, Edinburgh and Carlisle, PA: The Banner of Truth Trust, 1982.

Davidson, Richard M. *Typology In Scripture: A study of study of hermeneutical τύπος structures*. Berrien Springs, MI: Andrews University Press, 1981.

Dempster, Stephen G. *Dominion and dynasty: A theology of the Hebrew Bible*. Downers Grove, IL: InterVarsity Press, 2003, reprinted 2006.

Denault, Pascal. *The Distinctiveness of Baptist Covenant Theology: A Comparison Between Seventeenth-Century Particular Baptist and Paedobaptist Federalism*. Birmingham, AL: Solid Ground Christian Books, 2013.

Dennison, Charles G., editor. *Pressing Toward the Mark: Essays Commemorating Fifty Years of the Orthodox of the Presbyterian Church*. Willows Grove, PA: Orthodox Presbyterian Church, 1985.

Dumbrell, William J. *The End of the Beginning: Revelation 21–22 and the Old Testament*. Eugene, OR: Wipf and Stock Publishers, 2001; previously published by Baker Book House, 1985.

Edwards, Jonathan. *The Works of Jonathan Edwards*, Volume Two. Revised and corrected by Edward Hickman. 1834; reprint, Edinburgh and Carlisle, PA: The Banner of Truth Trust, 1992.

Estelle, Bryan D., J. V. Fesko, and David VanDrunen, editors. *The Law is not of Faith: Essays in Works and Grace in the Mosaic Covenant*. Phillipsburg, NJ: P&R Publishing, 2009.

Fairbairn, Patrick. *The Revelation of Law in Scripture*. Phillipsburg, NJ: P&R Publishing Company, 1996.

Fesko, J. V. *Last Things First: Unlocking Genesis 1–3 with the Christ of Eschatology*. Fearn, Ross-shire, Scotland: Mentor Imprint by Christian Focus Publications, 2007.

Frame, John M. *The Doctrine of the Christian Life*. Phillipsburg, NJ: P&R Publishing, 2008.

Gaffin, Jr., Richard B. *Resurrection and Redemption*. Phillipsburg, NJ: Presbyterian and Reformed Publishing, 1987.

Gill, John. *Exposition of the Old and New Testaments*, 9 vols. 1809; reprint, Paris, AR: The Baptist Standard Bearer, Inc., 1989.

Goppelt, Leonhard. *TYPOS: The Typological Interpretation of the Old Testament in the New*. 1939; reprint, Grand Rapids: William B. Eerdmans Publishing Company, 1982.

Hafemann, Scott J., editor. *Biblical Theology: Retrospect & Prospect*. Downers Grove, IL: InterVarsity Press, 2002.

Hamilton, Jr., James M. *God's Glory in Salvation through Judgment: A Biblical Theology*. Wheaton, IL: Crossway, 2010.

_____. *What is Biblical Theology? A Guide to the Bible's Story, Symbolism, and Patterns*. Wheaton, IL: Crossway, 2014.

Hodge, A. A. *The Confession of Faith*. 1869; reprint, Edinburgh; Carlisle, PA: The Banner of Truth Trust, 1983.

Hodge, Charles. *The Epistle to the Romans*. 1835; reprint, Edinburgh; Carlisle, PA: The Banner of Truth Trust, Reprinted 1983.

Holmes, Michael W., editor and translator. *The Apostolic Fathers: Greek Texts and English Translations*, third edition. Grand Rapids: Baker Academic, 2007.

Hoskins, Paul M. *Jesus as the Fulfillment of the Temple in the Gospel of John*. Eugene, OR: Wipf and Stock Publishers, 2006.

Hughes, Philip Edgcumbe. *A Commentary on the Epistle to the Hebrews*. 1990; reprint, Grand Rapids: Wm. B. Eerdmans Publishing Company, 1977.

Johnson, Dennis E. *Him We Proclaim: Preaching Christ from All the Scriptures*. Phillipsburg, NJ: P&R Publishing, 2007.

Kaiser, Jr., Walter J. *Toward An Exegetical Theology*. 1981; reprint, Grand Rapids: Baker Book House, Sixth printing, January 1987.

Keach, Benjamin. *The Jewish Sabbath Abrogated: or, the Saturday Sabbatarians confuted*. London: John Marshall, 1700.

Kelly, Douglas F. *Creation and Change: Genesis 1:1–2:4 in the Light of Changing Scientific Paradigms*. 1997; reprint, Fearn, Ross-shire, Scotland: Christian Focus Publications, Mentor Imprint, 2010.

Kline, Meredith G. *Kingdom Prologue: Genesis Foundations for a Covenantal Worldview*. Overland Park, KS: Two Age Press, 2000.

Kruger, Michael J. *Canon Revisited: Establishing the Origins and Authority of the New Testament Books*. Wheaton, IL: Crossway, 2012.

Lehrer, Steve. *New Covenant Theology: questions answered*. N. p., 2006.

Lillback, Peter A., editor. *Seeing Christ in all of Scripture: Hermeneutics at Westminster Theological Seminary*. Westminster Seminary Press, 2016.

Long, Gary D. *NCT: Time for a More Accurate Way*. N. p., 2013.

Martin, Oren R. *Bound for the Promised Land: The land promise in God's redemptive plan*. Downers Grove, IL: InterVarsity Press, 2015.

Martin, Robert Paul. *The Christian Sabbath: Its Redemptive-Historical Foundation, Present Obligation, and Practical Observance*. Montville, NJ: Trinity Pulpit Press, 2015.

Moo, Douglas J. *The Epistle to the Romans*, The New International Commentary on the New Testament. Grand Rapids: William B. Eerdmans Publishing Company, 1996.

Muller, Richard A. *Dictionary of Latin and Greek Theological Terms.* Grand Rapids: Baker Book House, 1985, Second printing, September 1986.

———. *Post-Reformation Reformed Dogmatics: The Rise and Development of Reformed Orthodoxy,* ca. 1520 to ca. 1725, Volume Two — Holy Scripture. Grand Rapids: Baker Academic, 2003 (Second Edition).

Muller, Richard A. and Rowland S. Ward. *Scripture and Worship: Biblical Interpretation & The Directory for Worship.* Phillipsburg, NJ: P&R Publishing, 2007.

Murray, John. *Collected Writings of John Murray,* 4 vols. Edinburgh: The Banner of Truth Trust, 1976.

———. *Epistle to the Romans.* 1959, 1965; reprint, Grand Rapids: Wm. B. Eerdmans Publishing Co., one-volume edition, 1984.

———. *Principles of Conduct.* 1957; reprint, Grand Rapids: William B. Eerdmans Publishing Company, 1999.

O'Brien, Peter T. *The Letter to the Ephesians,* PNTC. Grand Rapids: William B. Eerdmans Publishing Company, 1999.

———. *The Letter to the Hebrews,* The Pillar New Testament Commentary. Grand Rapids: Wm. B. Eerdmans Publishing Co., 2010.

Oswalt, John N. *The Book of Isaiah: Chapters 1–39,* NICOT. Robert L. Hubbard Jr., editor. Grand Rapids: Wm. B. Eerdmans, 1986.

Owen, John. *Biblical Theology or The Nature, Origin, Development, and Study of Theological Truth in Six Books.* Pittsburgh, PA: Soli Deo Gloria Publications, 1994.

———. *The Works of John Owen,* 23 vols. William H. Goold, editor. Edinburgh: The Banner of Truth Trust, 1987 edition.

Patzia, Arthur G. & Anthony J. Petrotta. *Pocket Dictionary of Biblical Studies.* Downers Grove, IL: InterVarsity Press, 2002.

Perkins, Williams. *A Golden Chain, or The Description of Theology.* 1597; reprint, n.p., Puritan Reprints, 2010.

Pipa, Joseph A. *The Lord's Day.* Ross-shire, Great Britain: Christian Focus, 1997.

Poole, Matthew. *Commentary on the Holy Bible*, 3 vols. 1683; reprint, London: The Banner of Truth Trust, 1968.

Porter, Stanley E. & Beth W. Stovell, editors. *Biblical Hermeneutics: Five Views*. Downers Grove, IL: IVP Academic, 2012.

Reisinger, John G. *Abraham's Four Seeds: A Biblical Examination of the Presuppositions of Covenant Theology and Dispensationalism*. Frederick, MD: New Covenant Media, 1998.

_____. *But I Say Unto You*. Southbridge, MA: Crown Publications, Inc., 1989.

_____. *Continuity and Discontinuity*. Frederick, MD: New Covenant Media, 2011.

_____. *In Defense of Jesus, the New Lawgiver*. Frederick, MD: New Covenant Media, 2008.

_____. *New Covenant Theology and Prophecy*. Frederick, MD: New Covenant Media, 2012.

_____. *Tablets of Stone & the History of Redemption*. Frederick, MD: New Covenant Media, 2004.

Ross, Philip S. *From the Finger of God: The Biblical and Theological Basis for the Threefold Division of the Law*. Fern, Ross-shire, Scotland: Christian Focus Publications Ltd., Mentor Imprint, 2010.

Rydelnik, Michael. *The Messianic Hope: Is the Hebrew Bible Really Messianic?*, NAC Studies in Bible & Theology, vol. 9. Nashville: B&H Publishing Group, 2010.

Ryken, Leland, James C. Wilhoit, and Tremper Longman III, editors. *Dictionary of Biblical Imagery*. Downers Grove, IL: InterVarstiy Press, 1998.

Sanday, William and Arthur C. Headlam. *A Critical and Exegetical Commentary on the Epistle to the Romans*, The International Critical Commentary. S. R. Driver, A. Plummer, and C. A. Briggs, editors. 1895; reprint, Edinburgh: T & T Clark, Fifth Edition, 1971.

Schreiner, Thomas R. *40 Questions about Christians and the Law*. Grand Rapids: Kregel Publications, 2010.

———. *Commentary on Hebrews, Biblical Theology for Christian Proclamation*. Nashville: B&H Publishing Group, 2015.

———. *The Law and Its Fulfillment: A Pauline Theology of Law*. Grand Rapids: Baker Books, 1993.

Shaw, Robert. *An Exposition of the Westminster Confession of Faith*. Fearn Ross-shire, Scotland: Christian Focus Publications, 1998.

Shedd, W. G. T. *Commentary on Romans*. Grand Rapids: Baker Book House, 1980.

Silva, Moisés, general editor. *Foundations of Contemporary Interpretation*. Grand Rapids: Zondervan Publishing House, 1996.

Silva, Moisés, revision editor. *New International Dictionary of New Testament Theology and Exegesis*, Second Edition. Grand Rapids: Zondervan, 2014.

Thompson, Alan J. *The Acts of the Risen Lord Jesus: Luke's account of God's unfolding plan*, New Studies in Biblical Theology. Downers Gove, IL: InterVarsity Press, 2011.

Trinity Hymnal—Baptist Edition. Suwanee, GA: Great Commission Publications, Inc., 1995.

Trueman, Carl R. *Histories and Fallacies: Problems Faced in the Writing of History*. Wheaton, IL: Crossway, 2010.

Turretin, Francis. *Institutes of Elenctic Theology*, 3 vols. James T. Dennison, Jr., editor and George Musgrave Giger, translator. Phillipsburg, NJ: P&R Publishing, 1992–97.

VanGemeren, Willem A., general editor. *New International Dictionary of Old Testament Theology and Exegesis*. Grand Rapids: Zondervan Publishing House, 1997.

Vanhoozer, Kevin J., general editor. *Dictionary for Theological Interpretation of the Bible*. Grand Rapids: Baker Academic, 2005.

Ventura, Rob, editor. *Going Beyond the Five Points: Pursuing a more Comprehensive Reformation*. N.p., 2015.

Vos, Geerhardus. *Biblical Theology: Old and New Testaments*. 1948; reprint, Grand Rapids: Wm. B. Eerdmans Publishing Company, 1988.

Bibliography

Waldron, Samuel E. *Lectures on the Lord's Day*. Unpublished.

———. *The End Times Made Simple*. Amityville, NY: Calvary Press, 2003.

Waldron, Samuel E. with Richard C. Barcellos. *A Reformed Baptist Manifesto: The New Covenant Constitution of the Church*. Palmdale, CA: Reformed Baptist Academic Press, 2004.

Ward, Rowland S. *God & Adam: Reformed Theology and the Creation Covenant*. Wantirna, Australia: New Melbourne Press, 2003.

Warfield, Benjamin B. *Selected Shorter Writings: Benjamin B. Warfield*, I. John E. Meeter, editor. Phillipsburg, NJ: P&R Publishing, Fourth Printing, January 2001.

Watson, Thomas. *A Body of Divinity: Contained in Sermons upon the Westminster Assembly's Catechism*. Edinburgh, The Banner of Truth Trust, Reprinted 1986.

Wells, Tom. *The Christian and the Sabbath*. Frederick, MD: New Covenant Media, 2010.

Wells, Tom and Fred Zaspel. *New Covenant Theology: Description, Definition, Defense*. Frederick, MD: New Covenant Media, 2002.

Wellum, Stephen J. and Brent E. Parker, editors. *Progressive Covenantalism: Charting a Course between Dispensational and Covenant Theologies*. Nashville: B&H Academic, 2016.

Wenham, Gordon J. *Genesis 1–15*, Word Biblical Commentary. Waco, TX: Word, 1987.

White, A. Blake. *The Law of Christ: A Theological Proposal*. Frederick, MD: New Covenant Media, 2010.

———. *The Newness of the New Covenant*. Frederick, MD: New Covenant Media, 2008.

———. *Theological Foundations for New Covenant Ethics*. Frederick, MD: New Covenant Media, 2013.

———. *What is New Covenant Theology? An Introduction*. Frederick, MD: New Covenant Media, 2012.

Wilson, Daniel. *The Lord's Day*. London: The Lord's Day Observance Society, 1988.

Witsius, Witsius. *The Economy of the Covenants Between God and Man: Comprehending A Complete Body of Divinity*, 2 vols. Escondido, CA: The den Dulk Christian Foundation, re. 1990.

Young, Edward J. *The Book of Isaiah, Chapters 19–39*, vol. 2. Grand Rapids: Wm. B. Eerdmans Publishing Co., 1969.

Zaspel, Fred G. *The New Covenant and New Covenant Theology*. Frederick, MD: New Covenant Media, 2011.

Articles

Barcellos, Richard C. "*Scopus Scripturae*: John Owen, Nehemiah Coxe, our Lord Jesus Christ, and a Few Early Disciples on Christ as the Scope of Scripture." *Journal of the Institute of Reformed Baptist Studies* (2015): 5–24.

_____. "*The Christian and the Sabbath*, Tom Wells: A Review Article (Part I)." *Reformed Baptist Theological Review* VII:1 (Spring 2010): 81–93.

_____. "*The Christian and the Sabbath*, Tom Wells: A Review Article (Part II)." *Reformed Baptist Theological Review* (RBTR) VII:2 (Fall 2010): 131–49.

Dennison, James T. "Vos on the Sabbath: A Close Reading." *Kerux* 2.1 (May 1987): 61–70.

Lee, Jon English. "An Examination of the Origins of English Puritan Sabbatarianism." *Puritan Reformed Journal* 7, 1 (2015): 103–19.

Mayhue, Richard L. "New Covenant Theology and Futuristic Premillennialism," *The Master's Seminary Journal*, 18.2 (Fall 2007): 221–32.

Moore, Nicholas J. "Jesus as 'The One who Entered his Rest': The Christological Reading of Hebrews 4:10." *Journal for the Study of the New Testament*, 2014, Vol. 36(4): 383–400.

Renihan, James M. "Theology on Target: The Scope of the Whole (which is to give all glory to God)." *Reformed Baptist Theological Review* II:2 (July 2005): 36–52.

Rudolph, David J. "Festivals in Genesis 1:14." *Tyndale Bulletin* 54.2 (2003): 23–40.

Steinmetz, David C. "The Superiority of Pre-Critical Exegesis." *Theology Today* (April 1980): 27–38.

Internet Links

Reisinger, John G. "A Covenant of Works?" http://resources.grantedministries.org/article/covenant_of_works_j_r.pdf. Accessed 31 March 2016.